Chapter 513:
BEYOND RESCUE!!!

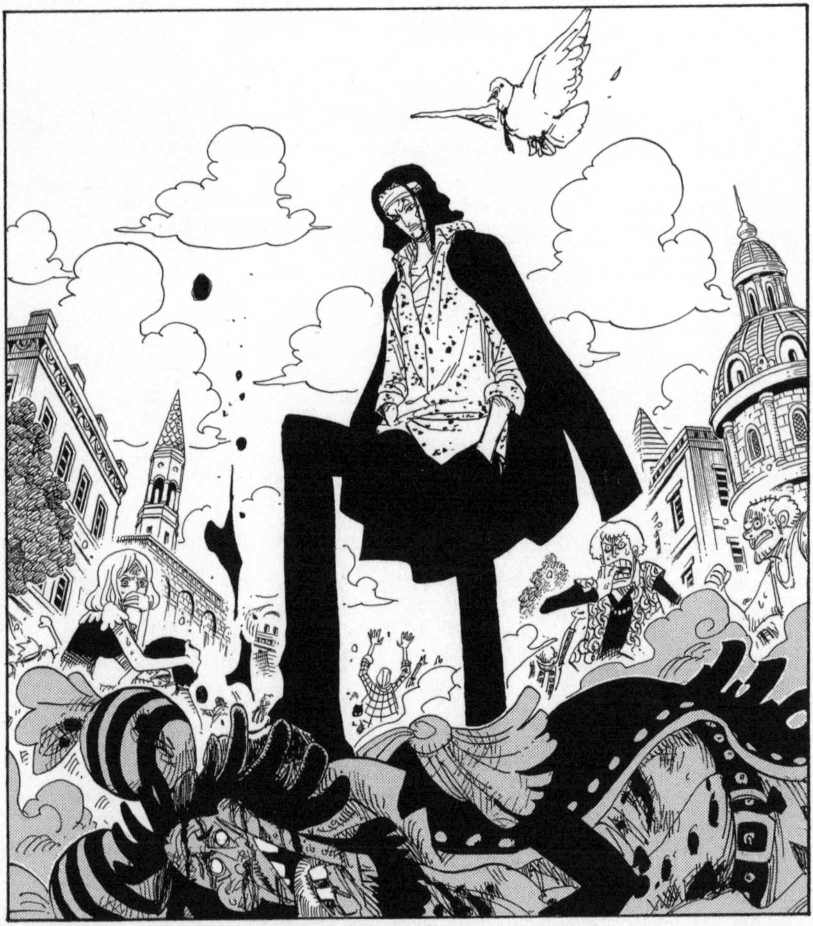

CP9'S INDEPENDENT REPORT, VOL. 21:
"EXCESSIVE JUSTICE"

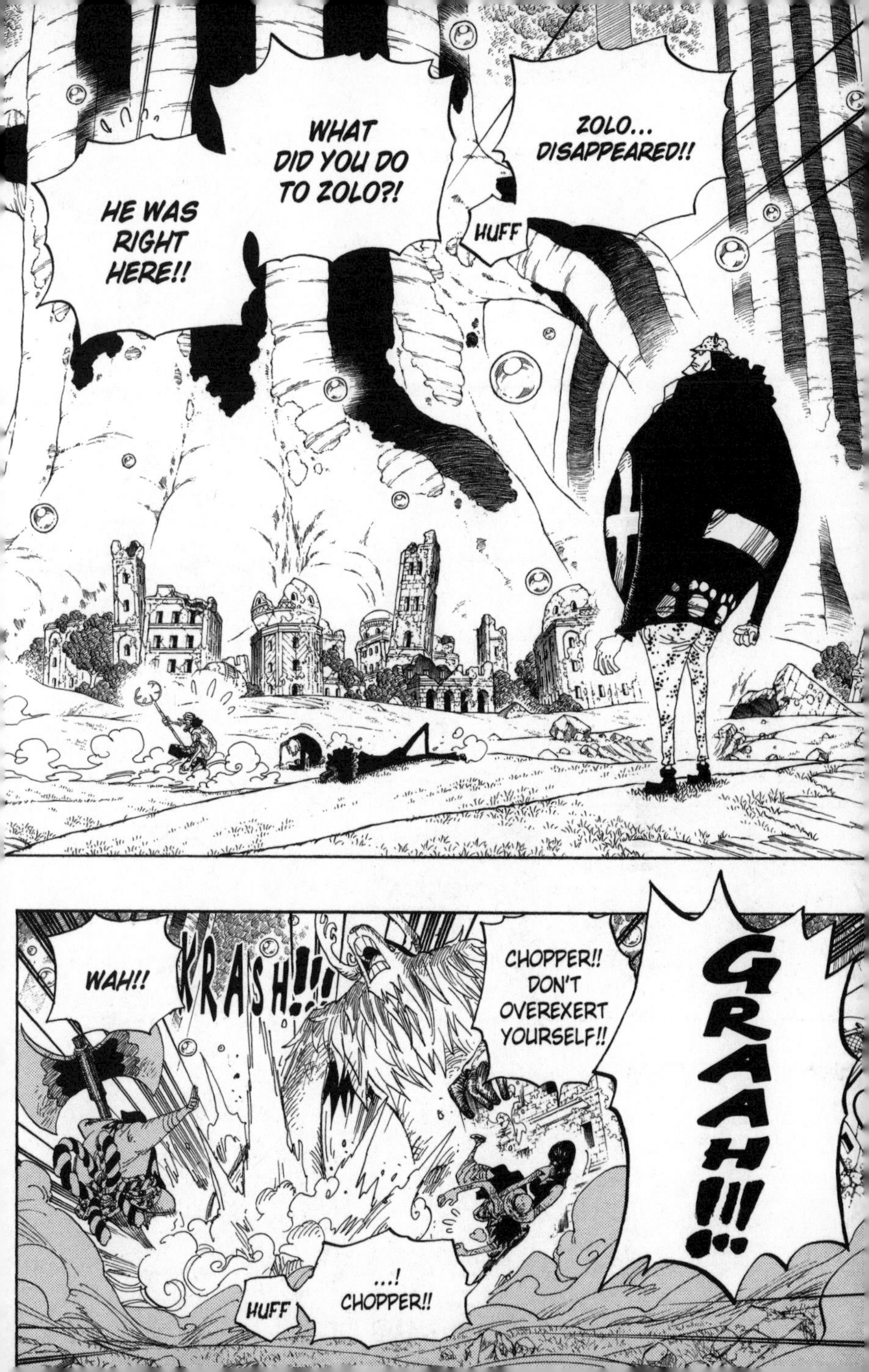
ZOLO... DISAPPEARED!!
HUFF
WHAT DID YOU DO TO ZOLO?!
HE WAS RIGHT HERE!!
GRAAH!!!
CHOPPER!! DON'T OVEREXERT YOURSELF!!
KRASH!!!
WAH!!
...! CHOPPER!!
HUFF

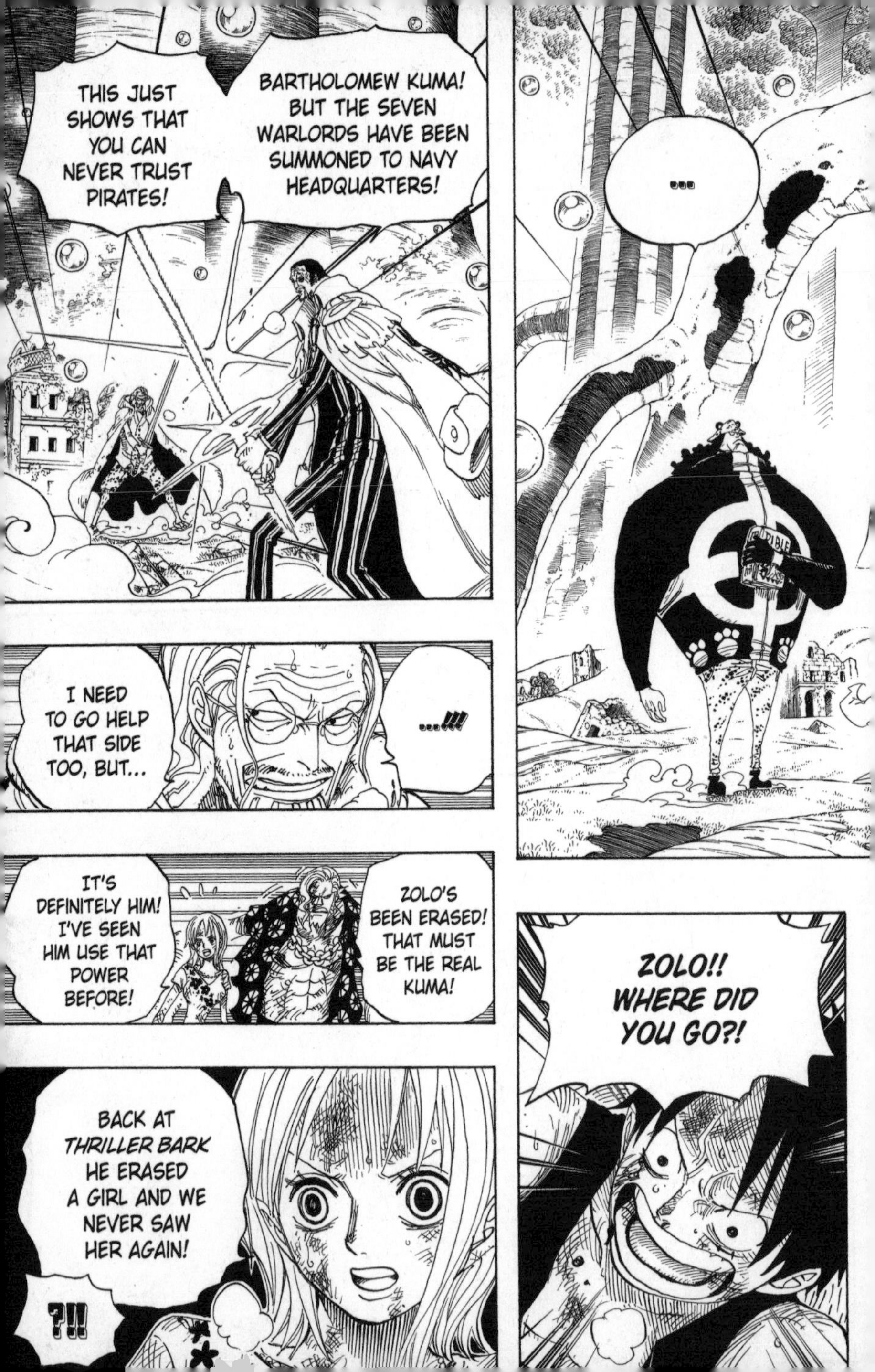
...
BARTHOLOMEW KUMA! BUT THE SEVEN WARLORDS HAVE BEEN SUMMONED TO NAVY HEADQUARTERS!
THIS JUST SHOWS THAT YOU CAN NEVER TRUST PIRATES!
...!!!
I NEED TO GO HELP THAT SIDE TOO, BUT...
ZOLO'S BEEN ERASED! THAT MUST BE THE REAL KUMA!
IT'S DEFINITELY HIM! I'VE SEEN HIM USE THAT POWER BEFORE!
ZOLO!! WHERE DID YOU GO?!
BACK AT *THRILLER BARK* HE ERASED A GIRL AND WE NEVER SAW HER AGAIN!
?!!

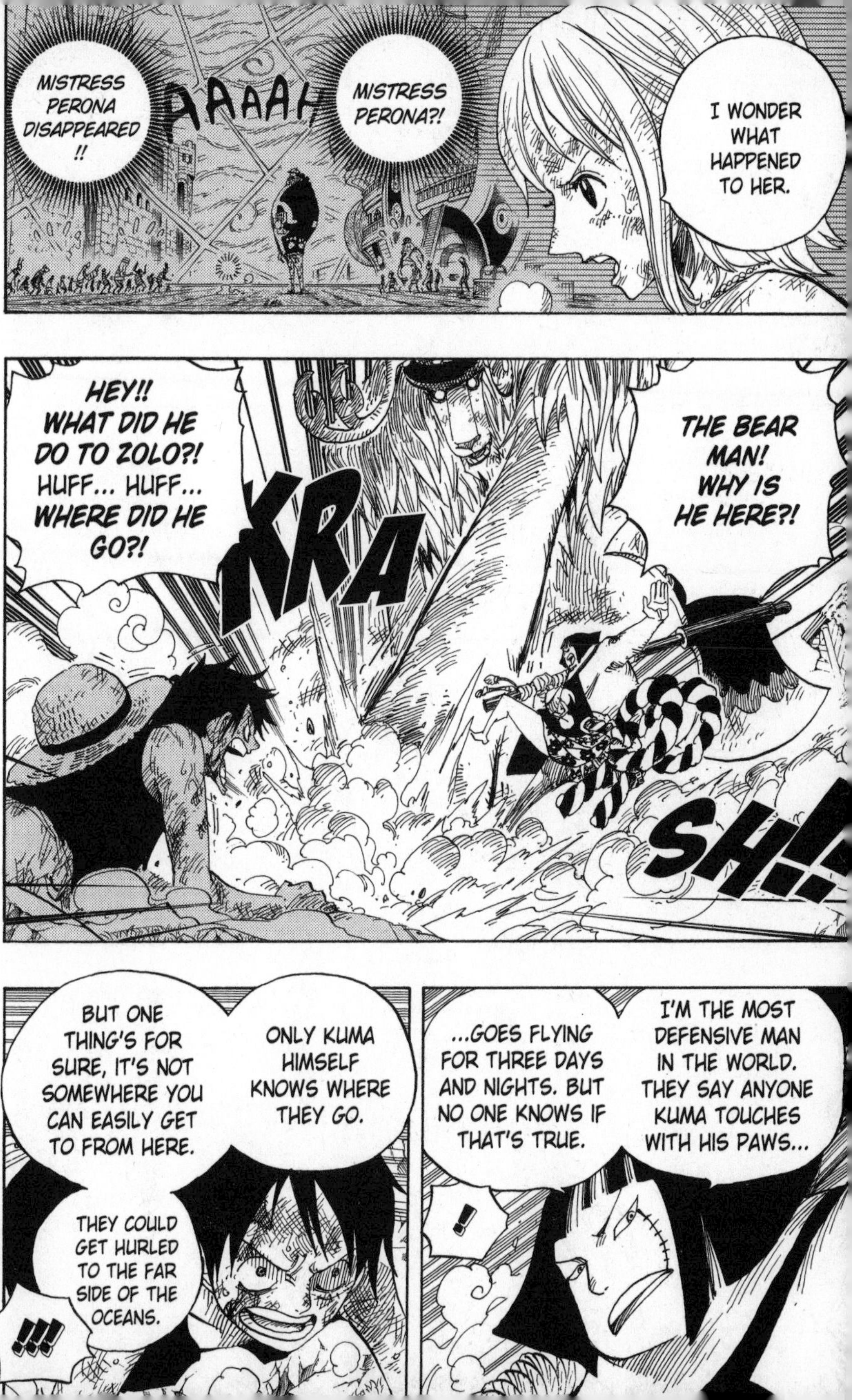

I WONDER WHAT HAPPENED TO HER.
MISTRESS PERONA?!
AAAAH
MISTRESS PERONA DISAPPEARED !!
THE BEAR MAN! WHY IS HE HERE?!
SH!!
KRA
HEY!! WHAT DID HE DO TO ZOLO?! HUFF... HUFF... WHERE DID HE GO?!
I'M THE MOST DEFENSIVE MAN IN THE WORLD. THEY SAY ANYONE KUMA TOUCHES WITH HIS PAWS...
...GOES FLYING FOR THREE DAYS AND NIGHTS. BUT NO ONE KNOWS IF THAT'S TRUE.
!
ONLY KUMA HIMSELF KNOWS WHERE THEY GO.
BUT ONE THING'S FOR SURE, IT'S NOT SOMEWHERE YOU CAN EASILY GET TO FROM HERE.
THEY COULD GET HURLED TO THE FAR SIDE OF THE OCEANS.
!!!

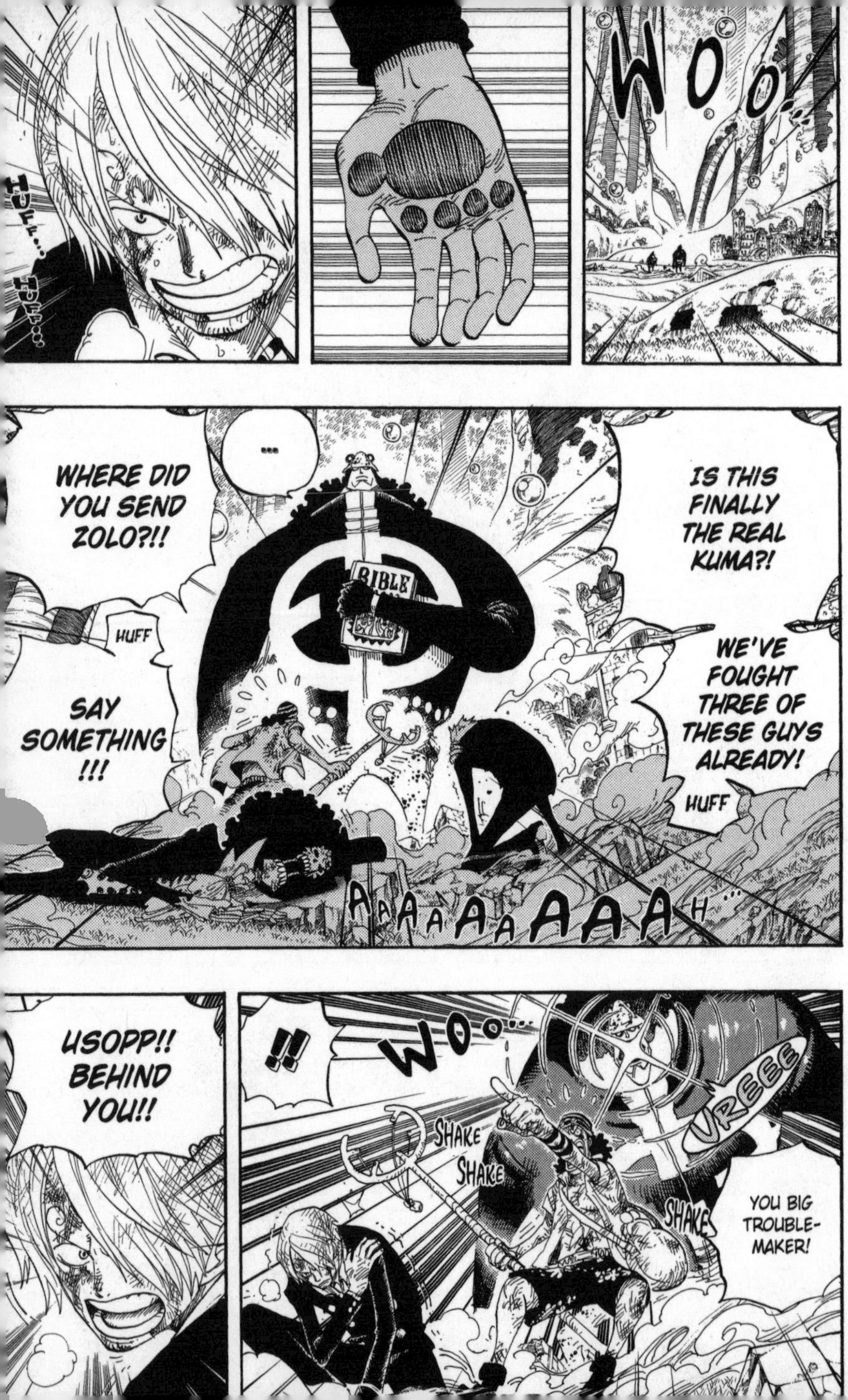
WOO...
HUFF... HUFF...
IS THIS FINALLY THE REAL KUMA?!
WE'VE FOUGHT THREE OF THESE GUYS ALREADY!
HUFF
...
WHERE DID YOU SEND ZOLO?!!
HUFF
SAY SOMETHING !!!
AAAAAAAAAAH...
!!
WOO...
UREEE
SHAKE
SHAKE
SHAKE
YOU BIG TROUBLE-MAKER!
USOPP!! BEHIND YOU!!

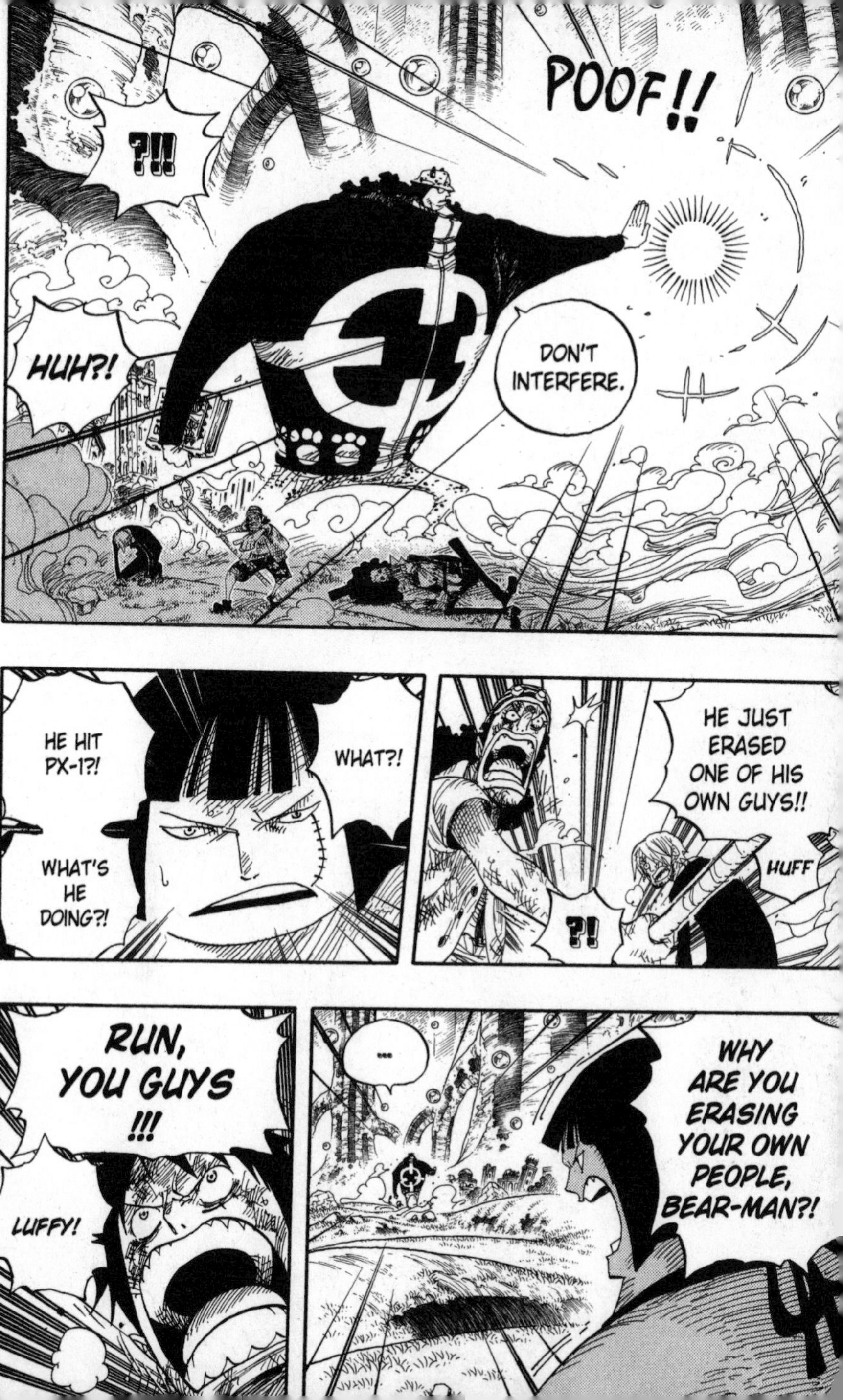
POOF!!
?!!
DON'T INTERFERE.
HUH?!
HE JUST ERASED ONE OF HIS OWN GUYS!!
HUFF
?!
WHAT?!
HE HIT PX-1?!
WHAT'S HE DOING?!
WHY ARE YOU ERASING YOUR OWN PEOPLE, BEAR-MAN?!
...
RUN, YOU GUYS!!!
LUFFY!

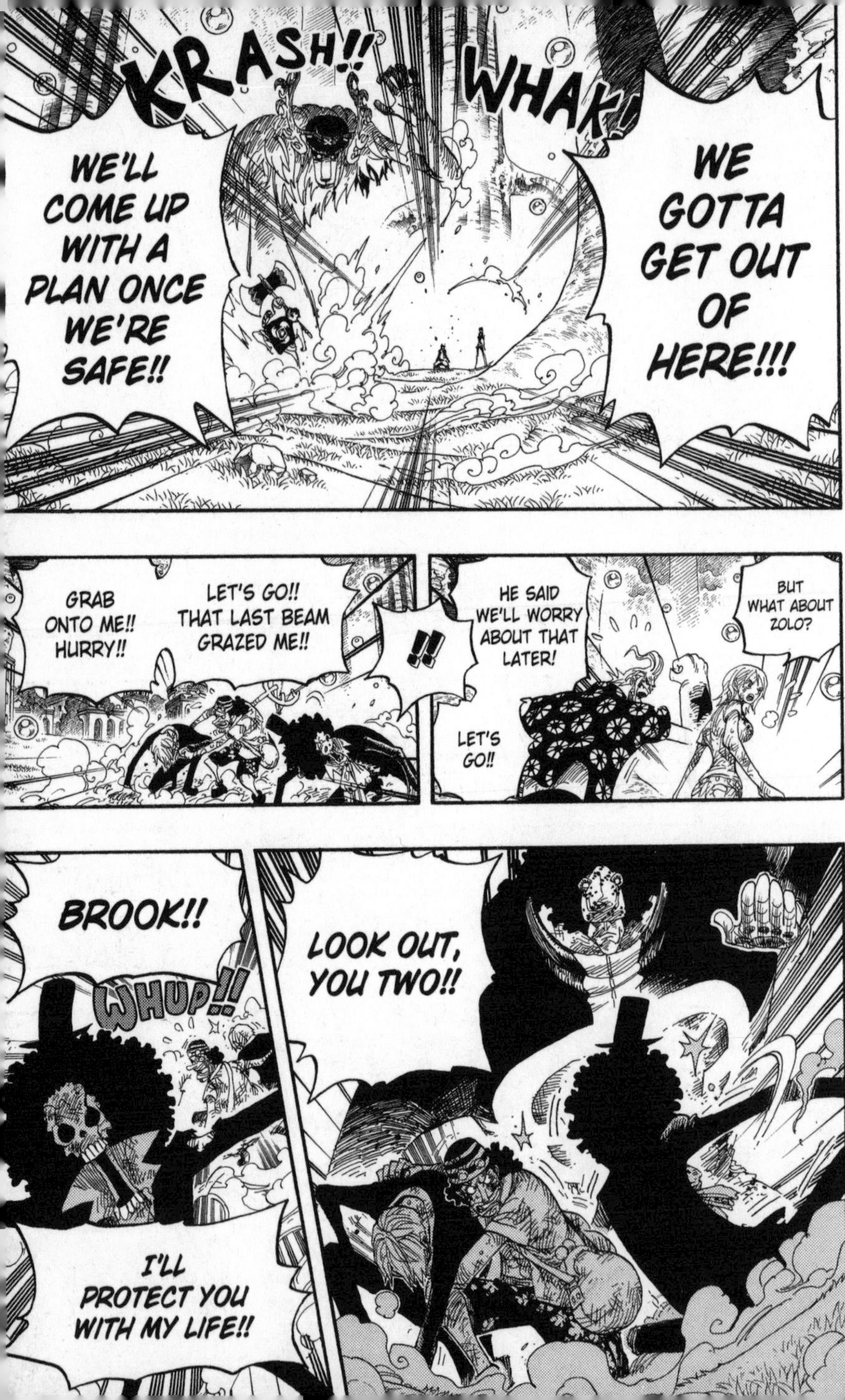
WHAK!
WE GOTTA GET OUT OF HERE!!!
KRASH!!
WE'LL COME UP WITH A PLAN ONCE WE'RE SAFE!!
BUT WHAT ABOUT ZOLO?
HE SAID WE'LL WORRY ABOUT THAT LATER!
LET'S GO!!
!!
LET'S GO!! THAT LAST BEAM GRAZED ME!!
GRAB ONTO ME!! HURRY!!
LOOK OUT, YOU TWO!!
BROOK!!
WHUP!!
I'LL PROTECT YOU WITH MY LIFE!!

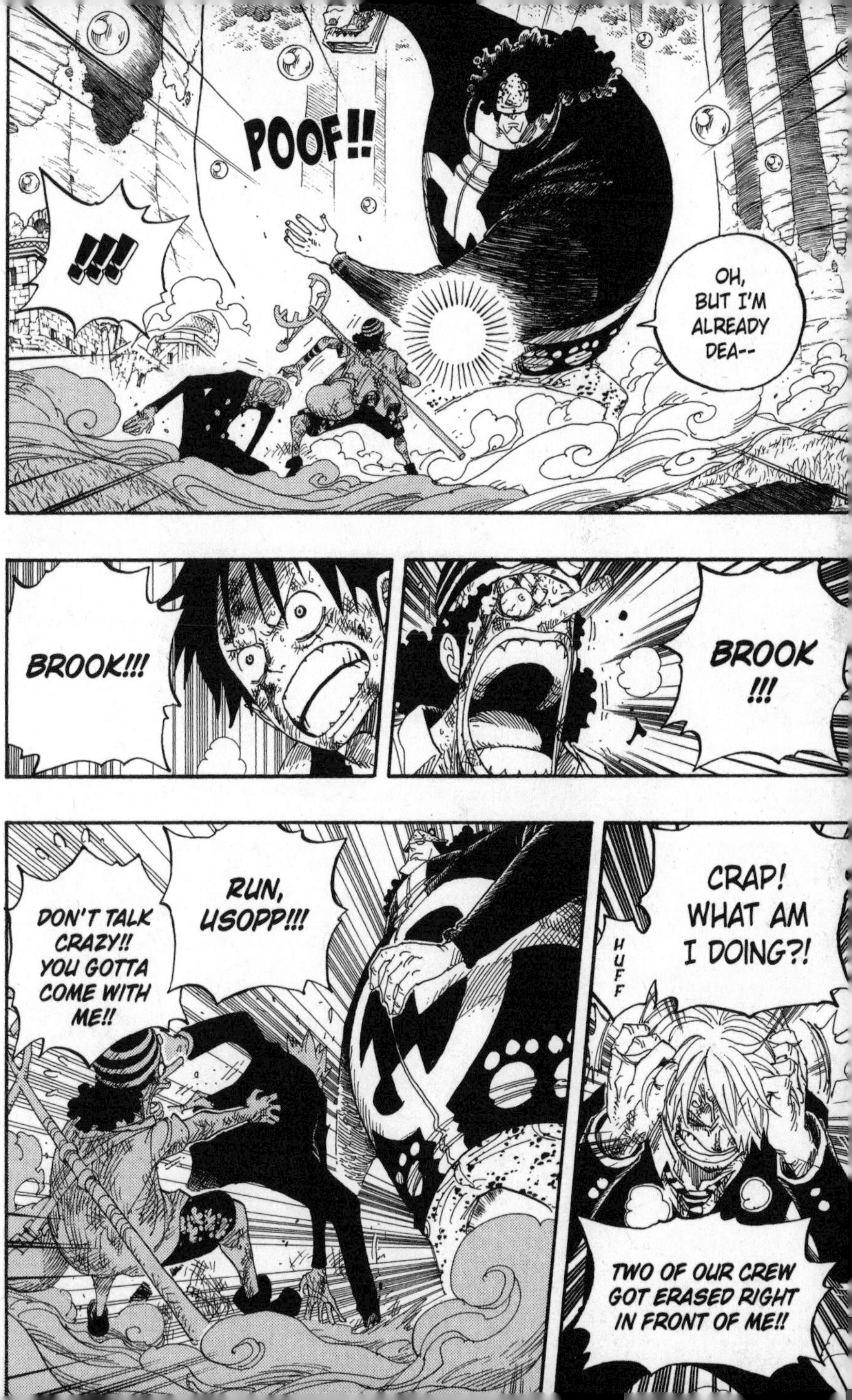
OH, BUT I'M ALREADY DEA--
POOF!!
!!!
BROOK !!!
BROOK!!!
CRAP! WHAT AM I DOING?!
HUFF
TWO OF OUR CREW GOT ERASED RIGHT IN FRONT OF ME!!
RUN, USOPP!!!
DON'T TALK CRAZY!! YOU GOTTA COME WITH ME!!

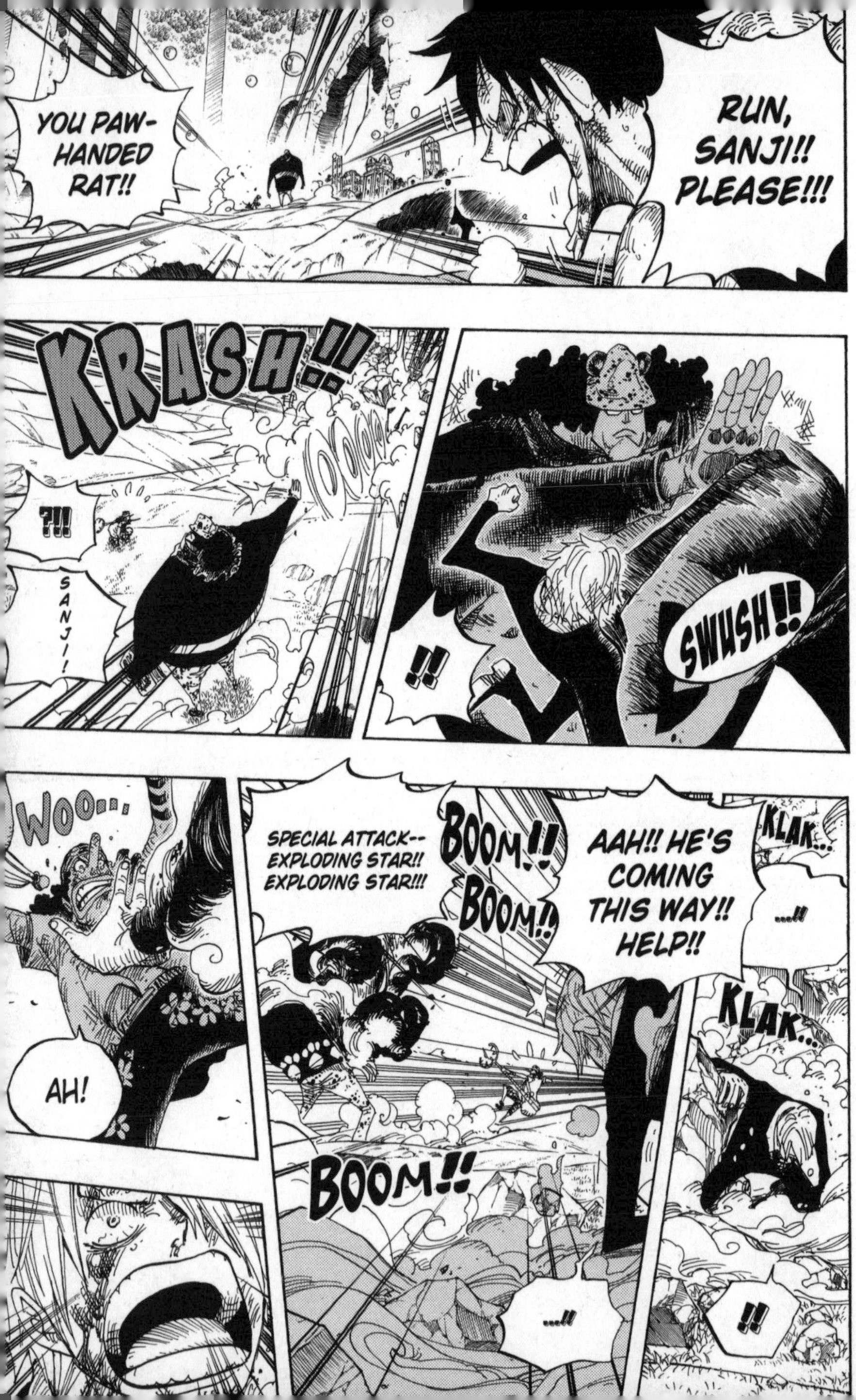
RUN, SANJI!! PLEASE!!!
YOU PAW-HANDED RAT!!
SWUSH!!
!!
KRASH!!
?!!
SANJI!
KLAK...
...!!
KLAK...
!!
AAH!! HE'S COMING THIS WAY!! HELP!!
BOOM!!
SPECIAL ATTACK-- EXPLODING STAR!! EXPLODING STAR!!!
BOOM!!
BOOM!!
...!!
WOO...
AH!

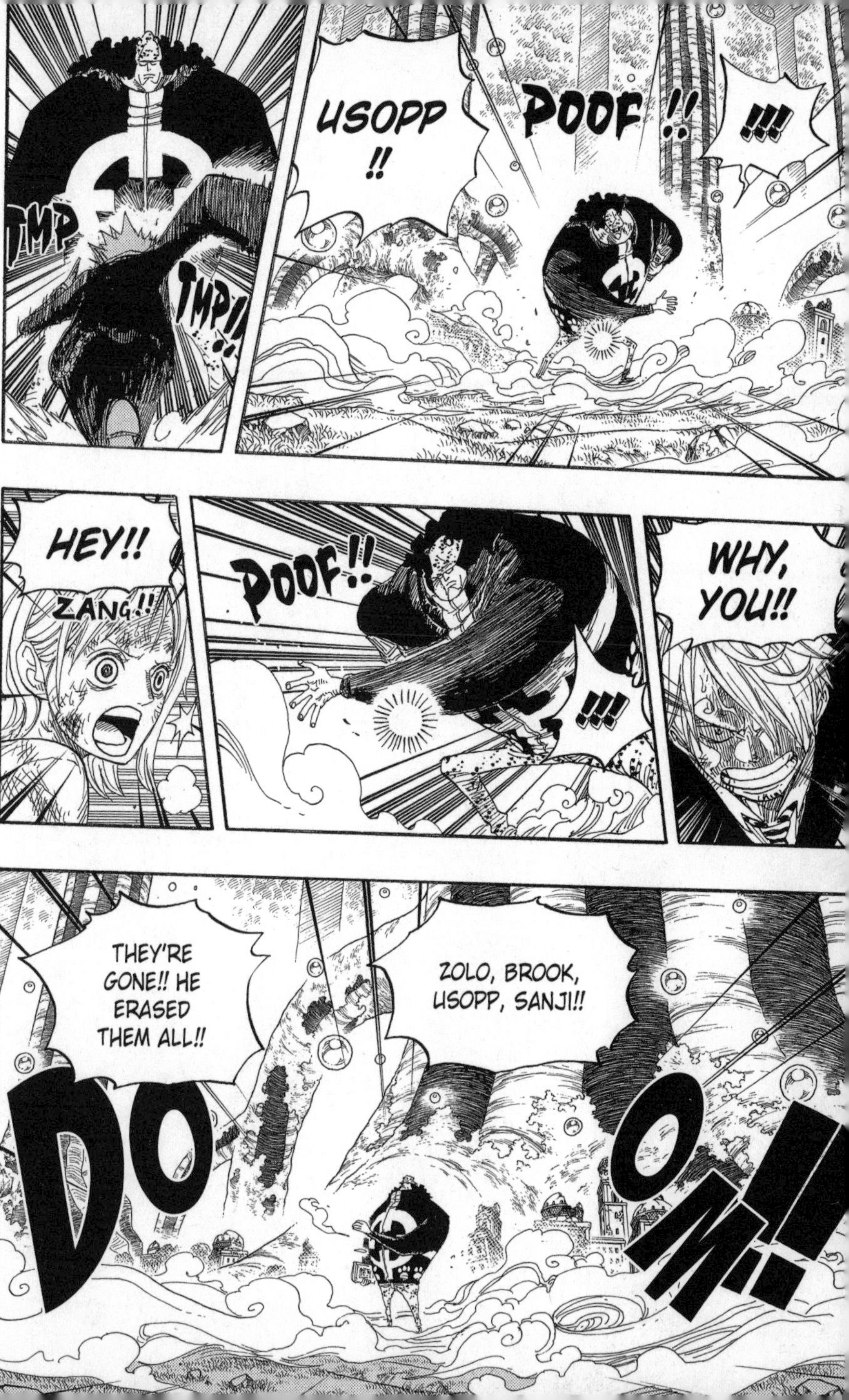
!!!
POOF!!
USOPP !!
TMP
TMP!!
WHY, YOU!!
POOF!!
!!!
HEY!!
ZANG!!
ZOLO, BROOK, USOPP, SANJI!!
THEY'RE GONE!! HE ERASED THEM ALL!!
DOOM!!

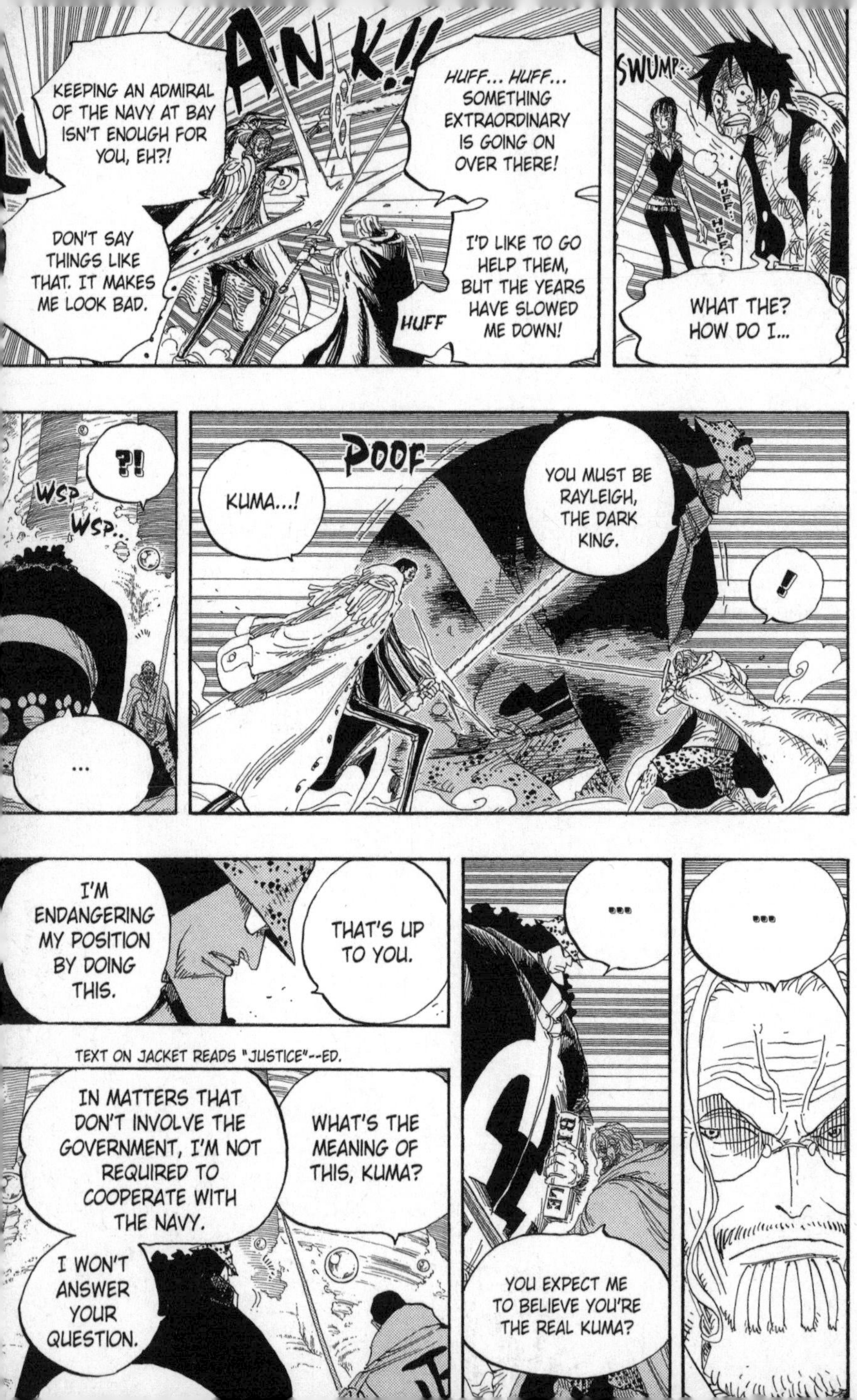
SWUMP
HUFF... HUFF...
WHAT THE? HOW DO I...
ANK!!
HUFF... HUFF... SOMETHING EXTRAORDINARY IS GOING ON OVER THERE!
I'D LIKE TO GO HELP THEM, BUT THE YEARS HAVE SLOWED ME DOWN!
HUFF
KEEPING AN ADMIRAL OF THE NAVY AT BAY ISN'T ENOUGH FOR YOU, EH?!
DON'T SAY THINGS LIKE THAT. IT MAKES ME LOOK BAD.
POOF
YOU MUST BE RAYLEIGH, THE DARK KING.
KUMA...!
!
?!
WSP
WSP...
...
...
...
YOU EXPECT ME TO BELIEVE YOU'RE THE REAL KUMA?
I'M ENDANGERING MY POSITION BY DOING THIS.
THAT'S UP TO YOU.
WHAT'S THE MEANING OF THIS, KUMA?
IN MATTERS THAT DON'T INVOLVE THE GOVERNMENT, I'M NOT REQUIRED TO COOPERATE WITH THE NAVY.
I WON'T ANSWER YOUR QUESTION.
TEXT ON JACKET READS "JUSTICE"--ED.

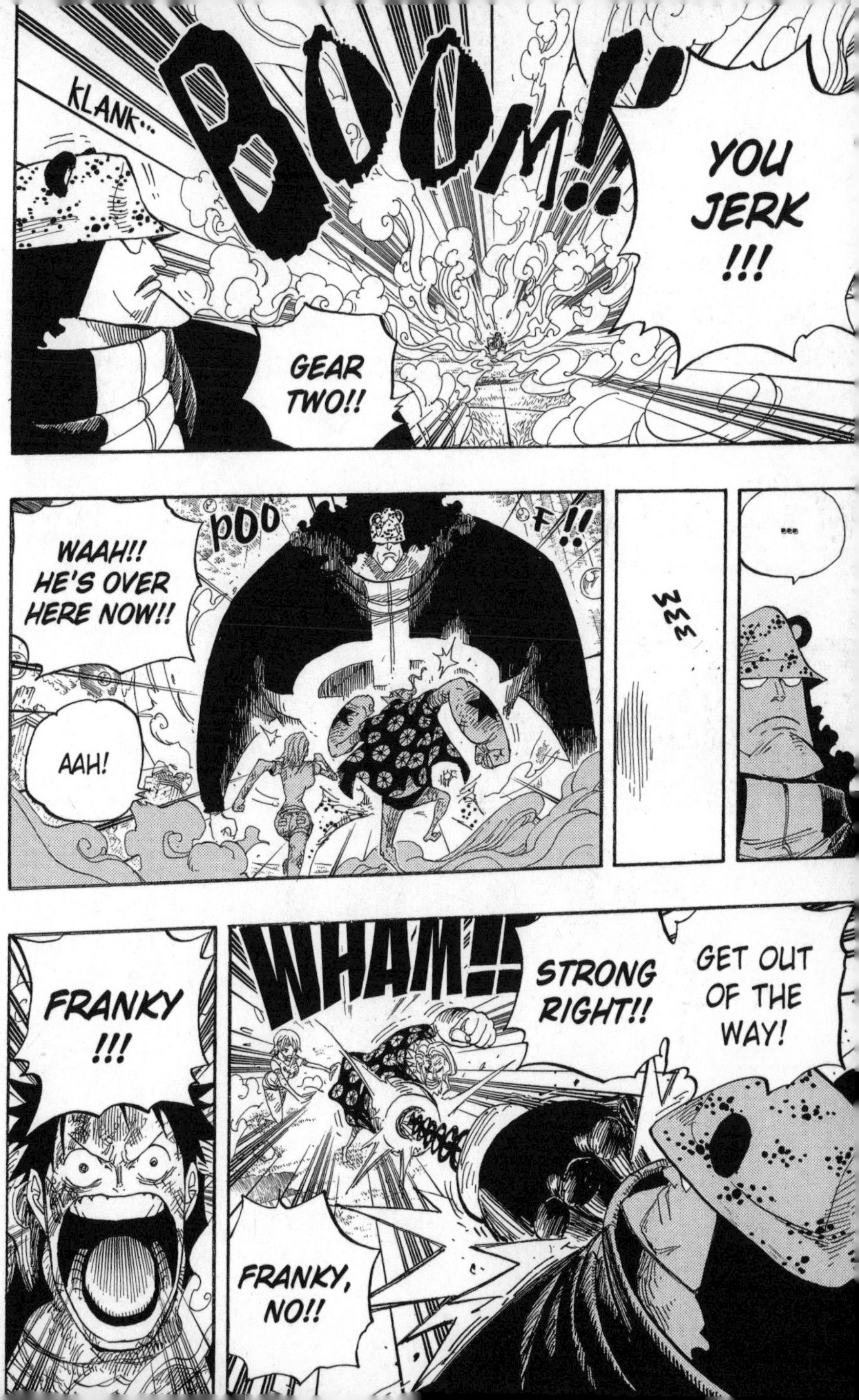
YOU JERK !!!
BOOM!!
KLANK...
GEAR TWO!!
...
POOF!!
WAAH!! HE'S OVER HERE NOW!!
AAH!
GET OUT OF THE WAY!
STRONG RIGHT!!
WHAM!!
FRANKY, NO!!
FRANKY !!!

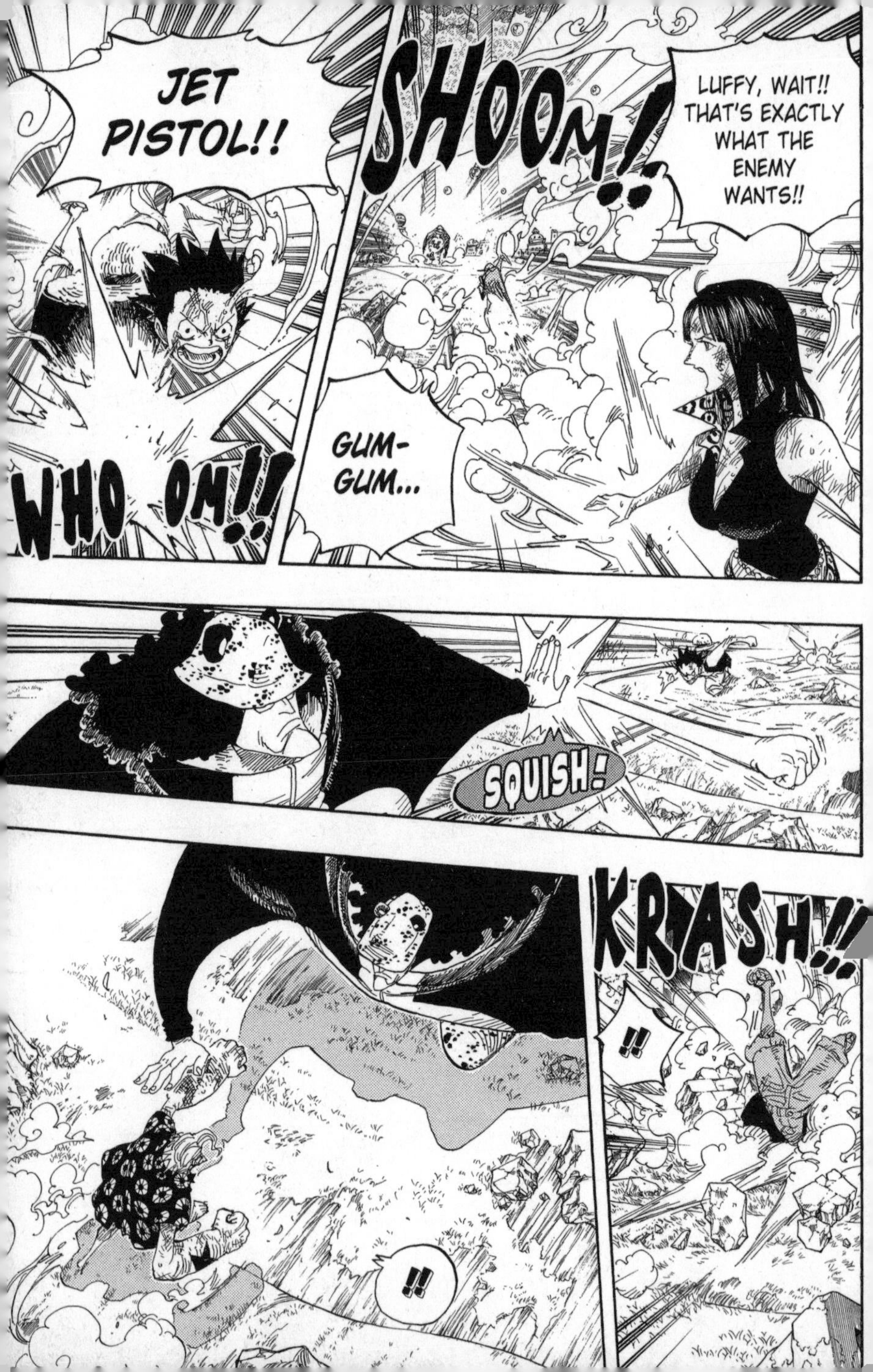
SHOOM!!
LUFFY, WAIT!! THAT'S EXACTLY WHAT THE ENEMY WANTS!!
GUM-GUM...
JET PISTOL!!
WHOOM!!
SQUISH!
KRASH!!!
!!
!!

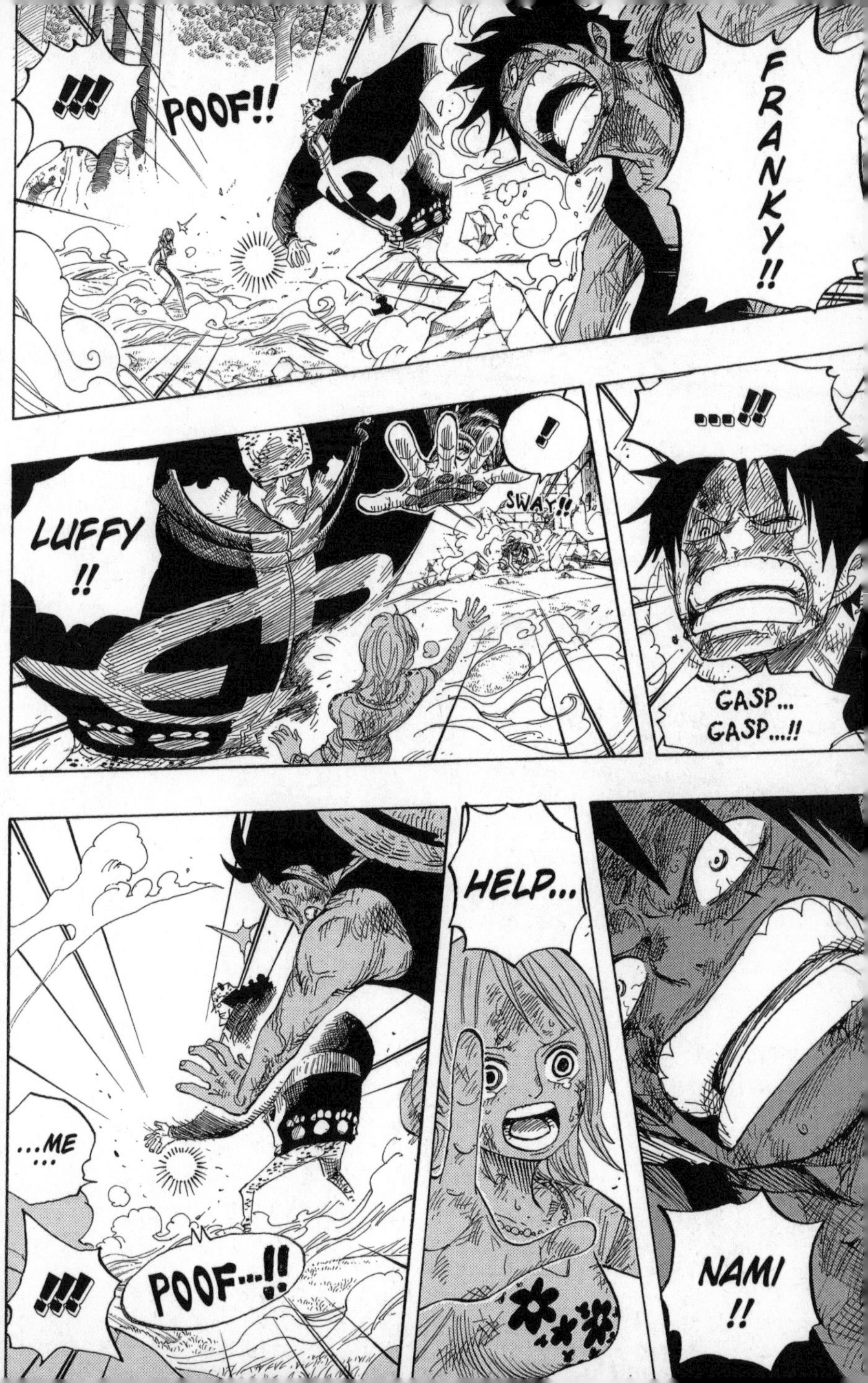
FRANKY!!
POOF!!
!!!
...!!
GASP... GASP...!!
!
SWAY!!
LUFFY!!
NAMI!!
HELP...
...ME...
POOF...!!
!!!

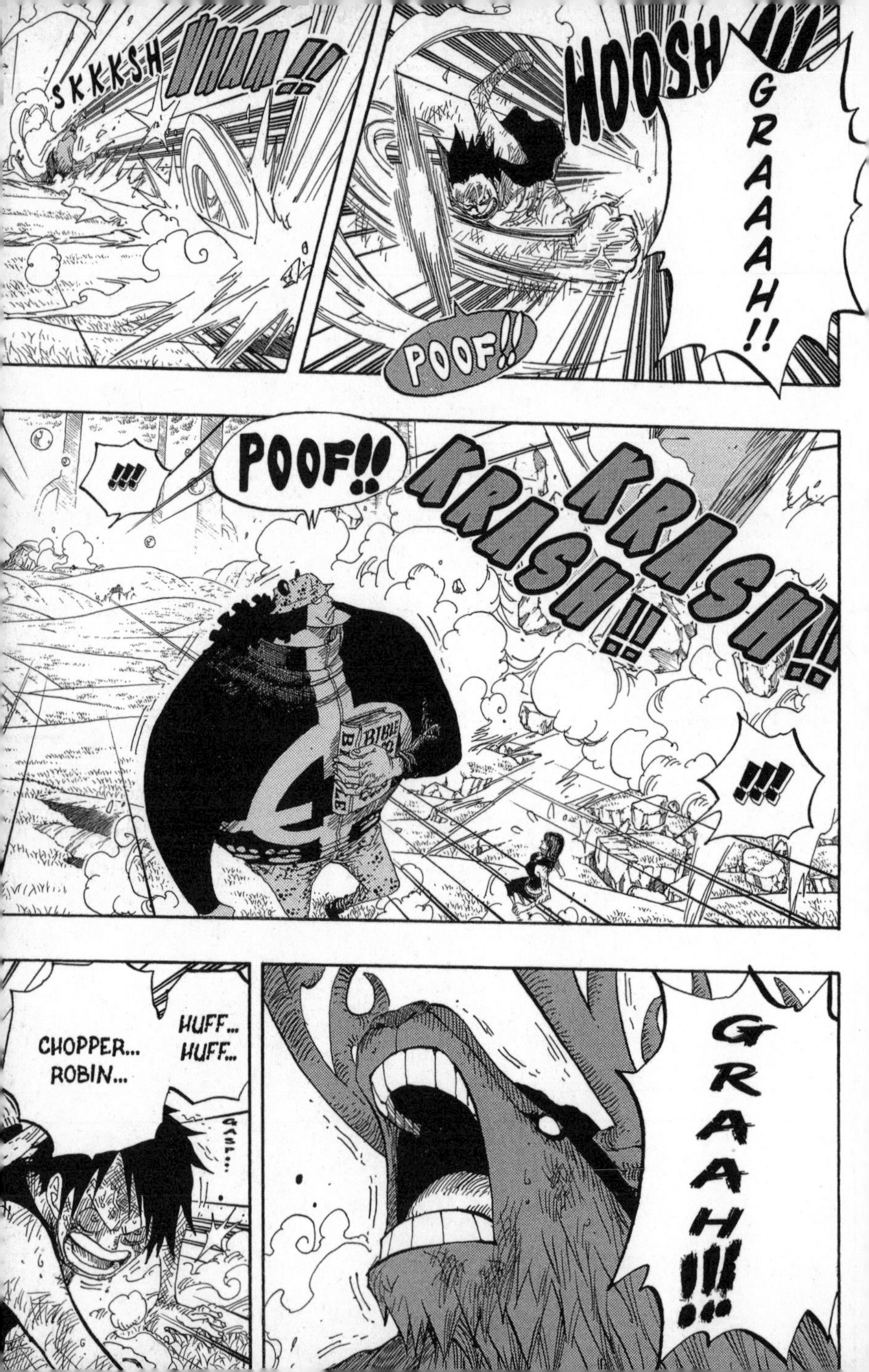
WHOOSH
GRAAAAH!!
POOF!!
SKKKSH
WHAM!!
KRASH
KRASH!!
!!!
POOF!!
!!!
GRAAH!!!
HUFF... HUFF...
CHOPPER... ROBIN...

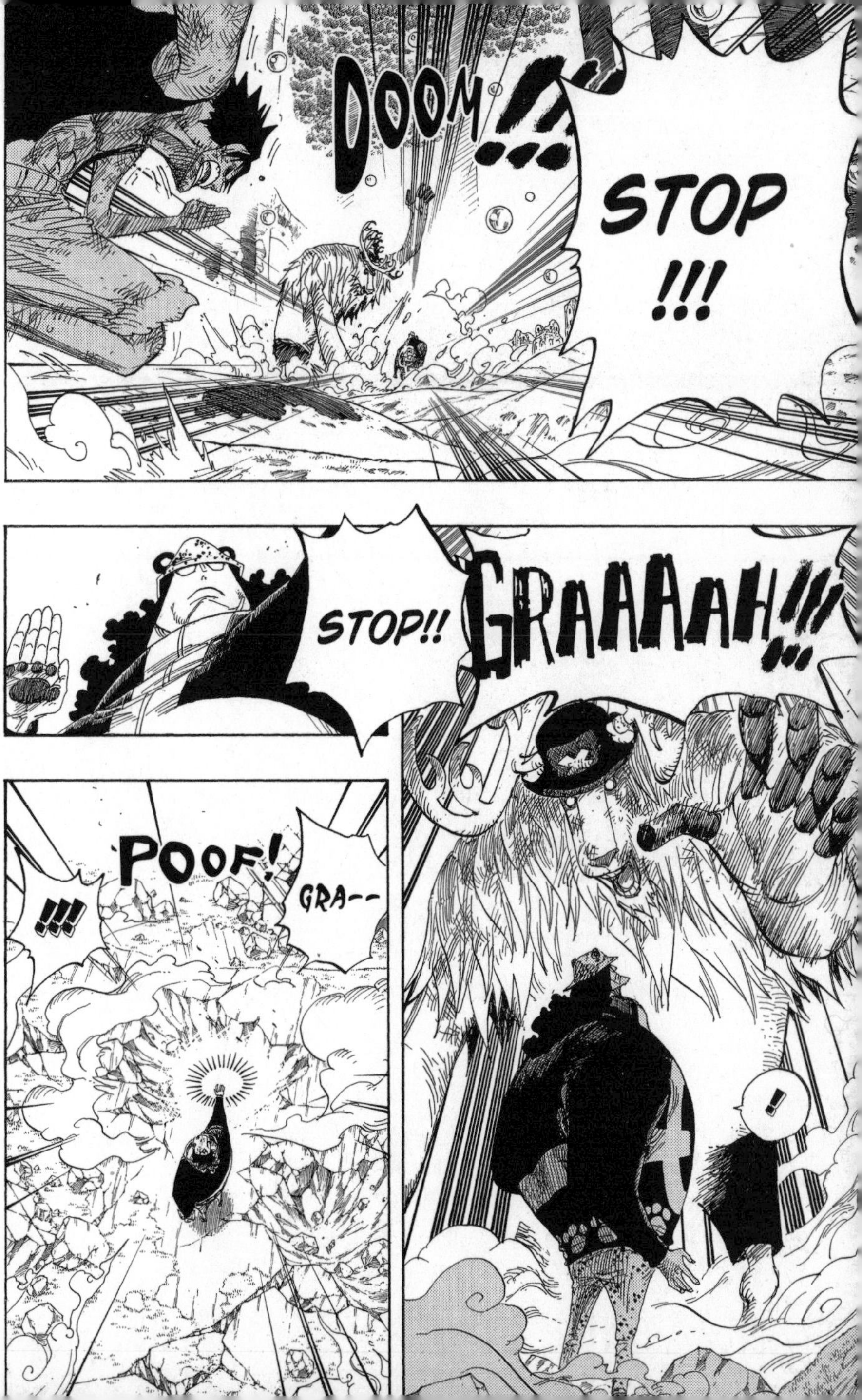
DOOM!!...
STOP !!!
GRAAAAH!!!...
!
STOP!!
POOF!
GRA--
!!!

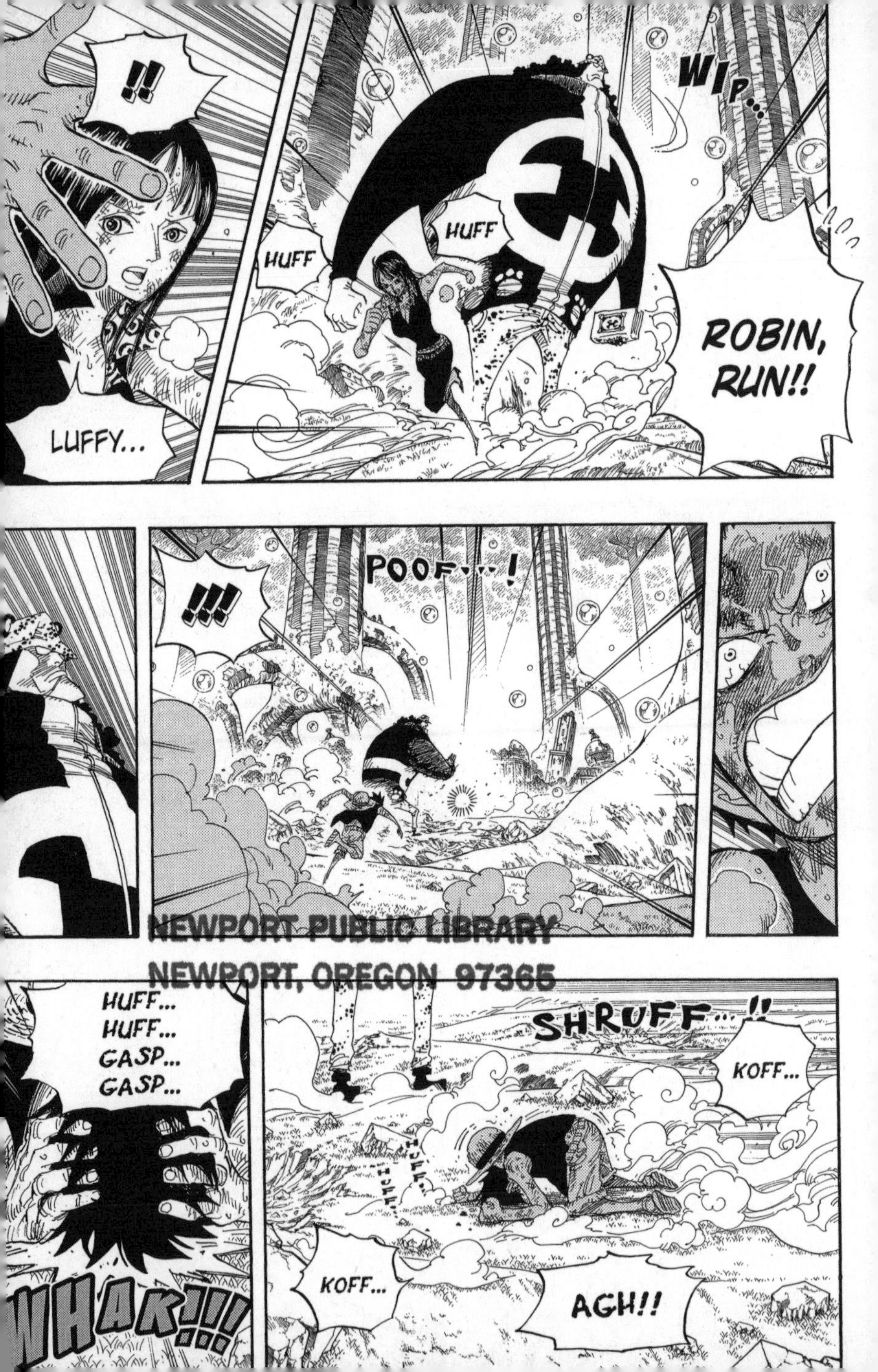
WIP...
ROBIN, RUN!!
HUFF
HUFF
!!
LUFFY...
POOF...!
!!!
SHRUFF...!!
KOFF...
HUFF...
HUFF...
AGH!!
KOFF...
HUFF... HUFF... GASP... GASP...
WHAK!!!!

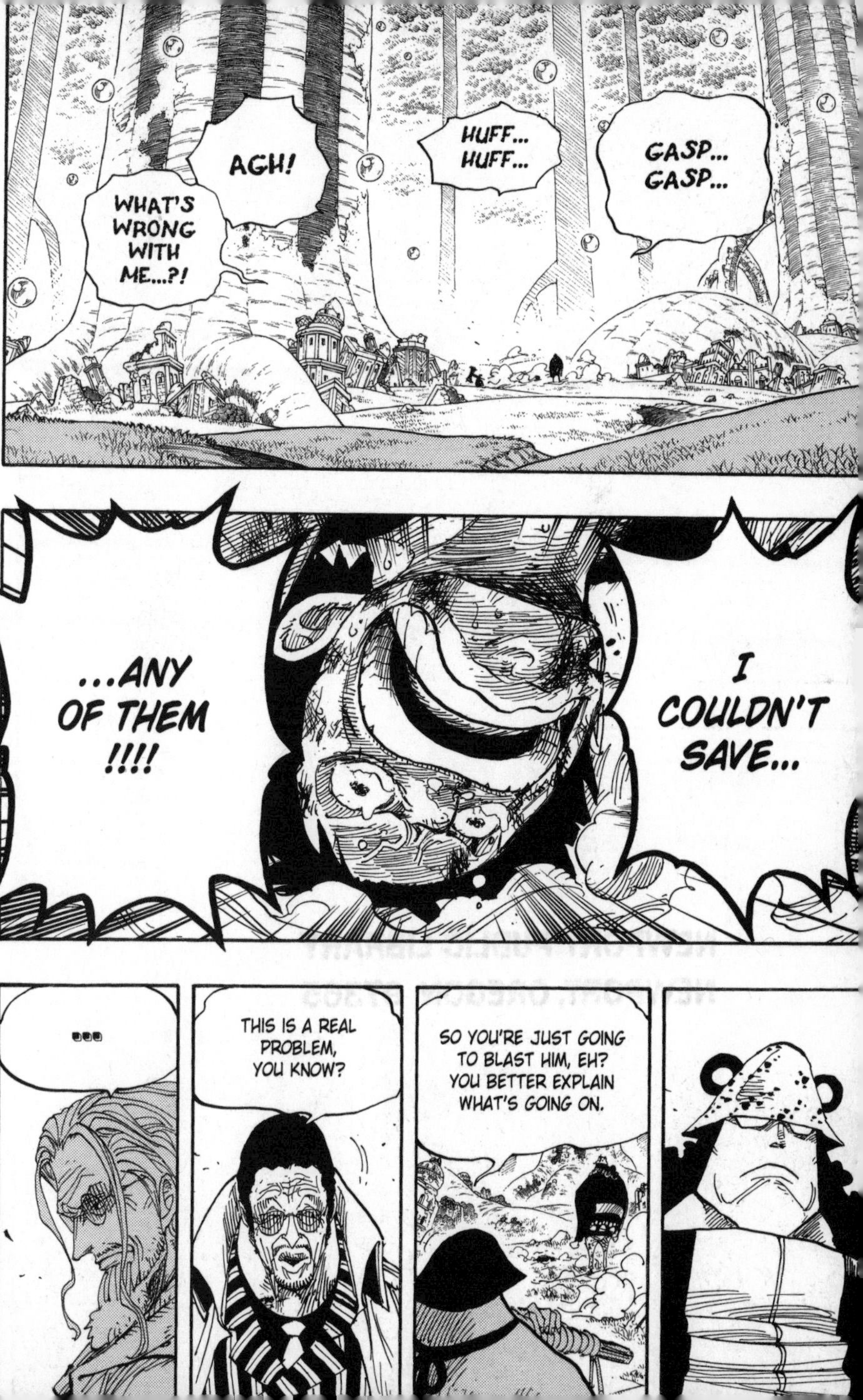
GASP... GASP...
HUFF... HUFF...
AGH!
WHAT'S WRONG WITH ME...?!
I COULDN'T SAVE...
...ANY OF THEM !!!!
SO YOU'RE JUST GOING TO BLAST HIM, EH? YOU BETTER EXPLAIN WHAT'S GOING ON.
THIS IS A REAL PROBLEM, YOU KNOW?
...

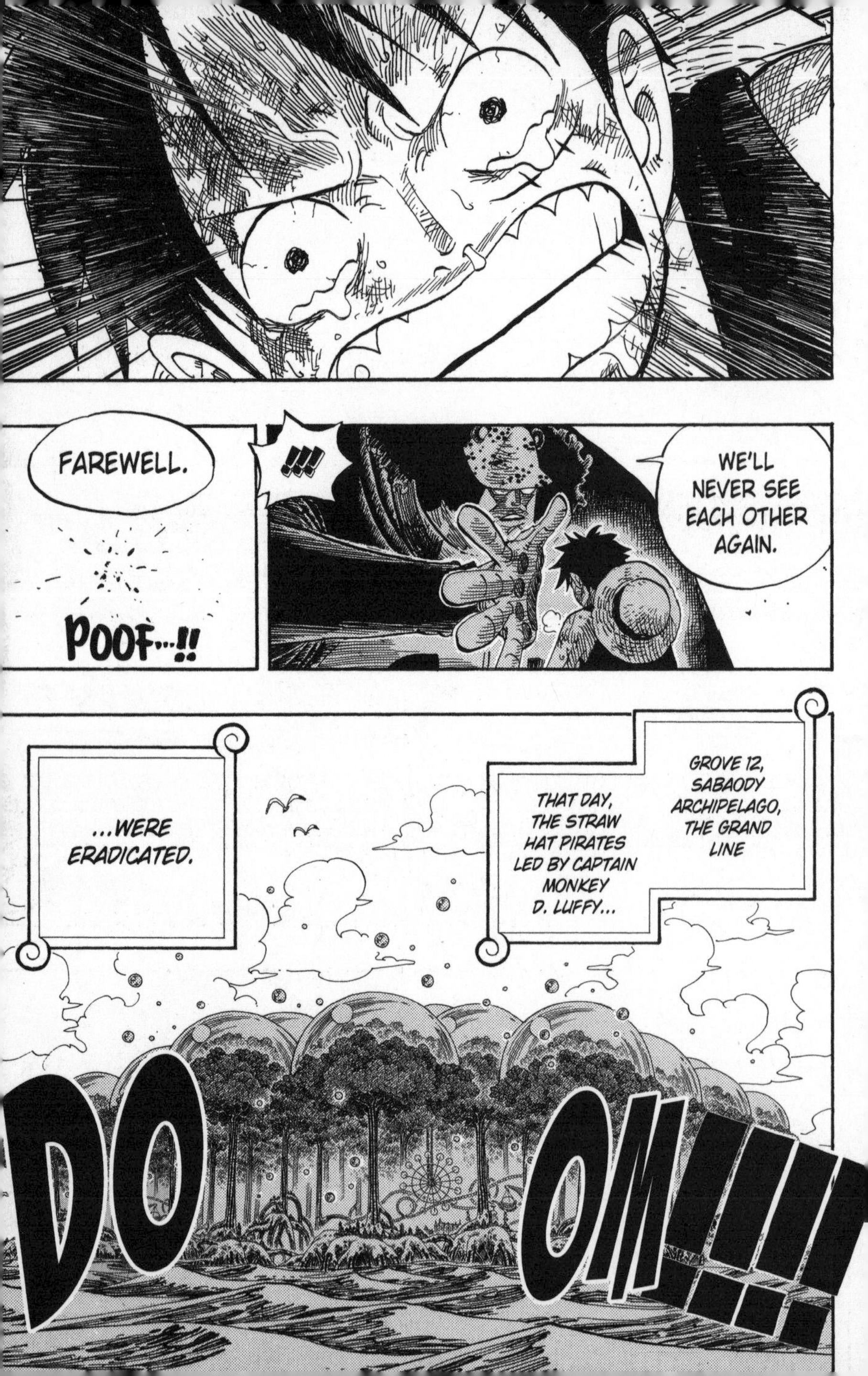
WE'LL NEVER SEE EACH OTHER AGAIN.
!!!
FAREWELL.
POOF...!!
GROVE 12, SABAODY ARCHIPELAGO, THE GRAND LINE
THAT DAY, THE STRAW HAT PIRATES LED BY CAPTAIN MONKEY D. LUFFY...
...WERE ERADICATED.
DOON!!!!!

Chapter 514:

BODY PARASITE MUSHROOMS

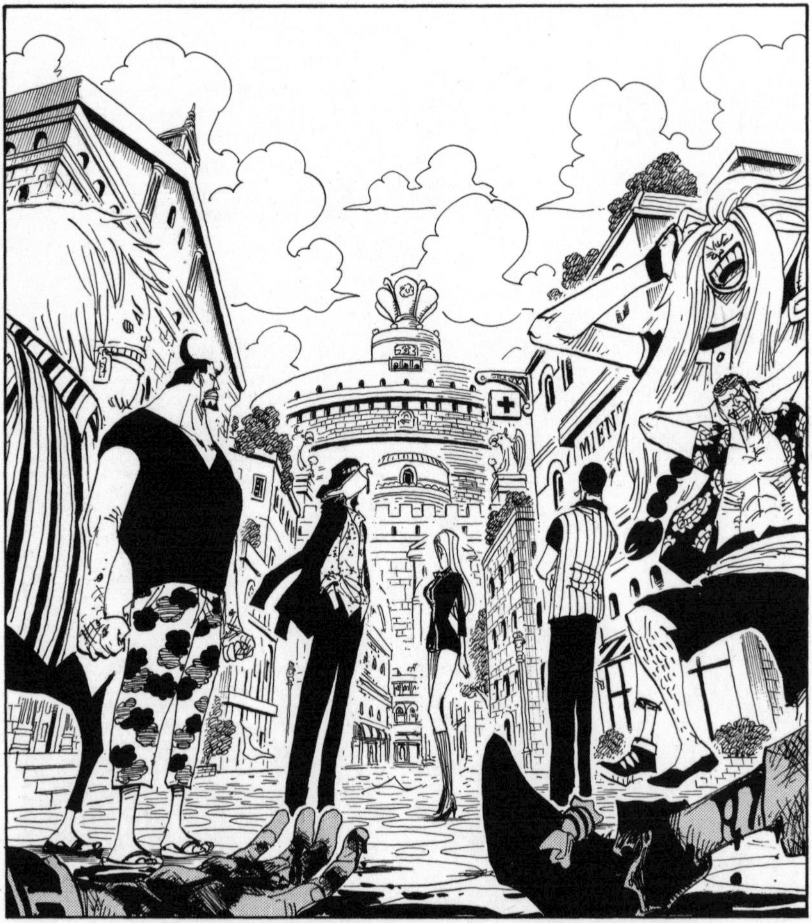
MIEN

CP9'S INDEPENDENT REPORT, VOL. 22:
"WE CAN'T STAY IN THIS TOWN ANY LONGER"

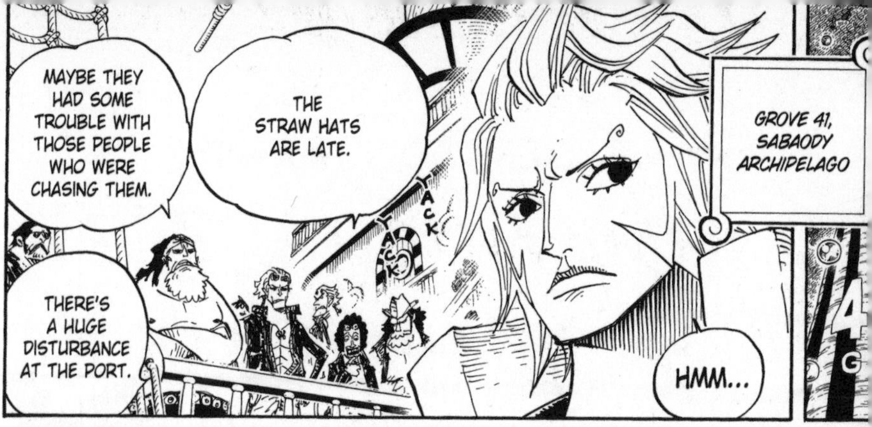
GROVE 41, SABAODY ARCHIPELAGO
HMM...
YACK
YACK
THE STRAW HATS ARE LATE.
MAYBE THEY HAD SOME TROUBLE WITH THOSE PEOPLE WHO WERE CHASING THEM.
THERE'S A HUGE DISTURBANCE AT THE PORT.

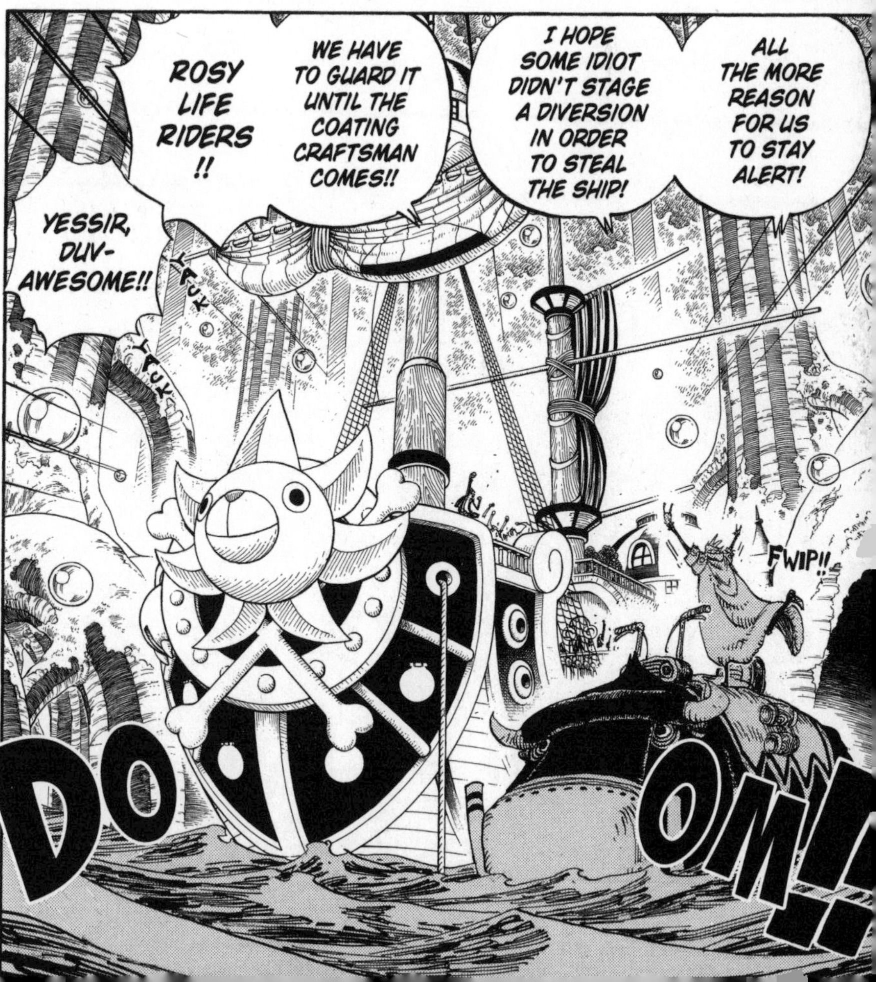
ALL THE MORE REASON FOR US TO STAY ALERT!
I HOPE SOME IDIOT DIDN'T STAGE A DIVERSION IN ORDER TO STEAL THE SHIP!
WE HAVE TO GUARD IT UNTIL THE COATING CRAFTSMAN COMES!!
ROSY LIFE RIDERS !!
YESSIR, DUV-AWESOME!!
YAUK
YAUK
FWIP!!
DOOM!!

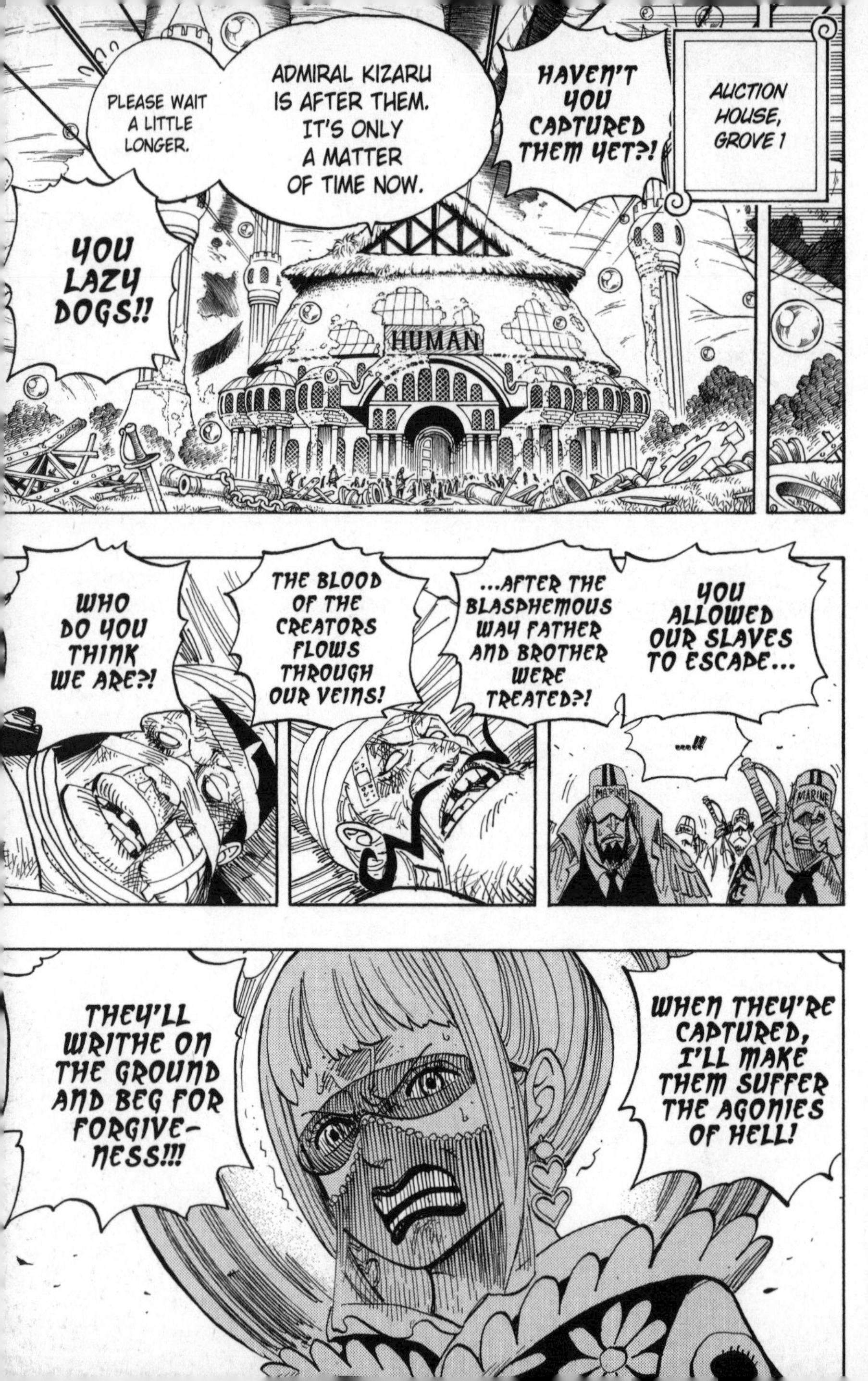
AUCTION HOUSE, GROVE 1
HAVEN'T YOU CAPTURED THEM YET?!
ADMIRAL KIZARU IS AFTER THEM. IT'S ONLY A MATTER OF TIME NOW.
PLEASE WAIT A LITTLE LONGER.
HUMAN
YOU LAZY DOGS!!
YOU ALLOWED OUR SLAVES TO ESCAPE...
...!!
...AFTER THE BLASPHEMOUS WAY FATHER AND BROTHER WERE TREATED?!
THE BLOOD OF THE CREATORS FLOWS THROUGH OUR VEINS!
WHO DO YOU THINK WE ARE?!
WHEN THEY'RE CAPTURED, I'LL MAKE THEM SUFFER THE AGONIES OF HELL!
THEY'LL WRITHE ON THE GROUND AND BEG FOR FORGIVENESS!!!

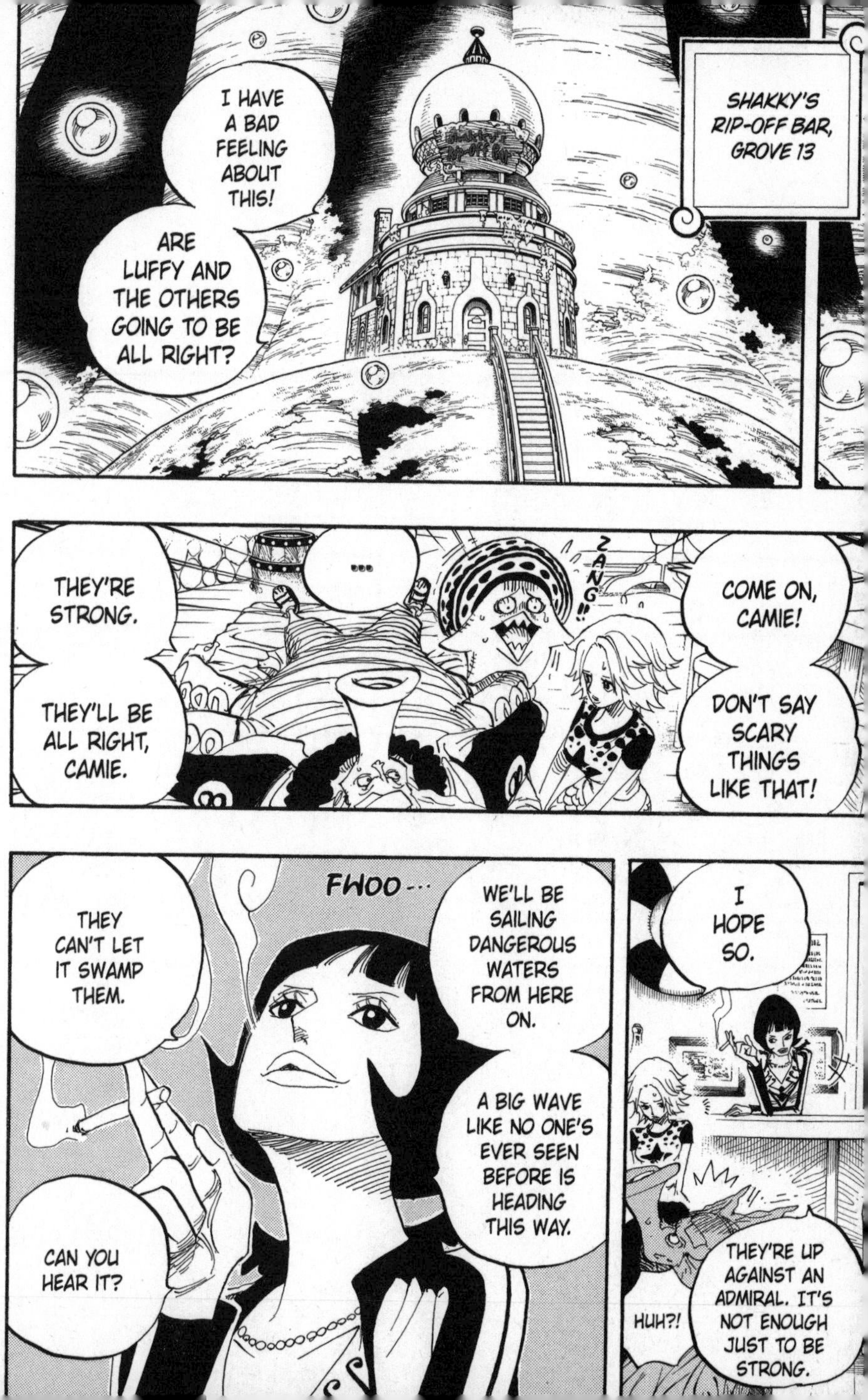
SHAKKY'S RIP-OFF BAR, GROVE 13
I HAVE A BAD FEELING ABOUT THIS!
ARE LUFFY AND THE OTHERS GOING TO BE ALL RIGHT?
COME ON, CAMIE!
DON'T SAY SCARY THINGS LIKE THAT!
ZANG!!
...
THEY'RE STRONG.
THEY'LL BE ALL RIGHT, CAMIE.
I HOPE SO.
THEY'RE UP AGAINST AN ADMIRAL. IT'S NOT ENOUGH JUST TO BE STRONG.
HUH?!
FWOO...
WE'LL BE SAILING DANGEROUS WATERS FROM HERE ON.
A BIG WAVE LIKE NO ONE'S EVER SEEN BEFORE IS HEADING THIS WAY.
THEY CAN'T LET IT SWAMP THEM.
CAN YOU HEAR IT?

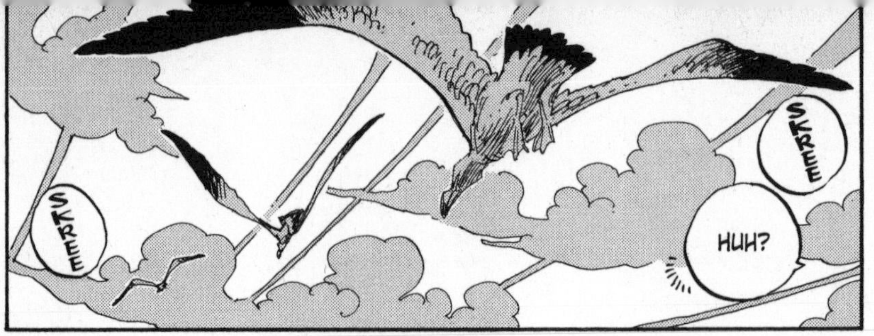
SKREE
HUH?
SKREE
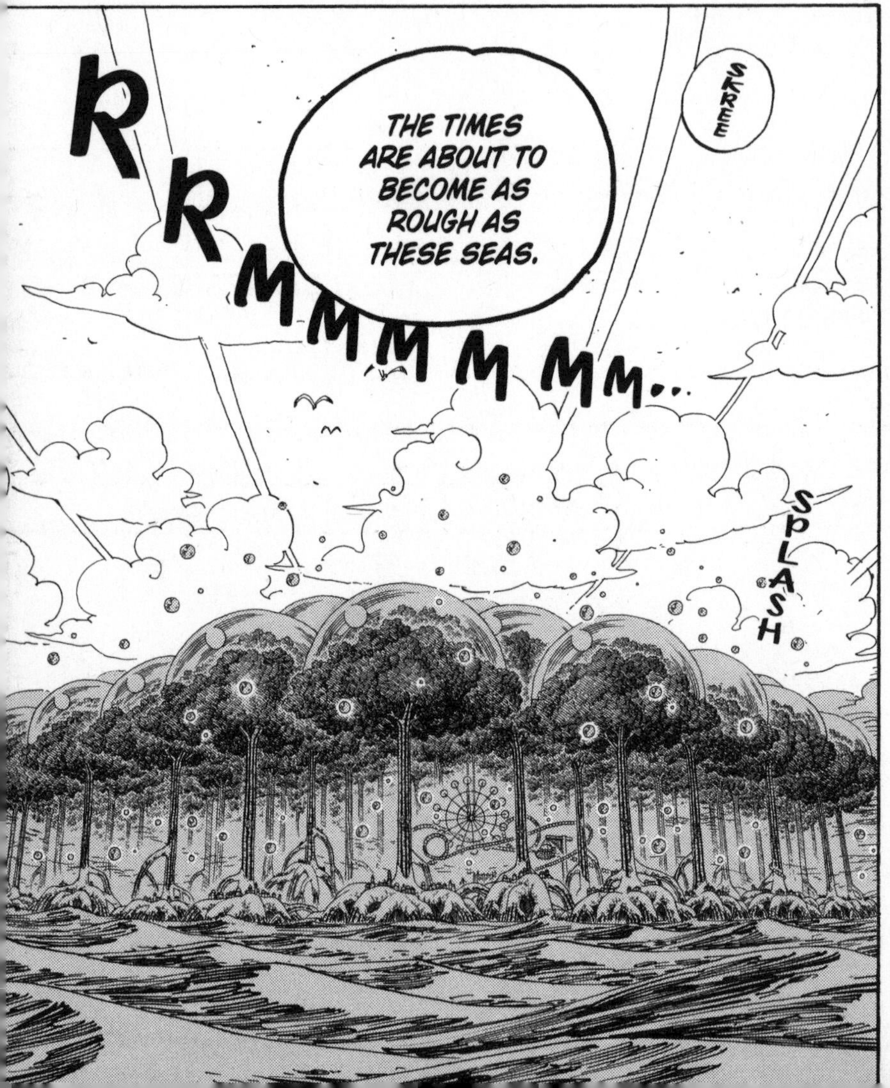
SKREE
THE TIMES ARE ABOUT TO BECOME AS ROUGH AS THESE SEAS.
RRMMMMM MMM...
SPLASH

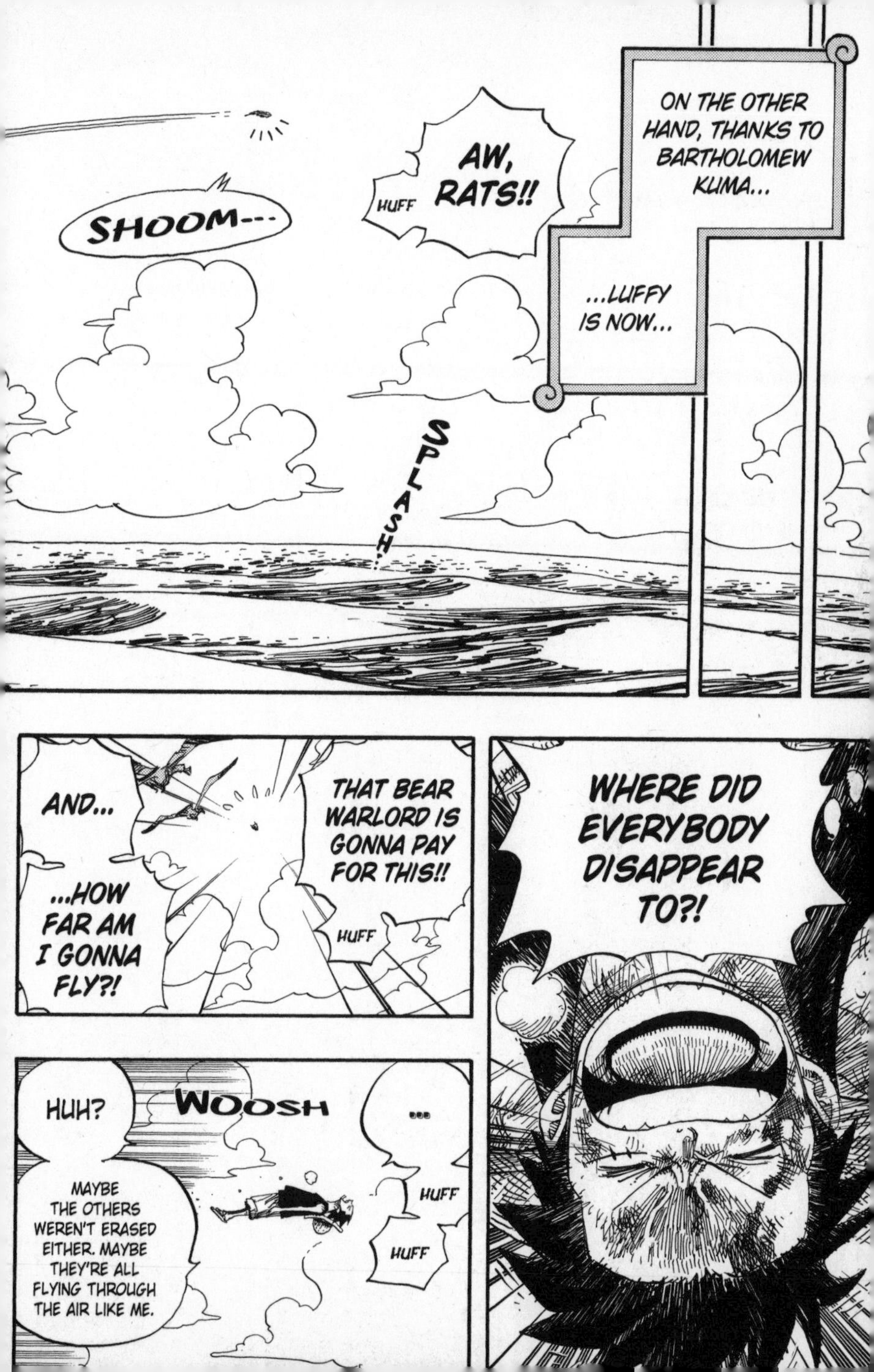
ON THE OTHER HAND, THANKS TO BARTHOLOMEW KUMA...
...LUFFY IS NOW...
AW, RATS!!
HUFF
SHOOM---
SPLASH
WHERE DID EVERYBODY DISAPPEAR TO?!
THAT BEAR WARLORD IS GONNA PAY FOR THIS!!
HUFF
AND...
...HOW FAR AM I GONNA FLY?!
...
HUFF
HUFF
WOOSH
HUH?
MAYBE THE OTHERS WEREN'T ERASED EITHER. MAYBE THEY'RE ALL FLYING THROUGH THE AIR LIKE ME.

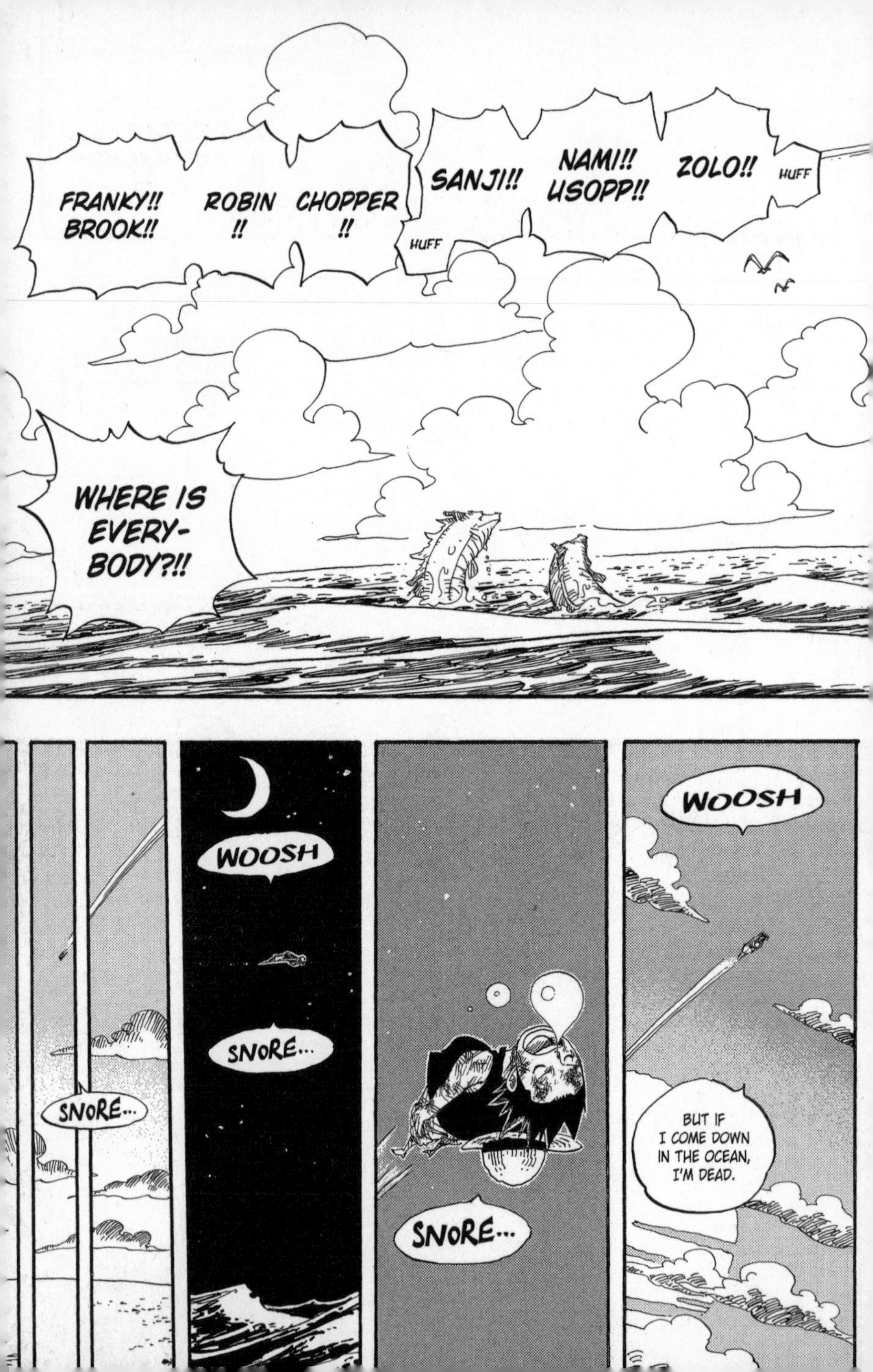
HUFF
ZOLO!!
NAMI!! USOPP!!
SANJI!!
HUFF
CHOPPER !!
ROBIN !!
FRANKY!! BROOK!!
WHERE IS EVERY-BODY?!!
WOOSH
BUT IF I COME DOWN IN THE OCEAN, I'M DEAD.
SNORE...
WOOSH
SNORE...
SNORE...

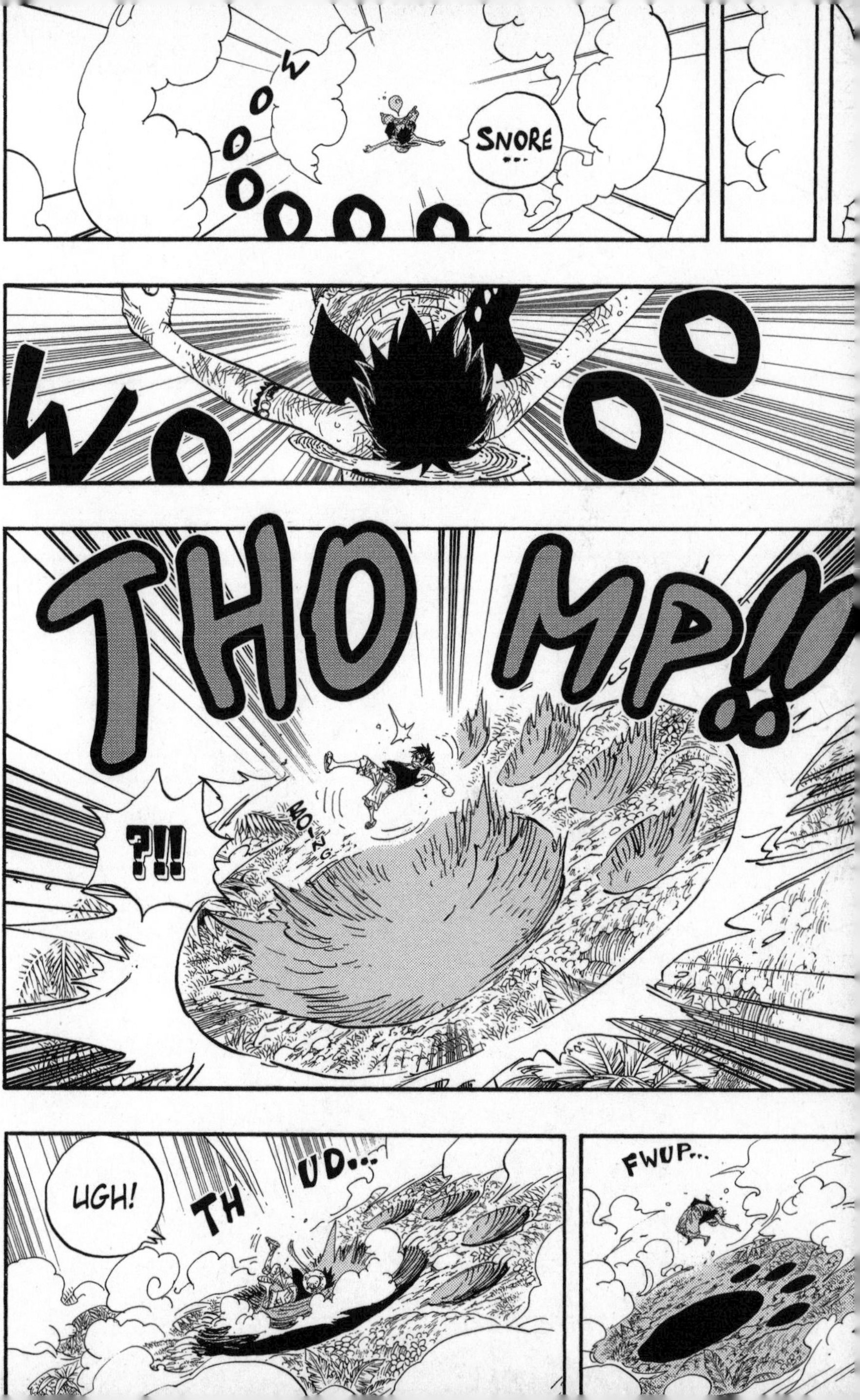
WOOOOOOO
SNORE...
WOOO
THOMP!!
?!!
BOING
UGH!
THUD...
FWUP...

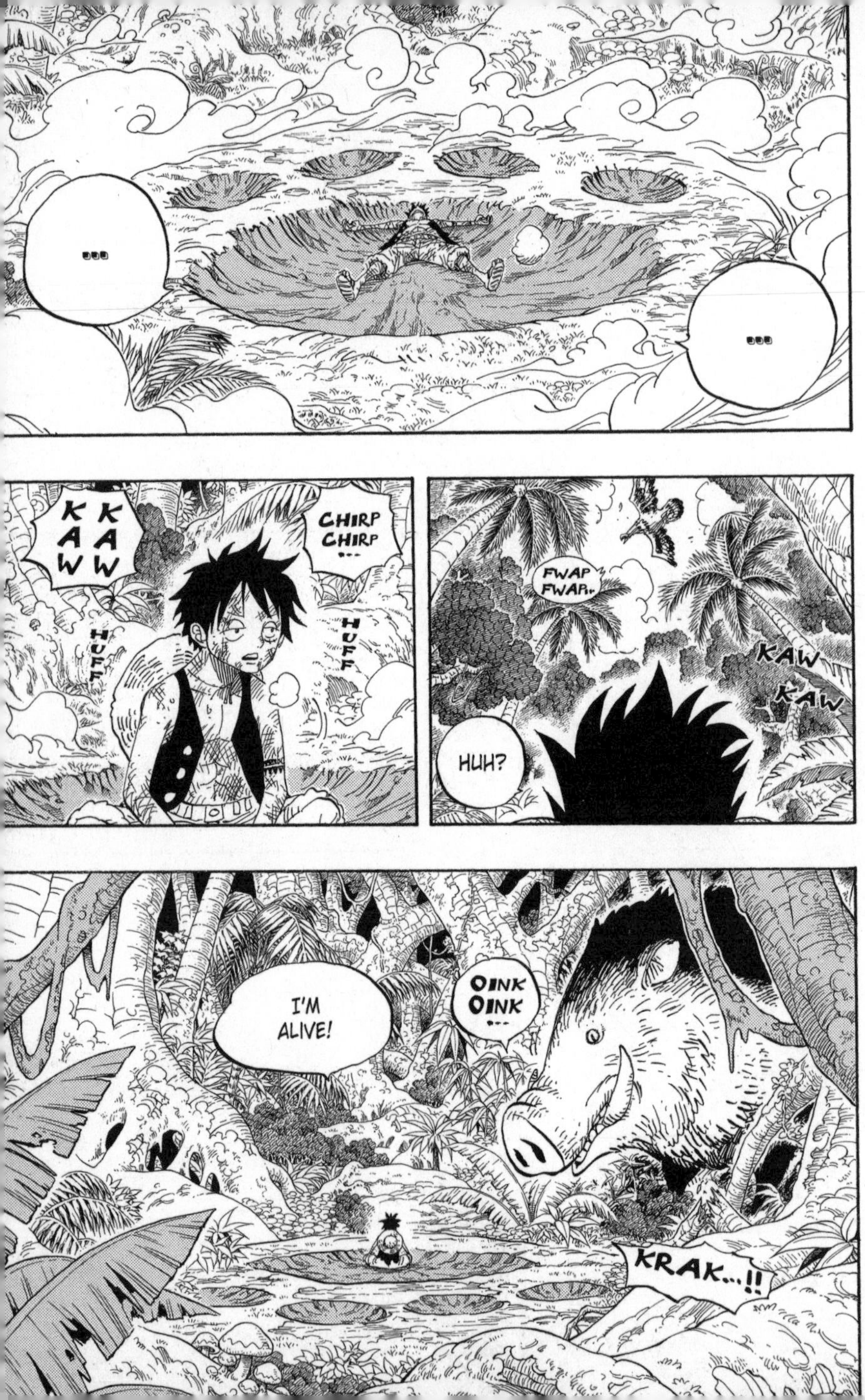
...
...
FWAP FWAP..
KAW KAW
HUH?
CHIRP CHIRP...
KAW KAW KAW KAW
HUFF HUFF
OINK OINK...
I'M ALIVE!
KRAK...!!

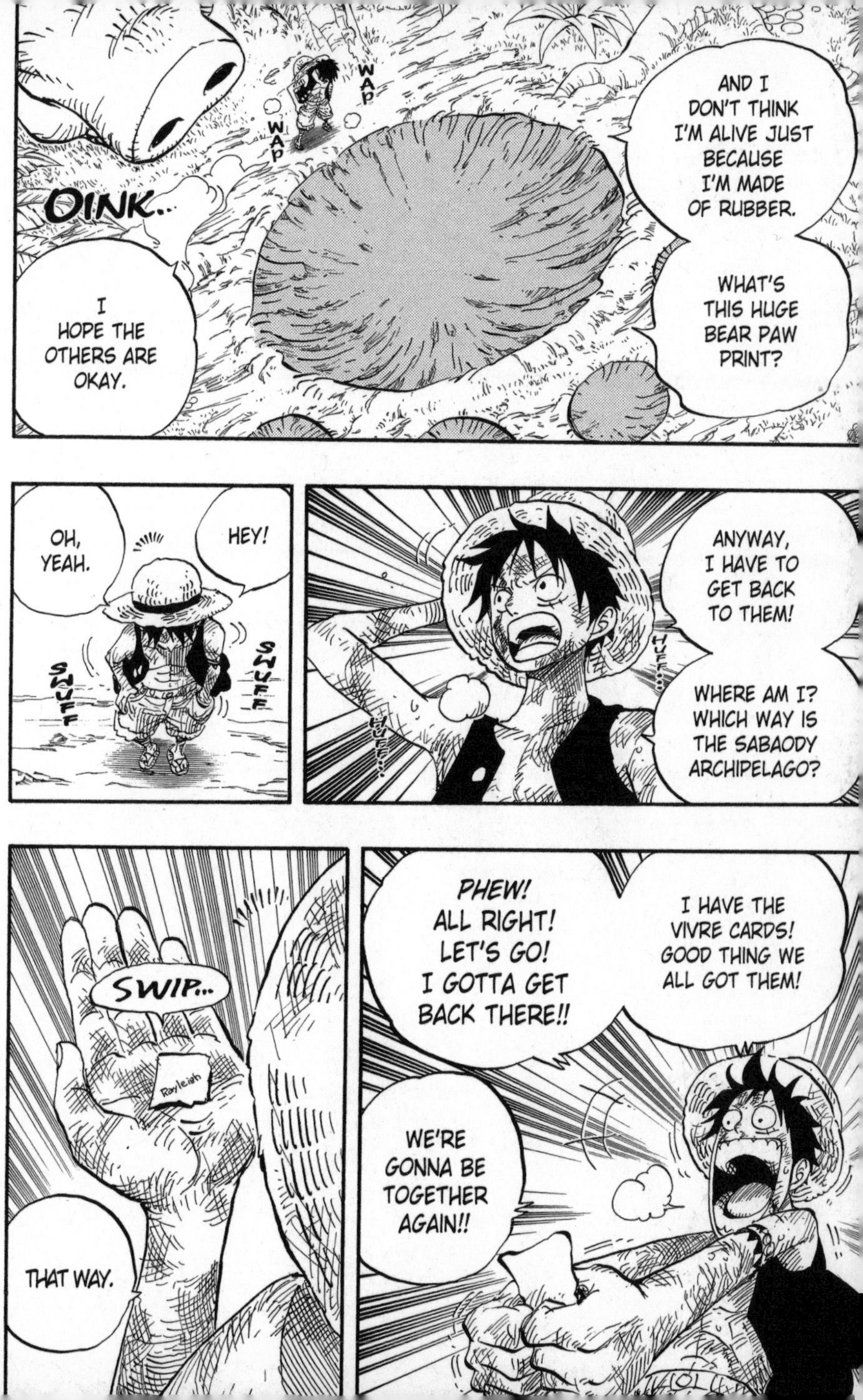
AND I DON'T THINK I'M ALIVE JUST BECAUSE I'M MADE OF RUBBER.
WHAT'S THIS HUGE BEAR PAW PRINT?
WAP
WAP
OINK...
I HOPE THE OTHERS ARE OKAY.
ANYWAY, I HAVE TO GET BACK TO THEM!
WHERE AM I? WHICH WAY IS THE SABAODY ARCHIPELAGO?
HUFF...
HUFF...
HEY!
OH, YEAH.
SHUFF
SHUFF
I HAVE THE VIVRE CARDS! GOOD THING WE ALL GOT THEM!
PHEW! ALL RIGHT! LET'S GO! I GOTTA GET BACK THERE!!
WE'RE GONNA BE TOGETHER AGAIN!!
SWIP...
Rayleigh
THAT WAY.

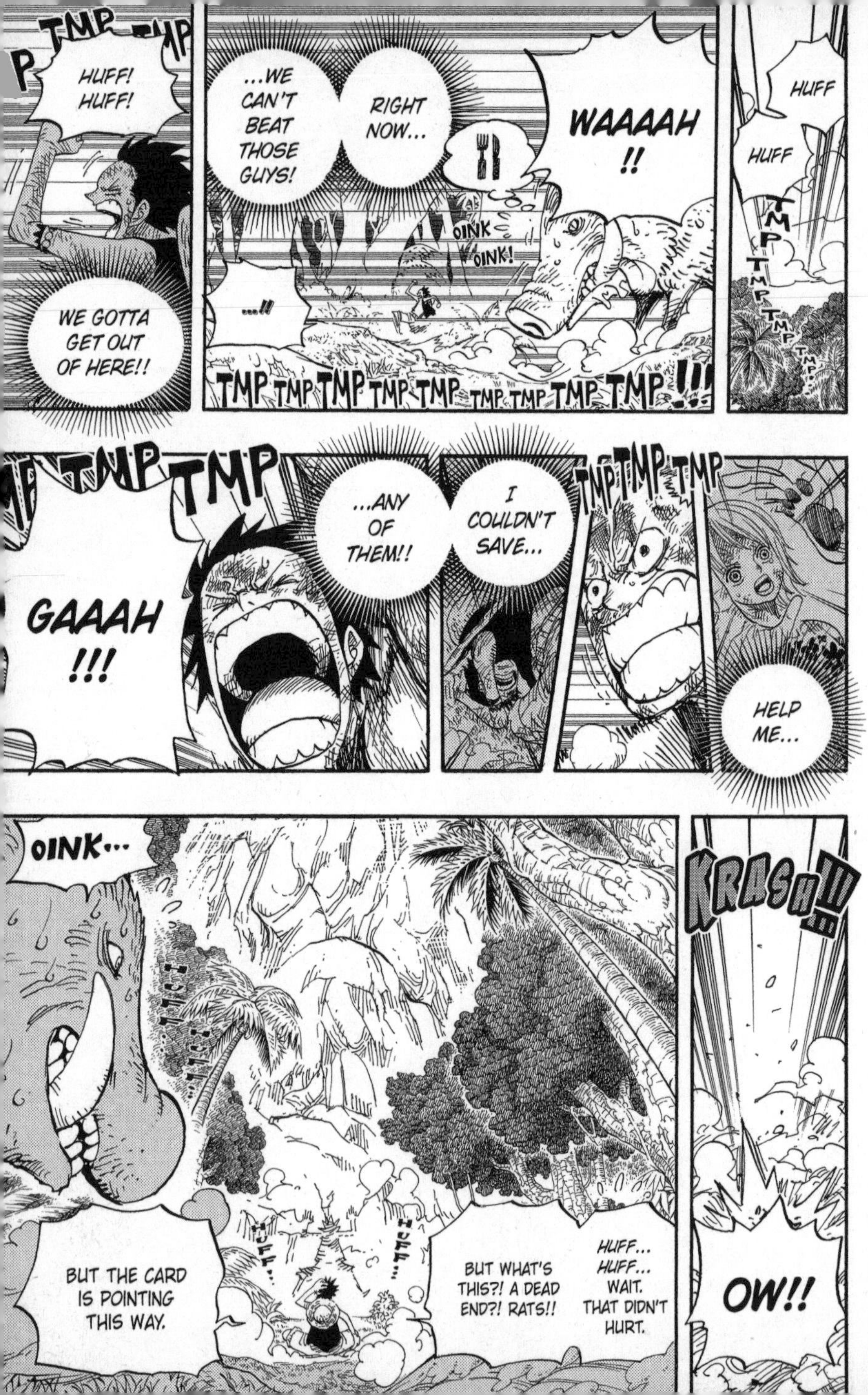
HUFF
HUFF
TMP TMP TMP TMP TMP TMP...
WAAAAH !!
OINK OINK!
RIGHT NOW...
...WE CAN'T BEAT THOSE GUYS!
...!!
TMP TMP TMP TMP TMP TMP TMP TMP TMP !!!
TMP TMP
HUFF! HUFF!
WE GOTTA GET OUT OF HERE!!
HELP ME...
TMP TMP TMP
I COULDN'T SAVE...
...ANY OF THEM!!
TMP TMP TMP
GAAAH !!!
KRASH!!!
OW!!
HUFF... HUFF... WAIT. THAT DIDN'T HURT.
BUT WHAT'S THIS?! A DEAD END?! RATS!!
HUFF...
HUFF...
BUT THE CARD IS POINTING THIS WAY.
HUFF HUFF
OINK...

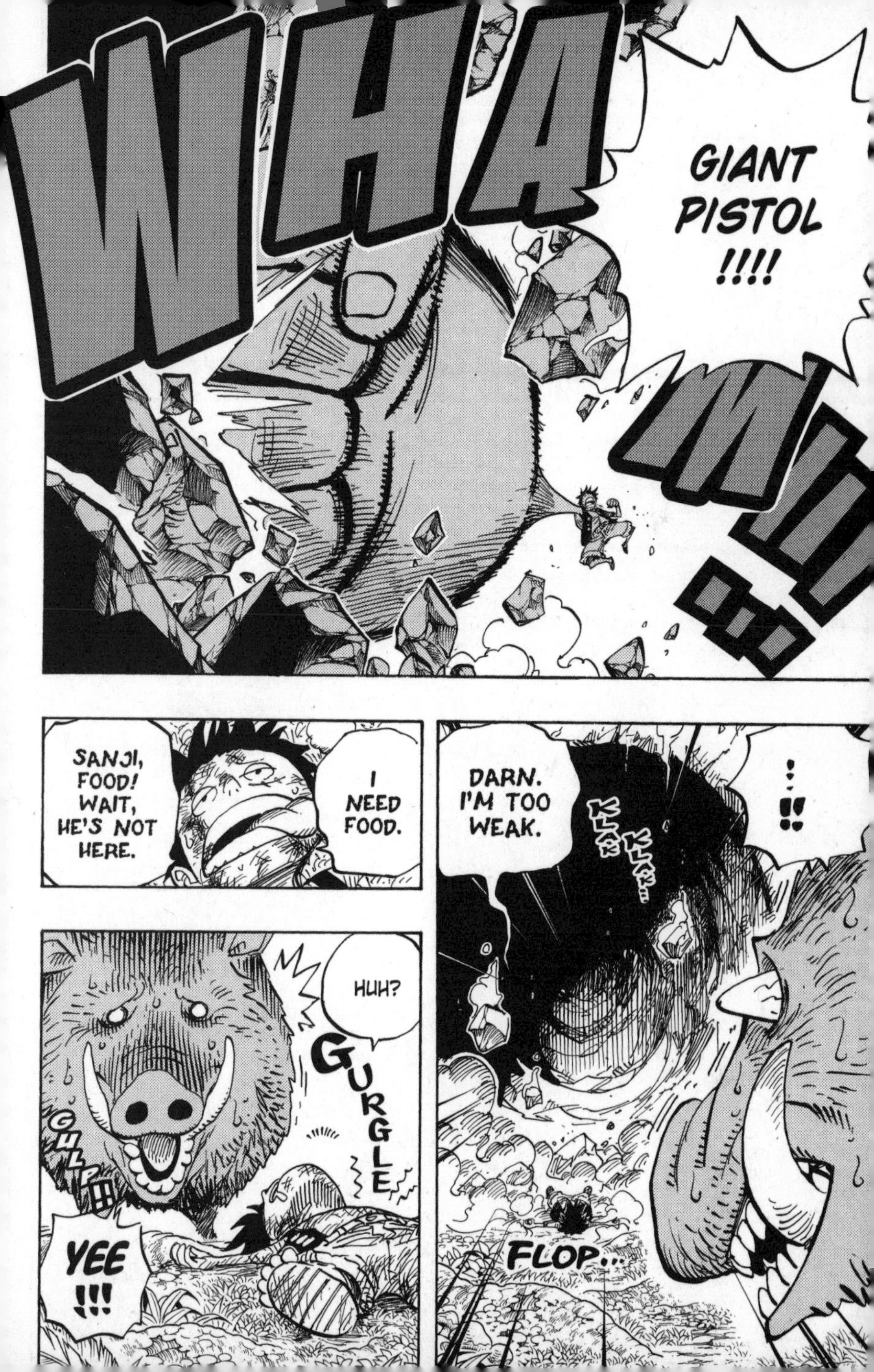

GIANT PISTOL !!!!
WHAM!!
!!
DARN. I'M TOO WEAK.
KLAK KLAK...
FLOP...
I NEED FOOD.
SANJI, FOOD! WAIT, HE'S NOT HERE.
HUH?
GURGLE
GULP!!
YEE !!!

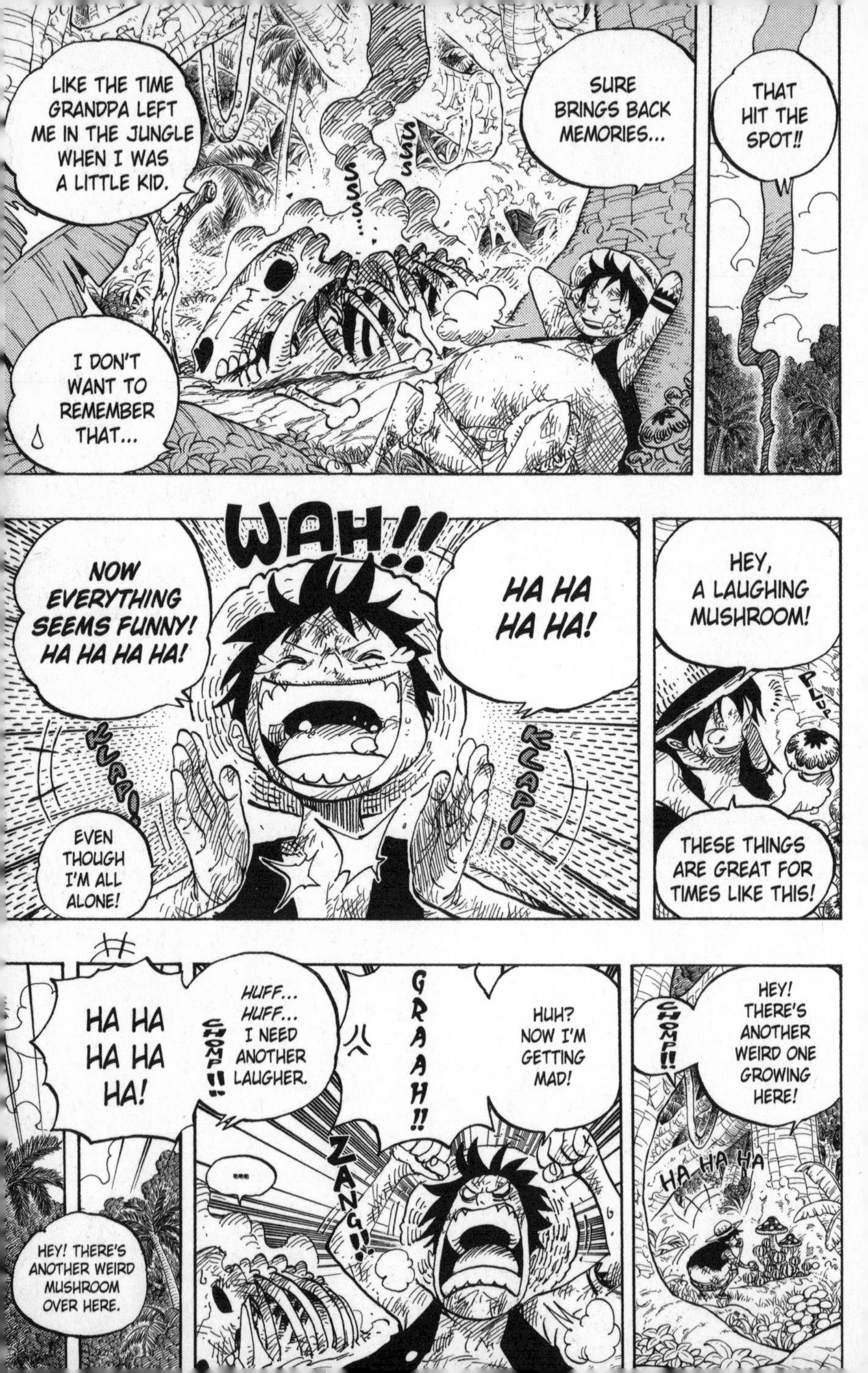
THAT HIT THE SPOT!!
SURE BRINGS BACK MEMORIES...
SSSS...
SSSS
LIKE THE TIME GRANDPA LEFT ME IN THE JUNGLE WHEN I WAS A LITTLE KID.
I DON'T WANT TO REMEMBER THAT...
HEY, A LAUGHING MUSHROOM!
PLUP
THESE THINGS ARE GREAT FOR TIMES LIKE THIS!
WAH!!
HA HA HA HA!
KLAP!
NOW EVERYTHING SEEMS FUNNY! HA HA HA HA!
KLAP!
EVEN THOUGH I'M ALL ALONE!
CHOMP!!
HEY! THERE'S ANOTHER WEIRD ONE GROWING HERE!
HA HA HA HA
HUH? NOW I'M GETTING MAD!
GRAAAH!!
ZANG!!
HUFF... HUFF... I NEED ANOTHER LAUGHER.
CHOMP!!
...
HA HA HA HA HA!
HEY! THERE'S ANOTHER WEIRD MUSHROOM OVER HERE.

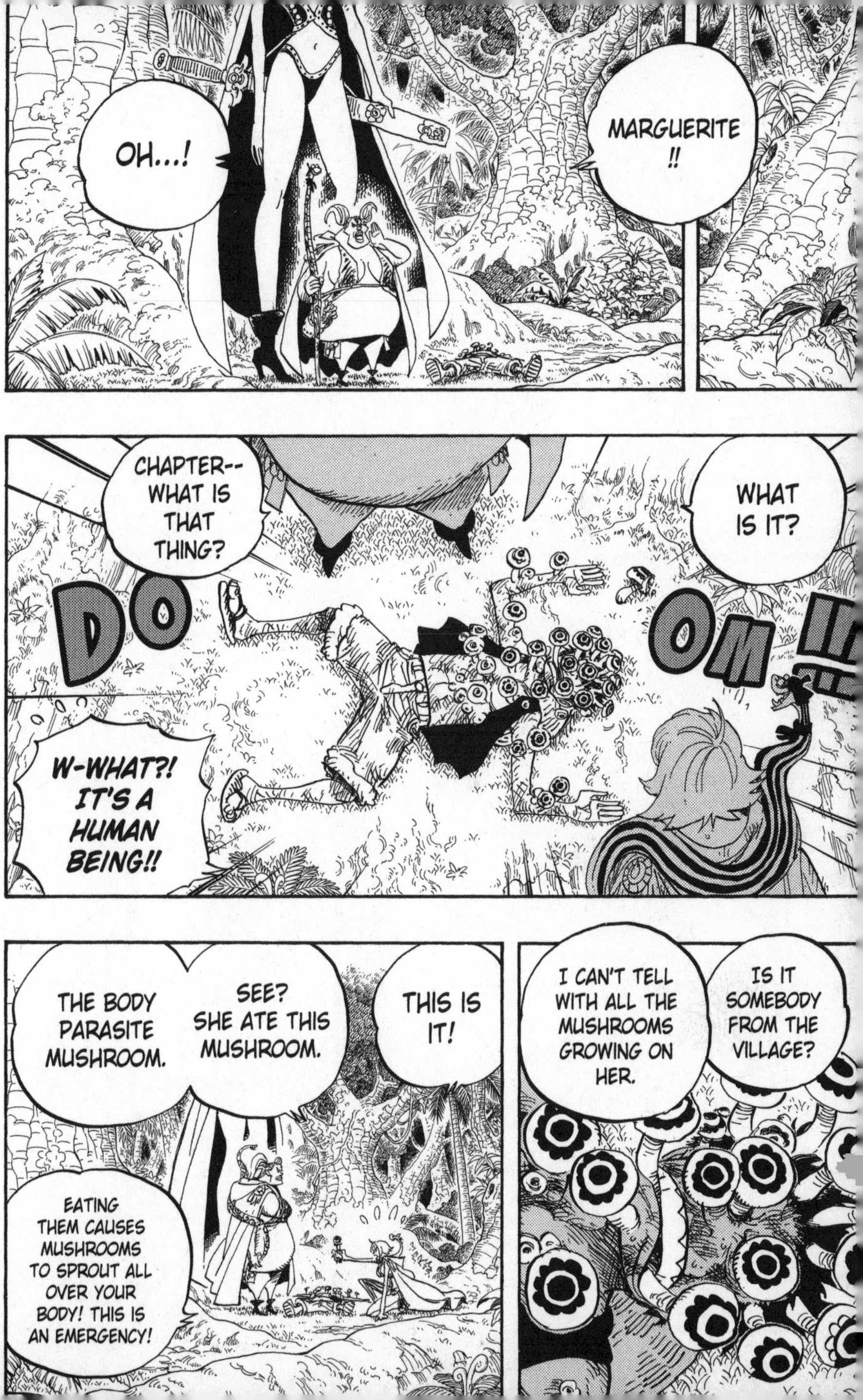
MARGUERITE !!
OH...!
WHAT IS IT?
CHAPTER-- WHAT IS THAT THING?
DO OM!!
W-WHAT?! IT'S A HUMAN BEING!!
IS IT SOMEBODY FROM THE VILLAGE?
I CAN'T TELL WITH ALL THE MUSHROOMS GROWING ON HER.
THIS IS IT!
SEE? SHE ATE THIS MUSHROOM.
THE BODY PARASITE MUSHROOM.
EATING THEM CAUSES MUSHROOMS TO SPROUT ALL OVER YOUR BODY! THIS IS AN EMERGENCY!

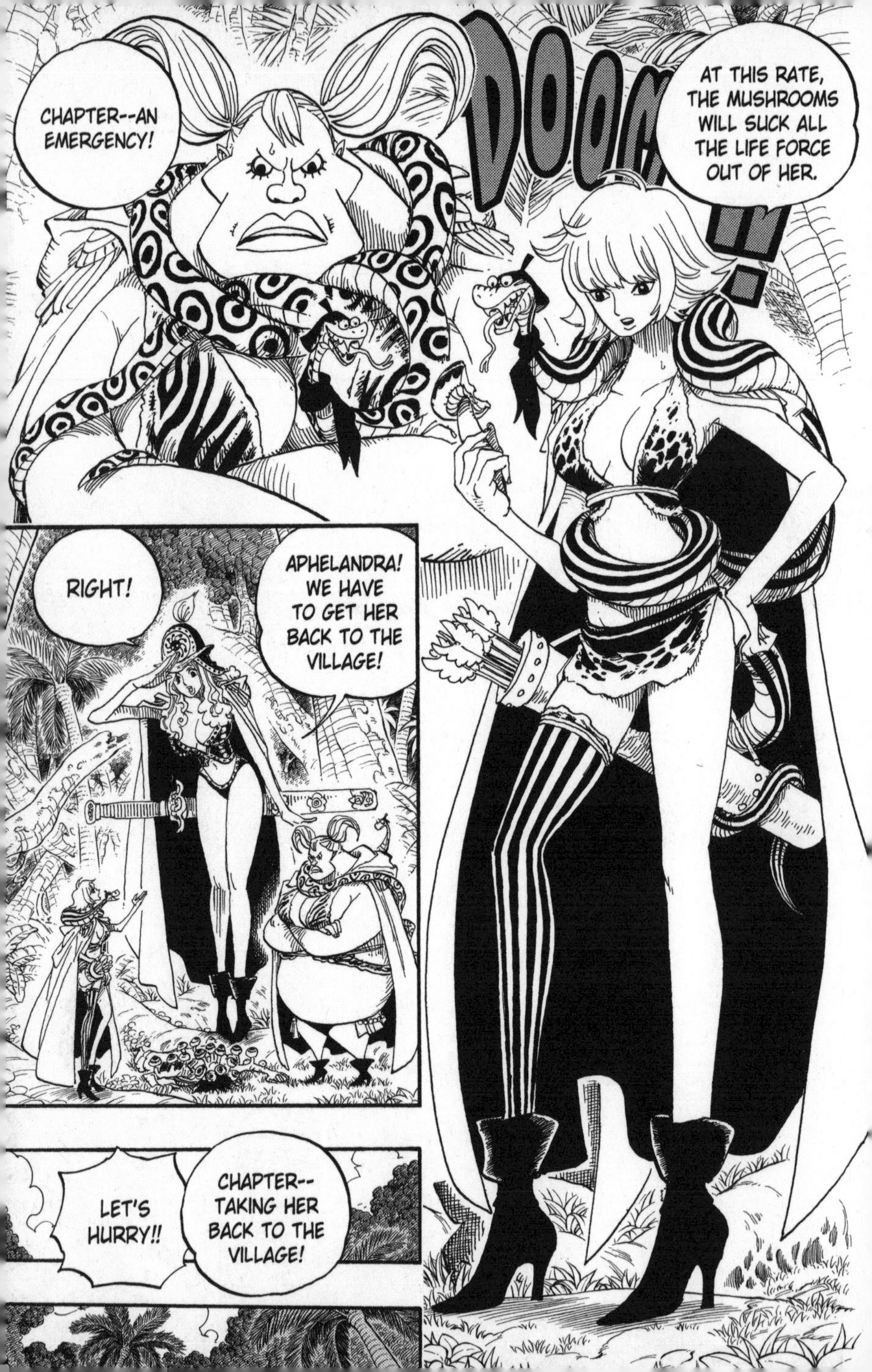
DOO
AT THIS RATE, THE MUSHROOMS WILL SUCK ALL THE LIFE FORCE OUT OF HER.
CHAPTER--AN EMERGENCY!
APHELANDRA! WE HAVE TO GET HER BACK TO THE VILLAGE!
RIGHT!
CHAPTER--TAKING HER BACK TO THE VILLAGE!
LET'S HURRY!!

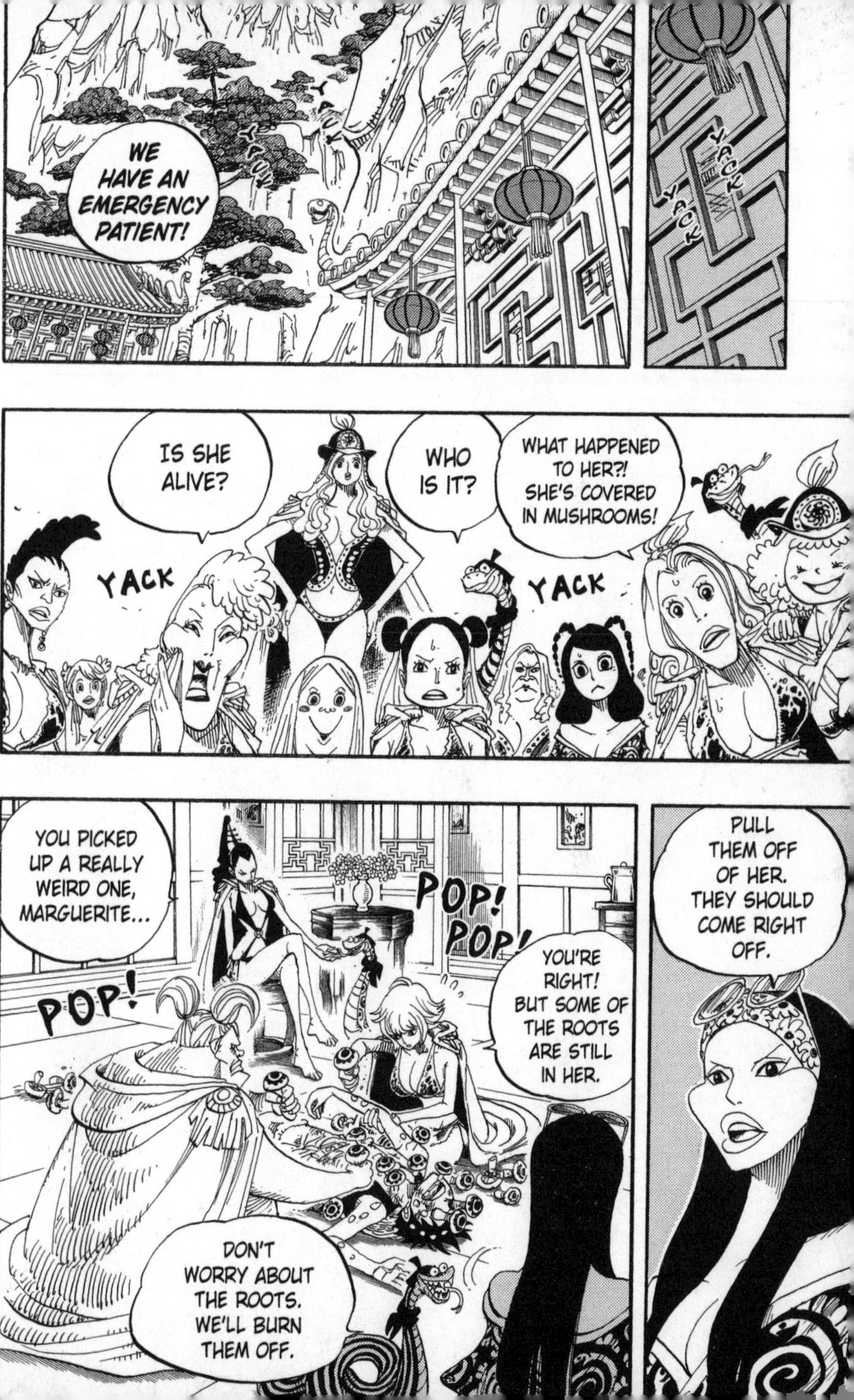
YACK
YACK
WE HAVE AN EMERGENCY PATIENT!
WHAT HAPPENED TO HER?! SHE'S COVERED IN MUSHROOMS!
YACK
WHO IS IT?
IS SHE ALIVE?
YACK
PULL THEM OFF OF HER. THEY SHOULD COME RIGHT OFF.
YOU'RE RIGHT! BUT SOME OF THE ROOTS ARE STILL IN HER.
POP! POP!
YOU PICKED UP A REALLY WEIRD ONE, MARGUERITE...
POP!
DON'T WORRY ABOUT THE ROOTS. WE'LL BURN THEM OFF.

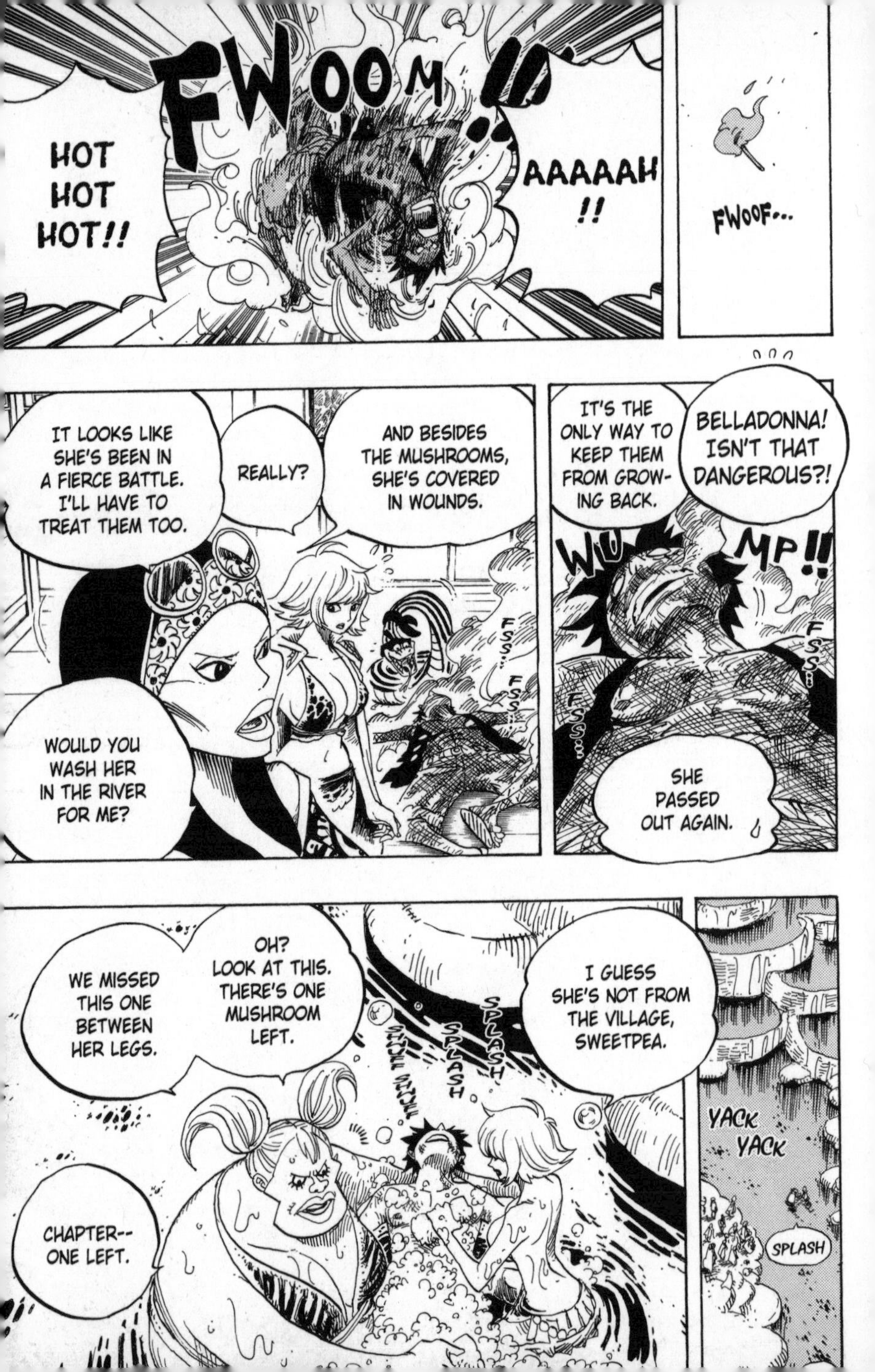
FWOOF...
FWOOM!!
AAAAAH!!
HOT HOT HOT!!
BELLADONNA! ISN'T THAT DANGEROUS?!
IT'S THE ONLY WAY TO KEEP THEM FROM GROWING BACK.
WUMP!!
FSS...
FSS...
SHE PASSED OUT AGAIN.
AND BESIDES THE MUSHROOMS, SHE'S COVERED IN WOUNDS.
REALLY?
IT LOOKS LIKE SHE'S BEEN IN A FIERCE BATTLE. I'LL HAVE TO TREAT THEM TOO.
FSS...
FSS...
WOULD YOU WASH HER IN THE RIVER FOR ME?
YACK YACK
SPLASH
I GUESS SHE'S NOT FROM THE VILLAGE, SWEETPEA.
SPLASH
SPLASH
OH? LOOK AT THIS. THERE'S ONE MUSHROOM LEFT.
WE MISSED THIS ONE BETWEEN HER LEGS.
CHAPTER-- ONE LEFT.

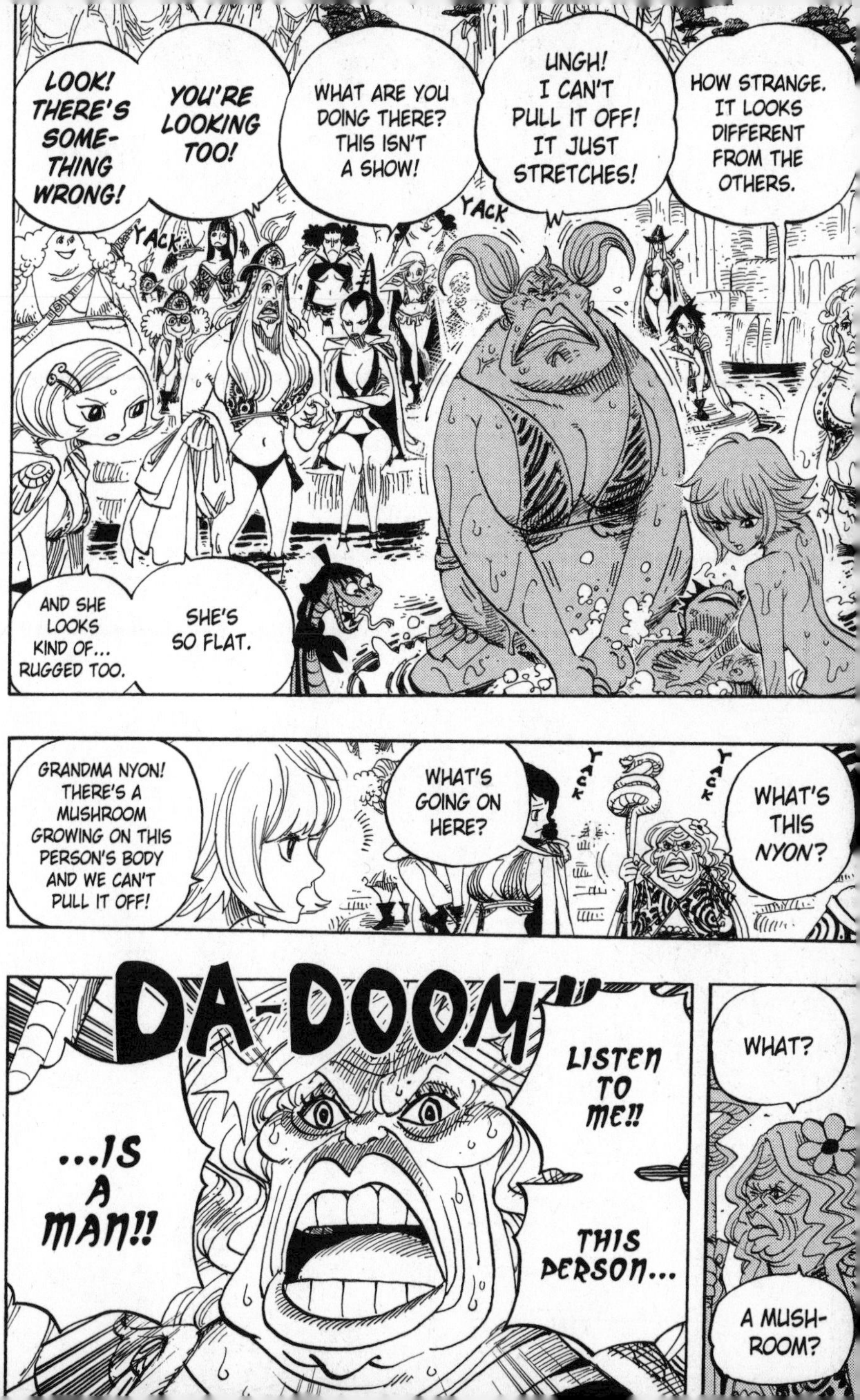
HOW STRANGE. IT LOOKS DIFFERENT FROM THE OTHERS.
UNGH! I CAN'T PULL IT OFF! IT JUST STRETCHES!
YACK
WHAT ARE YOU DOING THERE? THIS ISN'T A SHOW!
YOU'RE LOOKING TOO!
LOOK! THERE'S SOME-THING WRONG!
YACK
SHE'S SO FLAT.
AND SHE LOOKS KIND OF... RUGGED TOO.
WHAT'S THIS NYON?
YACK
YACK
WHAT'S GOING ON HERE?
GRANDMA NYON! THERE'S A MUSHROOM GROWING ON THIS PERSON'S BODY AND WE CAN'T PULL IT OFF!
WHAT?
A MUSH-ROOM?
DA-DOOM
LISTEN TO ME!!
THIS PERSON...
...IS A MAN!!

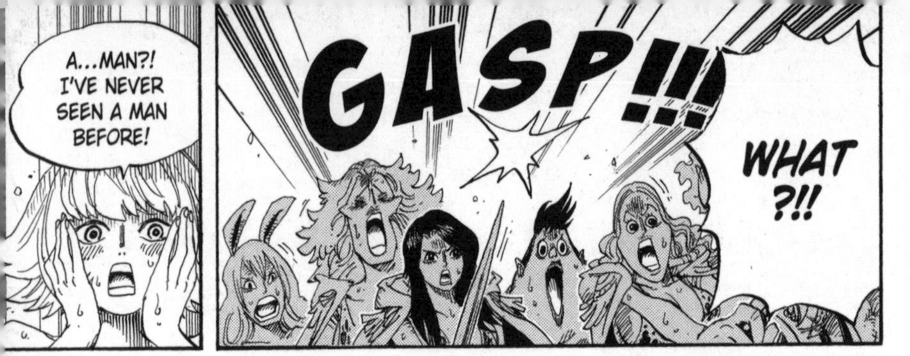
GASP!!!
WHAT ?!!
A...MAN?! I'VE NEVER SEEN A MAN BEFORE!

TEXT ON ISLAND SAYS "KUJA" (NINE SNAKES)--ED.

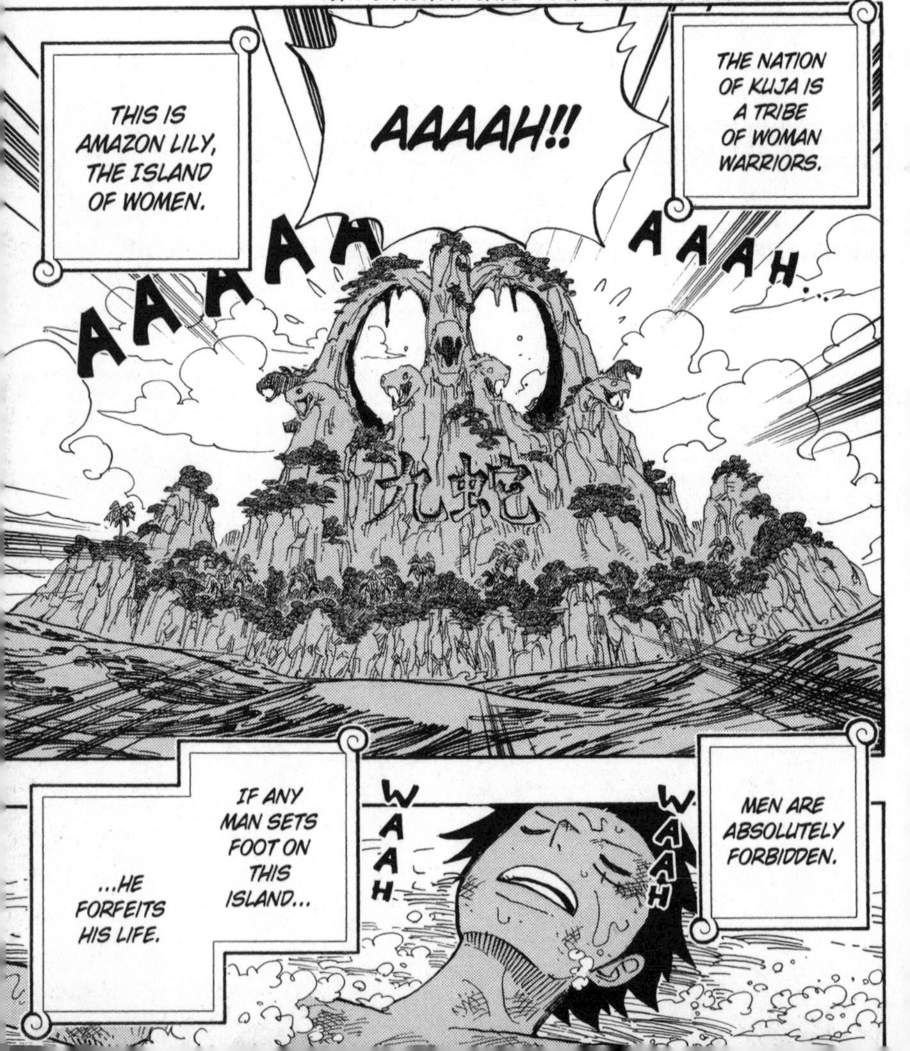
THE NATION OF KUJA IS A TRIBE OF WOMAN WARRIORS.
AAAAH!!
THIS IS AMAZON LILY, THE ISLAND OF WOMEN.
AAAAAA AAAAH.
MEN ARE ABSOLUTELY FORBIDDEN.
WAAAH
WAAAH
IF ANY MAN SETS FOOT ON THIS ISLAND...
...HE FORFEITS HIS LIFE.

SBS Question Corner

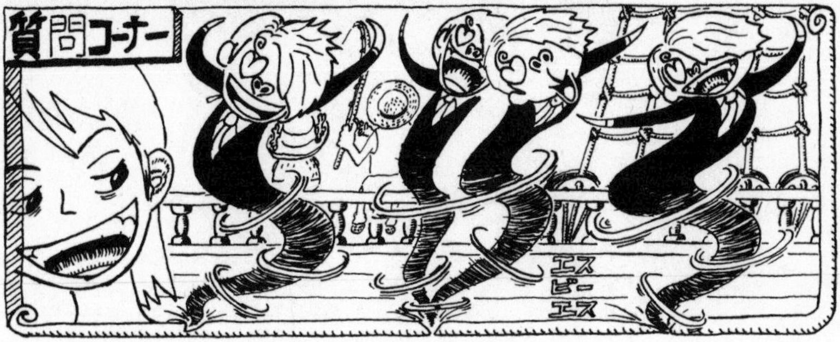
質問コーナー
エス
ビー
エス
(Yourikusai, Oita)

ader(Q): In volume 51, chapter 502, the CP9's Independent Report shows Kalifa wearing the Criminal brand that's popular on Fish-Man Island! Why would a human be wearing that? And does Kalifa like brand-name stuff?

--MOTO

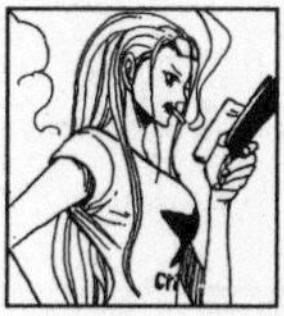

Oda(A): I'm glad you caught that. That is indeed a T-shirt of Pappagu's brand "Criminal." I get the feeling that Kalifa likes brand-name clothing. Criminal is very popular on Fish-Man Island, but it is sold on dry land too. Even Zolo was wearing it for a while. Now about the name "Criminal." The Japanese word for "criminal" can also mean "star." That's why it's star-shaped.

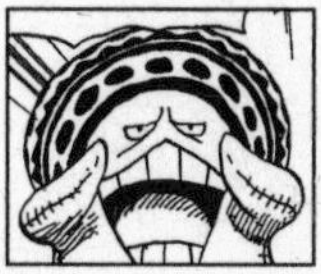

Q: Oda Sensei! Hello-Borsalino! This is about the super-cute mermaid Camie's birthday! The "Ca" in her name sounds like "K," the eleventh letter of the alphabet, so let's say it means eleven! Then "mie" rhymes with three (sort of)! So can her birthday be November 3?

--II TO ITTE!

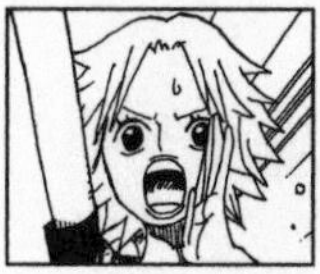

A: Hello-Borsalino! Sure. Sure-Borsalino!

Chapter 515:
ADVENTURE ON THE ISLAND OF WOMEN

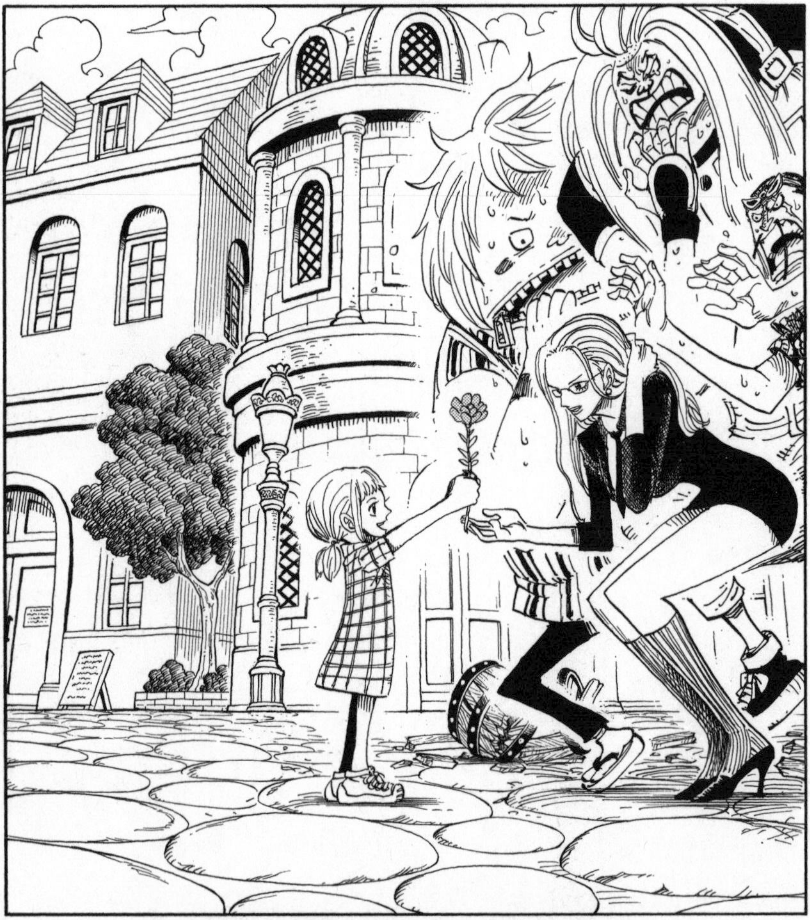

CP9'S INDEPENDENT REPORT, VOL. 23:
"A FLOWER IS A GIFT THAT SHINES BRIGHTLY"

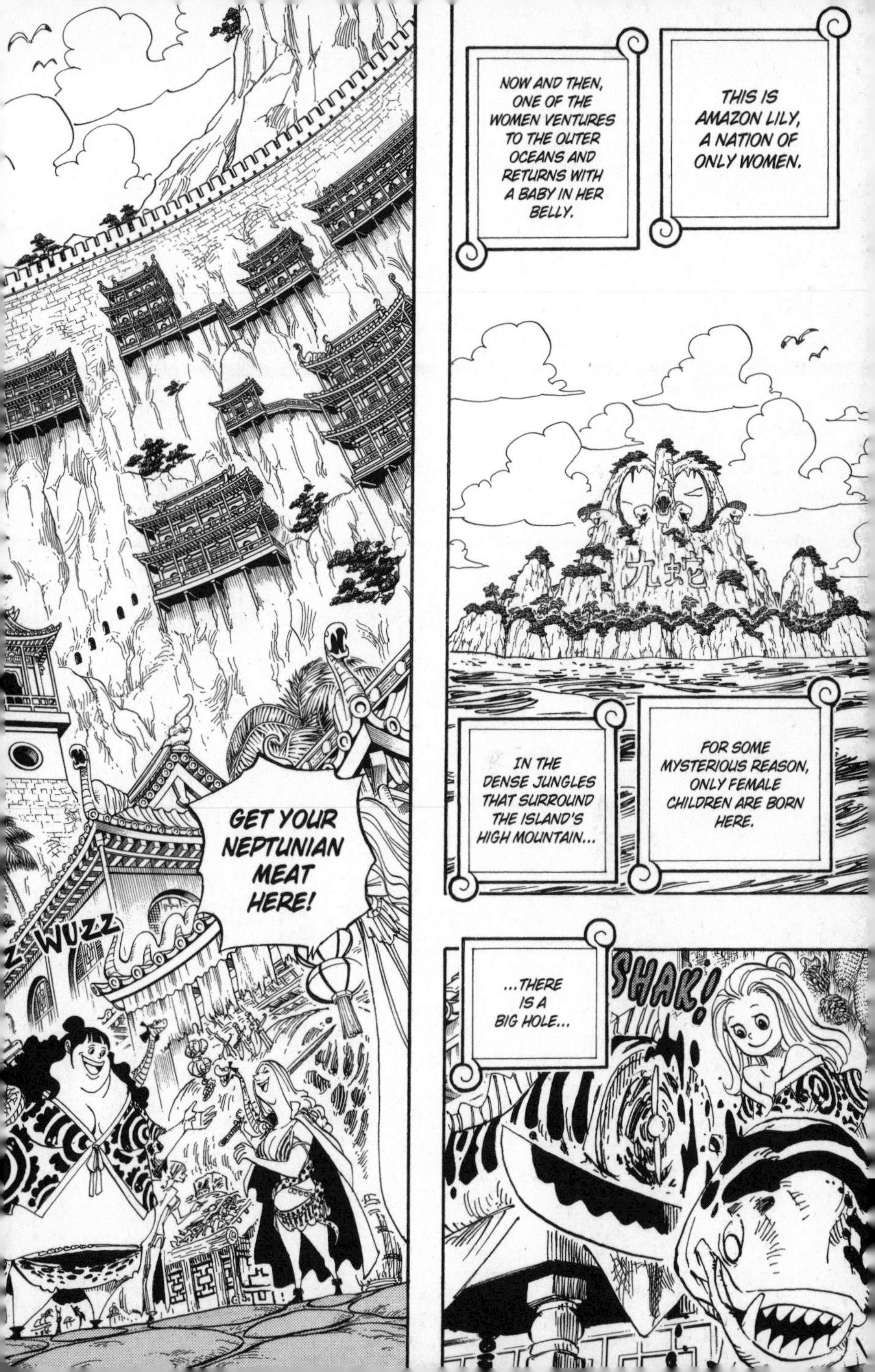
THIS IS AMAZON LILY, A NATION OF ONLY WOMEN.
NOW AND THEN, ONE OF THE WOMEN VENTURES TO THE OUTER OCEANS AND RETURNS WITH A BABY IN HER BELLY.
FOR SOME MYSTERIOUS REASON, ONLY FEMALE CHILDREN ARE BORN HERE.
IN THE DENSE JUNGLES THAT SURROUND THE ISLAND'S HIGH MOUNTAIN...
SHAK!
...THERE IS A BIG HOLE...
GET YOUR NEPTUNIAN MEAT HERE!
WUZZ

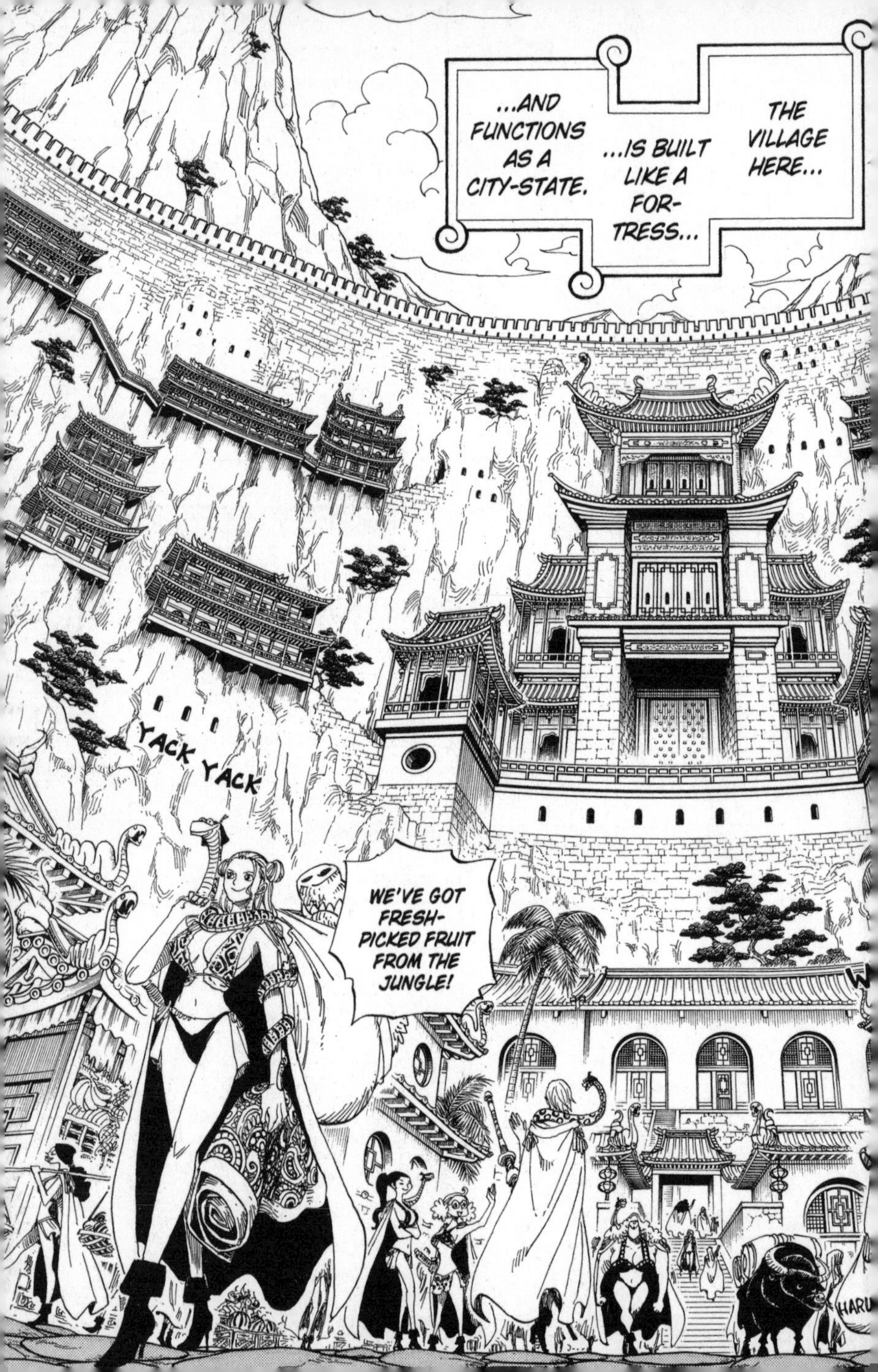
THE VILLAGE HERE...
...IS BUILT LIKE A FORTRESS...
...AND FUNCTIONS AS A CITY-STATE.
WE'VE GOT FRESH-PICKED FRUIT FROM THE JUNGLE!
YACK YACK

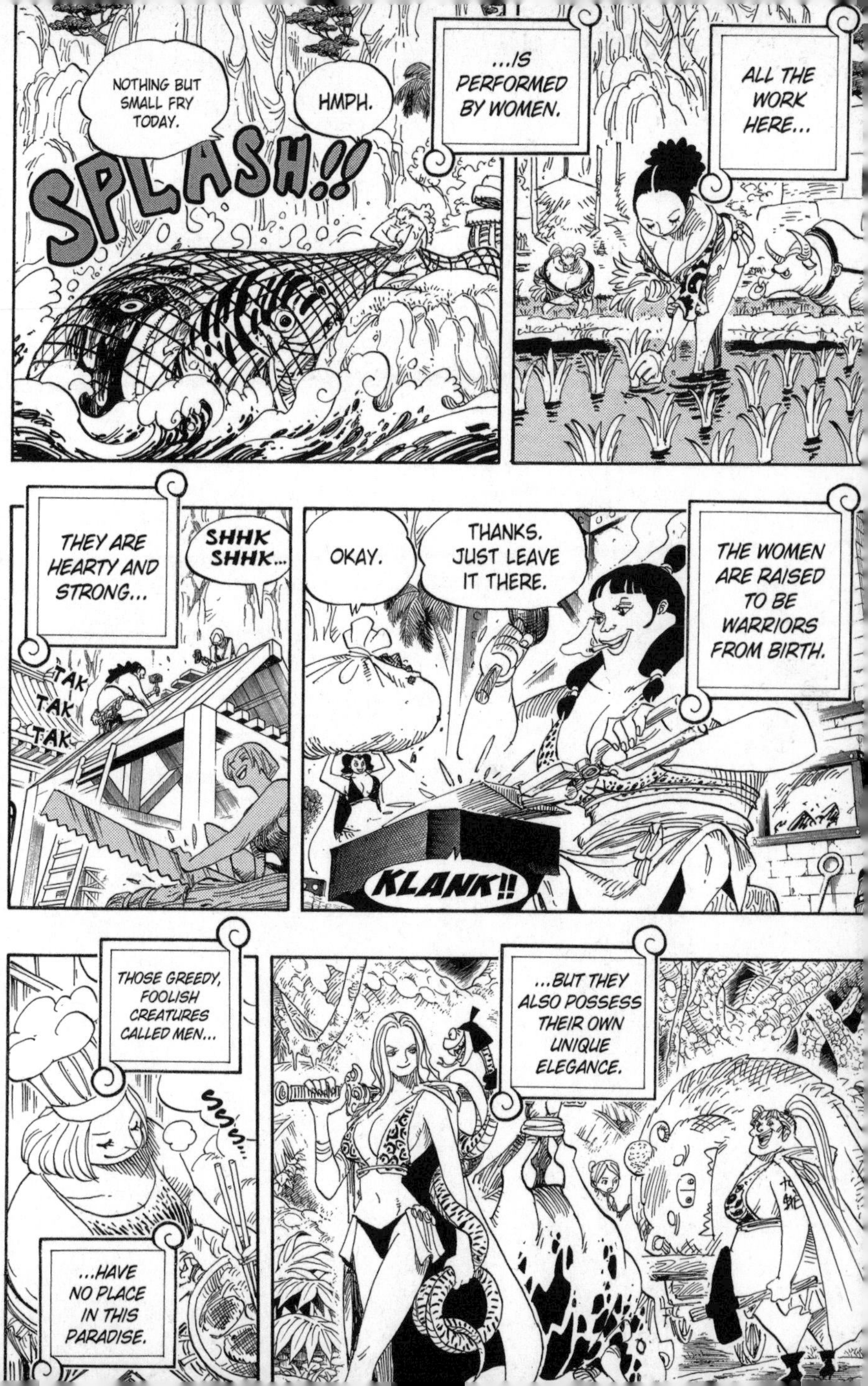
ALL THE WORK HERE...
...IS PERFORMED BY WOMEN.
HMPH.
NOTHING BUT SMALL FRY TODAY.
SPLASH!!
THE WOMEN ARE RAISED TO BE WARRIORS FROM BIRTH.
THANKS. JUST LEAVE IT THERE.
OKAY.
KLANK!!
SHHK SHHK...
THEY ARE HEARTY AND STRONG...
TAK TAK TAK
...BUT THEY ALSO POSSESS THEIR OWN UNIQUE ELEGANCE.
THOSE GREEDY, FOOLISH CREATURES CALLED MEN...
...HAVE NO PLACE IN THIS PARADISE.

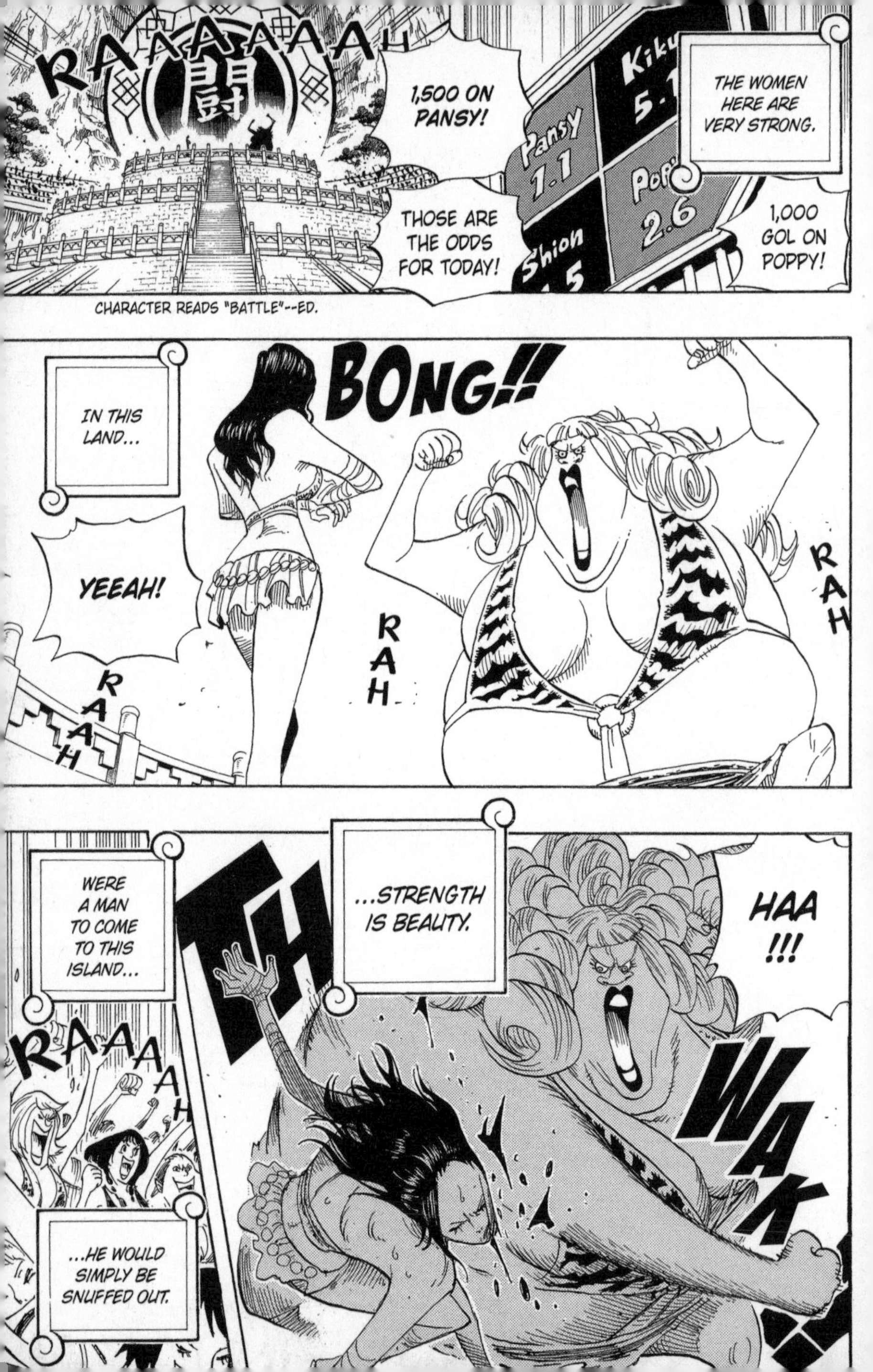
THE WOMEN HERE ARE VERY STRONG.
1,000 GOL ON POPPY!
Pansy 7.1
2.6
1,500 ON PANSY!
THOSE ARE THE ODDS FOR TODAY!
RAAAAAAH
BONG!!
RAH
RAH
IN THIS LAND...
YEEAH!
RAAH
HAA!!!
...STRENGTH IS BEAUTY.
WERE A MAN TO COME TO THIS ISLAND...
THWAK!!
RAAAAH
...HE WOULD SIMPLY BE SNUFFED OUT.

CHARACTER READS "BATTLE"--ED.

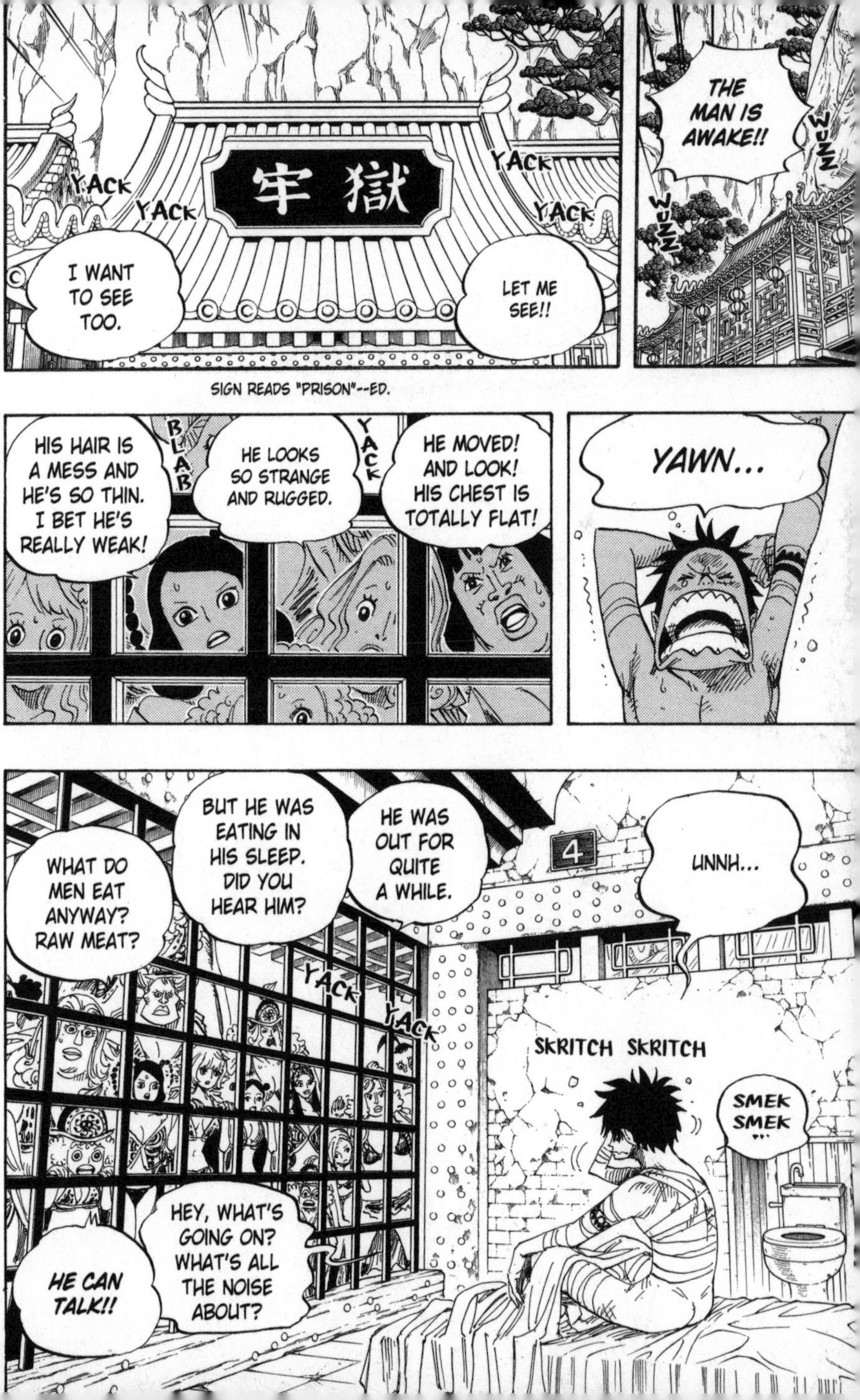
THE MAN IS AWAKE!!
WUZZ
WUZZ
YACK
YACK
LET ME SEE!!
牢獄
YACK
YACK
I WANT TO SEE TOO.
SIGN READS "PRISON"--ED.
YAWN...
HE MOVED! AND LOOK! HIS CHEST IS TOTALLY FLAT!
YACK
HE LOOKS SO STRANGE AND RUGGED.
BLAB
HIS HAIR IS A MESS AND HE'S SO THIN. I BET HE'S REALLY WEAK!
UNNH...
4
SMEK SMEK
SKRITCH SKRITCH
HE WAS OUT FOR QUITE A WHILE.
BUT HE WAS EATING IN HIS SLEEP. DID YOU HEAR HIM?
WHAT DO MEN EAT ANYWAY? RAW MEAT?
YACK
YACK
HEY, WHAT'S GOING ON? WHAT'S ALL THE NOISE ABOUT?
HE CAN TALK!!

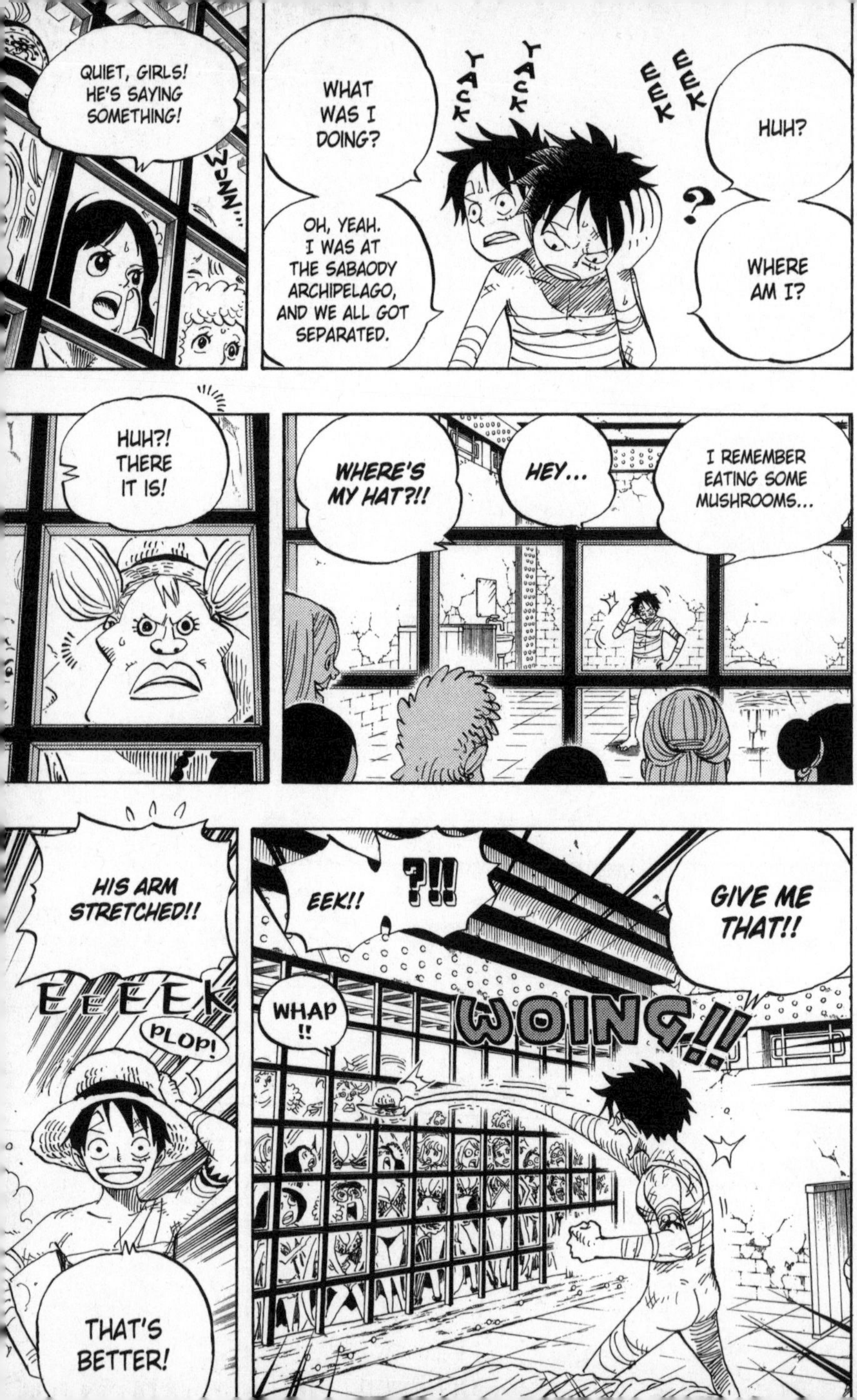
HUH?
?
WHERE AM I?
EEK EEK
YACK YACK
WHAT WAS I DOING?
OH, YEAH. I WAS AT THE SABAODY ARCHIPELAGO, AND WE ALL GOT SEPARATED.
QUIET, GIRLS! HE'S SAYING SOMETHING!
WUZZ...
I REMEMBER EATING SOME MUSHROOMS...
HEY...
WHERE'S MY HAT?!!
HUH?! THERE IT IS!
GIVE ME THAT!!
?!!
EEK!!
WOING!!
WHAP!!
HIS ARM STRETCHED!!
EEEEK
PLOP!
THAT'S BETTER!

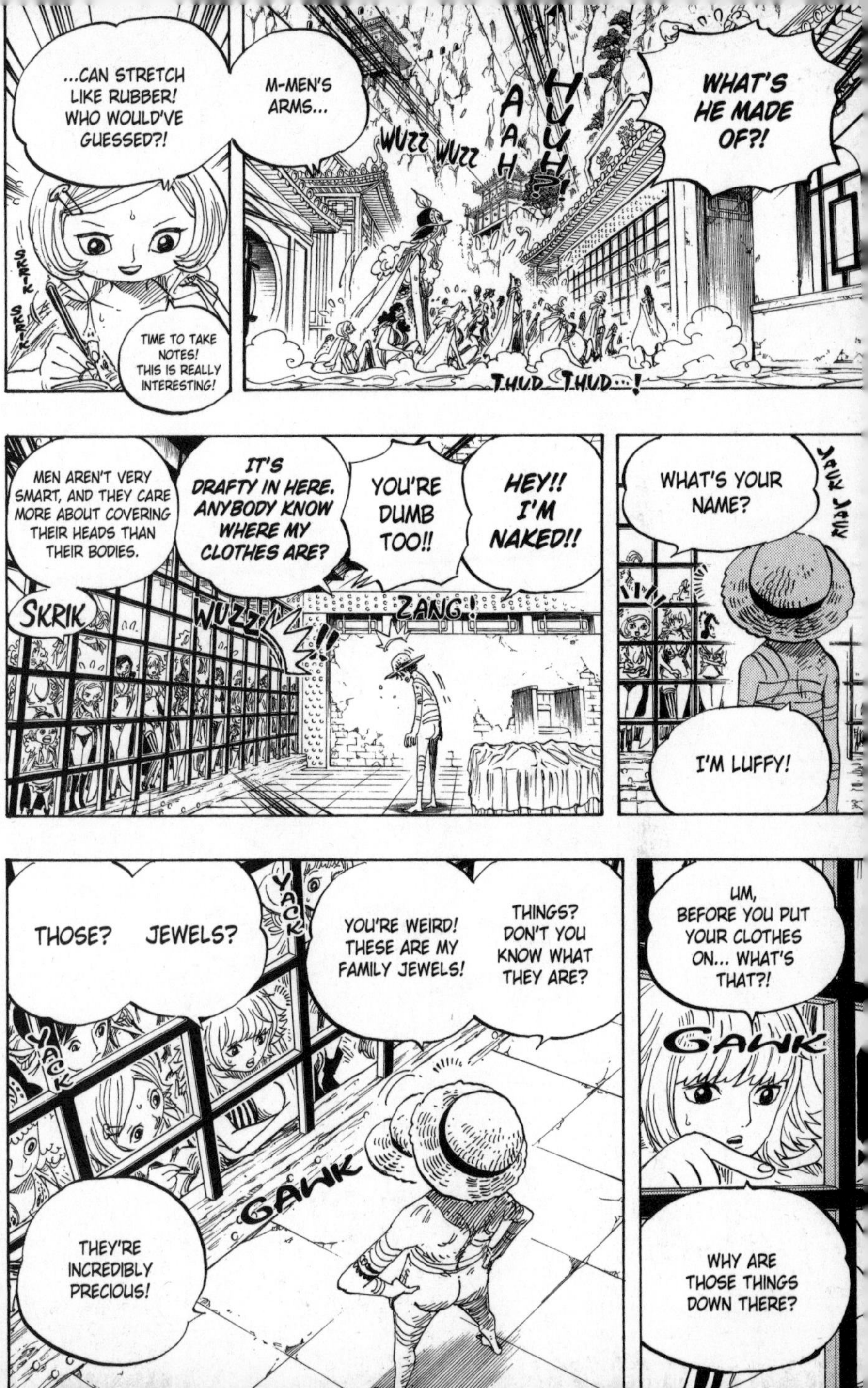
WHAT'S HE MADE OF?!
HUUH?!
AAAH
M-MEN'S ARMS...
WUZZ WUZZ
THUD THUD...!
...CAN STRETCH LIKE RUBBER! WHO WOULD'VE GUESSED?!
SKRIK
SKRIK
TIME TO TAKE NOTES! THIS IS REALLY INTERESTING!
YACK YACK
WHAT'S YOUR NAME?
I'M LUFFY!
HEY!! I'M NAKED!!
YOU'RE DUMB TOO!!
IT'S DRAFTY IN HERE. ANYBODY KNOW WHERE MY CLOTHES ARE?
ZANG!
!!
WUZZ
MEN AREN'T VERY SMART, AND THEY CARE MORE ABOUT COVERING THEIR HEADS THAN THEIR BODIES.
SKRIK
UM, BEFORE YOU PUT YOUR CLOTHES ON... WHAT'S THAT?!
GAWK
WHY ARE THOSE THINGS DOWN THERE?
THINGS? DON'T YOU KNOW WHAT THEY ARE?
YOU'RE WEIRD! THESE ARE MY FAMILY JEWELS!
YACK
JEWELS?
THOSE?
YACK
GAWK
THEY'RE INCREDIBLY PRECIOUS!

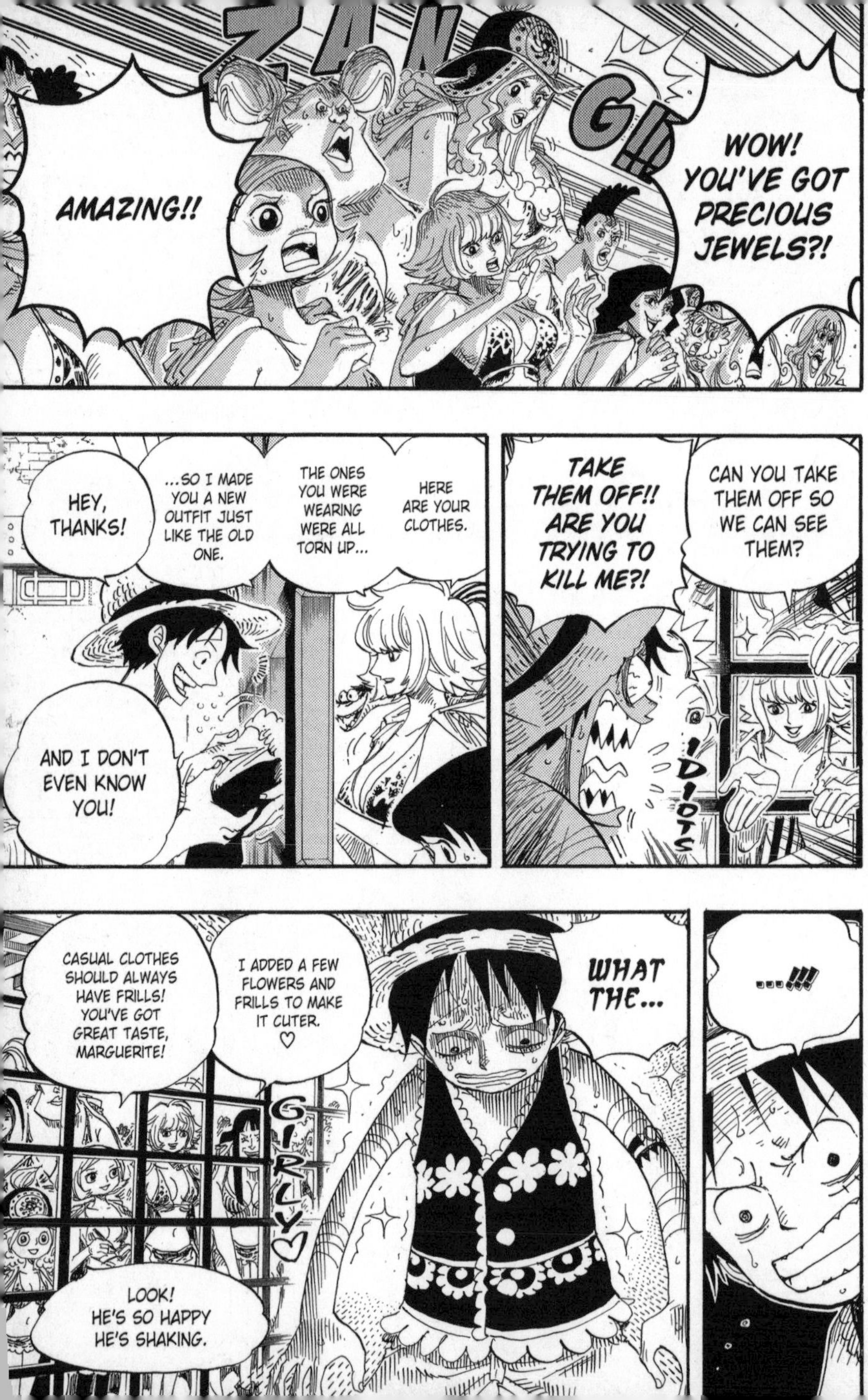

ZAN
GI
WOW! YOU'VE GOT PRECIOUS JEWELS?!
AMAZING!!
CAN YOU TAKE THEM OFF SO WE CAN SEE THEM?
TAKE THEM OFF!! ARE YOU TRYING TO KILL ME?!
IDIOTS
HERE ARE YOUR CLOTHES.
THE ONES YOU WERE WEARING WERE ALL TORN UP...
...SO I MADE YOU A NEW OUTFIT JUST LIKE THE OLD ONE.
HEY, THANKS!
AND I DON'T EVEN KNOW YOU!
...!!!
WHAT THE...
I ADDED A FEW FLOWERS AND FRILLS TO MAKE IT CUTER. ♡
CASUAL CLOTHES SHOULD ALWAYS HAVE FRILLS! YOU'VE GOT GREAT TASTE, MARGUERITE!
GIRLY♡
LOOK! HE'S SO HAPPY HE'S SHAKING.

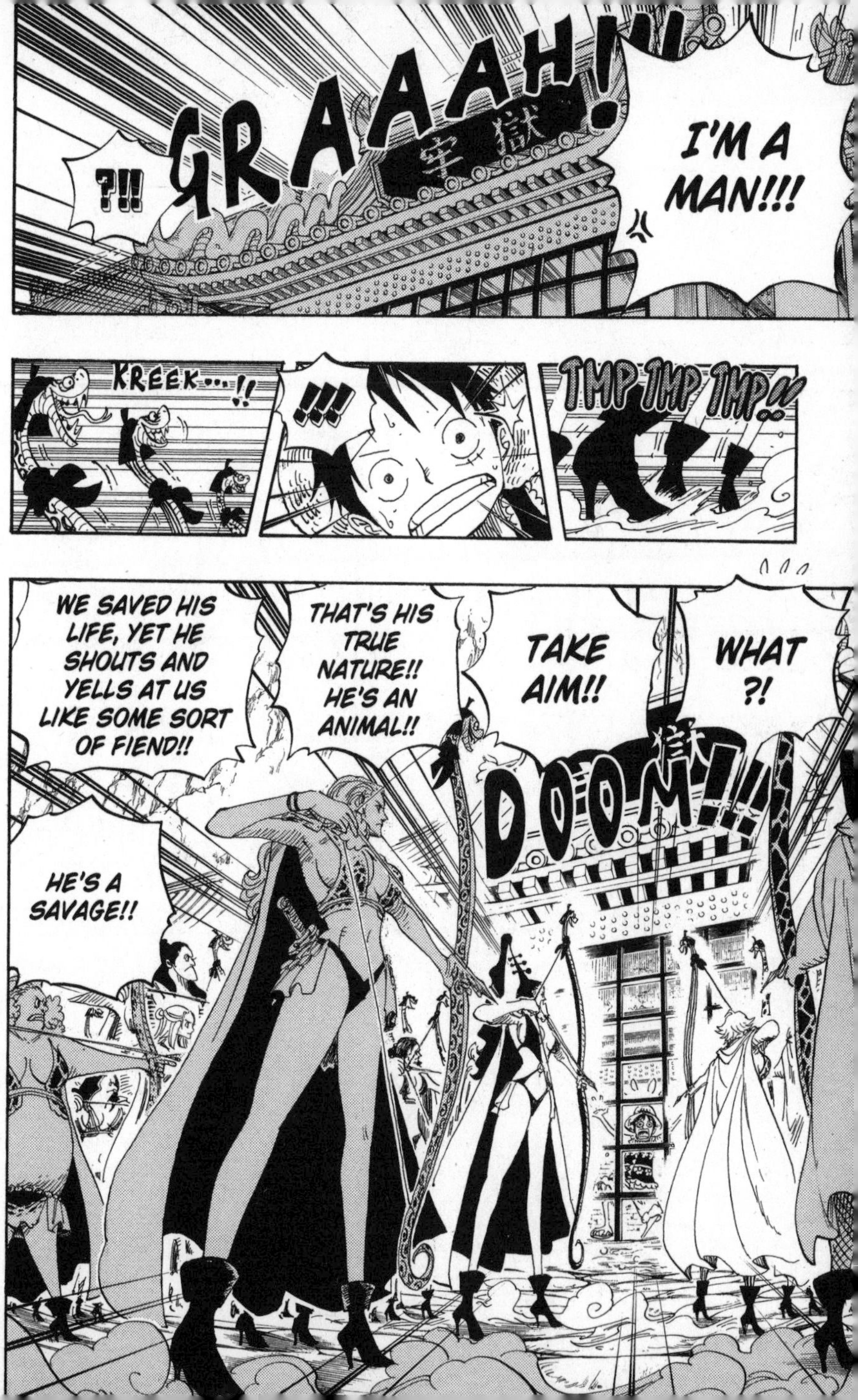
I'M A MAN!!!
GRAAAH!!!
?!!
TMP TMP TMP!!
!!!
KREEK...!!
WHAT?!
TAKE AIM!!
DOOM!!!
THAT'S HIS TRUE NATURE!! HE'S AN ANIMAL!!
WE SAVED HIS LIFE, YET HE SHOUTS AND YELLS AT US LIKE SOME SORT OF FIEND!!
HE'S A SAVAGE!!

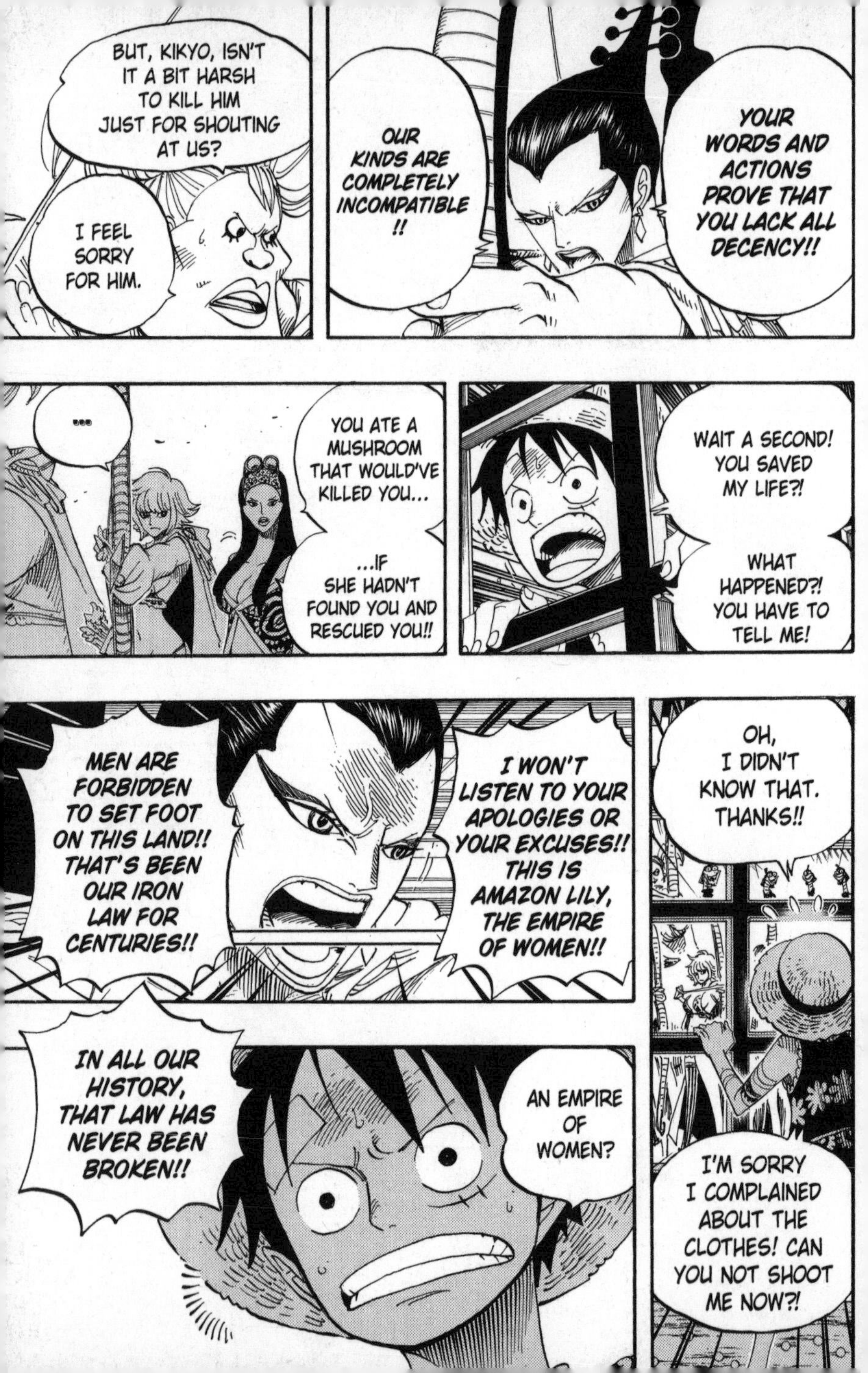
YOUR WORDS AND ACTIONS PROVE THAT YOU LACK ALL DECENCY!!
OUR KINDS ARE COMPLETELY INCOMPATIBLE!!
BUT, KIKYO, ISN'T IT A BIT HARSH TO KILL HIM JUST FOR SHOUTING AT US?
I FEEL SORRY FOR HIM.
WAIT A SECOND! YOU SAVED MY LIFE?!
WHAT HAPPENED?! YOU HAVE TO TELL ME!
YOU ATE A MUSHROOM THAT WOULD'VE KILLED YOU...
...IF SHE HADN'T FOUND YOU AND RESCUED YOU!!
...
OH, I DIDN'T KNOW THAT. THANKS!!
I'M SORRY I COMPLAINED ABOUT THE CLOTHES! CAN YOU NOT SHOOT ME NOW?!
I WON'T LISTEN TO YOUR APOLOGIES OR YOUR EXCUSES!! THIS IS AMAZON LILY, THE EMPIRE OF WOMEN!!
MEN ARE FORBIDDEN TO SET FOOT ON THIS LAND!! THAT'S BEEN OUR IRON LAW FOR CENTURIES!!
AN EMPIRE OF WOMEN?
IN ALL OUR HISTORY, THAT LAW HAS NEVER BEEN BROKEN!!

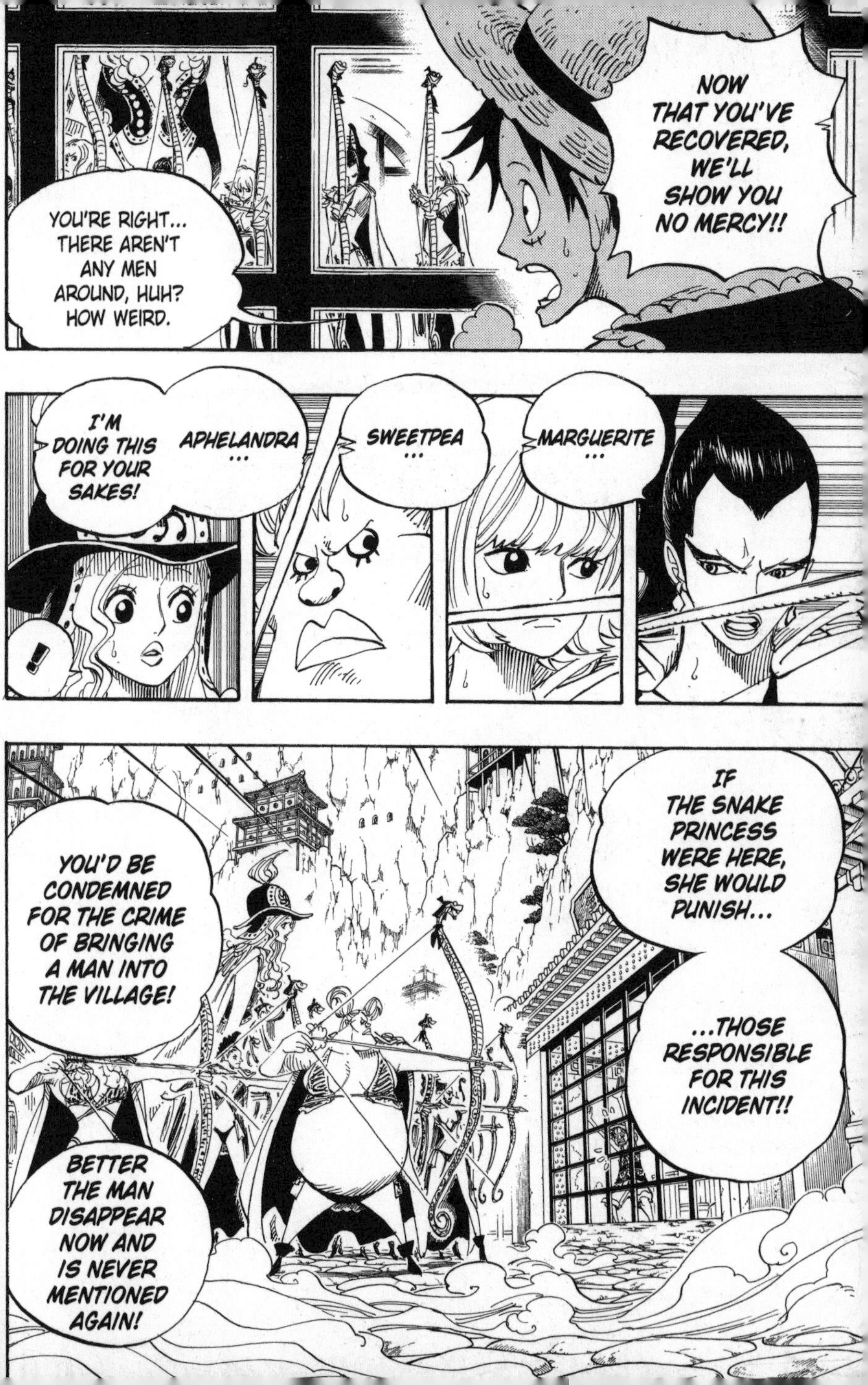
NOW THAT YOU'VE RECOVERED, WE'LL SHOW YOU NO MERCY!!
YOU'RE RIGHT... THERE AREN'T ANY MEN AROUND, HUH? HOW WEIRD.
MARGUERITE ...
SWEETPEA ...
APHELANDRA ...
I'M DOING THIS FOR YOUR SAKES!
!
IF THE SNAKE PRINCESS WERE HERE, SHE WOULD PUNISH...
...THOSE RESPONSIBLE FOR THIS INCIDENT!!
YOU'D BE CONDEMNED FOR THE CRIME OF BRINGING A MAN INTO THE VILLAGE!
BETTER THE MAN DISAPPEAR NOW AND IS NEVER MENTIONED AGAIN!

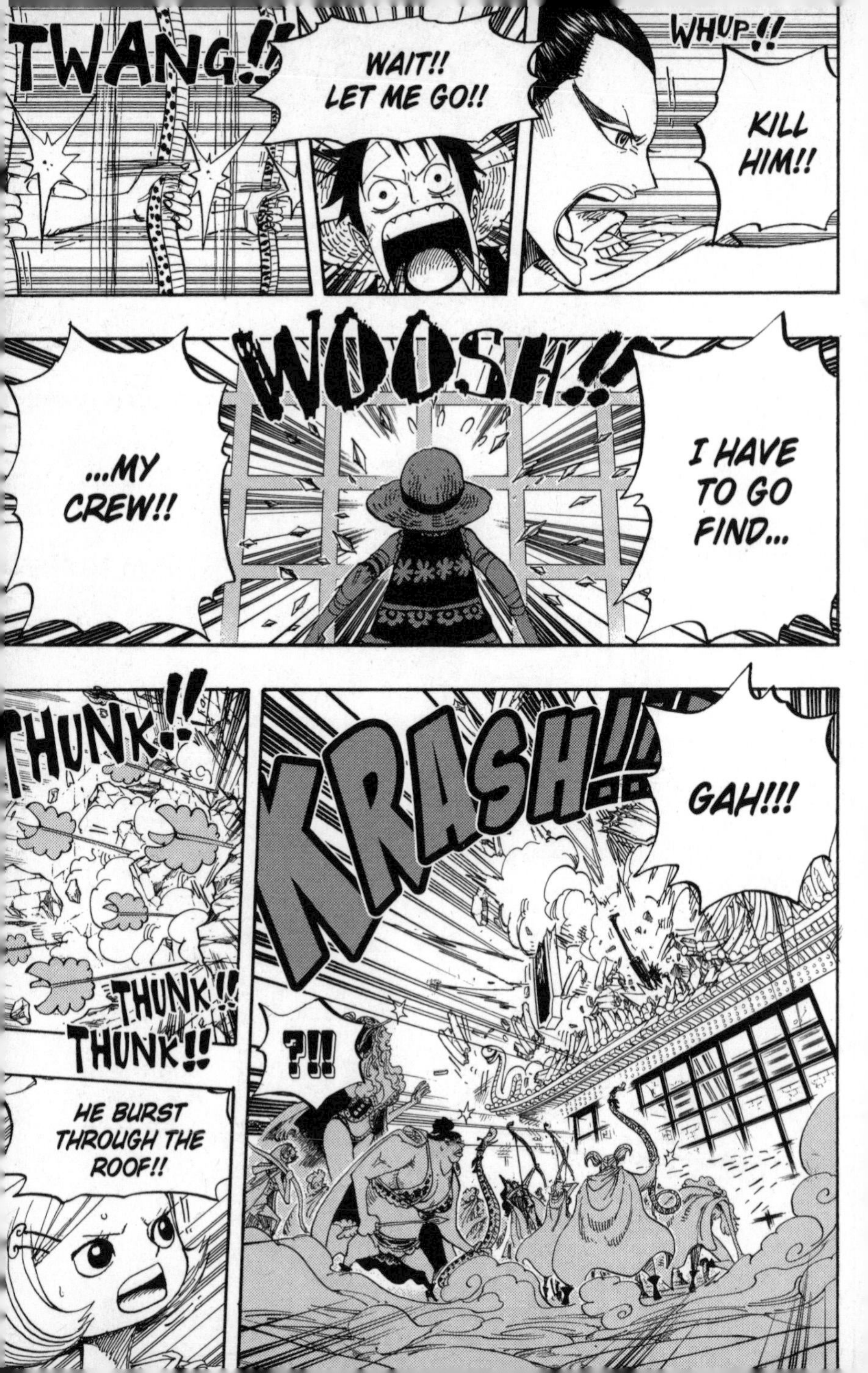
WHUP!!
KILL HIM!!
WAIT!! LET ME GO!!
TWANG!!
WOOSH!!
I HAVE TO GO FIND...
...MY CREW!!
KRASH!!
GAH!!!
?!!
THUNK!!
THUNK!!
THUNK!!
HE BURST THROUGH THE ROOF!!

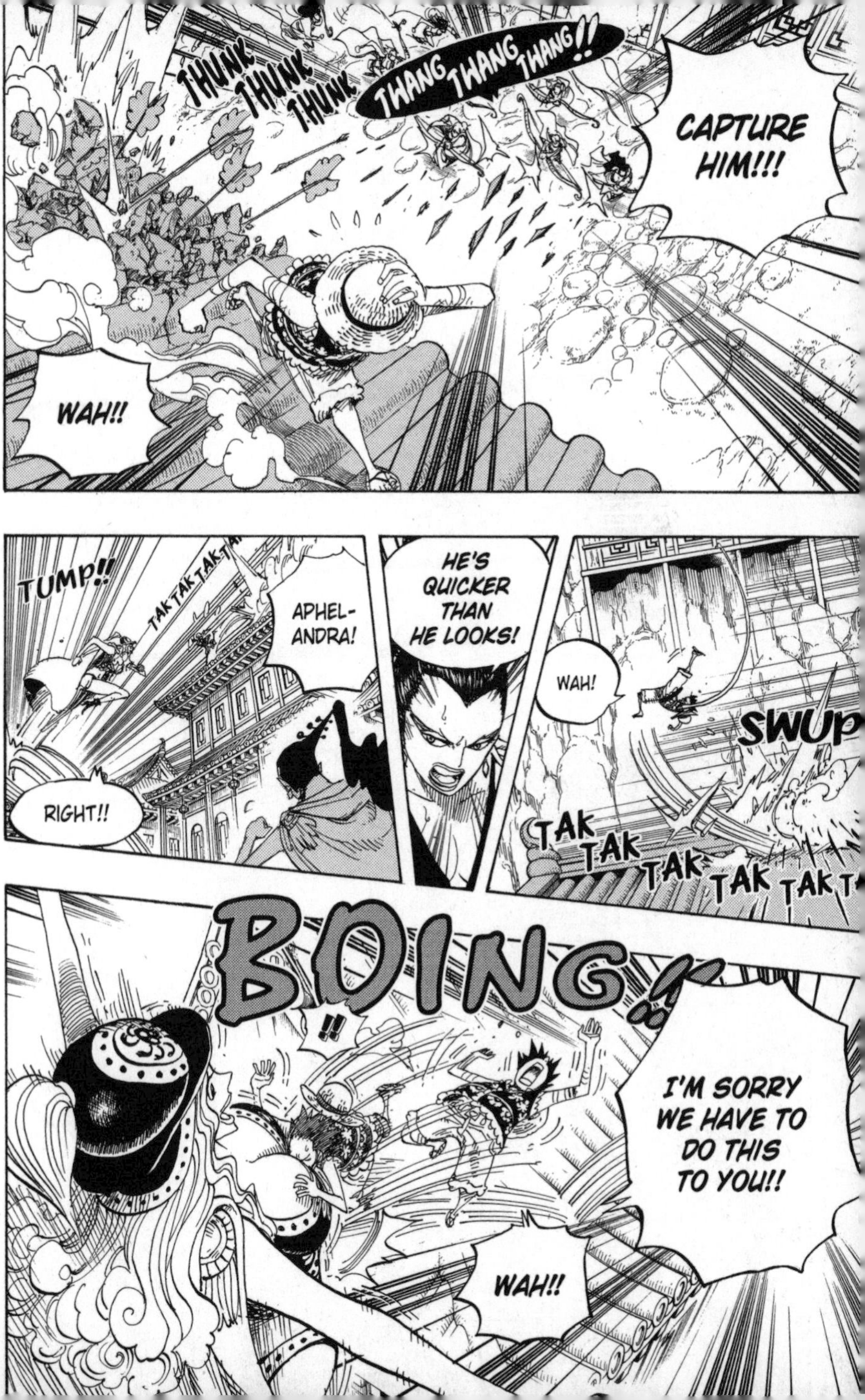
CAPTURE HIM!!!
THWANG TWANG THANG!!
THUNK THUNK THUNK
WAH!!
WAH!
SWUP
TAK TAK TAK TAK TAK
HE'S QUICKER THAN HE LOOKS!
APHEL- ANDRA!
TUMP!!
TAKTAKTAKTAK
RIGHT!!
BOING!!
!!
I'M SORRY WE HAVE TO DO THIS TO YOU!!
WAH!!

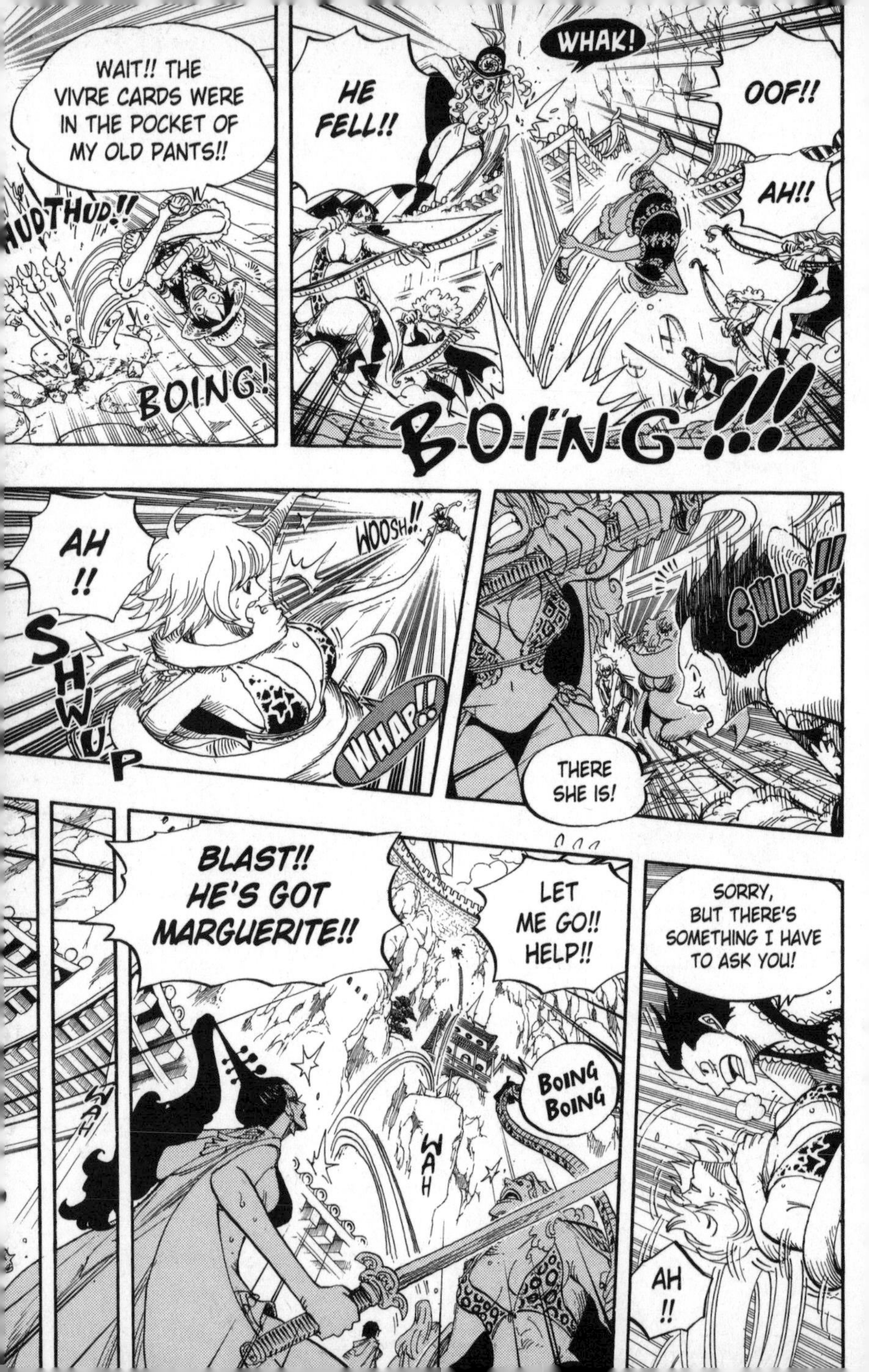

OOF!!
WHAK!
AH!!
HE FELL!!
BOING!!!
WAIT!! THE VIVRE CARDS WERE IN THE POCKET OF MY OLD PANTS!!
HUDTHUD!!
BOING!
SWIP!!
THERE SHE IS!
WOOSH!!
AH !!
SHWUP
WHAP!!
SORRY, BUT THERE'S SOMETHING I HAVE TO ASK YOU!
AH !!
LET ME GO!! HELP!!
BOING BOING
WAH
BLAST!! HE'S GOT MARGUERITE!!
WAH

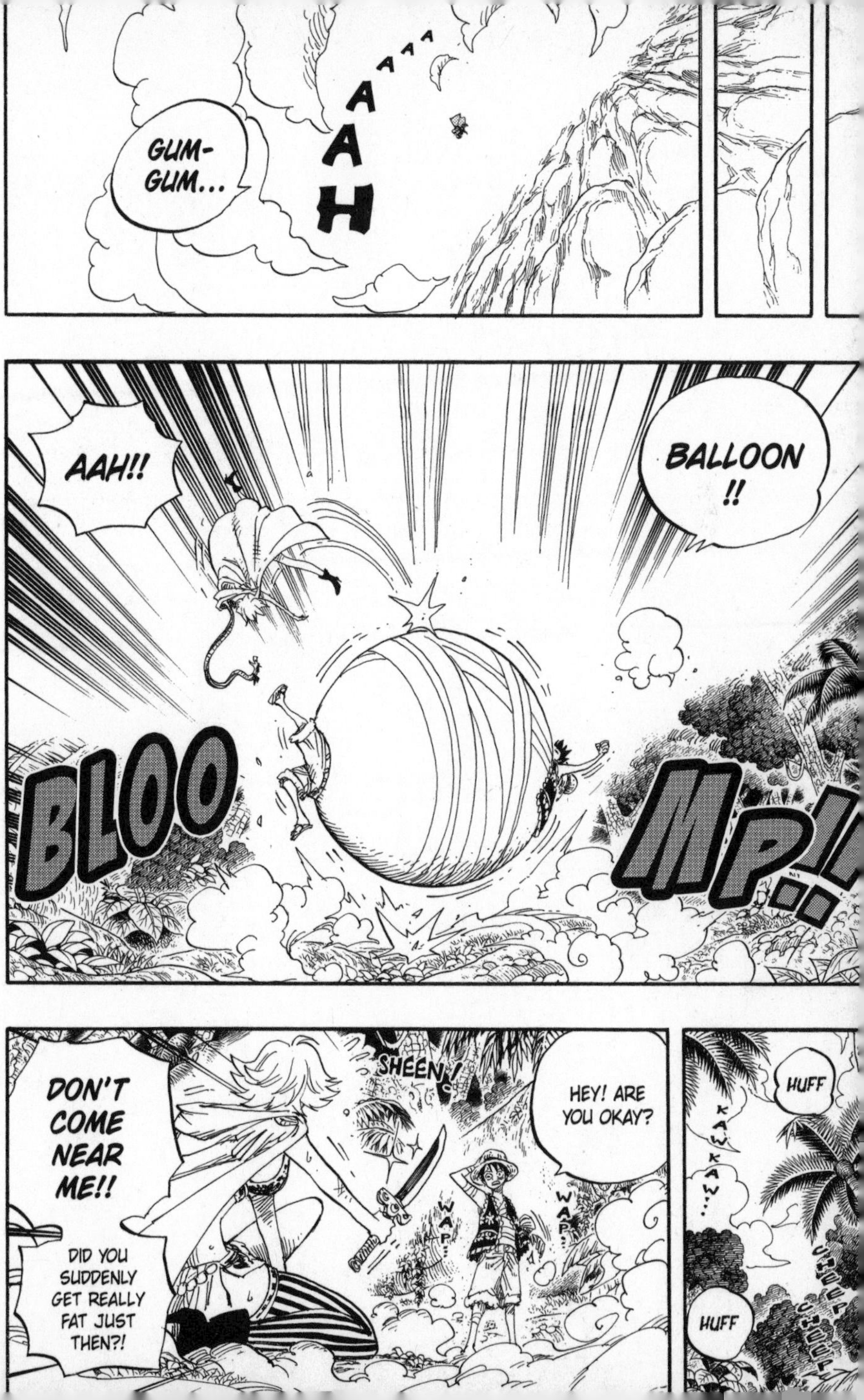
AAAAH
GUM-GUM...
BALLOON !!
AAH!!
BLOOMP!!
HUFF
KAW KAW...
HUFF
CHEEP CHEEP
HEY! ARE YOU OKAY?
WAP...
SHEEN!
WAP...
DON'T COME NEAR ME!!
DID YOU SUDDENLY GET REALLY FAT JUST THEN?!

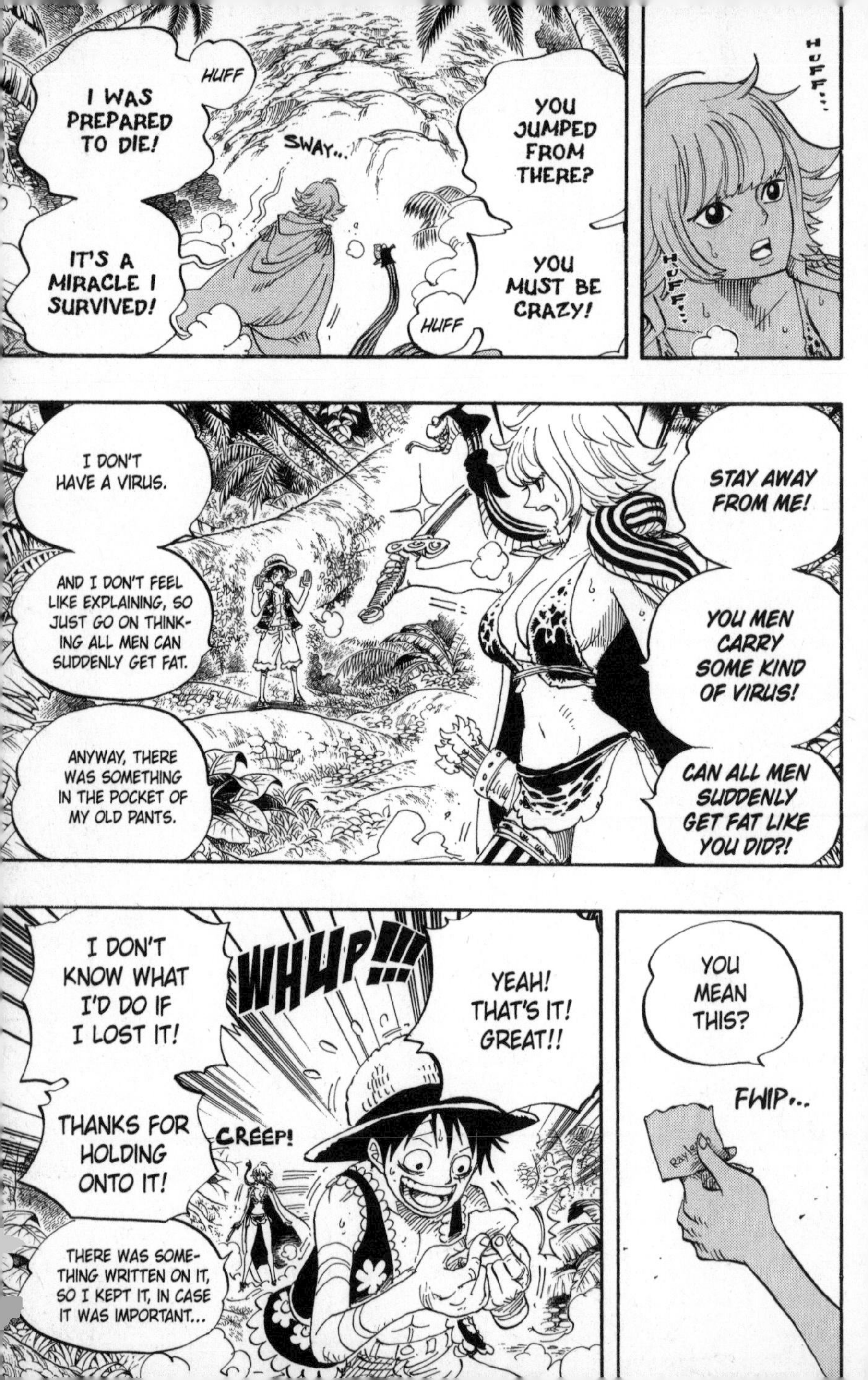
HUFF...
HUFF...
YOU JUMPED FROM THERE?
YOU MUST BE CRAZY!
HUFF
HUFF
I WAS PREPARED TO DIE!
SWAY...
IT'S A MIRACLE I SURVIVED!
STAY AWAY FROM ME!
YOU MEN CARRY SOME KIND OF VIRUS!
CAN ALL MEN SUDDENLY GET FAT LIKE YOU DID?!
I DON'T HAVE A VIRUS.
AND I DON'T FEEL LIKE EXPLAINING, SO JUST GO ON THINK-ING ALL MEN CAN SUDDENLY GET FAT.
ANYWAY, THERE WAS SOMETHING IN THE POCKET OF MY OLD PANTS.
YOU MEAN THIS?
FWIP...
WHUP!!!
YEAH! THAT'S IT! GREAT!!
I DON'T KNOW WHAT I'D DO IF I LOST IT!
THANKS FOR HOLDING ONTO IT!
CREEP!
THERE WAS SOME-THING WRITTEN ON IT, SO I KEPT IT, IN CASE IT WAS IMPORTANT...

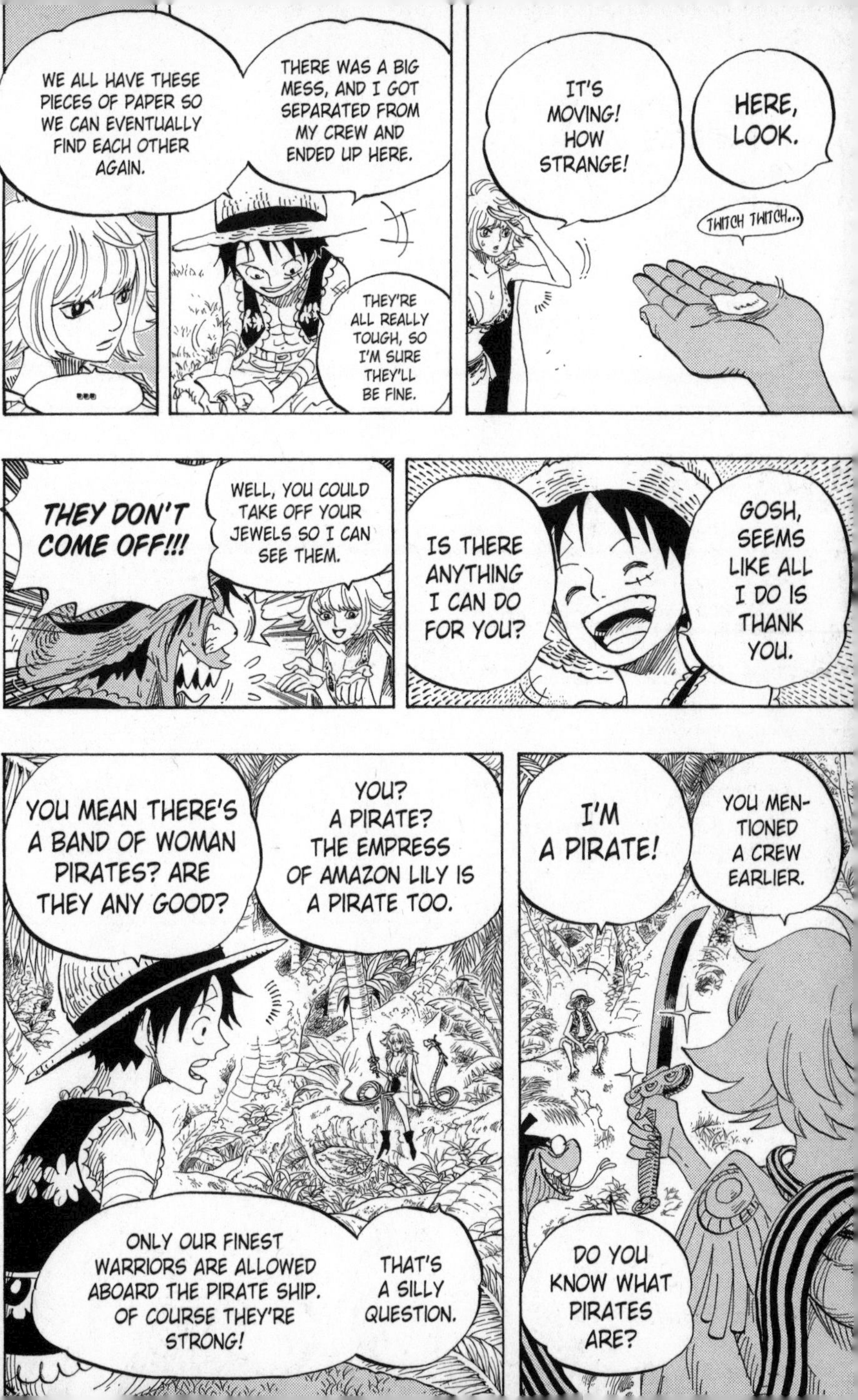
HERE, LOOK.
TWITCH TWITCH...
IT'S MOVING! HOW STRANGE!
THERE WAS A BIG MESS, AND I GOT SEPARATED FROM MY CREW AND ENDED UP HERE.
THEY'RE ALL REALLY TOUGH, SO I'M SURE THEY'LL BE FINE.
WE ALL HAVE THESE PIECES OF PAPER SO WE CAN EVENTUALLY FIND EACH OTHER AGAIN.
...
GOSH, SEEMS LIKE ALL I DO IS THANK YOU.
IS THERE ANYTHING I CAN DO FOR YOU?
WELL, YOU COULD TAKE OFF YOUR JEWELS SO I CAN SEE THEM.
THEY DON'T COME OFF!!!
YOU MENTIONED A CREW EARLIER.
I'M A PIRATE!
DO YOU KNOW WHAT PIRATES ARE?
YOU? A PIRATE? THE EMPRESS OF AMAZON LILY IS A PIRATE TOO.
YOU MEAN THERE'S A BAND OF WOMAN PIRATES? ARE THEY ANY GOOD?
THAT'S A SILLY QUESTION.
ONLY OUR FINEST WARRIORS ARE ALLOWED ABOARD THE PIRATE SHIP. OF COURSE THEY'RE STRONG!

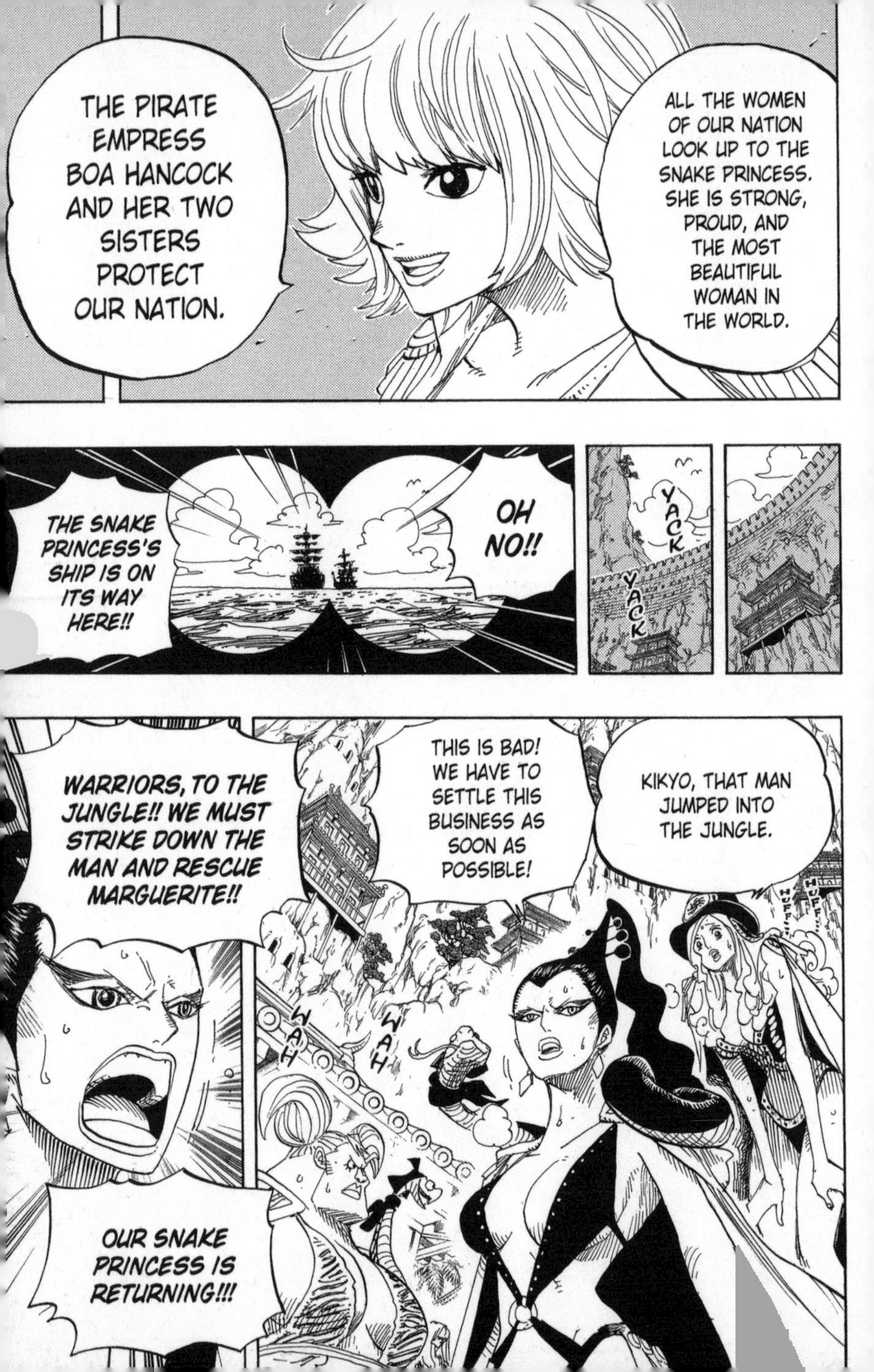
ALL THE WOMEN OF OUR NATION LOOK UP TO THE SNAKE PRINCESS. SHE IS STRONG, PROUD, AND THE MOST BEAUTIFUL WOMAN IN THE WORLD.
THE PIRATE EMPRESS BOA HANCOCK AND HER TWO SISTERS PROTECT OUR NATION.
YACK
YACK
OH NO!!
THE SNAKE PRINCESS'S SHIP IS ON ITS WAY HERE!!
KIKYO, THAT MAN JUMPED INTO THE JUNGLE.
HUFF... HUFF...
THIS IS BAD! WE HAVE TO SETTLE THIS BUSINESS AS SOON AS POSSIBLE!
WAH
WAH
WARRIORS, TO THE JUNGLE!! WE MUST STRIKE DOWN THE MAN AND RESCUE MARGUERITE!!
OUR SNAKE PRINCESS IS RETURNING!!!

EMPRESS BOA HANCOCK

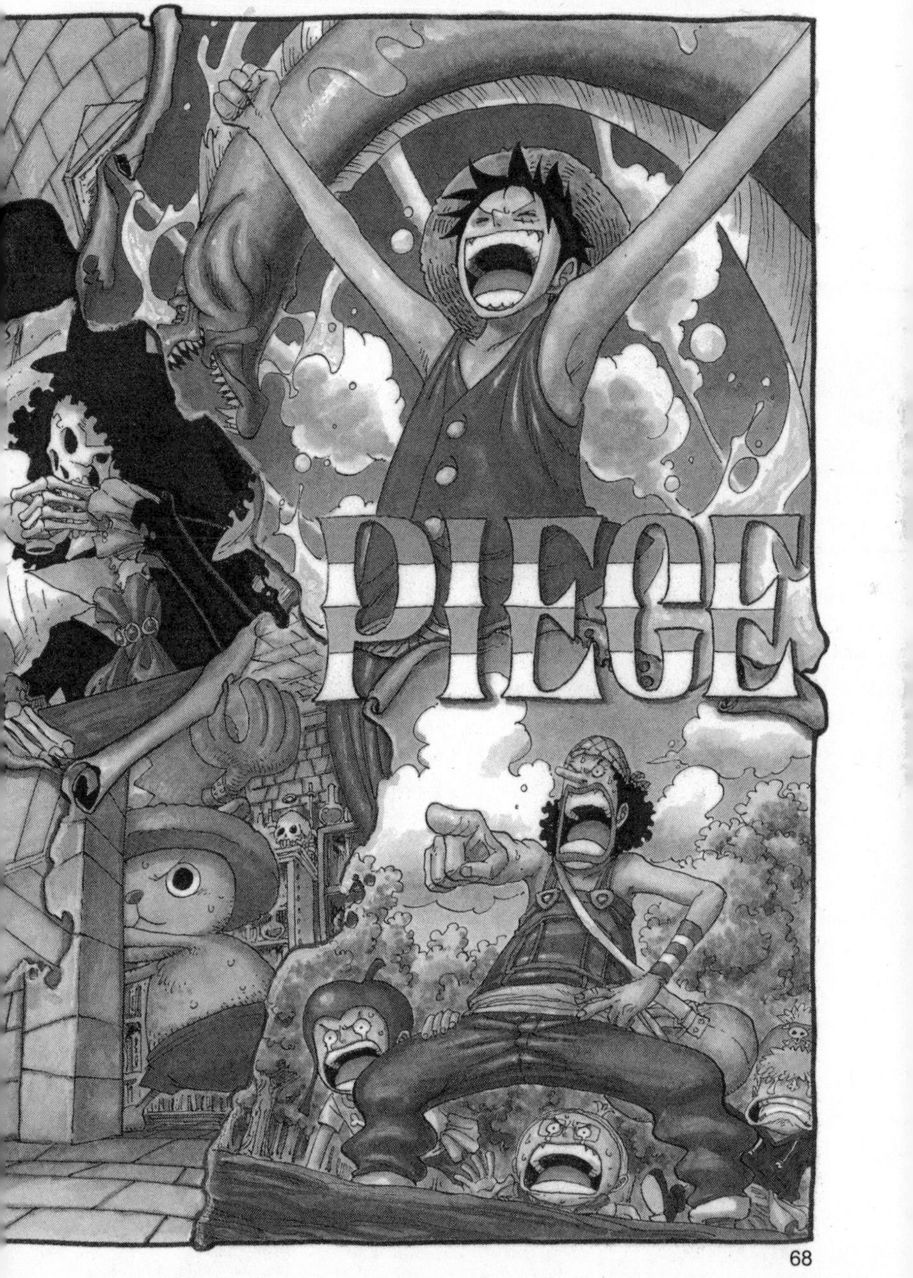
ONE PIECE

Chapter 516: PIRATE

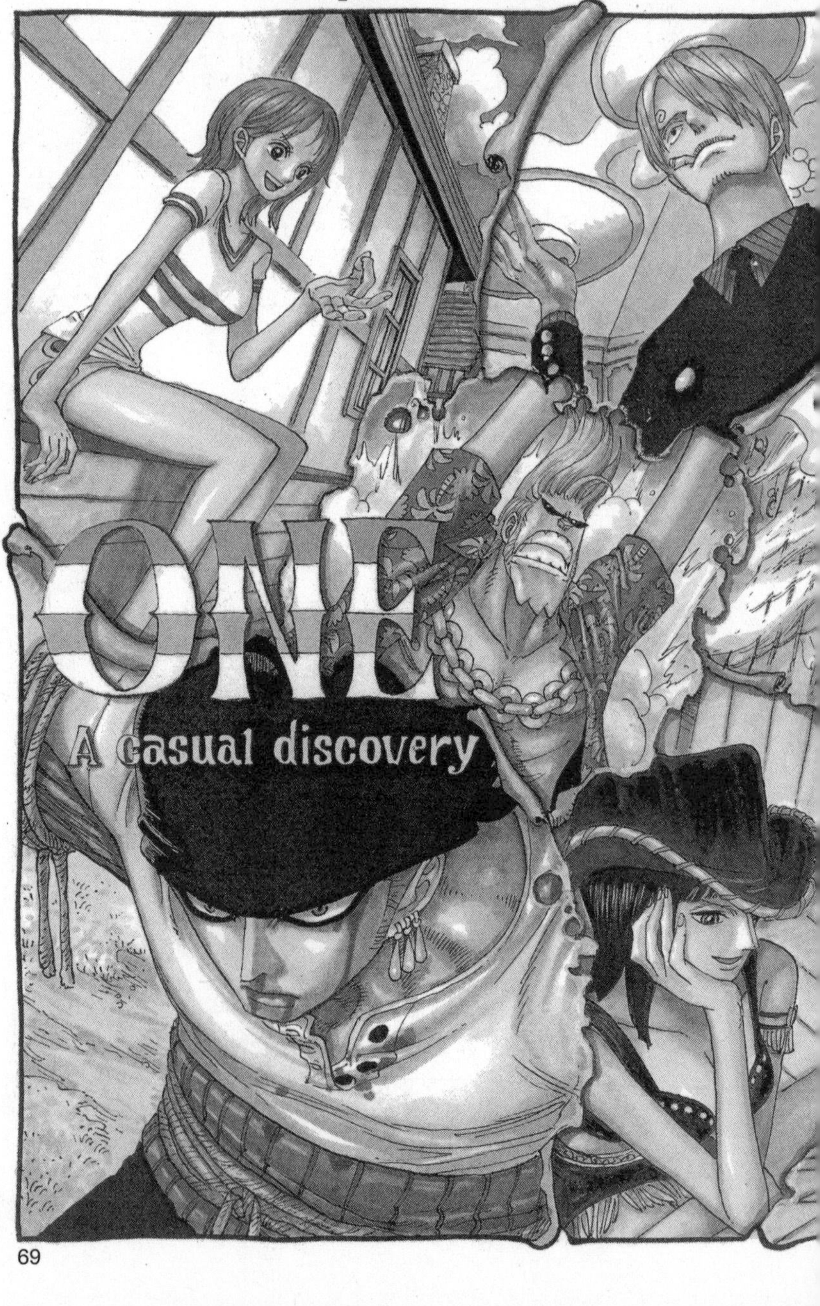
ONE
A casual discovery

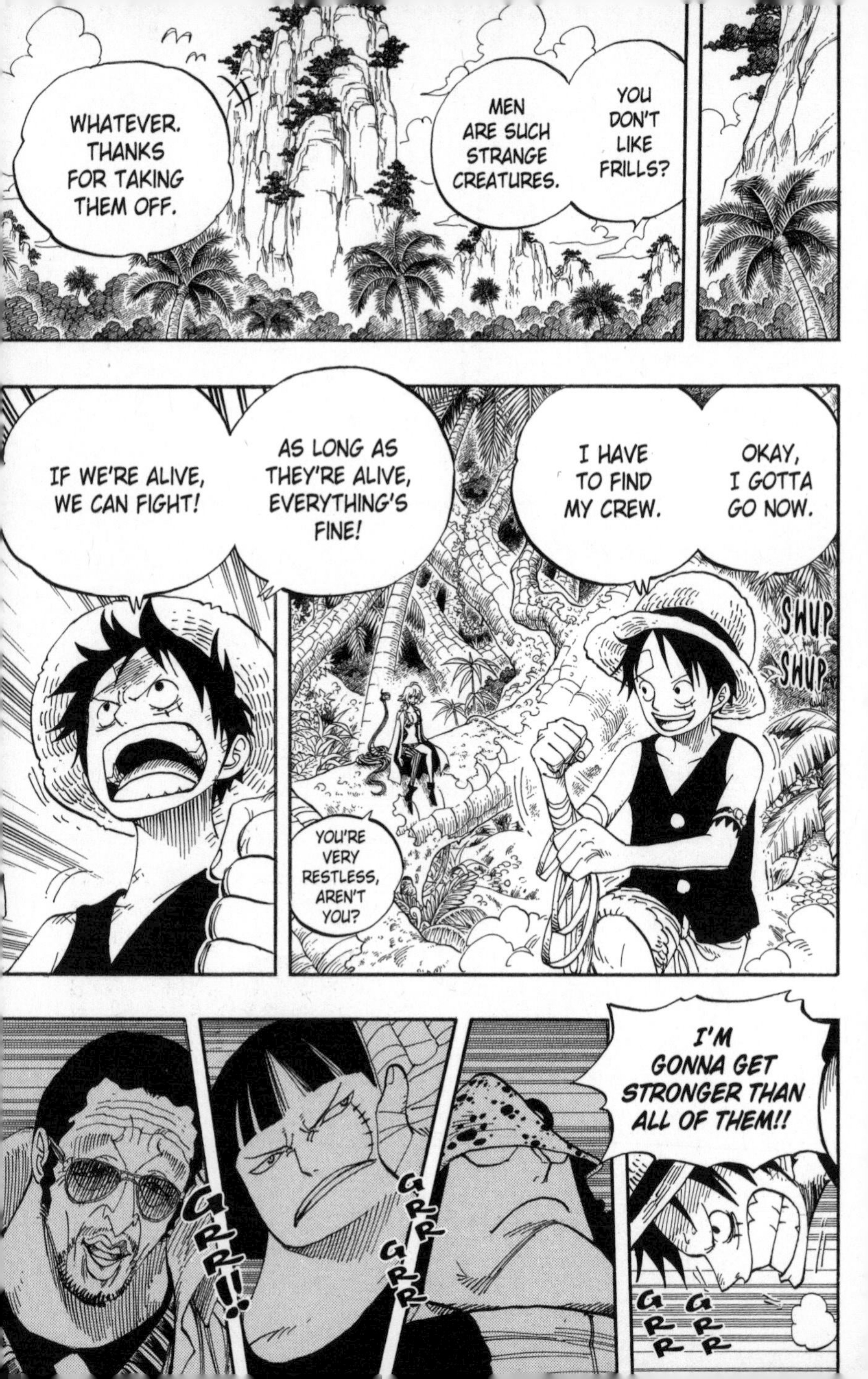
YOU DON'T LIKE FRILLS?
MEN ARE SUCH STRANGE CREATURES.
WHATEVER. THANKS FOR TAKING THEM OFF.
OKAY, I GOTTA GO NOW.
I HAVE TO FIND MY CREW.
SHUP SHUP
YOU'RE VERY RESTLESS, AREN'T YOU?
AS LONG AS THEY'RE ALIVE, EVERYTHING'S FINE!
IF WE'RE ALIVE, WE CAN FIGHT!
I'M GONNA GET STRONGER THAN ALL OF THEM!!
GRR GRR
GRR GRR
GRR GRR
GRR!!

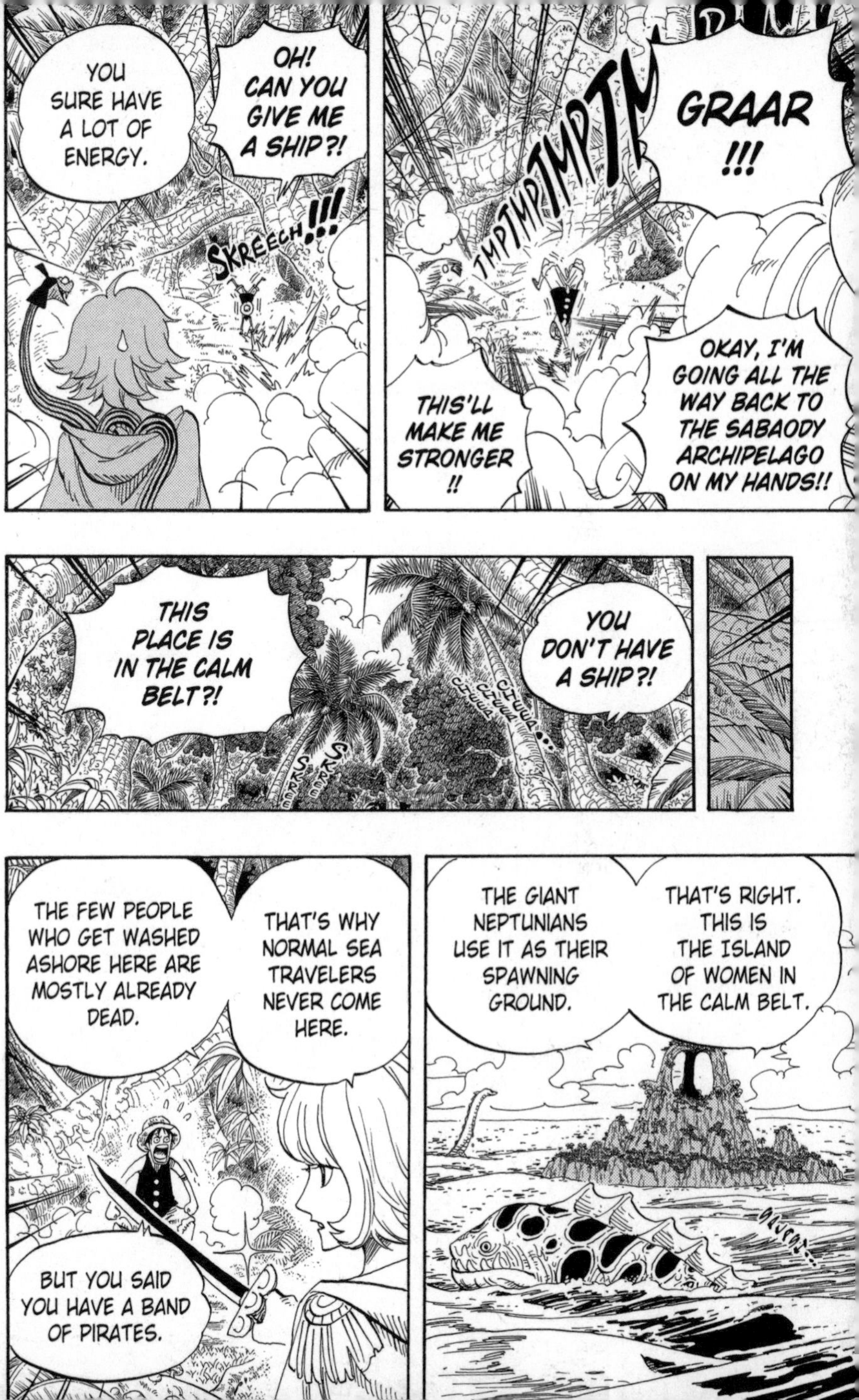
GRAAR!!!
TMPTMPTMPTMPTM
OKAY, I'M GOING ALL THE WAY BACK TO THE SABAODY ARCHIPELAGO ON MY HANDS!!
THIS'LL MAKE ME STRONGER !!
OH! CAN YOU GIVE ME A SHIP?!
YOU SURE HAVE A LOT OF ENERGY.
SKREECH!!!
YOU DON'T HAVE A SHIP?!
THIS PLACE IS IN THE CALM BELT?!
SKREE SKREE
THAT'S RIGHT. THIS IS THE ISLAND OF WOMEN IN THE CALM BELT.
THE GIANT NEPTUNIANS USE IT AS THEIR SPAWNING GROUND.
THAT'S WHY NORMAL SEA TRAVELERS NEVER COME HERE.
THE FEW PEOPLE WHO GET WASHED ASHORE HERE ARE MOSTLY ALREADY DEAD.
BUT YOU SAID YOU HAVE A BAND OF PIRATES.

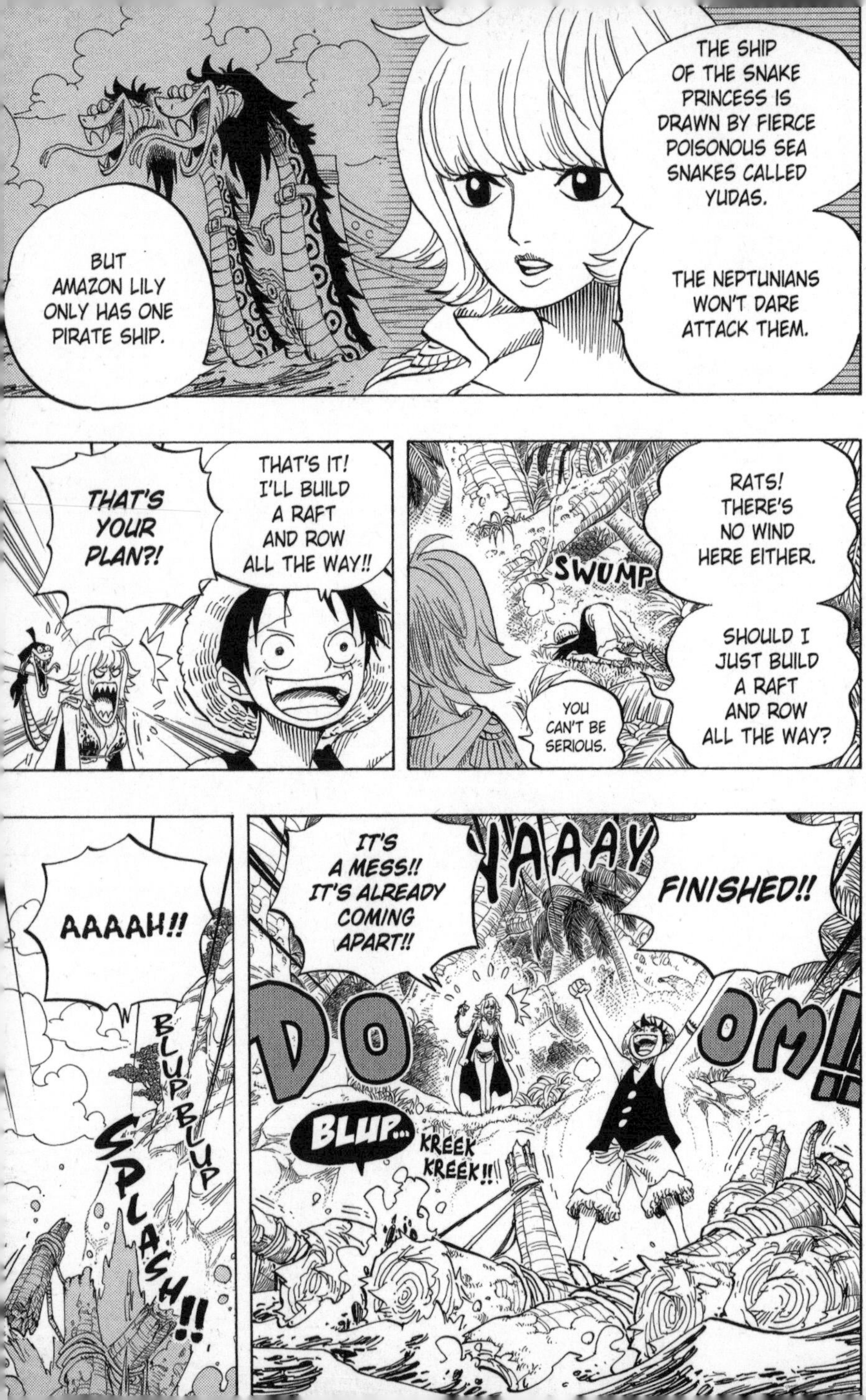
THE SHIP OF THE SNAKE PRINCESS IS DRAWN BY FIERCE POISONOUS SEA SNAKES CALLED YUDAS.
THE NEPTUNIANS WON'T DARE ATTACK THEM.
BUT AMAZON LILY ONLY HAS ONE PIRATE SHIP.
RATS! THERE'S NO WIND HERE EITHER.
SWUMP
SHOULD I JUST BUILD A RAFT AND ROW ALL THE WAY?
YOU CAN'T BE SERIOUS.
THAT'S IT! I'LL BUILD A RAFT AND ROW ALL THE WAY!!
THAT'S YOUR PLAN?!
FINISHED!!
YAAAY
IT'S A MESS!! IT'S ALREADY COMING APART!!
DOOM!!
BLUP...
KREEK KREEK!!
AAAAH!!
BLUP BLUP BLUP
SPLASH!!

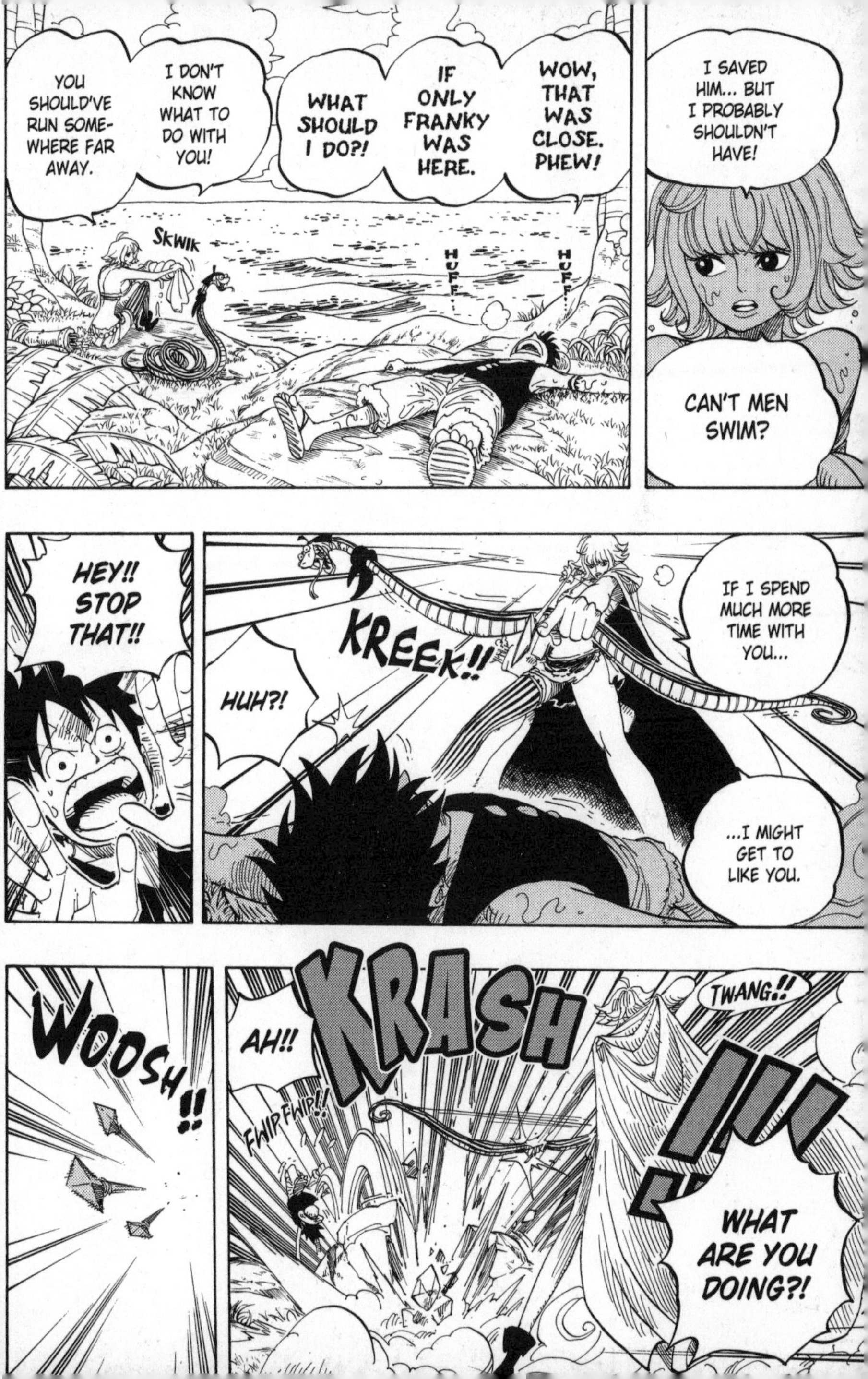
I SAVED HIM... BUT I PROBABLY SHOULDN'T HAVE!
CAN'T MEN SWIM?
WOW, THAT WAS CLOSE. PHEW!
IF ONLY FRANKY WAS HERE.
WHAT SHOULD I DO?!
I DON'T KNOW WHAT TO DO WITH YOU!
YOU SHOULD'VE RUN SOME-WHERE FAR AWAY.
HUFF...
HUFF...
SKWIK
IF I SPEND MUCH MORE TIME WITH YOU...
...I MIGHT GET TO LIKE YOU.
KREEK!!
HUH?!
HEY!! STOP THAT!!
TWANG!!
KRASH
AH!!
FWIP FWIP!!
WHAT ARE YOU DOING?!
WOOSH!!

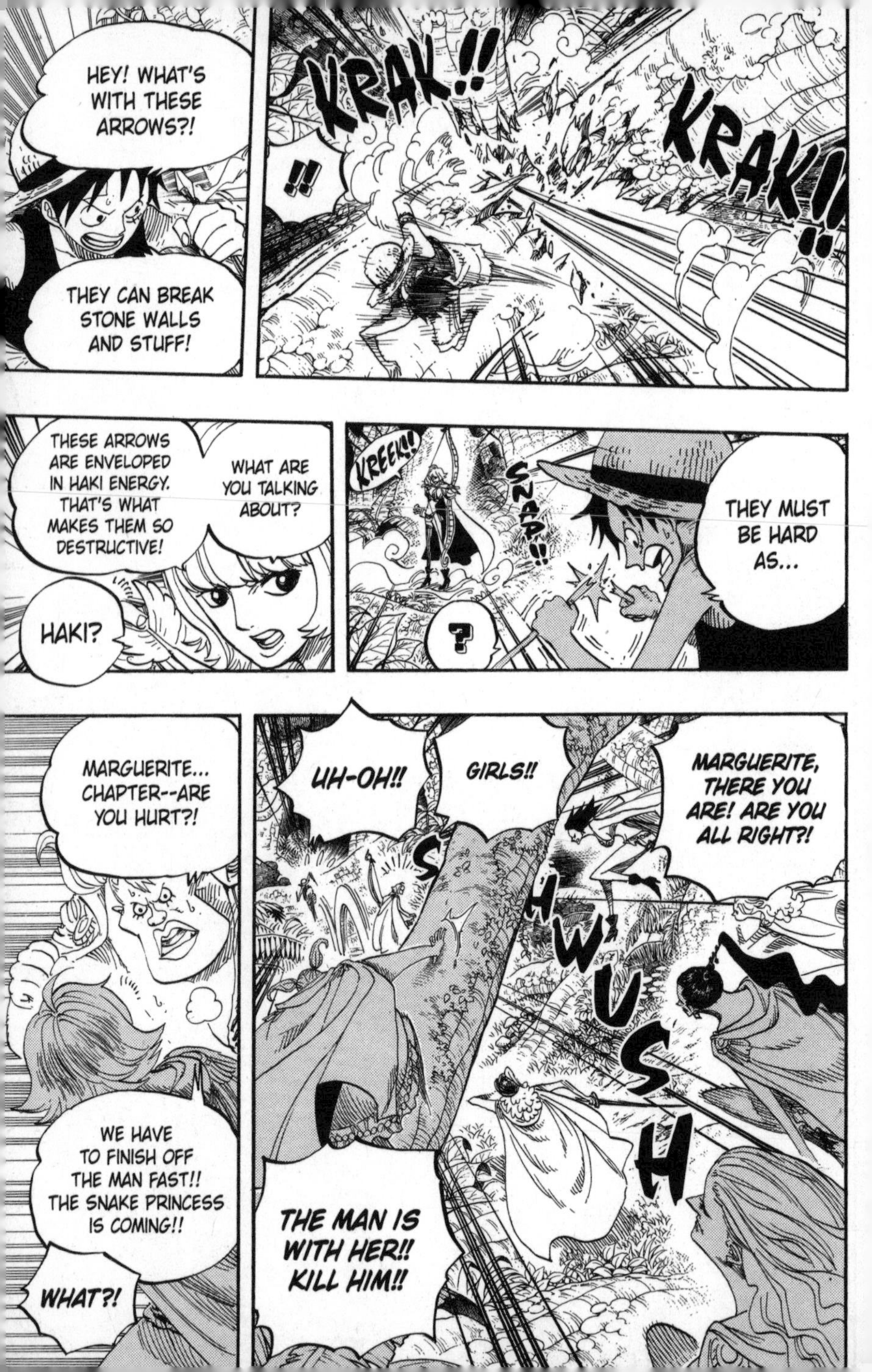
KRAK!!
KRAK!!
!!
HEY! WHAT'S WITH THESE ARROWS?!
THEY CAN BREAK STONE WALLS AND STUFF!
THEY MUST BE HARD AS...
SNAP!!
KREEK!!
?
WHAT ARE YOU TALKING ABOUT?
THESE ARROWS ARE ENVELOPED IN HAKI ENERGY. THAT'S WHAT MAKES THEM SO DESTRUCTIVE!
HAKI?
MARGUERITE, THERE YOU ARE! ARE YOU ALL RIGHT?!
GIRLS!!
UH-OH!!
SHWUSH
THE MAN IS WITH HER!! KILL HIM!!
MARGUERITE... CHAPTER--ARE YOU HURT?!
WE HAVE TO FINISH OFF THE MAN FAST!! THE SNAKE PRINCESS IS COMING!!
WHAT?!

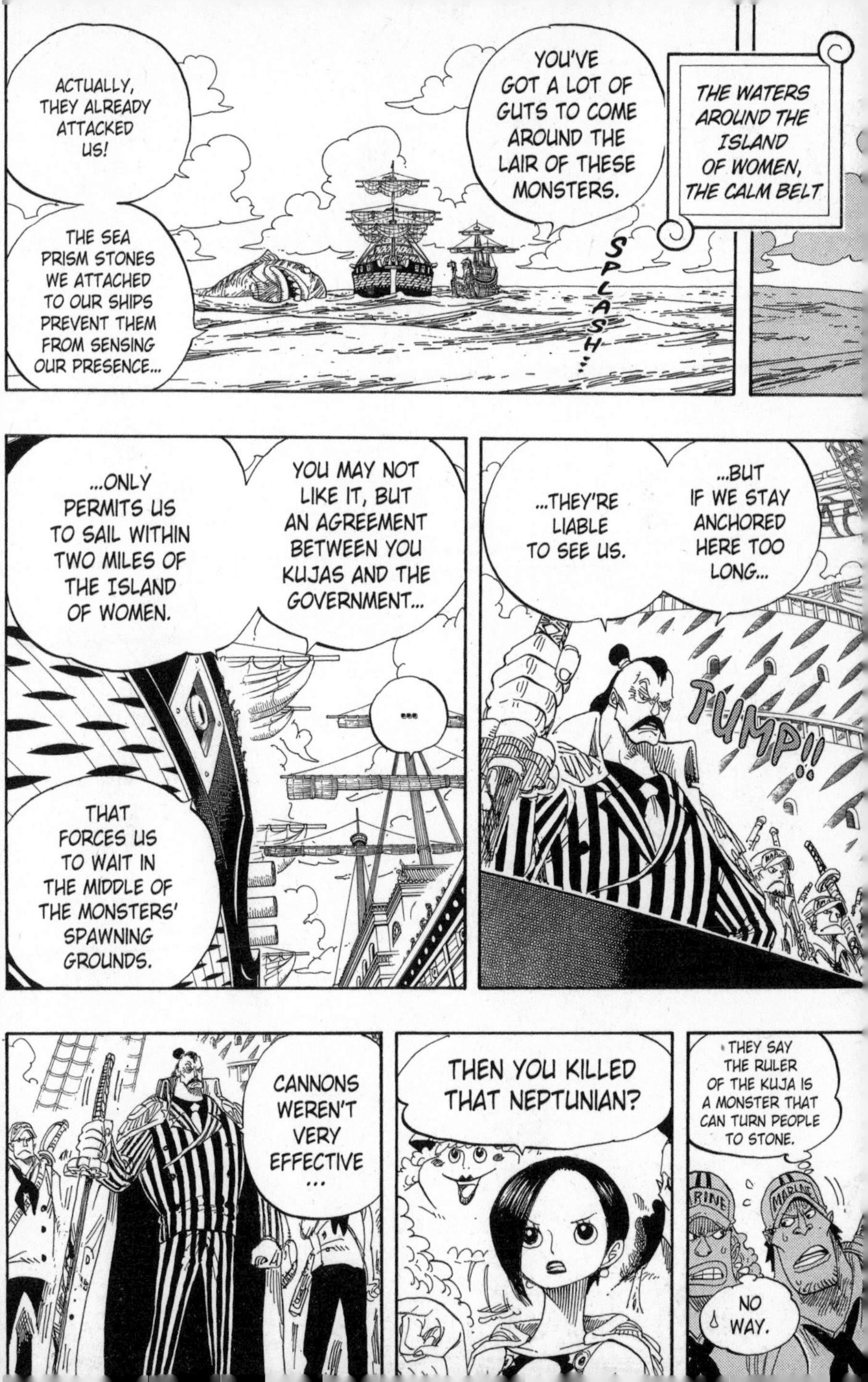
THE WATERS AROUND THE ISLAND OF WOMEN, THE CALM BELT
YOU'VE GOT A LOT OF GUTS TO COME AROUND THE LAIR OF THESE MONSTERS.
SPLASH...
ACTUALLY, THEY ALREADY ATTACKED US!
THE SEA PRISM STONES WE ATTACHED TO OUR SHIPS PREVENT THEM FROM SENSING OUR PRESENCE...
...BUT IF WE STAY ANCHORED HERE TOO LONG...
...THEY'RE LIABLE TO SEE US.
TUMP!!
YOU MAY NOT LIKE IT, BUT AN AGREEMENT BETWEEN YOU KUJAS AND THE GOVERNMENT...
...ONLY PERMITS US TO SAIL WITHIN TWO MILES OF THE ISLAND OF WOMEN.
...
THAT FORCES US TO WAIT IN THE MIDDLE OF THE MONSTERS' SPAWNING GROUNDS.
THEY SAY THE RULER OF THE KUJA IS A MONSTER THAT CAN TURN PEOPLE TO STONE.
NO WAY.
THEN YOU KILLED THAT NEPTUNIAN?
CANNONS WEREN'T VERY EFFECTIVE ...

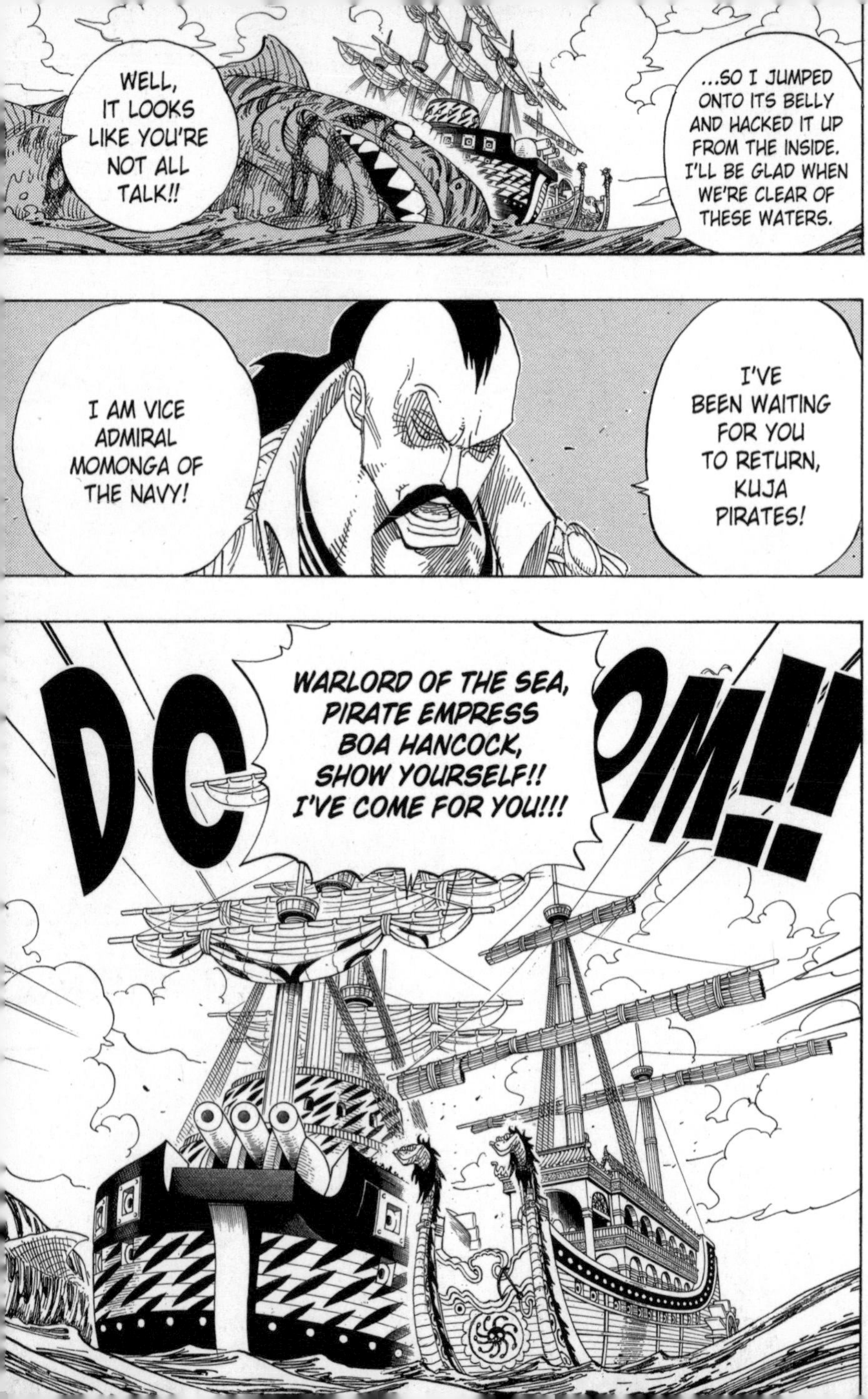
...SO I JUMPED ONTO ITS BELLY AND HACKED IT UP FROM THE INSIDE. I'LL BE GLAD WHEN WE'RE CLEAR OF THESE WATERS.
WELL, IT LOOKS LIKE YOU'RE NOT ALL TALK!!
I'VE BEEN WAITING FOR YOU TO RETURN, KUJA PIRATES!
I AM VICE ADMIRAL MOMONGA OF THE NAVY!
DO
WARLORD OF THE SEA, PIRATE EMPRESS BOA HANCOCK, SHOW YOURSELF!! I'VE COME FOR YOU!!!
OM!!

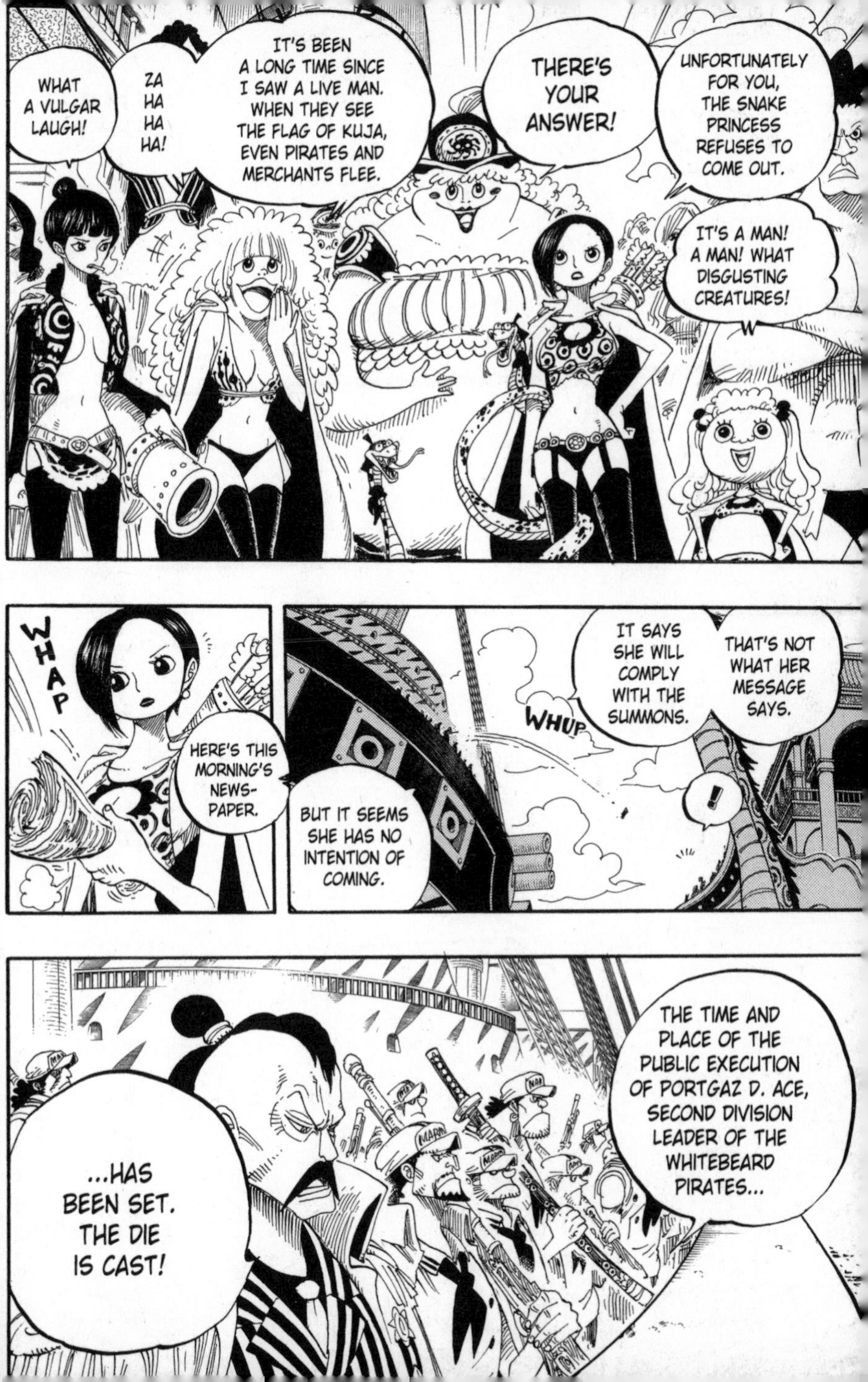
UNFORTUNATELY FOR YOU, THE SNAKE PRINCESS REFUSES TO COME OUT.
IT'S A MAN! A MAN! WHAT DISGUSTING CREATURES!
THERE'S YOUR ANSWER!
IT'S BEEN A LONG TIME SINCE I SAW A LIVE MAN. WHEN THEY SEE THE FLAG OF KUJA, EVEN PIRATES AND MERCHANTS FLEE.
ZA HA HA HA!
WHAT A VULGAR LAUGH!
THAT'S NOT WHAT HER MESSAGE SAYS.
IT SAYS SHE WILL COMPLY WITH THE SUMMONS.
WHUP
!
BUT IT SEEMS SHE HAS NO INTENTION OF COMING.
WHAP
HERE'S THIS MORNING'S NEWS-PAPER.
THE TIME AND PLACE OF THE PUBLIC EXECUTION OF PORTGAZ D. ACE, SECOND DIVISION LEADER OF THE WHITEBEARD PIRATES...
...HAS BEEN SET. THE DIE IS CAST!

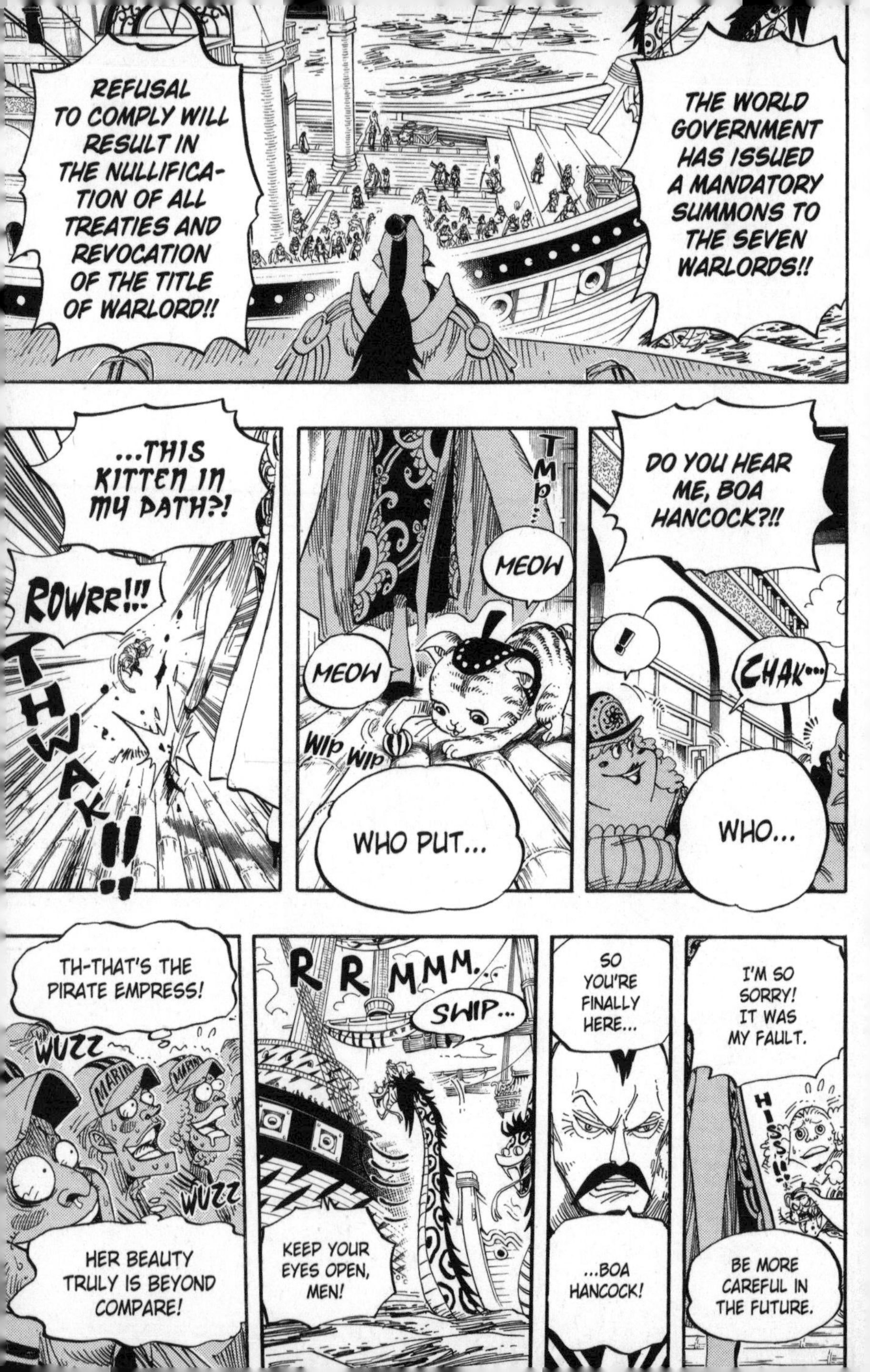
THE WORLD GOVERNMENT HAS ISSUED A MANDATORY SUMMONS TO THE SEVEN WARLORDS!!
REFUSAL TO COMPLY WILL RESULT IN THE NULLIFICATION OF ALL TREATIES AND REVOCATION OF THE TITLE OF WARLORD!!
DO YOU HEAR ME, BOA HANCOCK?!!
!
CHAK...
WHO...
TMP...
MEOW
MEOW
WIP WIP
WHO PUT...
...THIS KITTEN IN MY PATH?!
ROWRR!!
THWAK!!
I'M SO SORRY! IT WAS MY FAULT.
HISS!!
BE MORE CAREFUL IN THE FUTURE.
SO YOU'RE FINALLY HERE...
...BOA HANCOCK!
RRMMM.
SWIP...
KEEP YOUR EYES OPEN, MEN!
TH-THAT'S THE PIRATE EMPRESS!
WUZZ
WUZZ
HER BEAUTY TRULY IS BEYOND COMPARE!

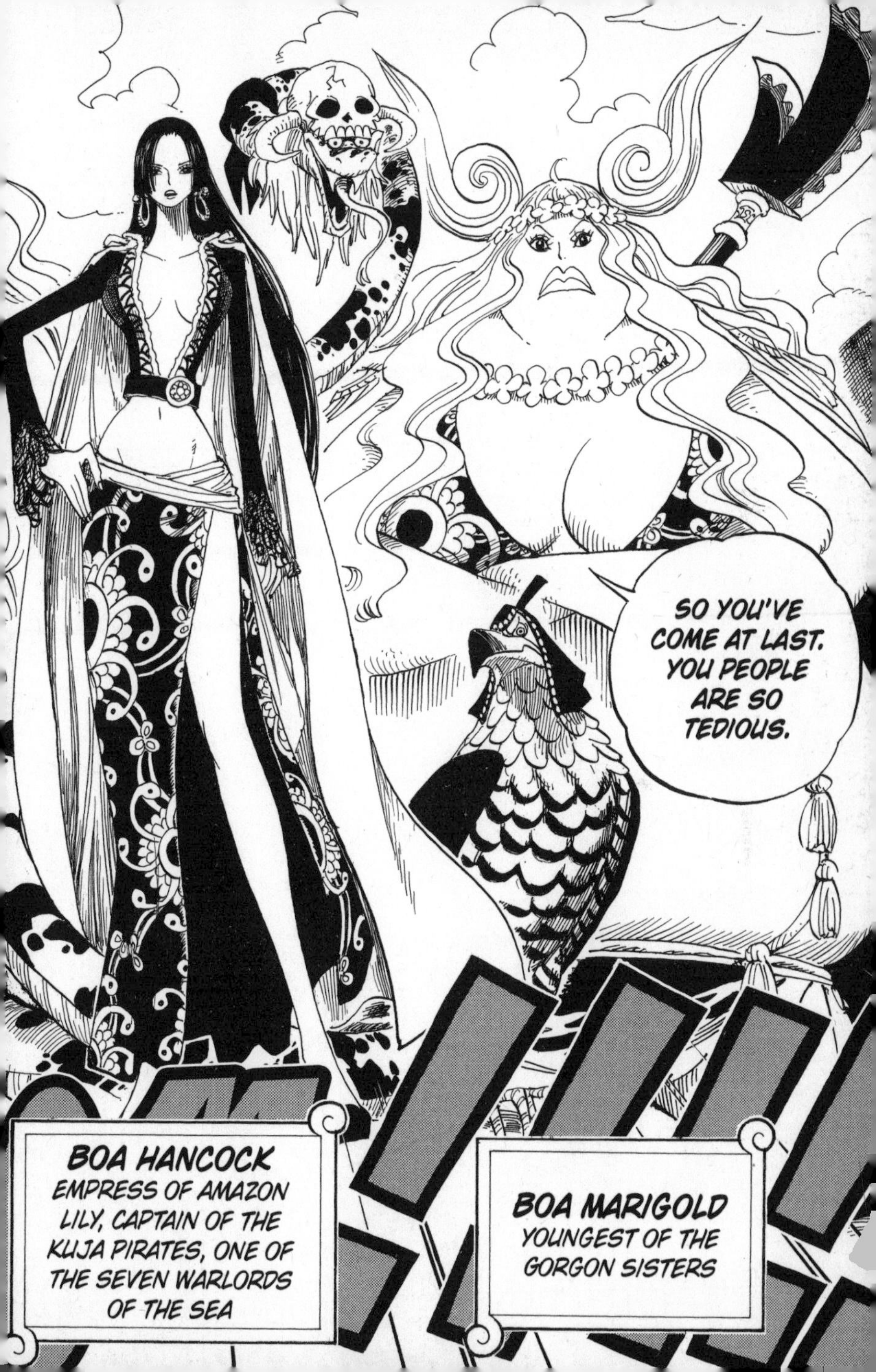
SO YOU'VE COME AT LAST. YOU PEOPLE ARE SO TEDIOUS.
BOA MARIGOLD
YOUNGEST OF THE GORGON SISTERS
BOA HANCOCK
EMPRESS OF AMAZON LILY, CAPTAIN OF THE KUJA PIRATES, ONE OF THE SEVEN WARLORDS OF THE SEA

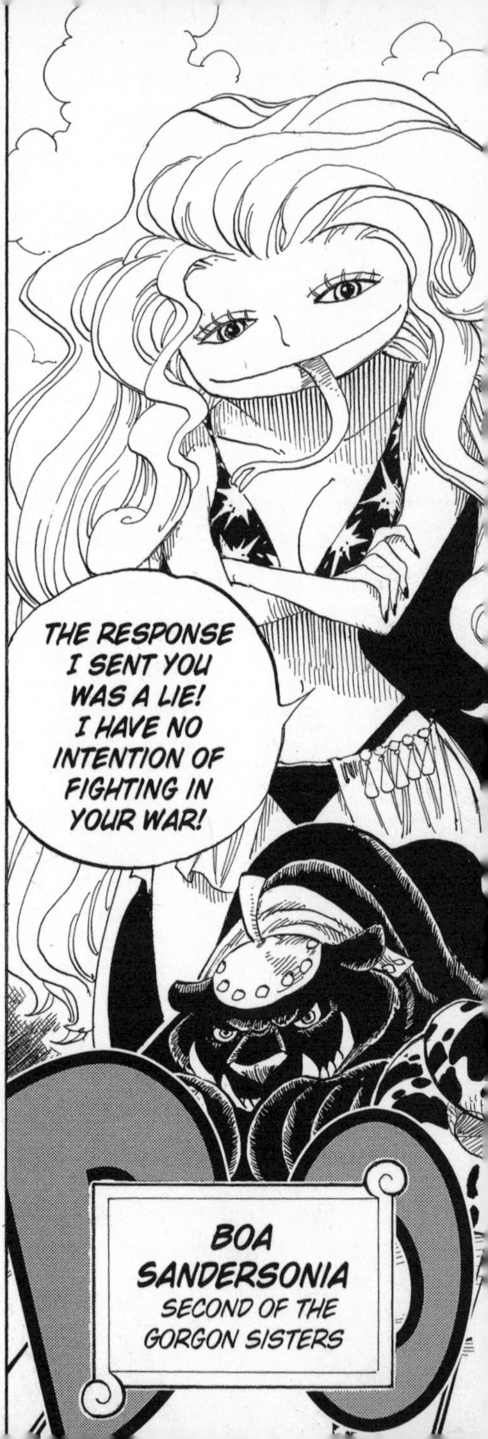
THE RESPONSE I SENT YOU WAS A LIE! I HAVE NO INTENTION OF FIGHTING IN YOUR WAR!
BOA SANDERSONIA
SECOND OF THE GORGON SISTERS

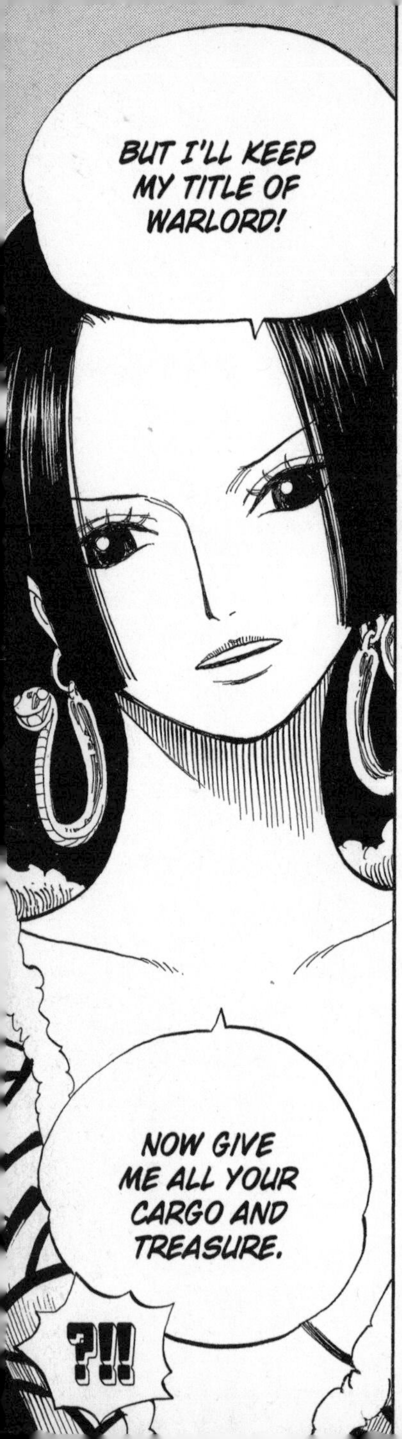
BUT I'LL KEEP MY TITLE OF WARLORD!
NOW GIVE ME ALL YOUR CARGO AND TREASURE.
?!!

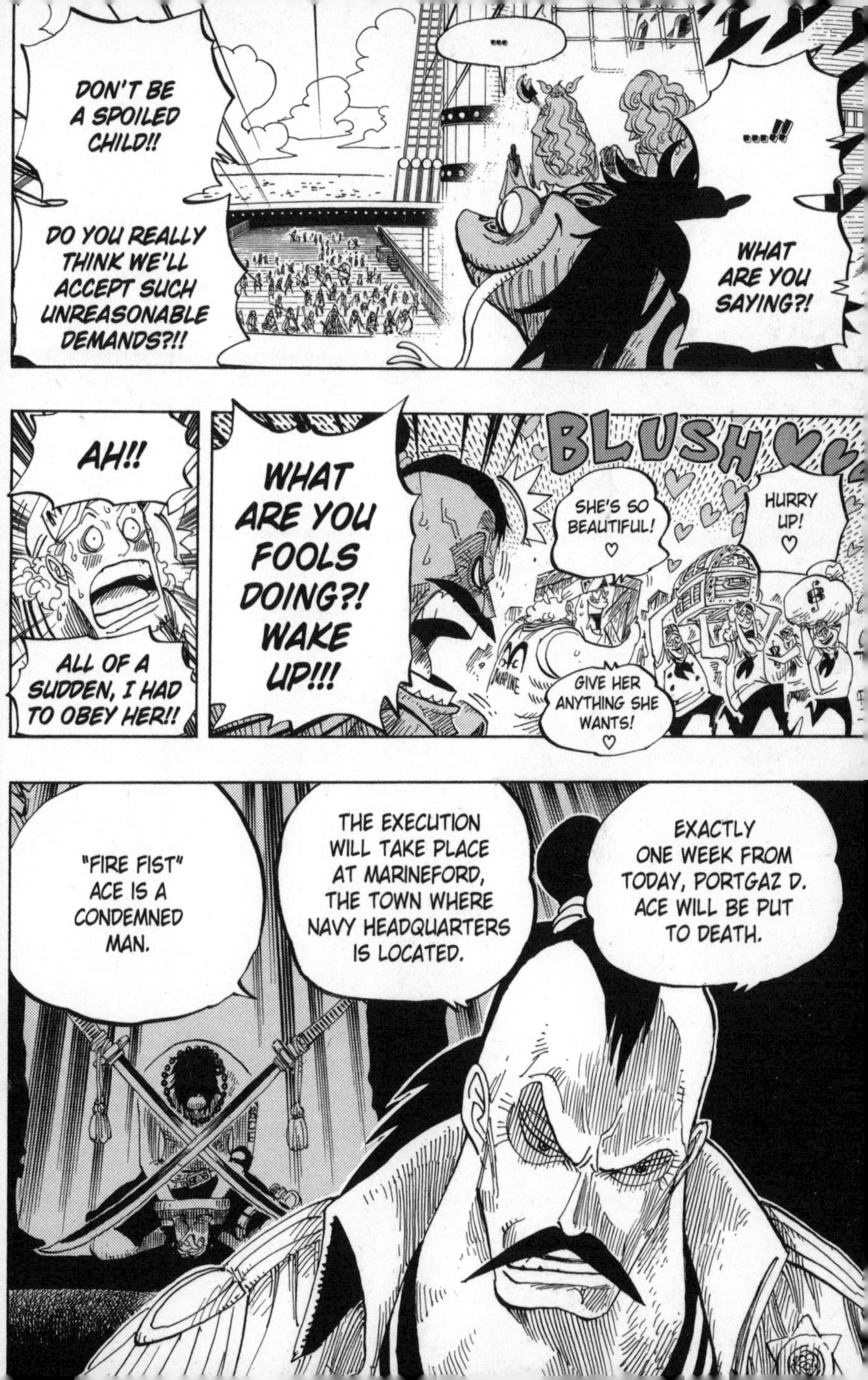
...
...!!
WHAT ARE YOU SAYING?!
DON'T BE A SPOILED CHILD!!
DO YOU REALLY THINK WE'LL ACCEPT SUCH UNREASONABLE DEMANDS?!!
BLUSH
HURRY UP! ♡
SHE'S SO BEAUTIFUL! ♡
GIVE HER ANYTHING SHE WANTS! ♡
WHAT ARE YOU FOOLS DOING?! WAKE UP!!!
AH!!
ALL OF A SUDDEN, I HAD TO OBEY HER!!
EXACTLY ONE WEEK FROM TODAY, PORTGAZ D. ACE WILL BE PUT TO DEATH.
THE EXECUTION WILL TAKE PLACE AT MARINEFORD, THE TOWN WHERE NAVY HEADQUARTERS IS LOCATED.
"FIRE FIST" ACE IS A CONDEMNED MAN.

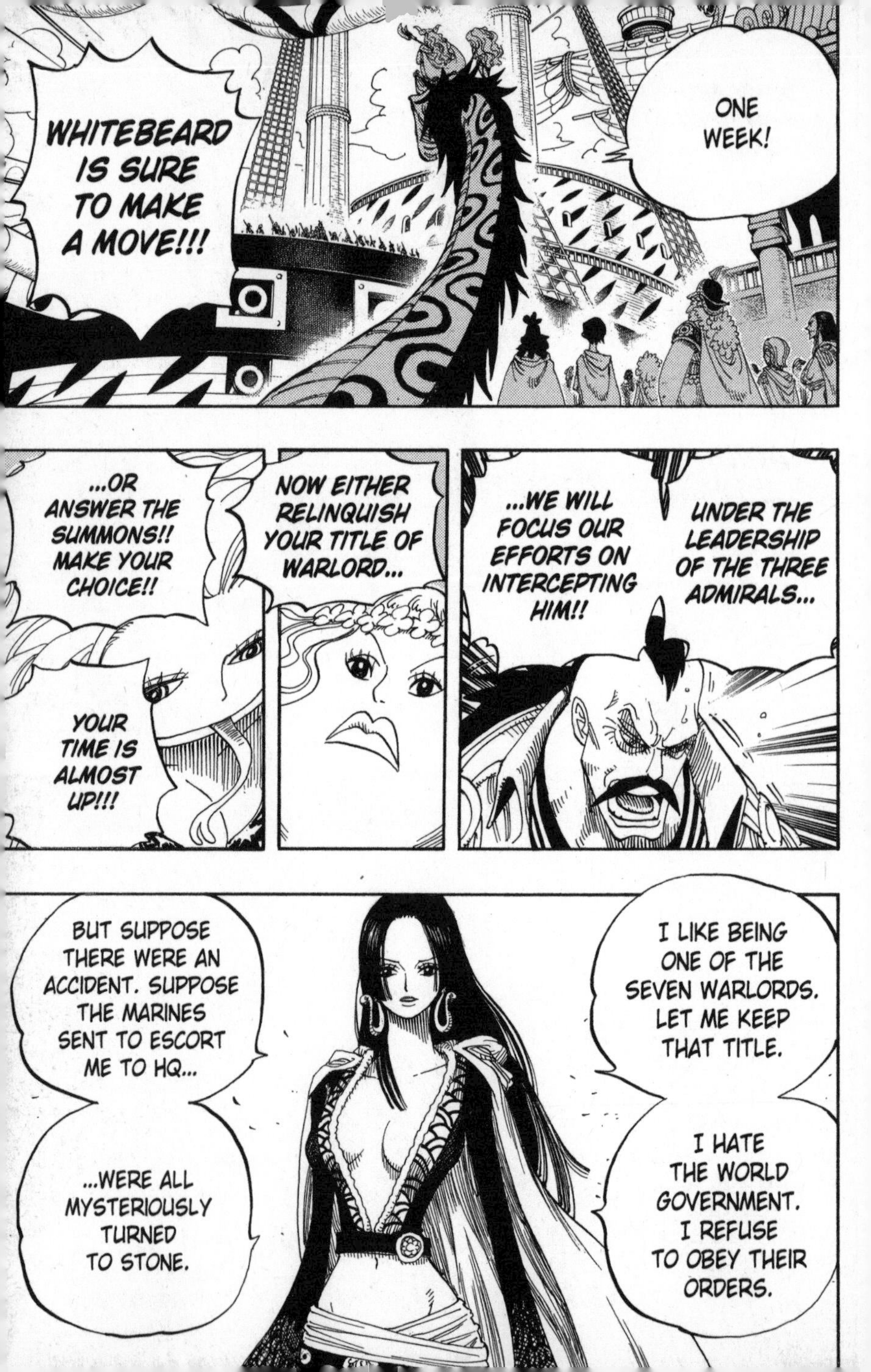
ONE WEEK!
WHITEBEARD IS SURE TO MAKE A MOVE!!!
UNDER THE LEADERSHIP OF THE THREE ADMIRALS...
...WE WILL FOCUS OUR EFFORTS ON INTERCEPTING HIM!!
NOW EITHER RELINQUISH YOUR TITLE OF WARLORD...
...OR ANSWER THE SUMMONS!! MAKE YOUR CHOICE!!
YOUR TIME IS ALMOST UP!!!
I LIKE BEING ONE OF THE SEVEN WARLORDS. LET ME KEEP THAT TITLE.
I HATE THE WORLD GOVERNMENT. I REFUSE TO OBEY THEIR ORDERS.
BUT SUPPOSE THERE WERE AN ACCIDENT. SUPPOSE THE MARINES SENT TO ESCORT ME TO HQ...
...WERE ALL MYSTERIOUSLY TURNED TO STONE.

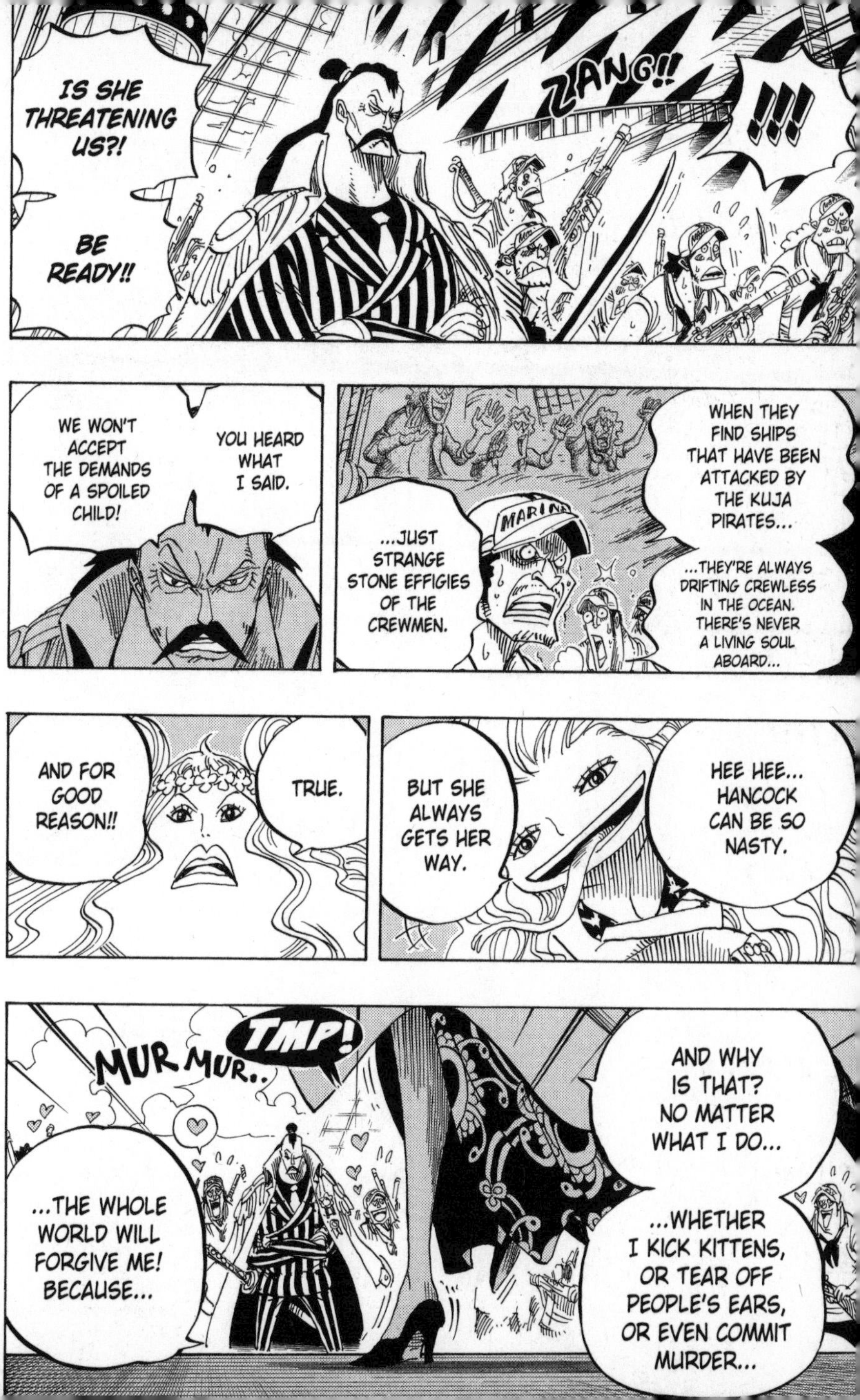
ZANG!!
!!!
IS SHE THREATENING US?!
BE READY!!
WHEN THEY FIND SHIPS THAT HAVE BEEN ATTACKED BY THE KUJA PIRATES...
...THEY'RE ALWAYS DRIFTING CREWLESS IN THE OCEAN. THERE'S NEVER A LIVING SOUL ABOARD...
...JUST STRANGE STONE EFFIGIES OF THE CREWMEN.
MARINE
YOU HEARD WHAT I SAID.
WE WON'T ACCEPT THE DEMANDS OF A SPOILED CHILD!
HEE HEE... HANCOCK CAN BE SO NASTY.
BUT SHE ALWAYS GETS HER WAY.
TRUE.
AND FOR GOOD REASON!!
AND WHY IS THAT? NO MATTER WHAT I DO...
...WHETHER I KICK KITTENS, OR TEAR OFF PEOPLE'S EARS, OR EVEN COMMIT MURDER...
TMP!
MUR MUR..
...THE WHOLE WORLD WILL FORGIVE ME! BECAUSE...

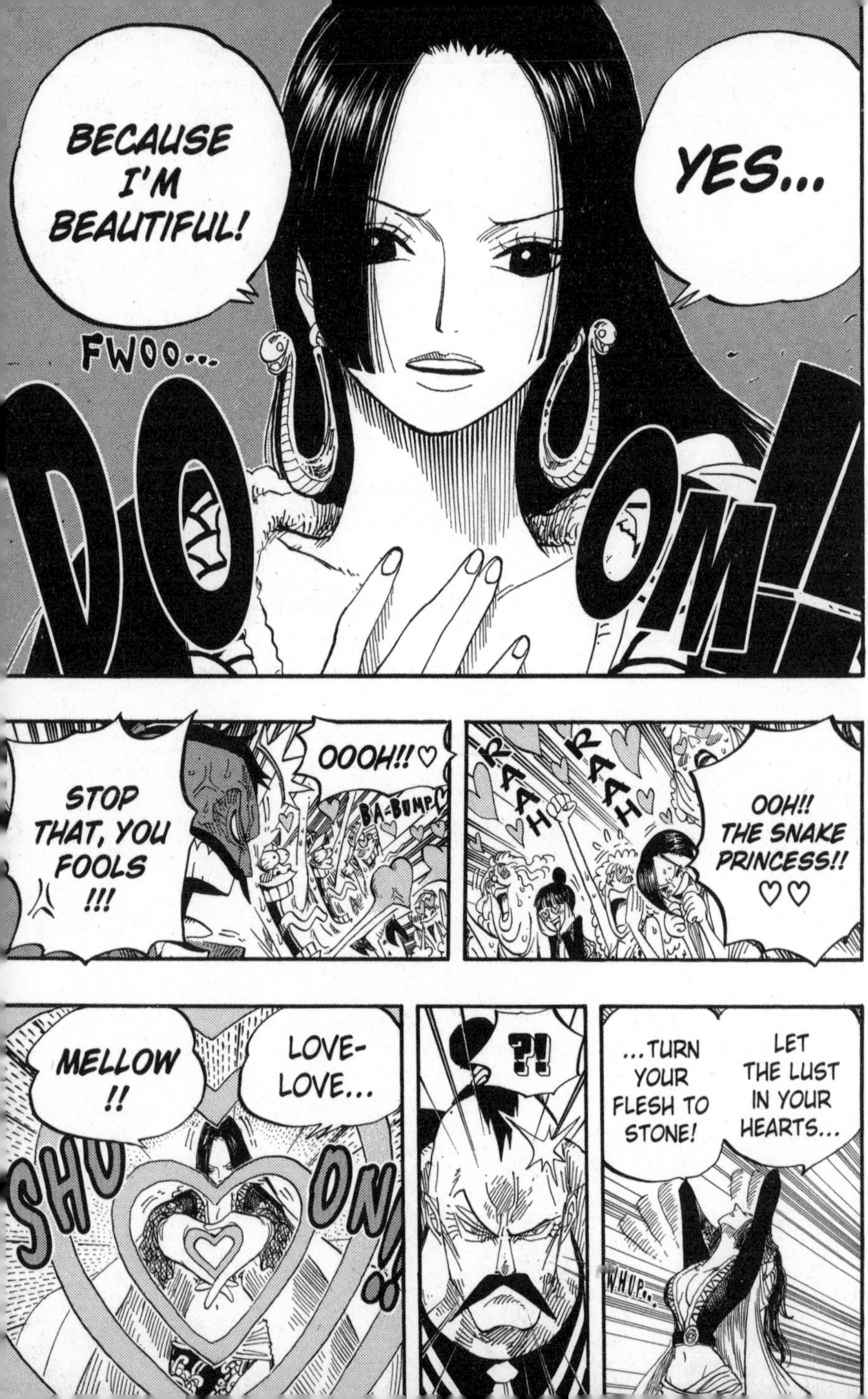
YES...
BECAUSE I'M BEAUTIFUL!
FWOO...
DOOM!!
OOH!! THE SNAKE PRINCESS!! ♡♡
RAAH
RAAH
OOOH!! ♡
BA-BUMP
STOP THAT, YOU FOOLS!!!
LET THE LUST IN YOUR HEARTS...
...TURN YOUR FLESH TO STONE!
WHUP...
?!
LOVE-LOVE...
MELLOW!!
SHO ON!!

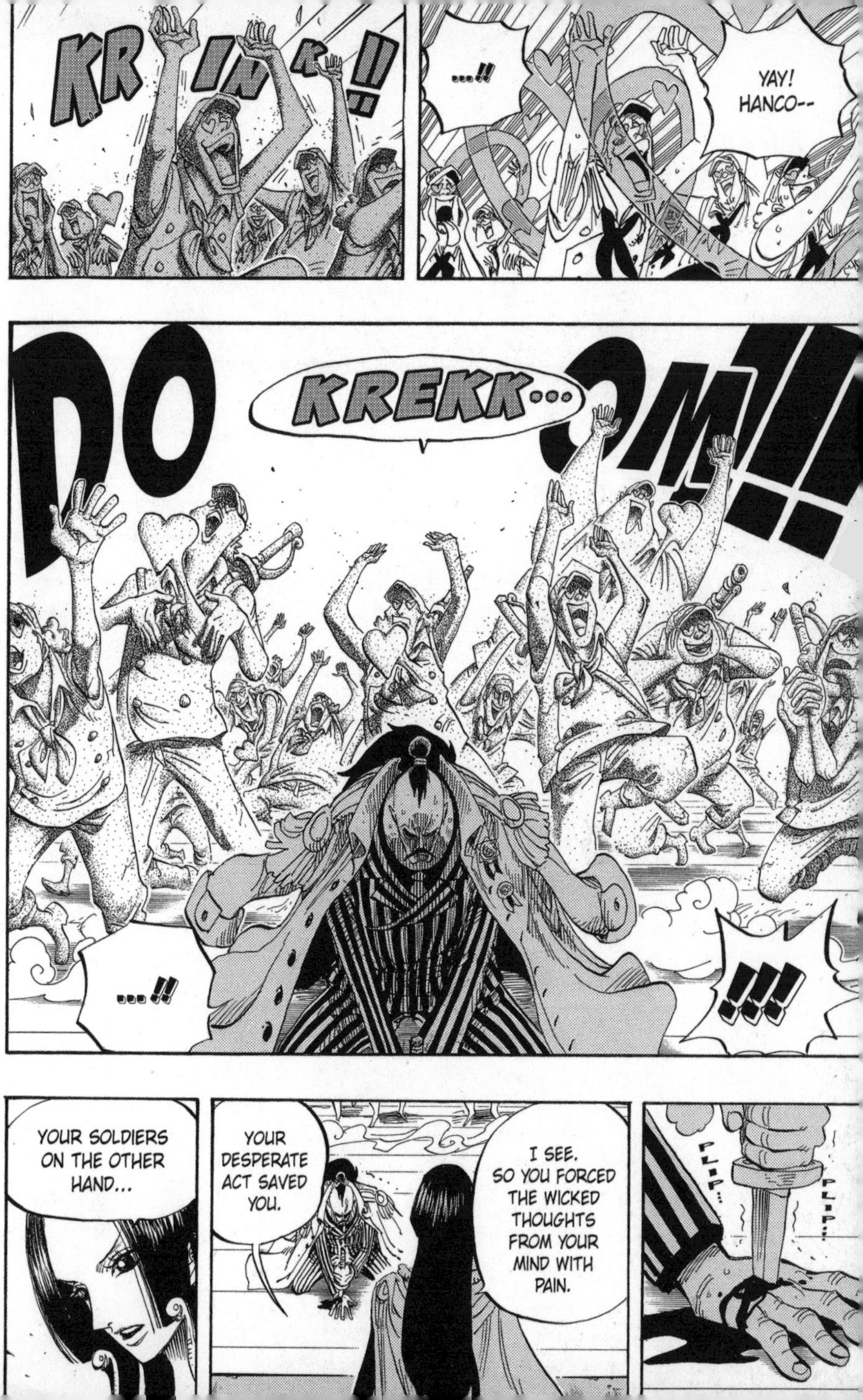
YAY! HANCO--
...!!
KRINK!!
DOOM!!!
KREKK...
!!!
...!!
PLIP...
PLIP...
I SEE. SO YOU FORCED THE WICKED THOUGHTS FROM YOUR MIND WITH PAIN.
YOUR DESPERATE ACT SAVED YOU.
YOUR SOLDIERS ON THE OTHER HAND...

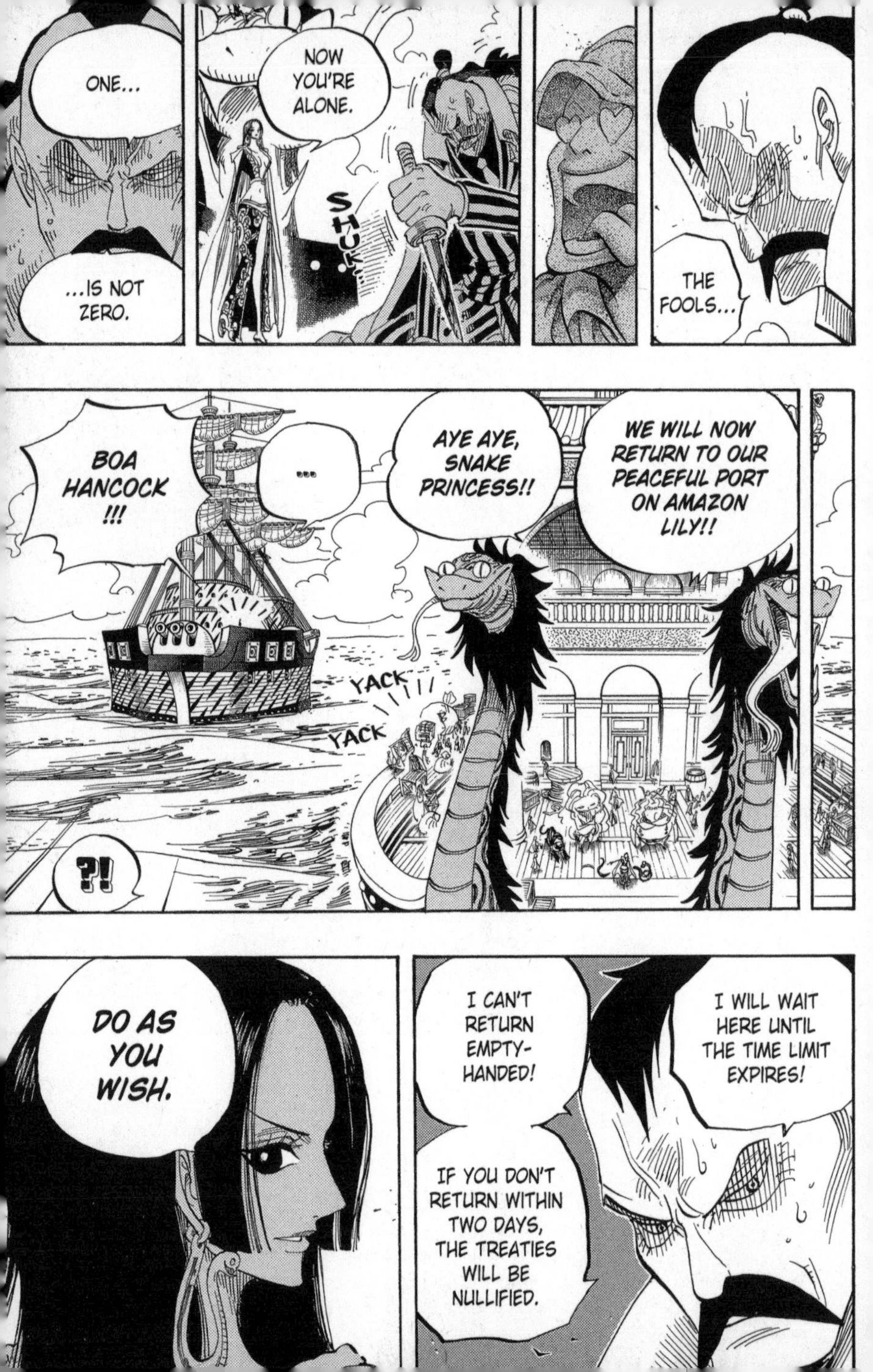
THE FOOLS...
SHUK
NOW YOU'RE ALONE.
ONE...
...IS NOT ZERO.
WE WILL NOW RETURN TO OUR PEACEFUL PORT ON AMAZON LILY!!
AYE AYE, SNAKE PRINCESS!!
...
BOA HANCOCK!!!
YACK
YACK
?!
I WILL WAIT HERE UNTIL THE TIME LIMIT EXPIRES!
I CAN'T RETURN EMPTY-HANDED!
IF YOU DON'T RETURN WITHIN TWO DAYS, THE TREATIES WILL BE NULLIFIED.
DO AS YOU WISH.

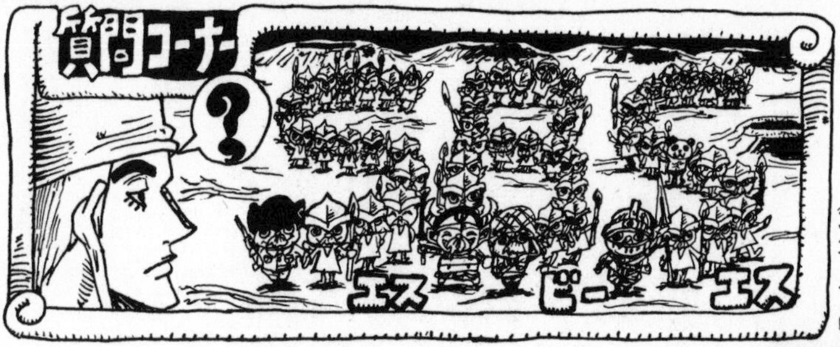
質問コーナー
エス ピー エス
(Ponio, Aichi)

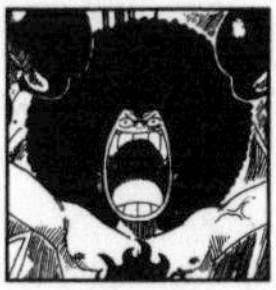

Q: Oda Sensei, aren't you going to get an afro? I think you'd look great with one.
--Hiromu

A: No! When did I ever say I would?!

Q: Oddachi, why do you want to be a pirate? You're a grown-up now! ♡
--Ulmol

A: I never said I did! What's with you people today?

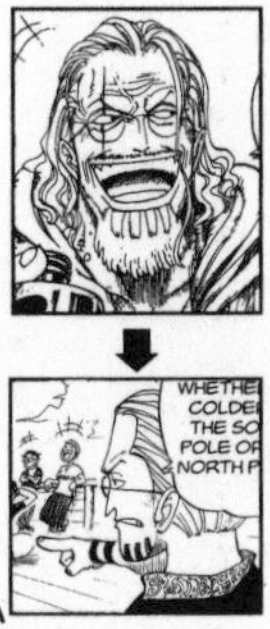
WHETHE
COLDE
THE SO
POLE OF
NORTH P

Q: Rayleigh, the Dark King, is too wicked. (I guess people don't use that word anymore.) By the way, in Buggy's flashback in chapter 19, I found a somewhat younger Rayleigh (volume 3, page 34). I was surprised to see you'd already designed the character that long ago.
--Kanpla

A: I got a lot of letters about this. I really feel that this manga is worth drawing when people remember such tiny details from the early episodes. I explained that this person was the first mate in an earlier Question Corner, but that would mean that Silvers Rayleigh was the Pirate King's right-hand man! So, Kanpla, you're a 48-year-old man. I'm happy to know that even someone your age can be impressed by Rayleigh.

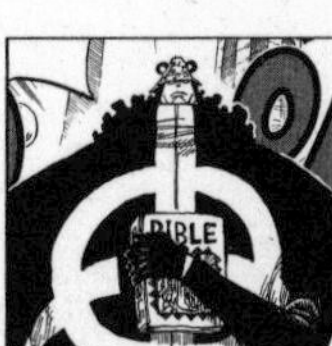
BIBLE

Q: Is the book Kuma's holding *One Piece* volume 12? My friend says it's definitely volume 13! I don't know what to tell him. Which is it, Mr. Oda?
--YUMAx527

A: It would be right around the time the crew entered the Grand Line in volumes 12 and 13. Kuma always has that bored look on his face, so maybe he's reading the Davy Back Fight in volume 33 and laughing to himself. Or maybe he's holding volume 25, in which he debuted. I wonder which volume it is! I don't know. Let's all take a guess! Bye!

Chapter 517:
BATH TIME

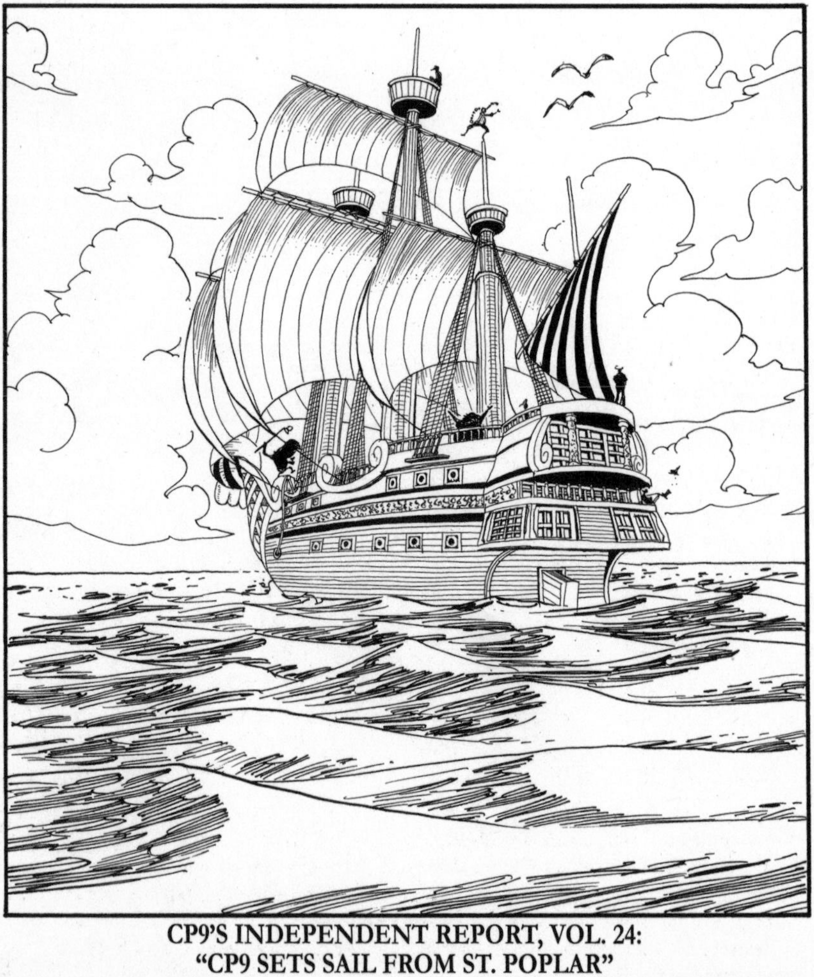

CP9'S INDEPENDENT REPORT, VOL. 24:
"CP9 SETS SAIL FROM ST. POPLAR"

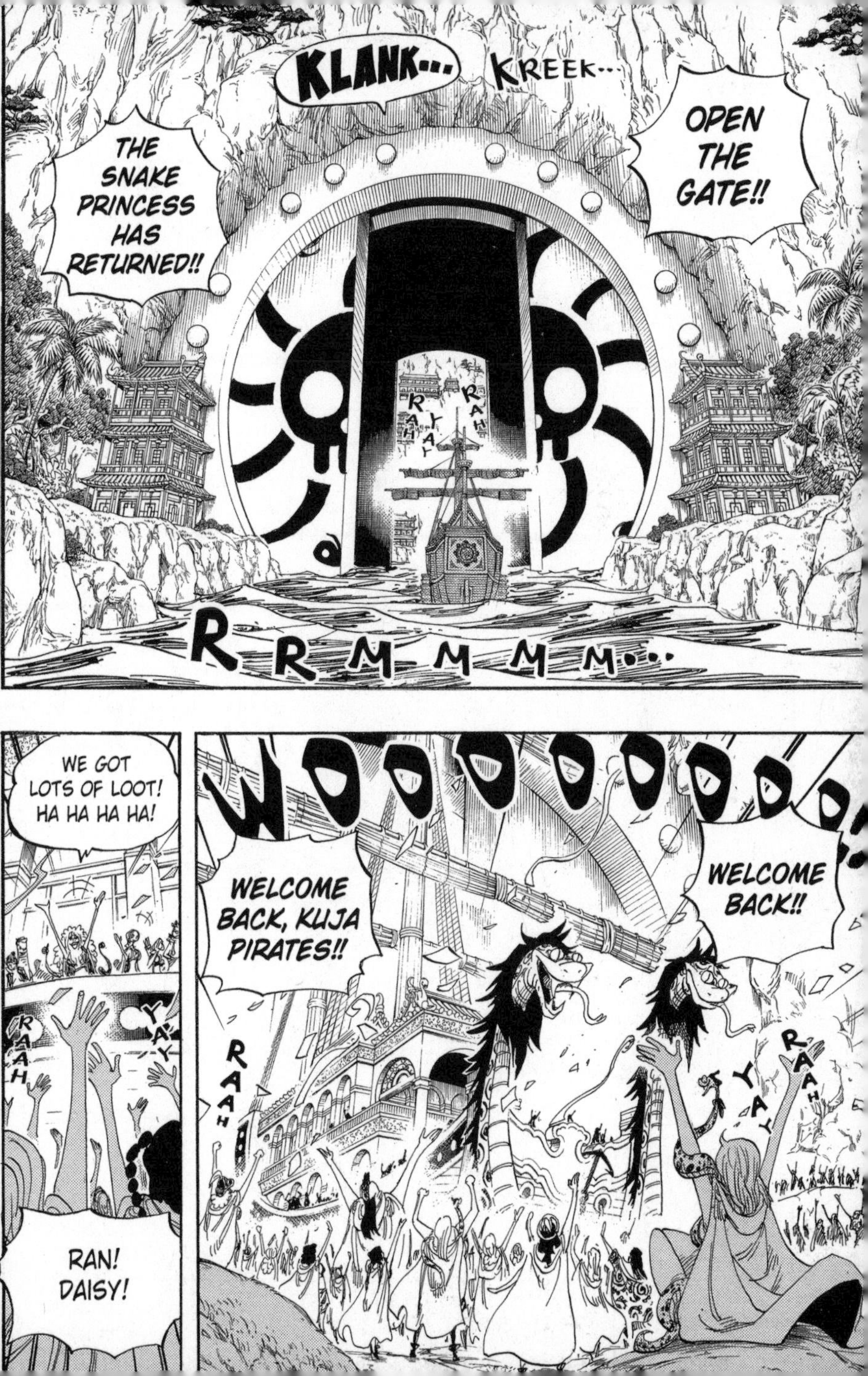
KREEK...
KLANK...
OPEN THE GATE!!
THE SNAKE PRINCESS HAS RETURNED!!
RAH
YAY
RAAH
RRMMMM...
WOOOOOOOO!
WELCOME BACK!!
WELCOME BACK, KUJA PIRATES!!
RAAH
YAY
RAAH
WE GOT LOTS OF LOOT! HA HA HA HA!
YAY
RAAH
RAN! DAISY!

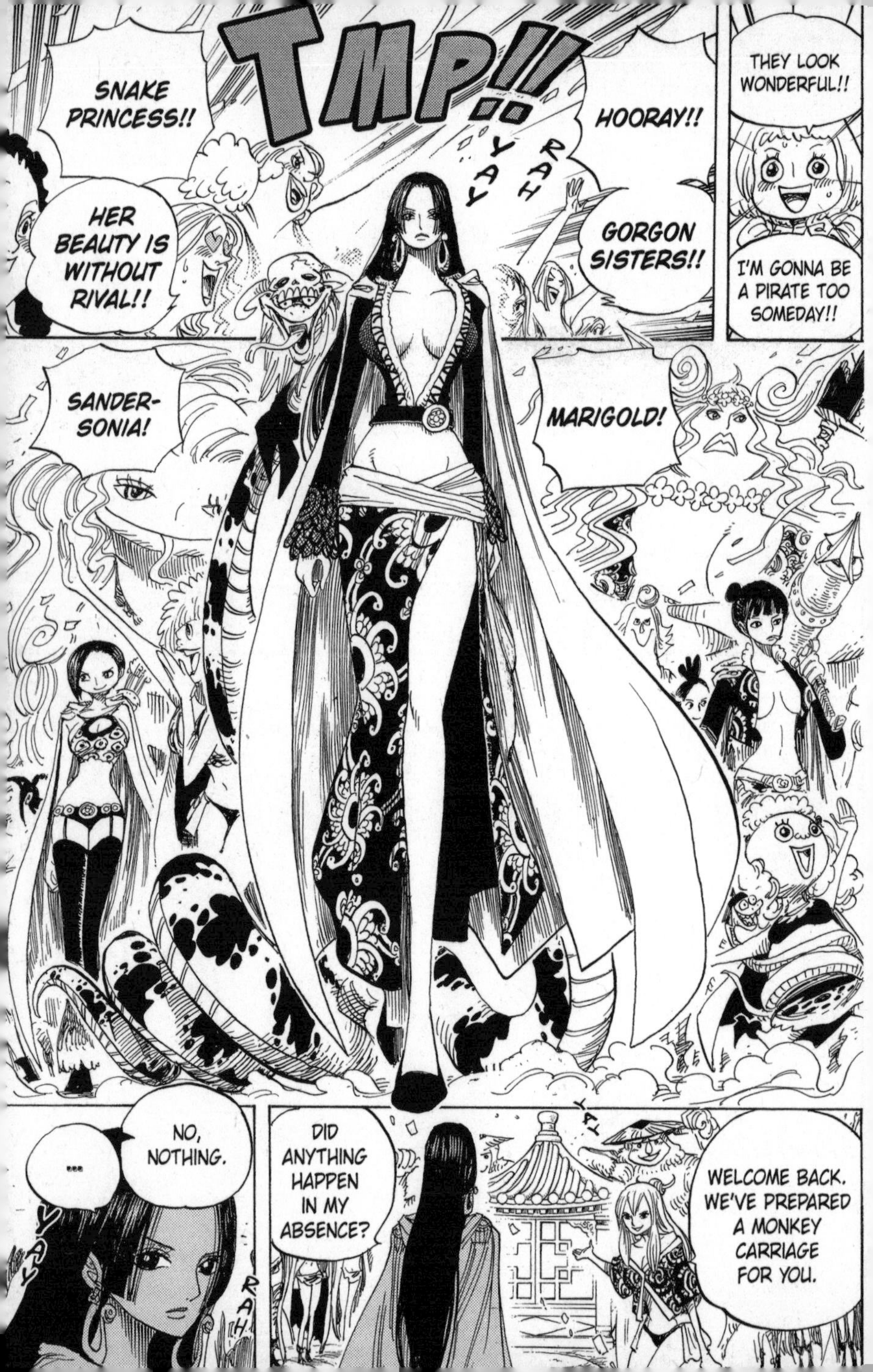
THEY LOOK WONDERFUL!!
I'M GONNA BE A PIRATE TOO SOMEDAY!!
TMP!!
HOORAY!!
RAH
YAY
GORGON SISTERS!!
SNAKE PRINCESS!!
HER BEAUTY IS WITHOUT RIVAL!!
MARIGOLD!
SANDER-SONIA!
WELCOME BACK. WE'VE PREPARED A MONKEY CARRIAGE FOR YOU.
YAY
DID ANYTHING HAPPEN IN MY ABSENCE?
NO, NOTHING.
...
YAY
RAH

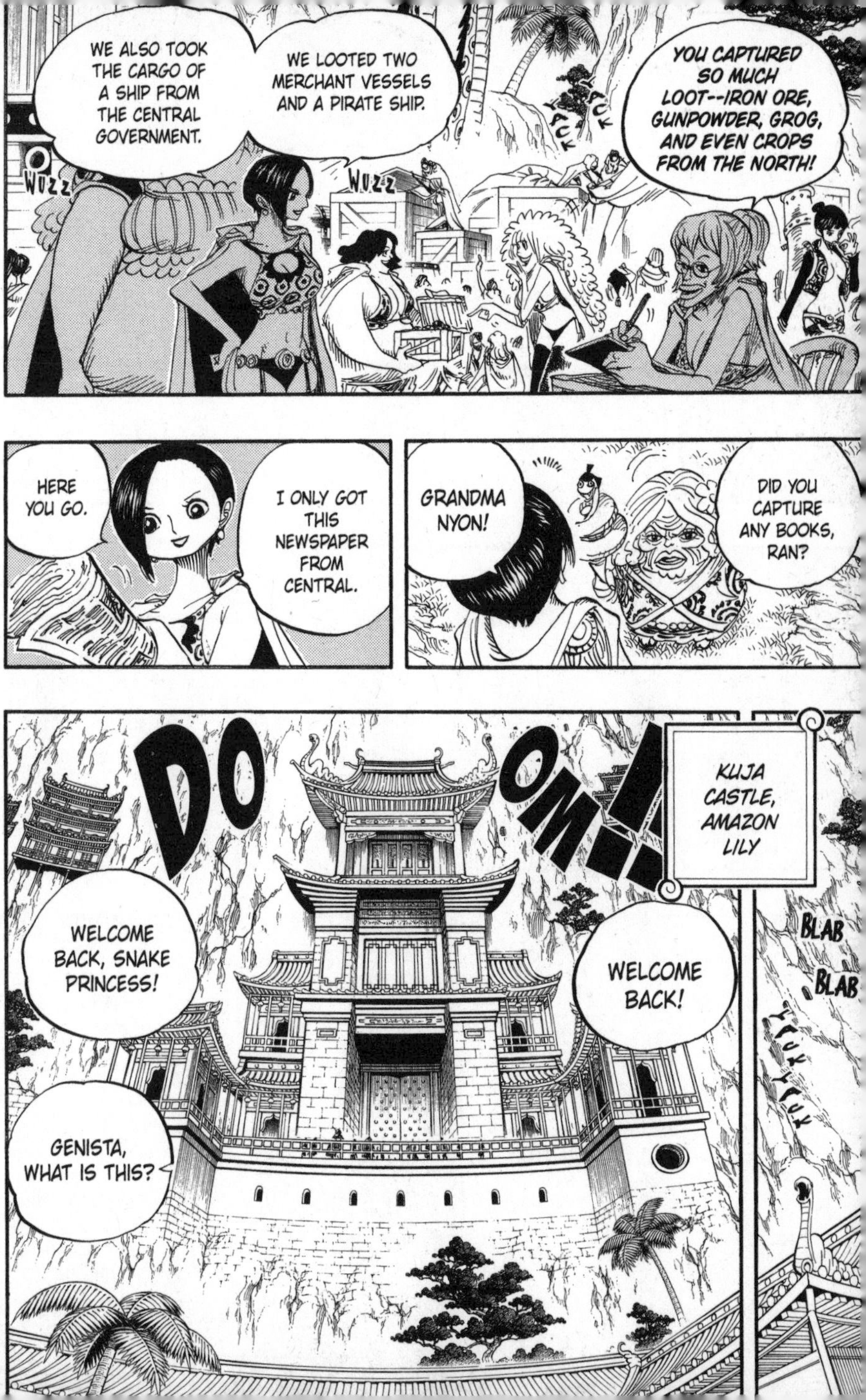
YOU CAPTURED SO MUCH LOOT--IRON ORE, GUNPOWDER, GROG, AND EVEN CROPS FROM THE NORTH!
YACK YACK
WE LOOTED TWO MERCHANT VESSELS AND A PIRATE SHIP.
WUZZ
WE ALSO TOOK THE CARGO OF A SHIP FROM THE CENTRAL GOVERNMENT.
WUZZ
DID YOU CAPTURE ANY BOOKS, RAN?
GRANDMA NYON!
I ONLY GOT THIS NEWSPAPER FROM CENTRAL.
HERE YOU GO.
KUJA CASTLE, AMAZON LILY
DOOM!!
BLAB
BLAB
YACK YACK
WELCOME BACK!
WELCOME BACK, SNAKE PRINCESS!
GENISTA, WHAT IS THIS?

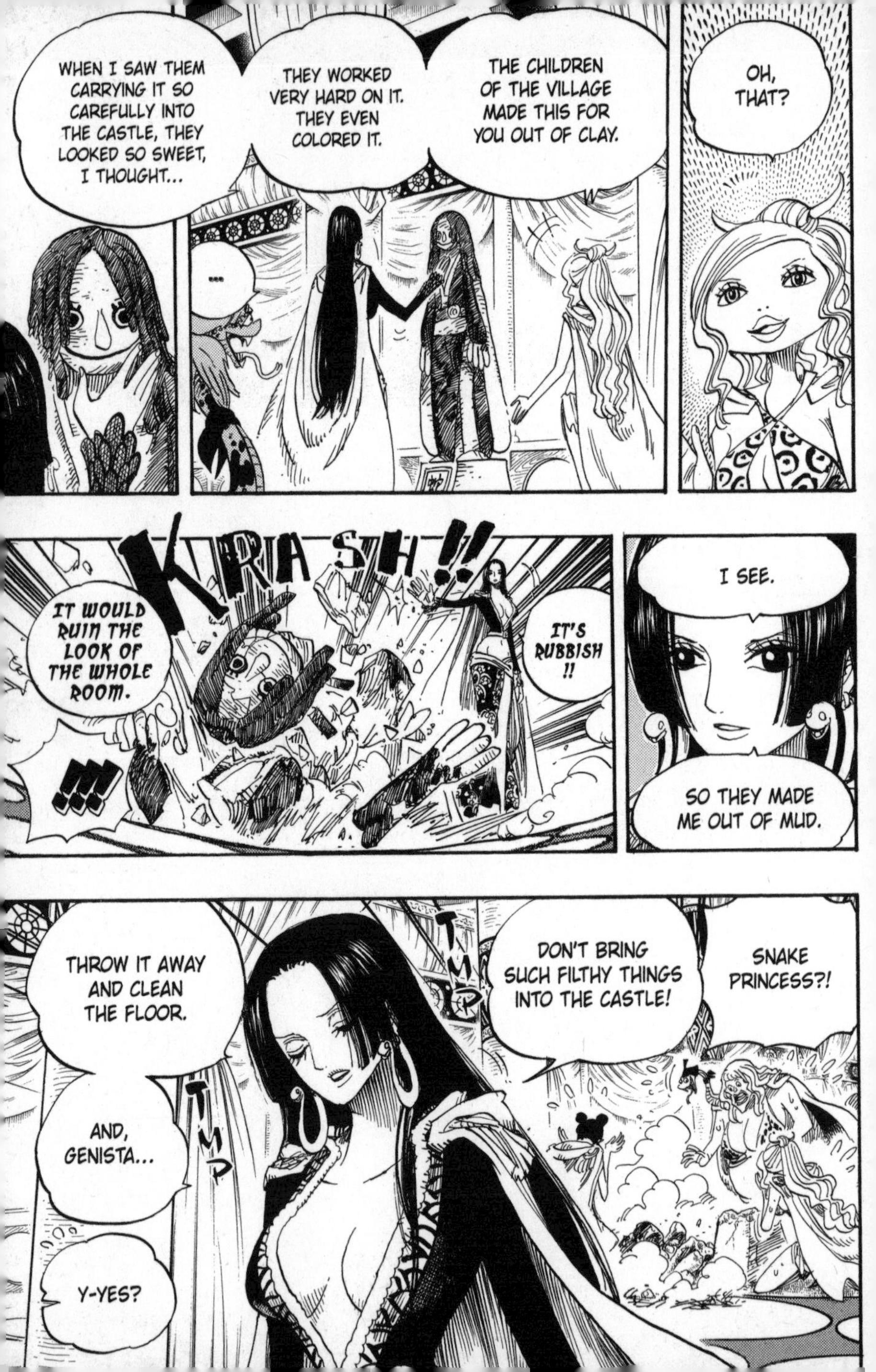
OH, THAT?
THE CHILDREN OF THE VILLAGE MADE THIS FOR YOU OUT OF CLAY.
THEY WORKED VERY HARD ON IT. THEY EVEN COLORED IT.
...
WHEN I SAW THEM CARRYING IT SO CAREFULLY INTO THE CASTLE, THEY LOOKED SO SWEET, I THOUGHT...
I SEE.
SO THEY MADE ME OUT OF MUD.
KRASH!!
IT'S RUBBISH!!
IT WOULD RUIN THE LOOK OF THE WHOLE ROOM.
!!!
SNAKE PRINCESS?!
DON'T BRING SUCH FILTHY THINGS INTO THE CASTLE!
TMP
THROW IT AWAY AND CLEAN THE FLOOR.
TMP
AND, GENISTA...
Y-YES?

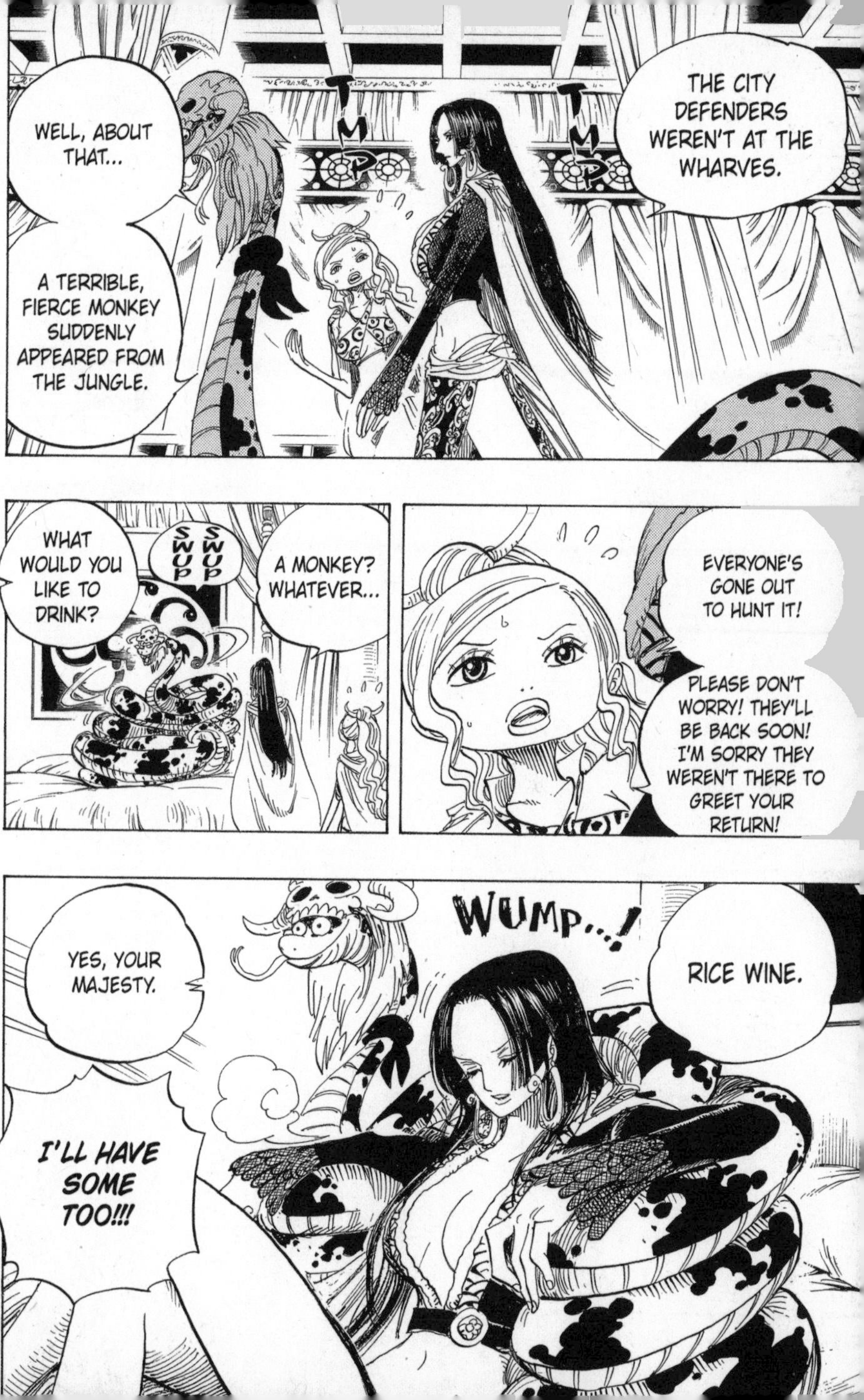
THE CITY DEFENDERS WEREN'T AT THE WHARVES.
TMP
TMP
WELL, ABOUT THAT...
A TERRIBLE, FIERCE MONKEY SUDDENLY APPEARED FROM THE JUNGLE.
EVERYONE'S GONE OUT TO HUNT IT!
PLEASE DON'T WORRY! THEY'LL BE BACK SOON! I'M SORRY THEY WEREN'T THERE TO GREET YOUR RETURN!
A MONKEY? WHATEVER...
SWUP
SWUP
WHAT WOULD YOU LIKE TO DRINK?
RICE WINE.
WUMP...!
YES, YOUR MAJESTY.
I'LL HAVE SOME TOO!!!

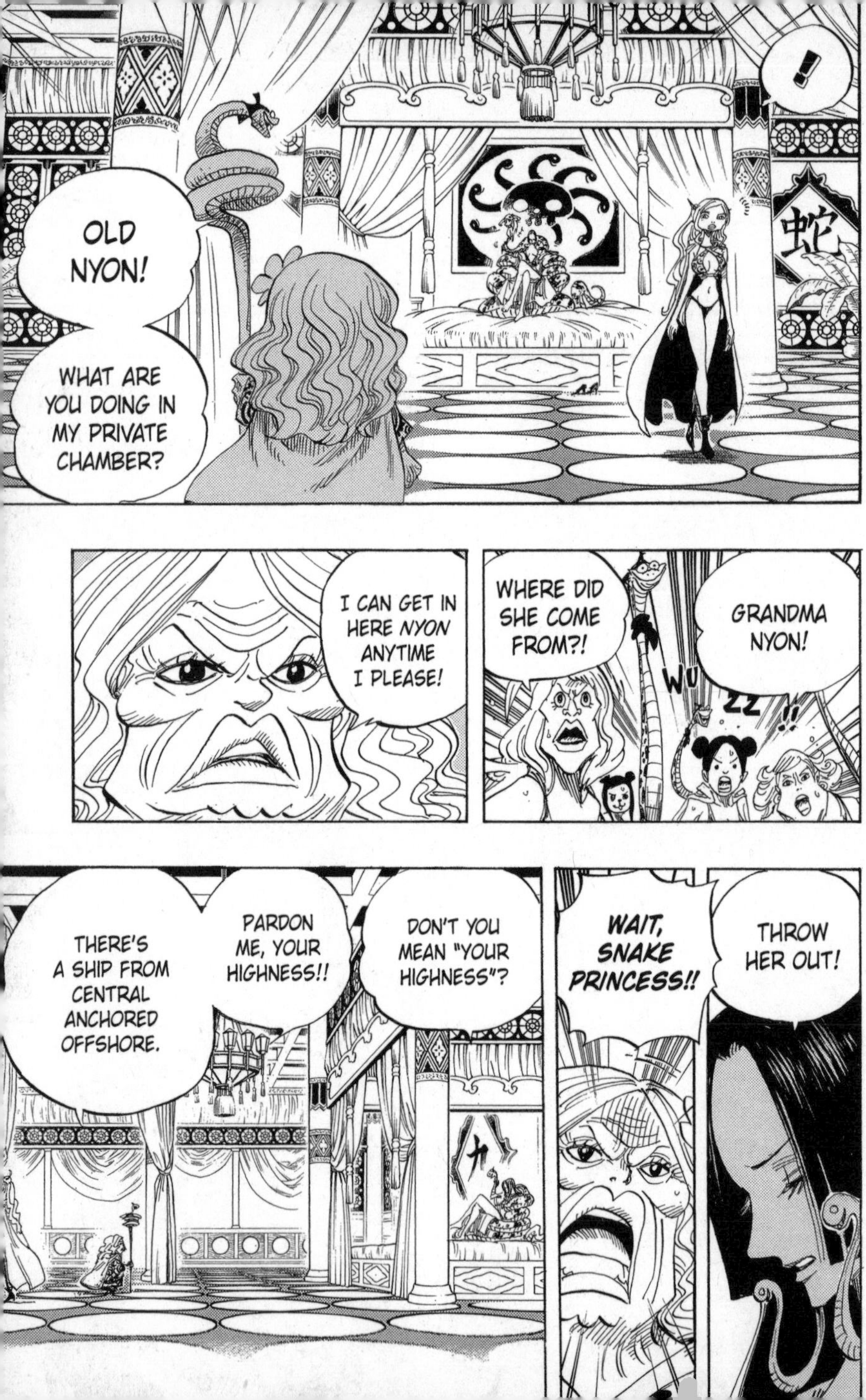
!
蛇
OLD NYON!
WHAT ARE YOU DOING IN MY PRIVATE CHAMBER?
GRANDMA NYON!
WHERE DID SHE COME FROM?!
WU
ZZ
I CAN GET IN HERE *NYON* ANYTIME I PLEASE!
THROW HER OUT!
WAIT, SNAKE PRINCESS!!
DON'T YOU MEAN "YOUR HIGHNESS"?
PARDON ME, YOUR HIGHNESS!!
THERE'S A SHIP FROM CENTRAL ANCHORED OFFSHORE.

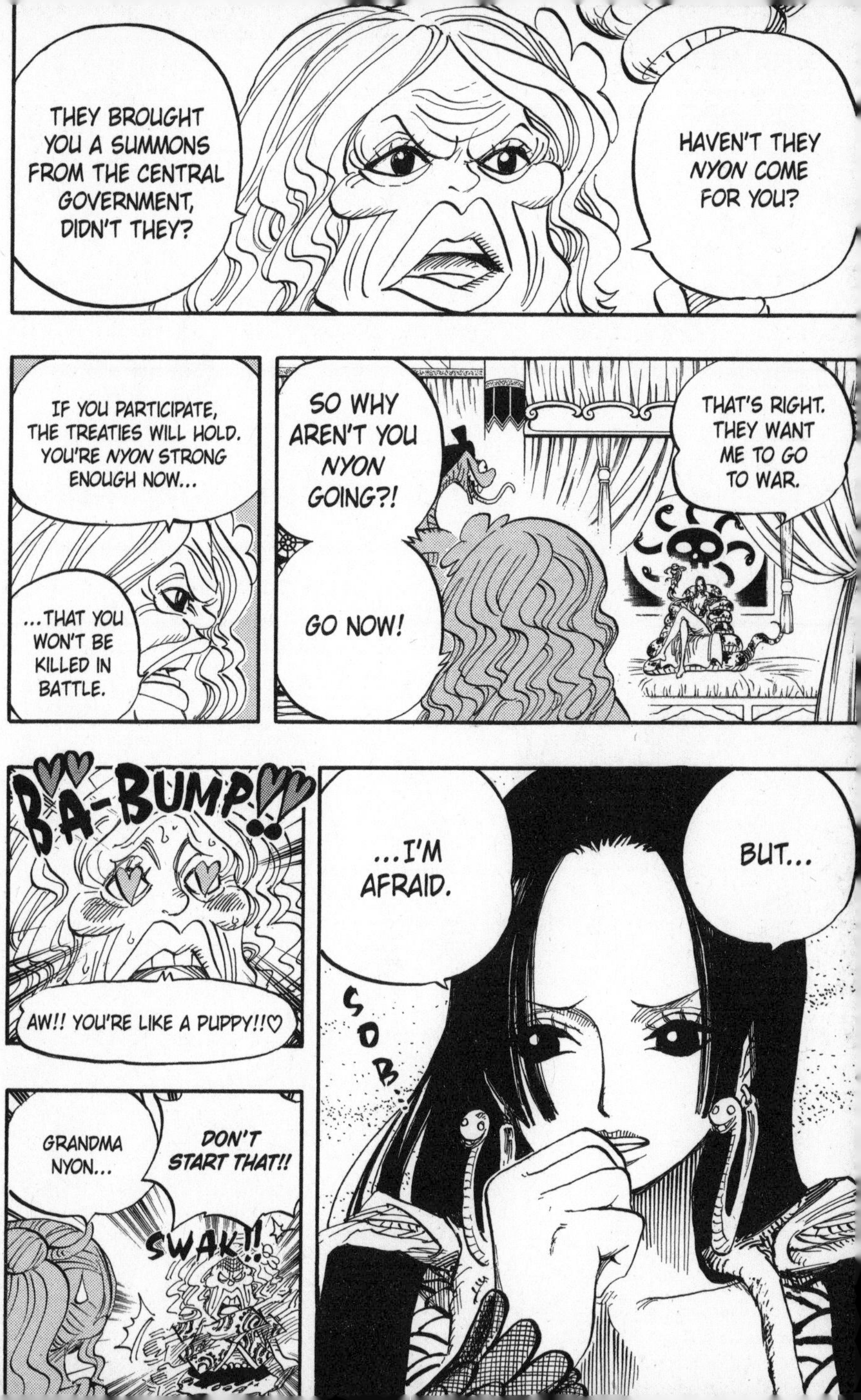
HAVEN'T THEY NYON COME FOR YOU?
THEY BROUGHT YOU A SUMMONS FROM THE CENTRAL GOVERNMENT, DIDN'T THEY?
THAT'S RIGHT. THEY WANT ME TO GO TO WAR.
SO WHY AREN'T YOU NYON GOING?!
GO NOW!
IF YOU PARTICIPATE, THE TREATIES WILL HOLD. YOU'RE NYON STRONG ENOUGH NOW...
...THAT YOU WON'T BE KILLED IN BATTLE.
BUT...
...I'M AFRAID.
SOB
BA-BUMP!!
AW!! YOU'RE LIKE A PUPPY!!♡
GRANDMA NYON...
DON'T START THAT!!
SWAK!!

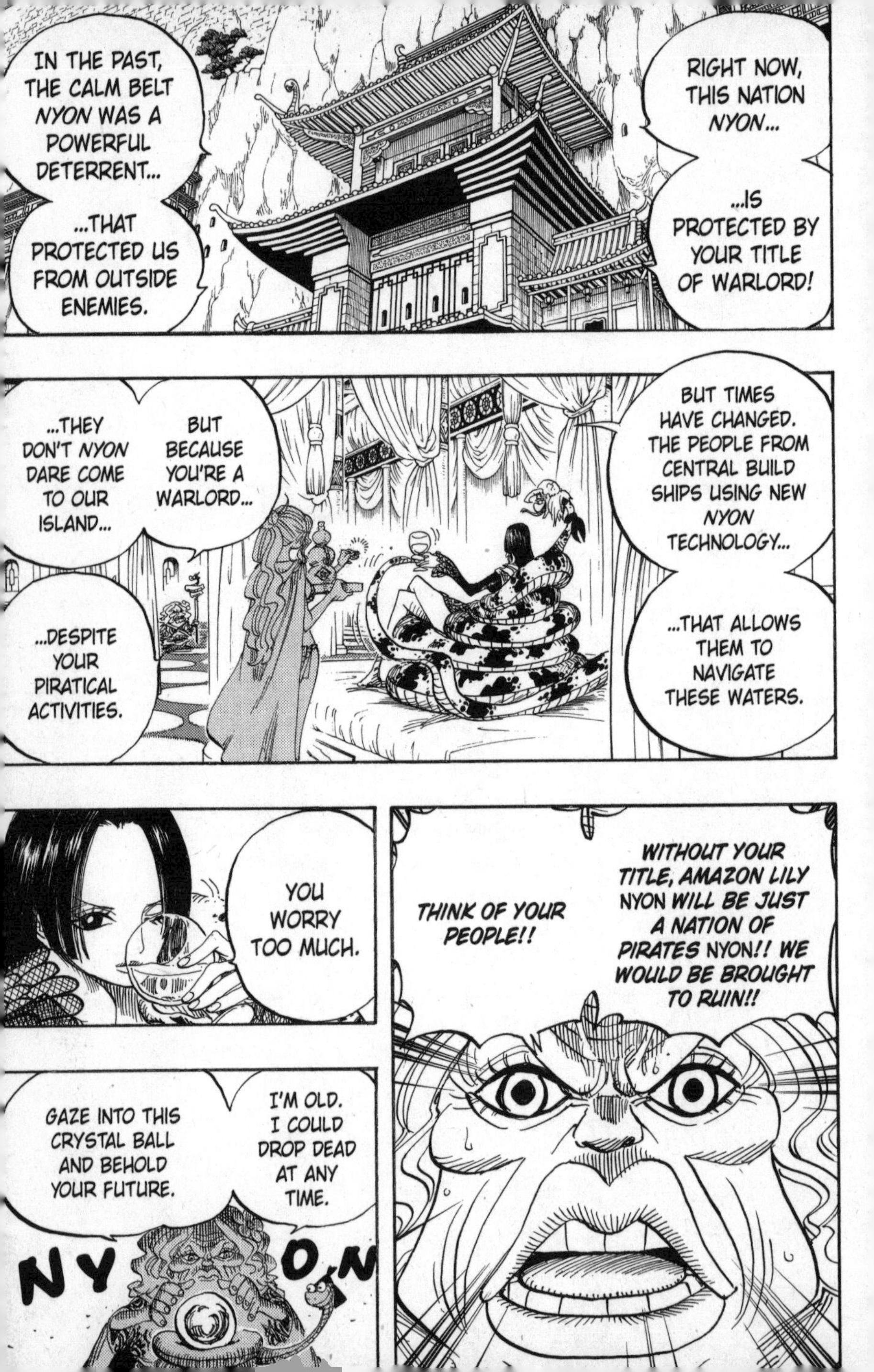
RIGHT NOW, THIS NATION NYON...
...IS PROTECTED BY YOUR TITLE OF WARLORD!
IN THE PAST, THE CALM BELT NYON WAS A POWERFUL DETERRENT...
...THAT PROTECTED US FROM OUTSIDE ENEMIES.
BUT TIMES HAVE CHANGED. THE PEOPLE FROM CENTRAL BUILD SHIPS USING NEW NYON TECHNOLOGY...
...THAT ALLOWS THEM TO NAVIGATE THESE WATERS.
BUT BECAUSE YOU'RE A WARLORD...
...THEY DON'T NYON DARE COME TO OUR ISLAND...
...DESPITE YOUR PIRATICAL ACTIVITIES.
WITHOUT YOUR TITLE, AMAZON LILY NYON WILL BE JUST A NATION OF PIRATES NYON!! WE WOULD BE BROUGHT TO RUIN!!
THINK OF YOUR PEOPLE!!
YOU WORRY TOO MUCH.
I'M OLD. I COULD DROP DEAD AT ANY TIME.
GAZE INTO THIS CRYSTAL BALL AND BEHOLD YOUR FUTURE.
NYON

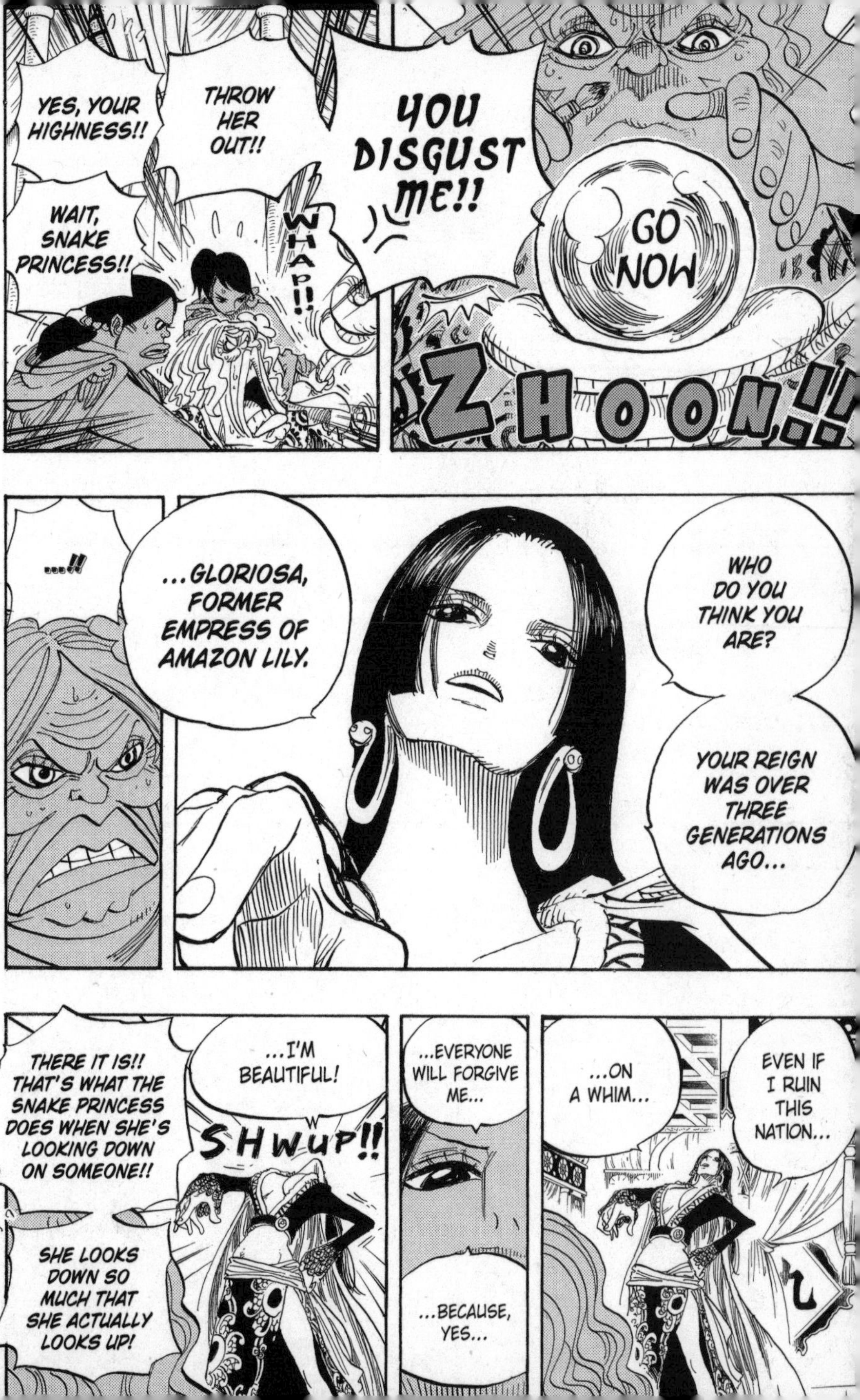
YOU DISGUST ME!!
GO NOW
ZHOON!!
THROW HER OUT!!
YES, YOUR HIGHNESS!!
WAIT, SNAKE PRINCESS!!
WHAP!!
WHO DO YOU THINK YOU ARE?
YOUR REIGN WAS OVER THREE GENERATIONS AGO...
...GLORIOSA, FORMER EMPRESS OF AMAZON LILY.
...!!
EVEN IF I RUIN THIS NATION...
...ON A WHIM...
...EVERYONE WILL FORGIVE ME...
...BECAUSE, YES...
...I'M BEAUTIFUL!
SHWUP!!
THERE IT IS!! THAT'S WHAT THE SNAKE PRINCESS DOES WHEN SHE'S LOOKING DOWN ON SOMEONE!!
SHE LOOKS DOWN SO MUCH THAT SHE ACTUALLY LOOKS UP!

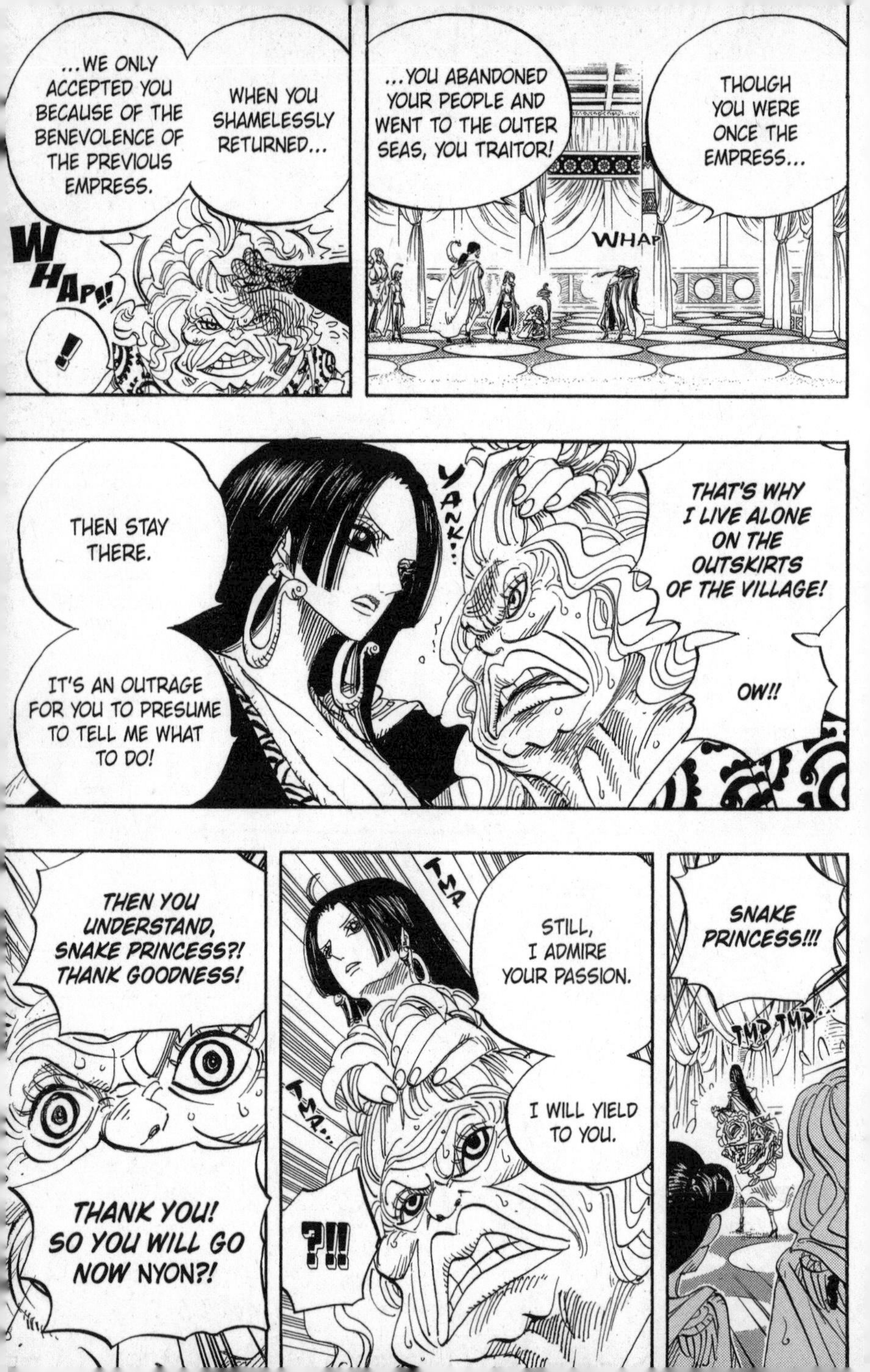
THOUGH YOU WERE ONCE THE EMPRESS...
...YOU ABANDONED YOUR PEOPLE AND WENT TO THE OUTER SEAS, YOU TRAITOR!
WHAP
WHEN YOU SHAMELESSLY RETURNED...
...WE ONLY ACCEPTED YOU BECAUSE OF THE BENEVOLENCE OF THE PREVIOUS EMPRESS.
WHAP!!
!
THAT'S WHY I LIVE ALONE ON THE OUTSKIRTS OF THE VILLAGE!
OW!!
YANK...
THEN STAY THERE.
IT'S AN OUTRAGE FOR YOU TO PRESUME TO TELL ME WHAT TO DO!
SNAKE PRINCESS!!!
TMP TMP...
TMP
STILL, I ADMIRE YOUR PASSION.
I WILL YIELD TO YOU.
?!!
THEN YOU UNDERSTAND, SNAKE PRINCESS?! THANK GOODNESS!
THANK YOU! SO YOU WILL GO NOW NYON?!

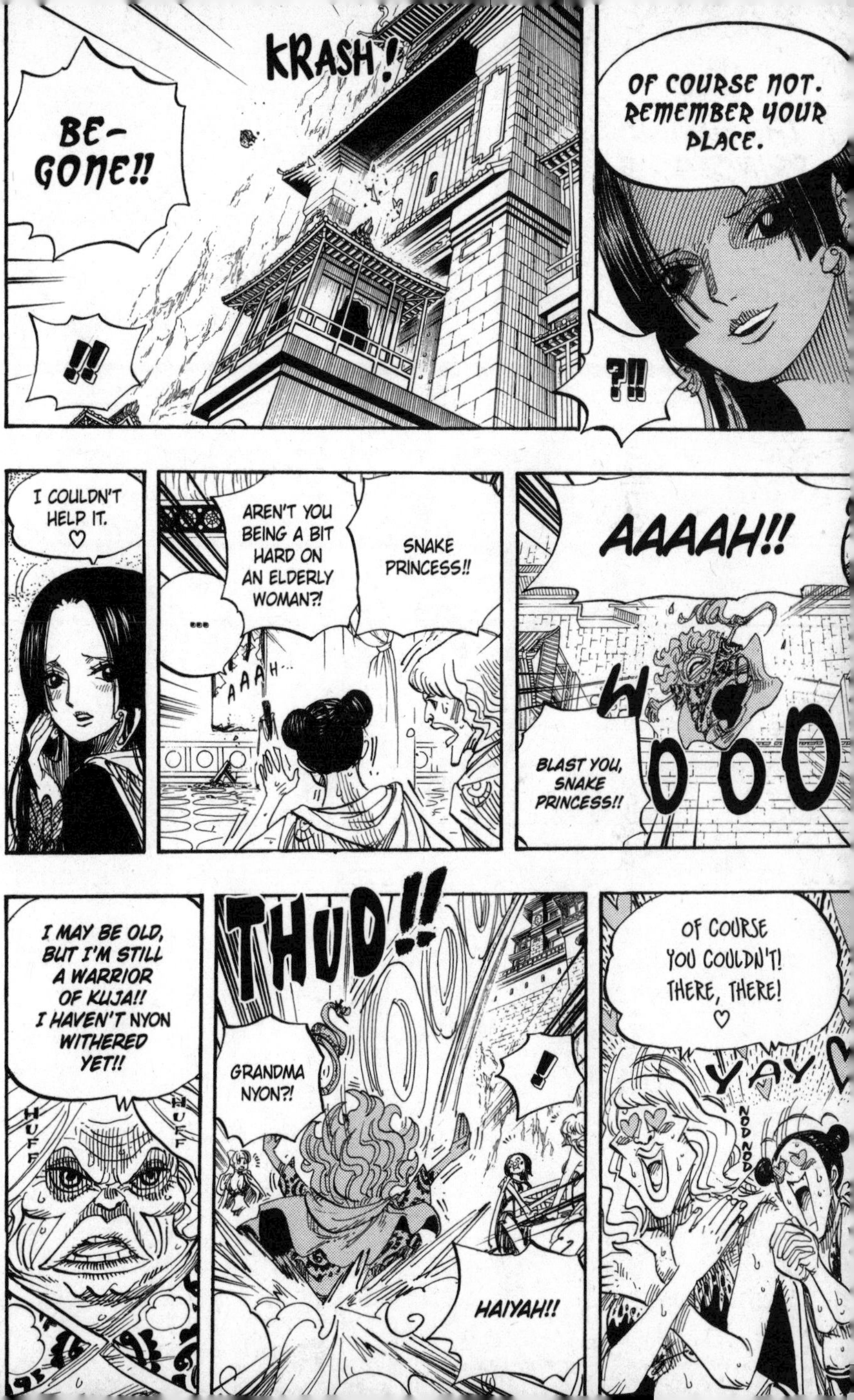
OF COURSE NOT. REMEMBER YOUR PLACE.
?!!
KRASH!
BE-GONE!!
!!
AAAAH!!
HOOOO
BLAST YOU, SNAKE PRINCESS!!
SNAKE PRINCESS!!
AREN'T YOU BEING A BIT HARD ON AN ELDERLY WOMAN?!
...
AAAAH...
I COULDN'T HELP IT. ♡
OF COURSE YOU COULDN'T! THERE, THERE! ♡
YAY
NOD NOD
THUD!!
!
GRANDMA NYON?!
HAIYAH!!
I MAY BE OLD, BUT I'M STILL A WARRIOR OF KUJA!! I HAVEN'T NYON WITHERED YET!!
HUFF
HUFF

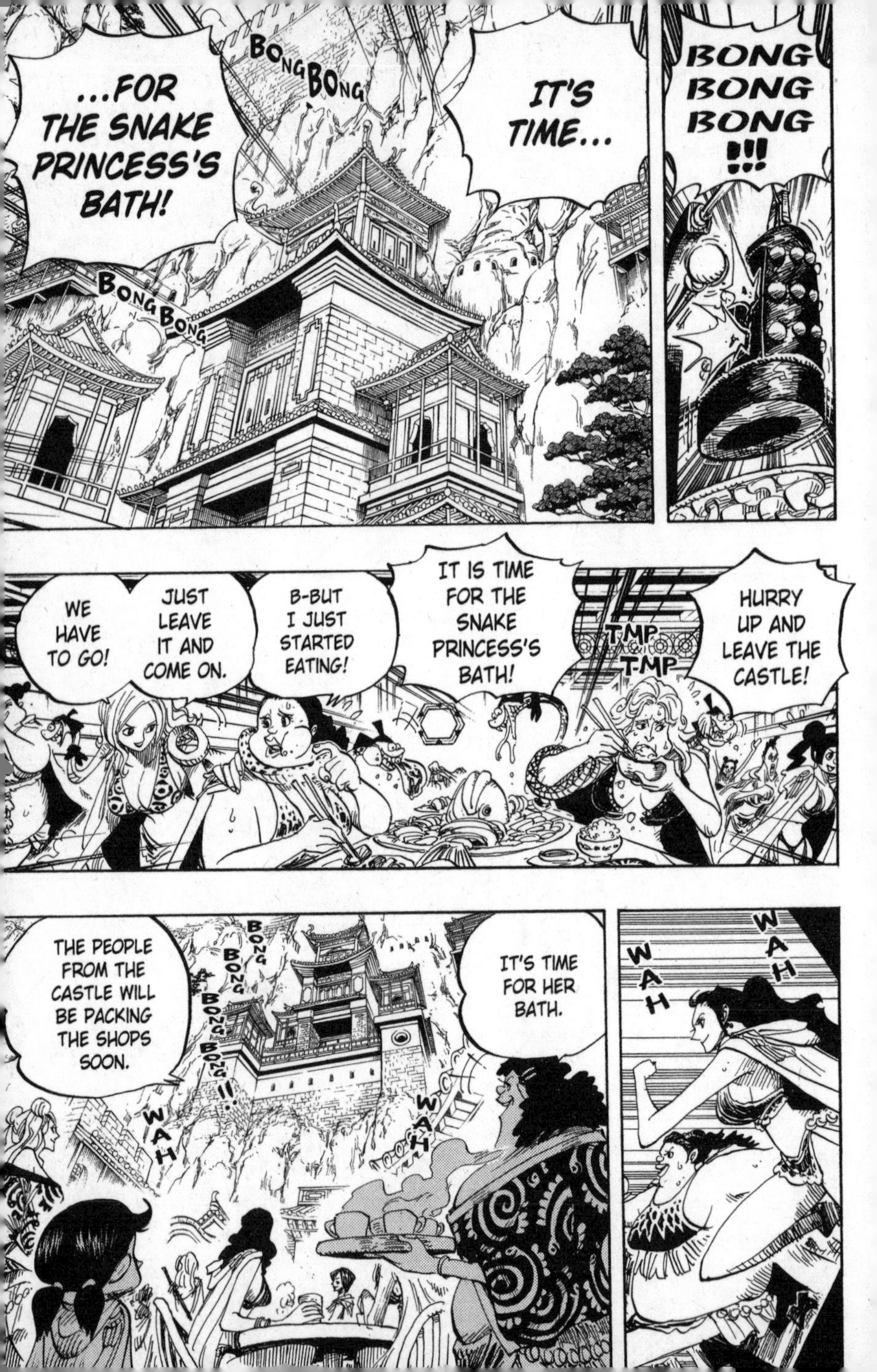
BONG BONG BONG!!!
IT'S TIME...
...FOR THE SNAKE PRINCESS'S BATH!
BONG BONG
BONG BONG
HURRY UP AND LEAVE THE CASTLE!
T-MP T-MP
IT IS TIME FOR THE SNAKE PRINCESS'S BATH!
B-BUT I JUST STARTED EATING!
JUST LEAVE IT AND COME ON.
WE HAVE TO GO!
WAH
WAH
IT'S TIME FOR HER BATH.
WAH
BONG BONG BONG BONG!!
THE PEOPLE FROM THE CASTLE WILL BE PACKING THE SHOPS SOON.
WAH

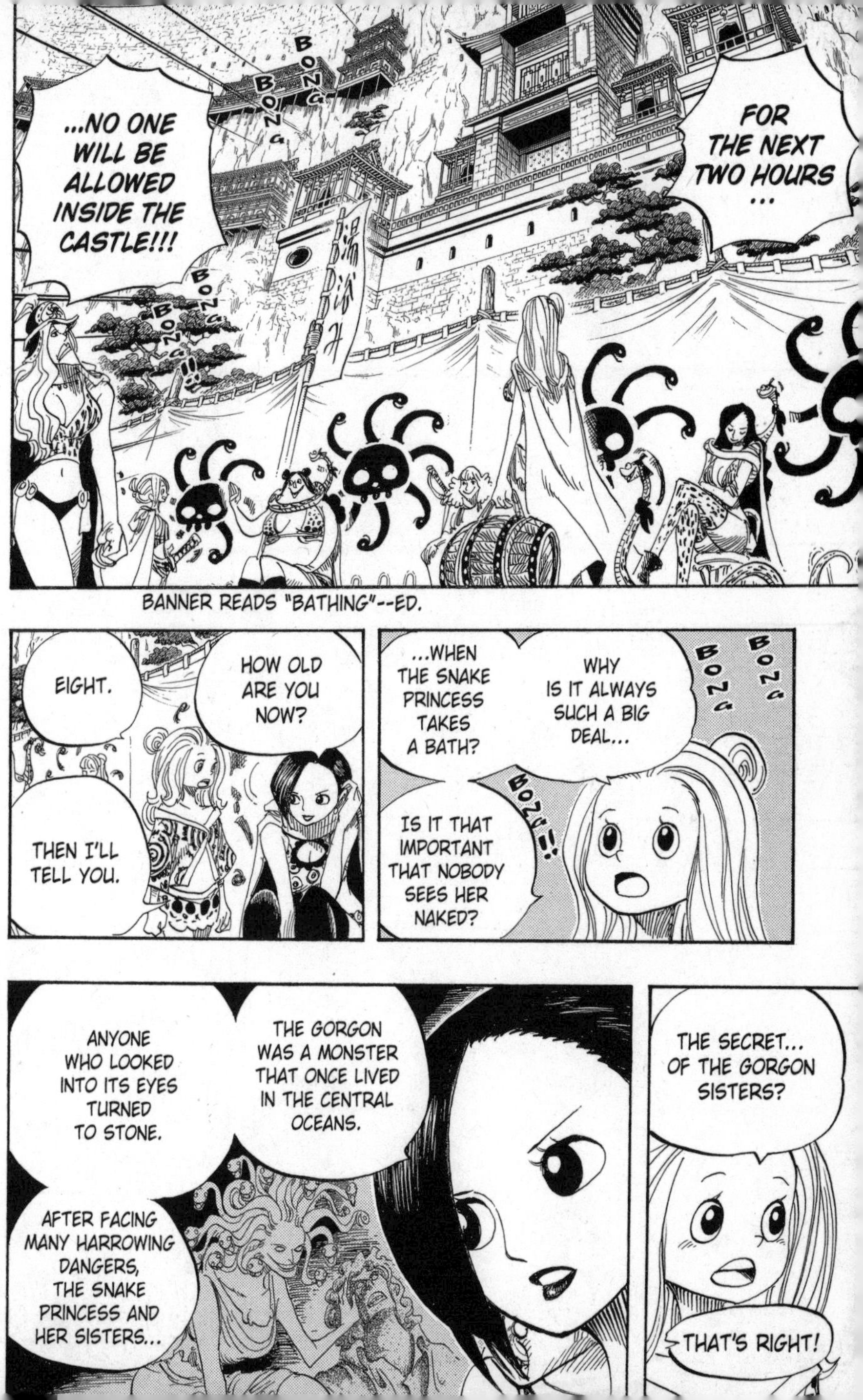

FOR THE NEXT TWO HOURS ...
...NO ONE WILL BE ALLOWED INSIDE THE CASTLE!!!
BONG BONG
BONG BONG!!
BANNER READS "BATHING"--ED.
BONG BONG
WHY IS IT ALWAYS SUCH A BIG DEAL...
...WHEN THE SNAKE PRINCESS TAKES A BATH?
BONG!!
IS IT THAT IMPORTANT THAT NOBODY SEES HER NAKED?
HOW OLD ARE YOU NOW?
EIGHT.
THEN I'LL TELL YOU.
THE SECRET... OF THE GORGON SISTERS?
THAT'S RIGHT!
THE GORGON WAS A MONSTER THAT ONCE LIVED IN THE CENTRAL OCEANS.
ANYONE WHO LOOKED INTO ITS EYES TURNED TO STONE.
AFTER FACING MANY HARROWING DANGERS, THE SNAKE PRINCESS AND HER SISTERS...

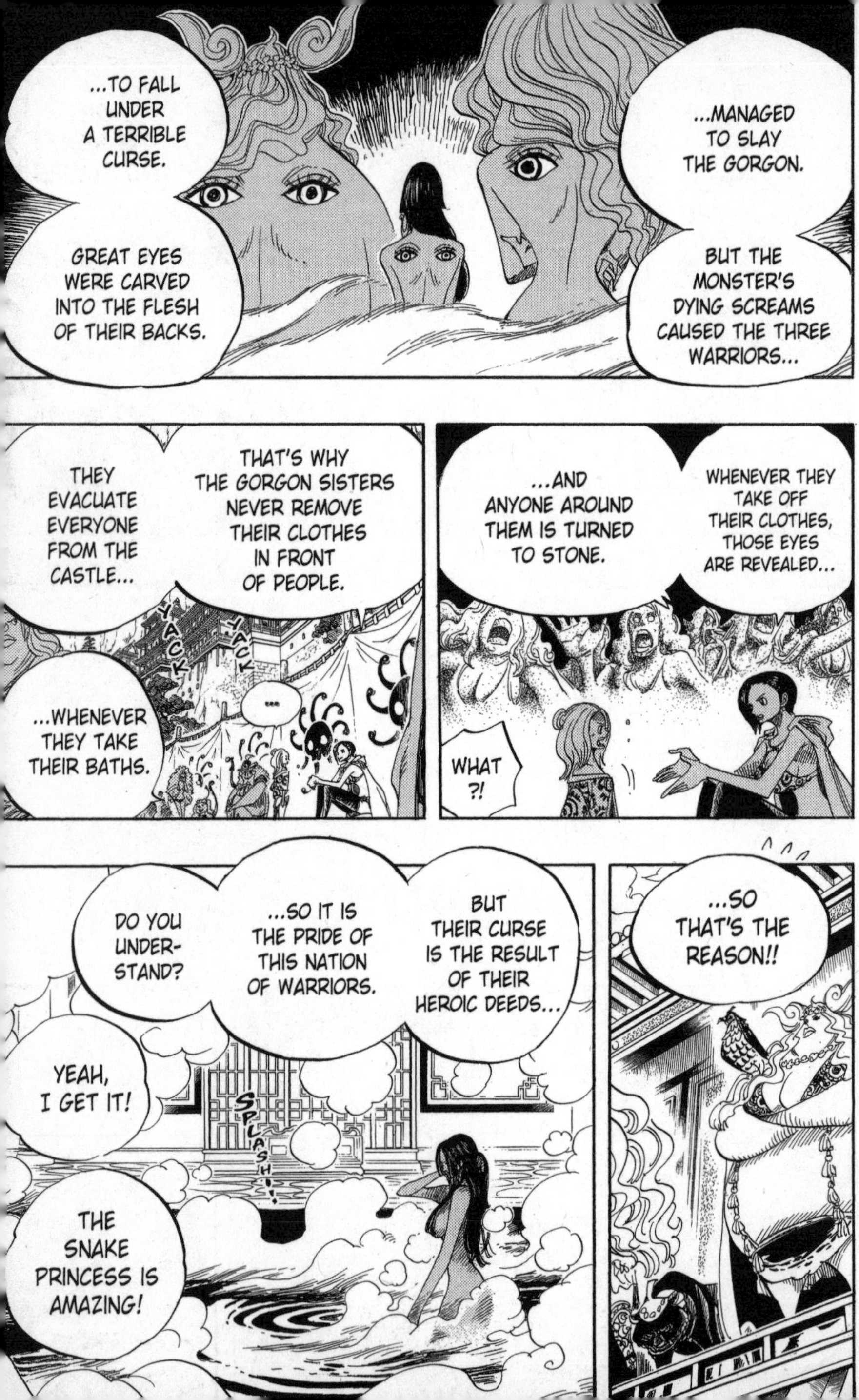
...MANAGED TO SLAY THE GORGON.
BUT THE MONSTER'S DYING SCREAMS CAUSED THE THREE WARRIORS...
...TO FALL UNDER A TERRIBLE CURSE.
GREAT EYES WERE CARVED INTO THE FLESH OF THEIR BACKS.
WHENEVER THEY TAKE OFF THEIR CLOTHES, THOSE EYES ARE REVEALED...
...AND ANYONE AROUND THEM IS TURNED TO STONE.
WHAT ?!
THAT'S WHY THE GORGON SISTERS NEVER REMOVE THEIR CLOTHES IN FRONT OF PEOPLE.
THEY EVACUATE EVERYONE FROM THE CASTLE...
YACK
YACK
...
...WHENEVER THEY TAKE THEIR BATHS.
...SO THAT'S THE REASON!!
BUT THEIR CURSE IS THE RESULT OF THEIR HEROIC DEEDS...
...SO IT IS THE PRIDE OF THIS NATION OF WARRIORS.
DO YOU UNDER-STAND?
YEAH, I GET IT!
SPLASH!!
THE SNAKE PRINCESS IS AMAZING!

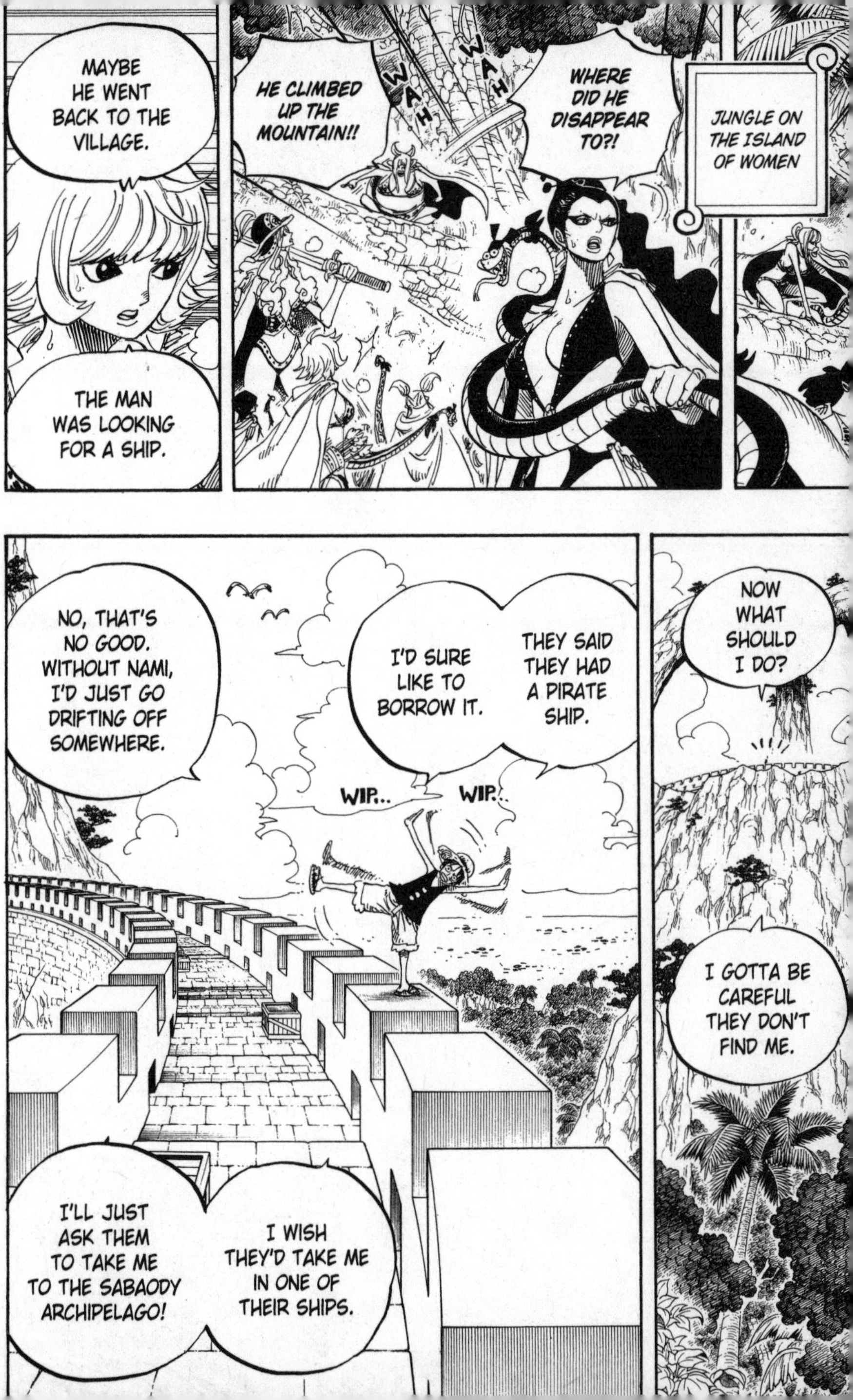
JUNGLE ON THE ISLAND OF WOMEN
WHERE DID HE DISAPPEAR TO?!
WAH WAH
HE CLIMBED UP THE MOUNTAIN!!
MAYBE HE WENT BACK TO THE VILLAGE.
THE MAN WAS LOOKING FOR A SHIP.
NOW WHAT SHOULD I DO?
I GOTTA BE CAREFUL THEY DON'T FIND ME.
THEY SAID THEY HAD A PIRATE SHIP.
I'D SURE LIKE TO BORROW IT.
WIP... WIP...
NO, THAT'S NO GOOD. WITHOUT NAMI, I'D JUST GO DRIFTING OFF SOMEWHERE.
I WISH THEY'D TAKE ME IN ONE OF THEIR SHIPS.
I'LL JUST ASK THEM TO TAKE ME TO THE SABAODY ARCHIPELAGO!

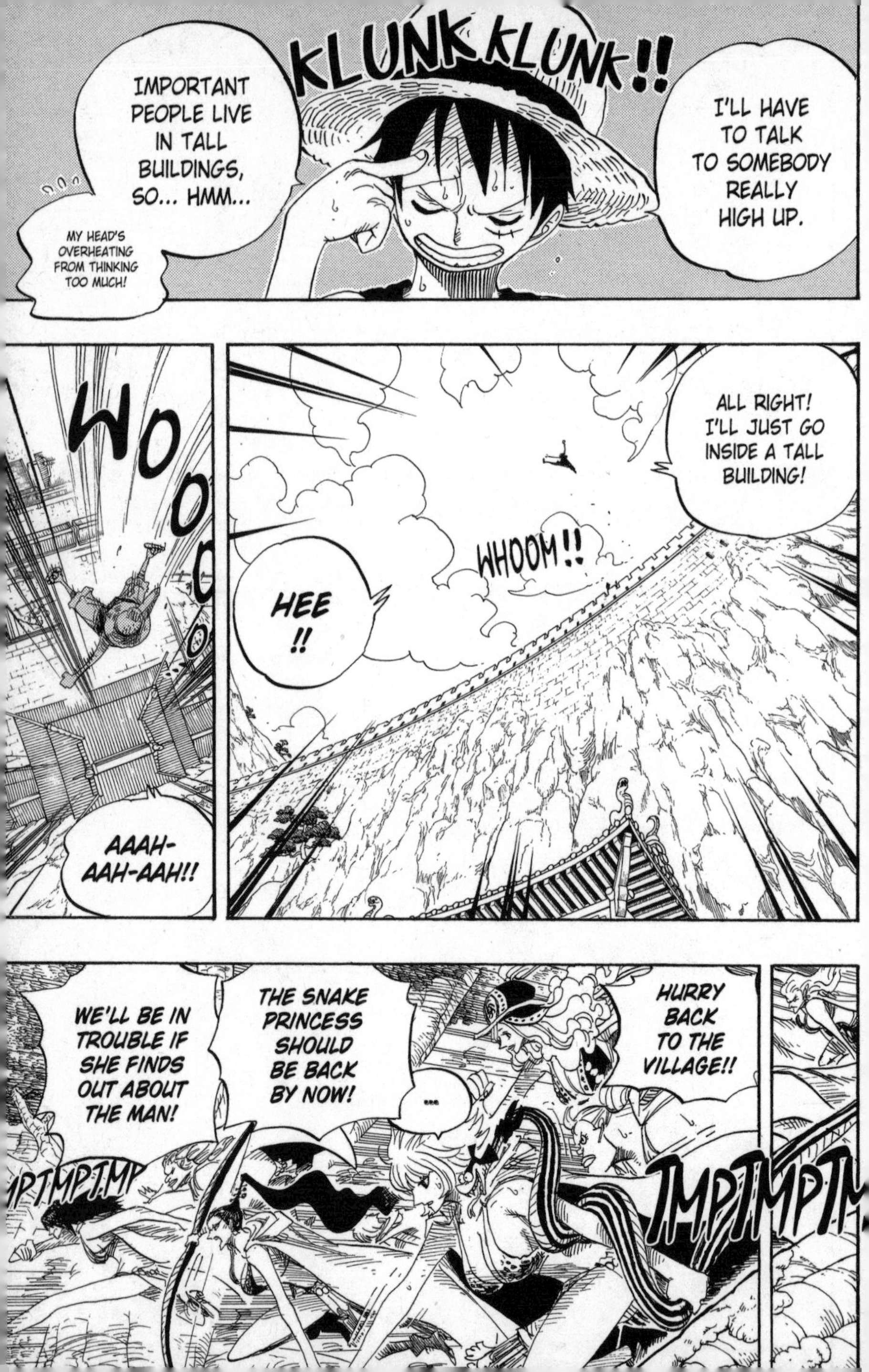
I'LL HAVE TO TALK TO SOMEBODY REALLY HIGH UP.
KLUNK KLUNK!!
IMPORTANT PEOPLE LIVE IN TALL BUILDINGS, SO... HMM...
MY HEAD'S OVERHEATING FROM THINKING TOO MUCH!
ALL RIGHT! I'LL JUST GO INSIDE A TALL BUILDING!
WHOOM!!
HEE!!
WOOOO
AAAH-AAH-AAH!!
HURRY BACK TO THE VILLAGE!!
THE SNAKE PRINCESS SHOULD BE BACK BY NOW!
...
WE'LL BE IN TROUBLE IF SHE FINDS OUT ABOUT THE MAN!

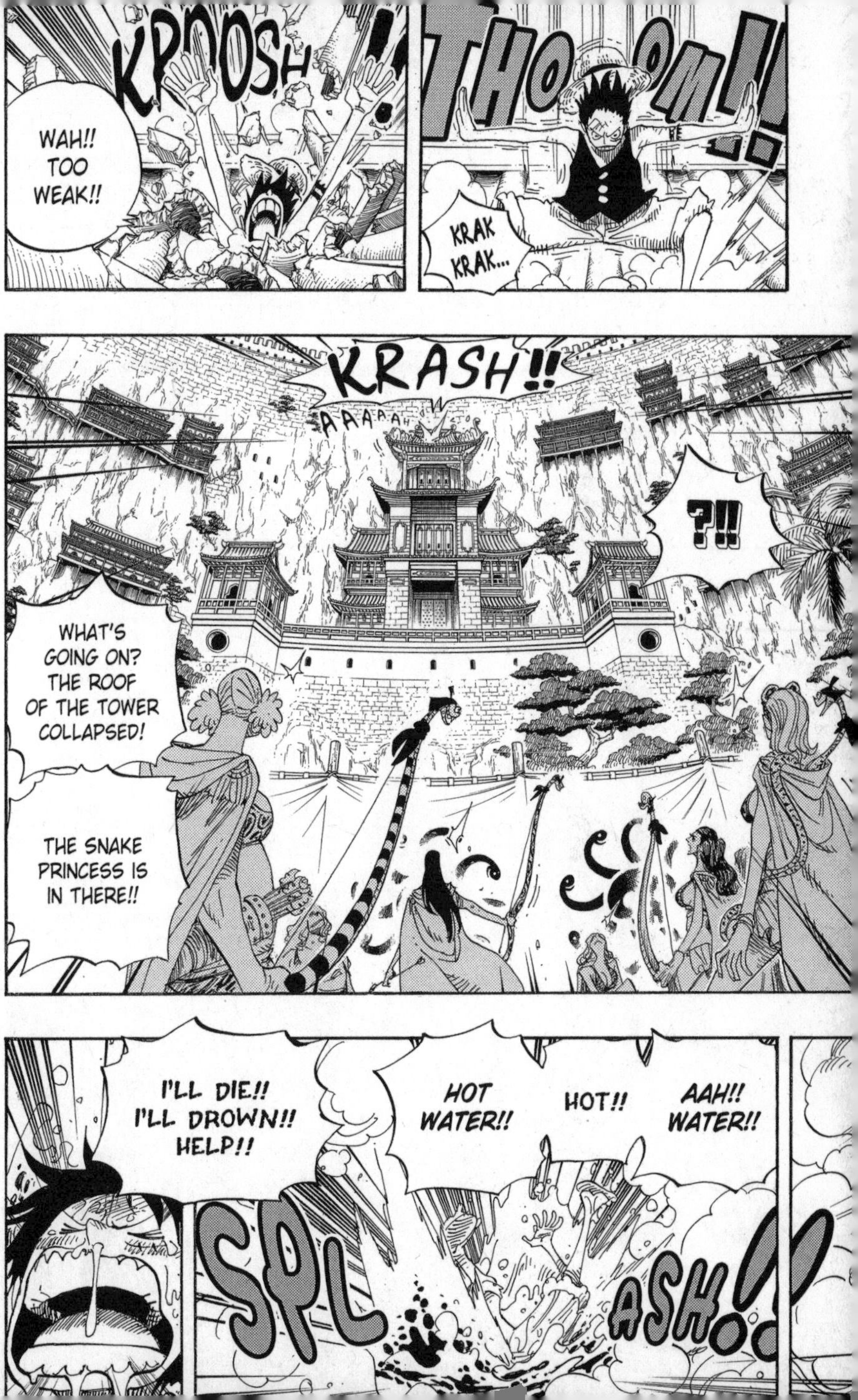
THO OM!!
KRAK KRAK...
KPNOSH!!
WAH!! TOO WEAK!!
KRASH!!
AAAAAH
?!!
WHAT'S GOING ON? THE ROOF OF THE TOWER COLLAPSED!
THE SNAKE PRINCESS IS IN THERE!!
AAH!! WATER!!
HOT!!
HOT WATER!!
I'LL DIE!! I'LL DROWN!! HELP!!
SPL ASH!!

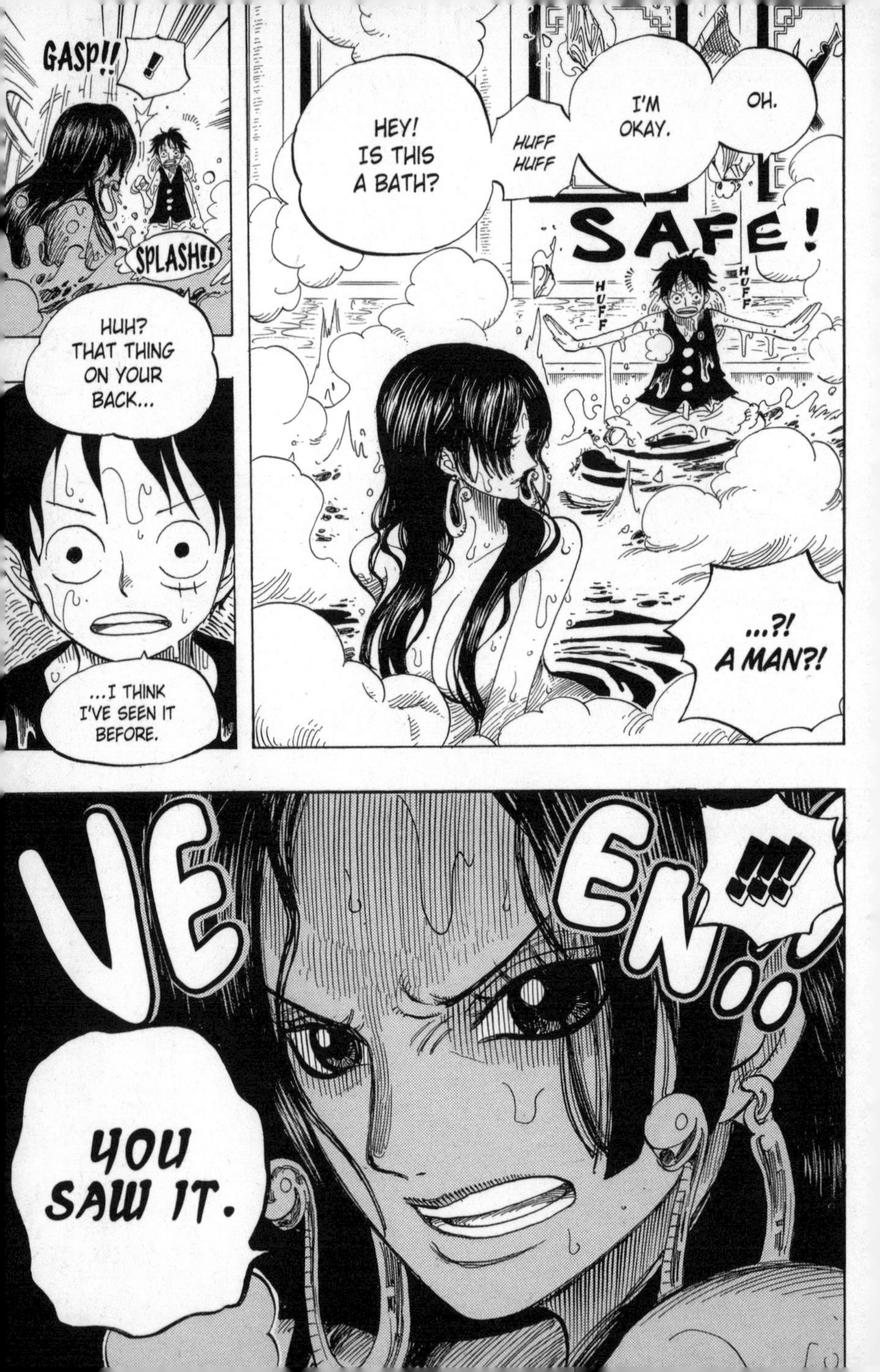
OH.
I'M OKAY.
HUFF HUFF
HEY! IS THIS A BATH?
SAFE!
HUFF HUFF
...?! A MAN?!
GASP!!
!
SPLASH!!
HUH? THAT THING ON YOUR BACK...
...I THINK I'VE SEEN IT BEFORE.
VE
EN...!!!
YOU SAW IT.

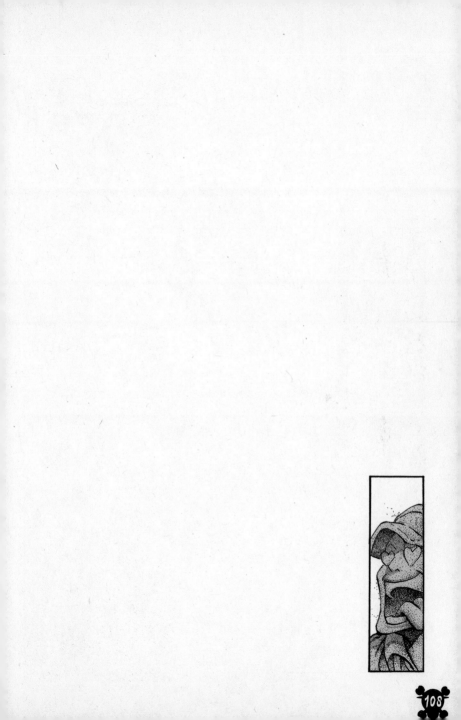

Chapter 518:
COLISEUM

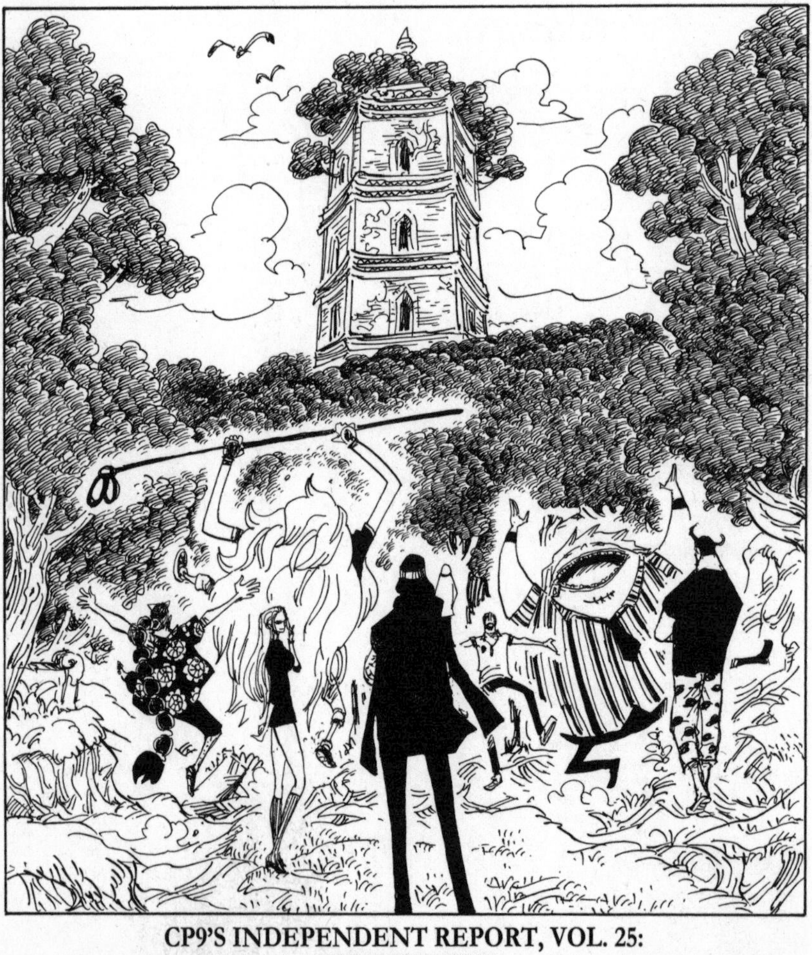

CP9'S INDEPENDENT REPORT, VOL. 25:
"HOMETOWN"

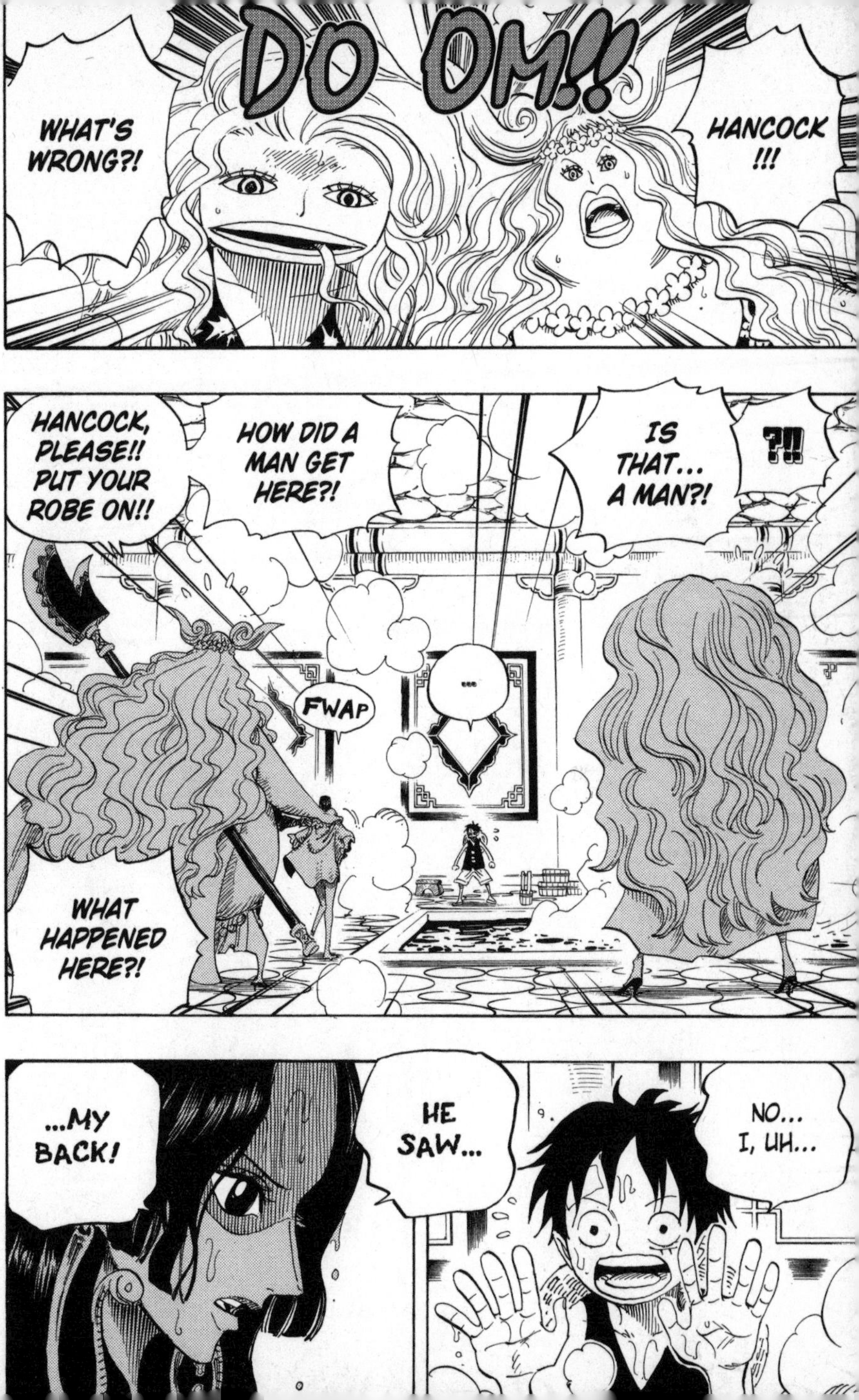
DO OM!!
HANCOCK !!!
WHAT'S WRONG?!
?!!
IS THAT... A MAN?!
HOW DID A MAN GET HERE?!
HANCOCK, PLEASE!! PUT YOUR ROBE ON!!
...
FWAP
WHAT HAPPENED HERE?!
NO... I, UH...
HE SAW...
...MY BACK!

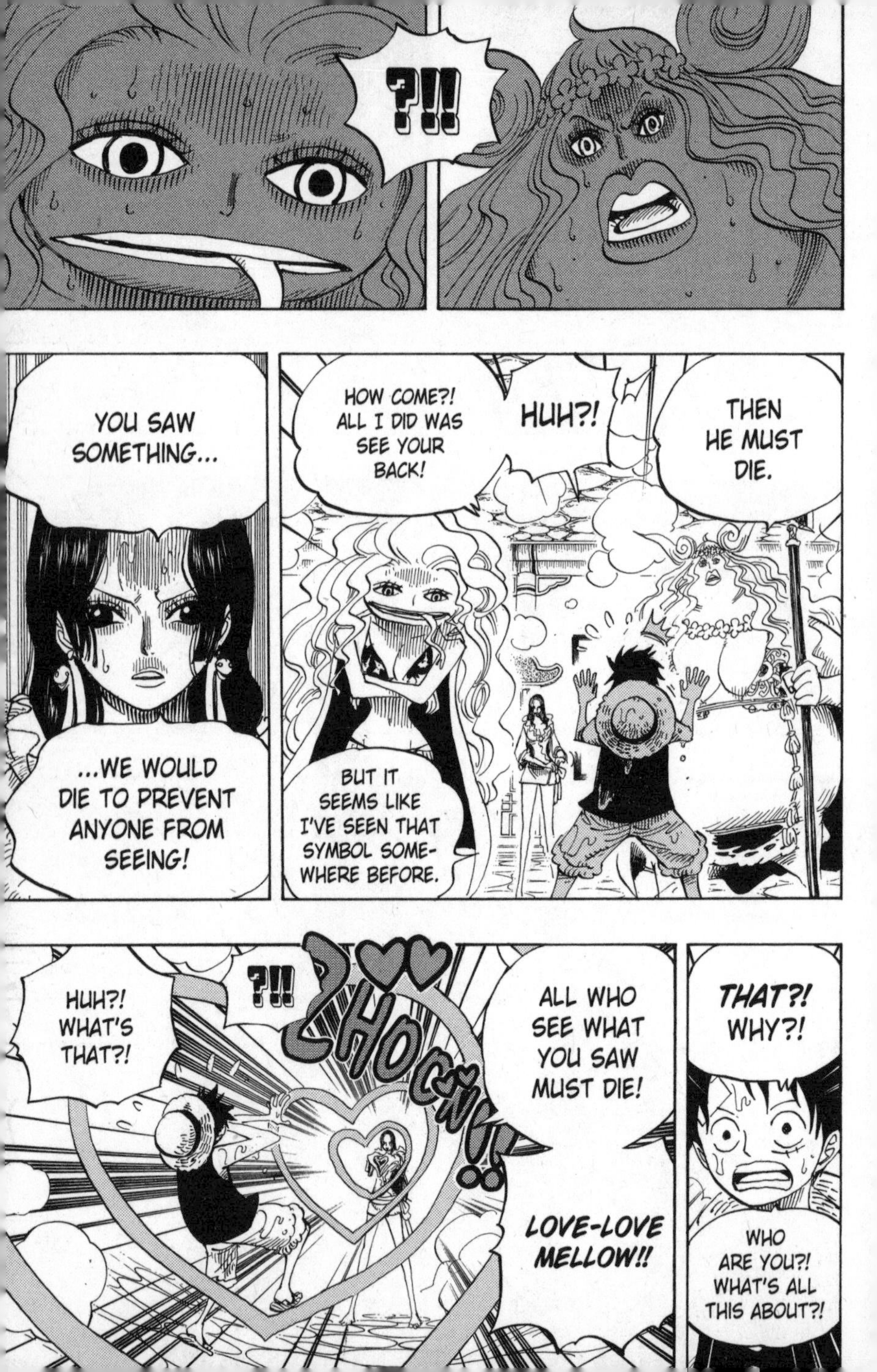
?!!
THEN HE MUST DIE.
HUH?!
HOW COME?! ALL I DID WAS SEE YOUR BACK!
BUT IT SEEMS LIKE I'VE SEEN THAT SYMBOL SOME-WHERE BEFORE.
YOU SAW SOMETHING...
...WE WOULD DIE TO PREVENT ANYONE FROM SEEING!
THAT?! WHY?!
WHO ARE YOU?! WHAT'S ALL THIS ABOUT?!
ALL WHO SEE WHAT YOU SAW MUST DIE!
LOVE-LOVE MELLOW!!
?!!
HUH?! WHAT'S THAT?!

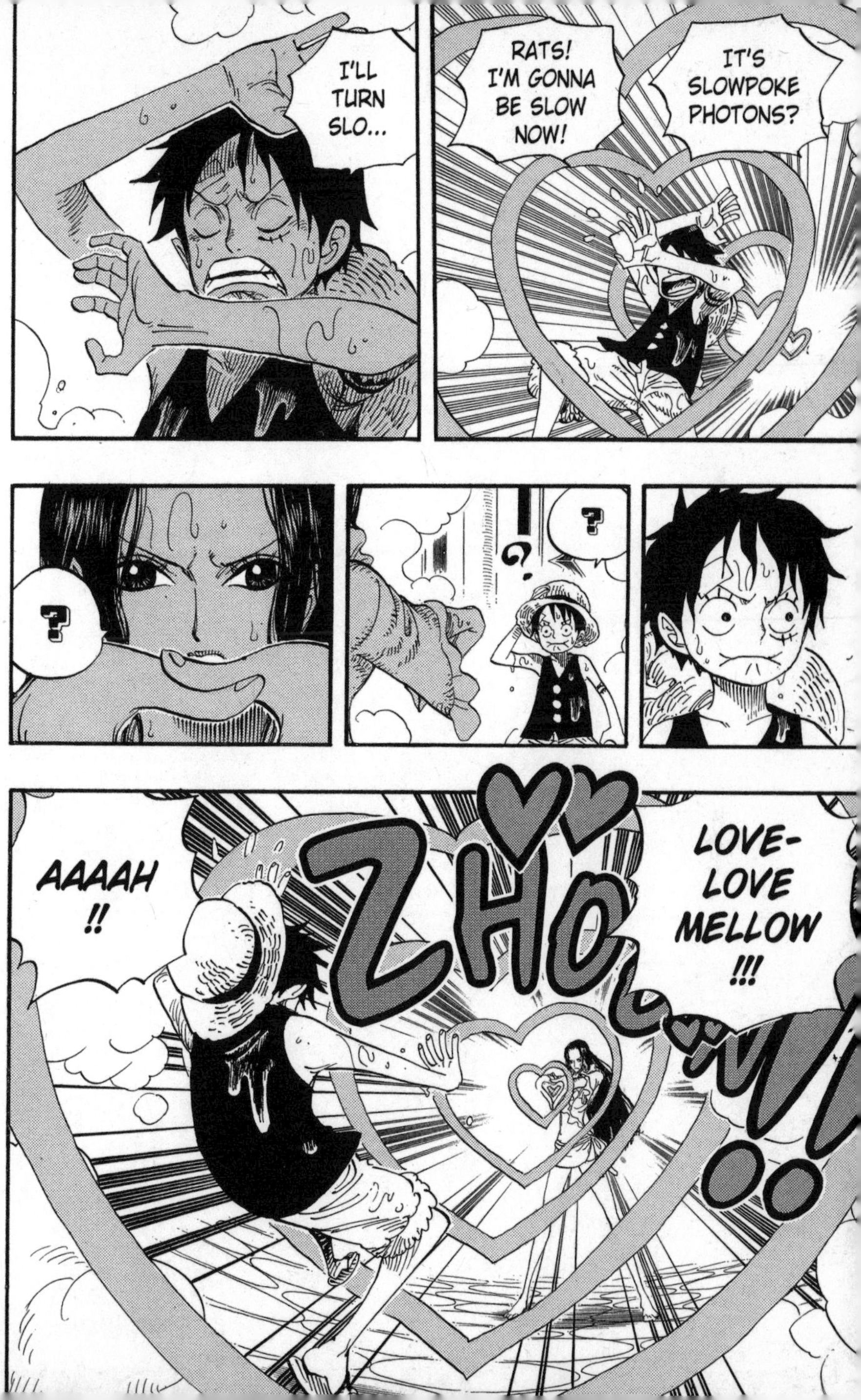
IT'S SLOWPOKE PHOTONS?
RATS! I'M GONNA BE SLOW NOW!
I'LL TURN SLO...
?
!?
?
LOVE-LOVE MELLOW !!!
AAAAH !!

WHY DOESN'T HE TURN TO STONE?!
HE SAW ME IN THE BATH, YET MY POWERS HAVE NO EFFECT ON HIM!!
BUT THAT'S IMPOSSIBLE, SISTER!
YOUR BODY IS SO BEAUTIFUL THAT PEOPLE OF ALL AGES AND GENDERS FALL IN LOVE WITH YOU!
HIS FEAR OF DEATH MUST'VE ERASED ANY IMPURE THOUGHTS FROM HIS MIND.
SWIP
HE'S A PITIFUL MAN, BUT LUCKY.
I DON'T KNOW WHAT'S GOING ON, BUT I'D BETTER RUN!
DASH!!
!
I JUST WANTED TO TALK TO WHOEVER'S IN CHARGE AROUND HERE!!

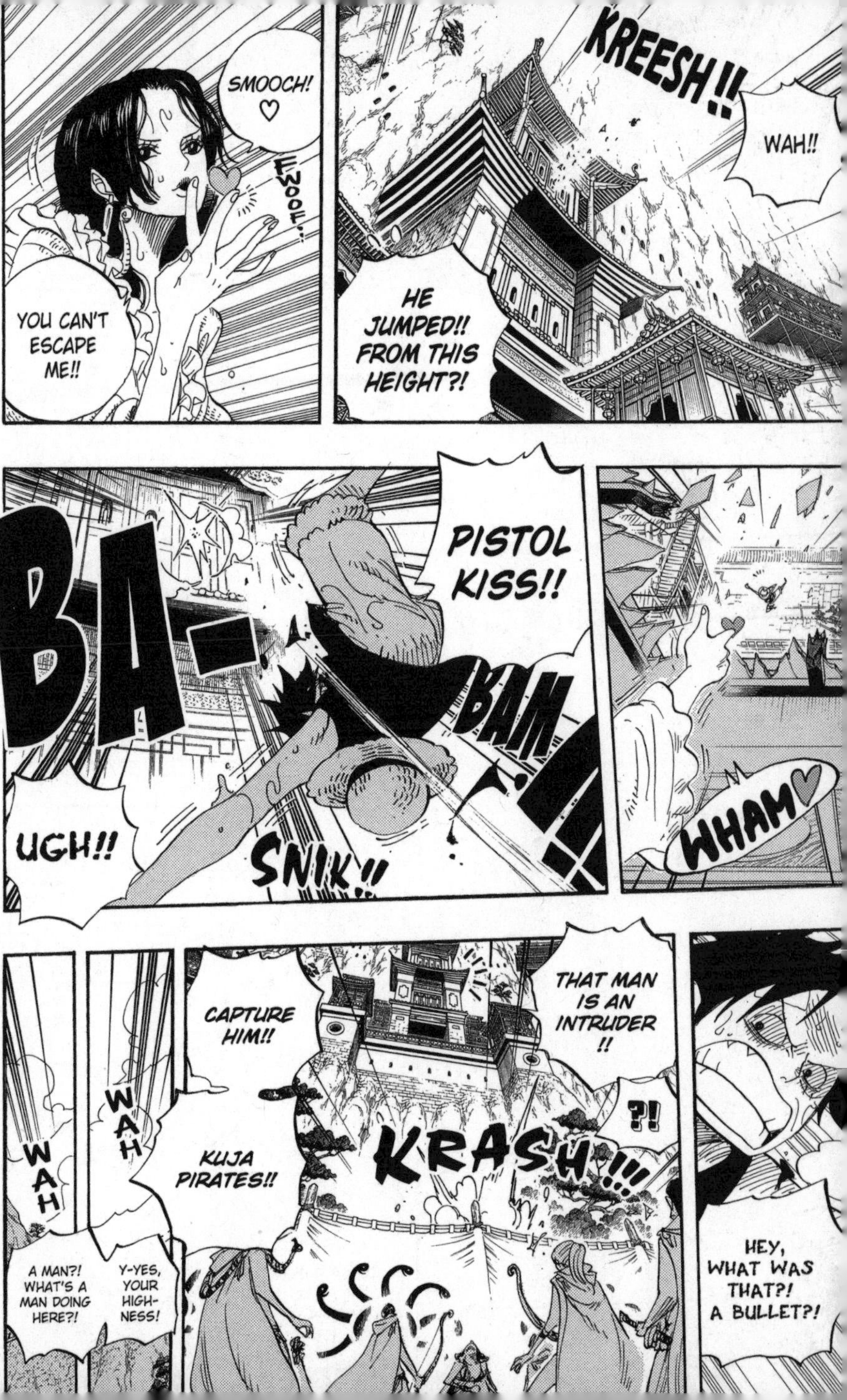
KREESH!!
WAH!!
HE JUMPED!! FROM THIS HEIGHT?!
SMOOCH! ♡
FWOOF..
YOU CAN'T ESCAPE ME!!
WHAM♡
PISTOL KISS!!
BA-BAM!!
UGH!!
SNIK!!
HEY, WHAT WAS THAT?! A BULLET?!
THAT MAN IS AN INTRUDER!!
?!
KRASH!!!
CAPTURE HIM!!
KUJA PIRATES!!
WAH
Y-YES, YOUR HIGH-NESS!
WAH
A MAN?! WHAT'S A MAN DOING HERE?!

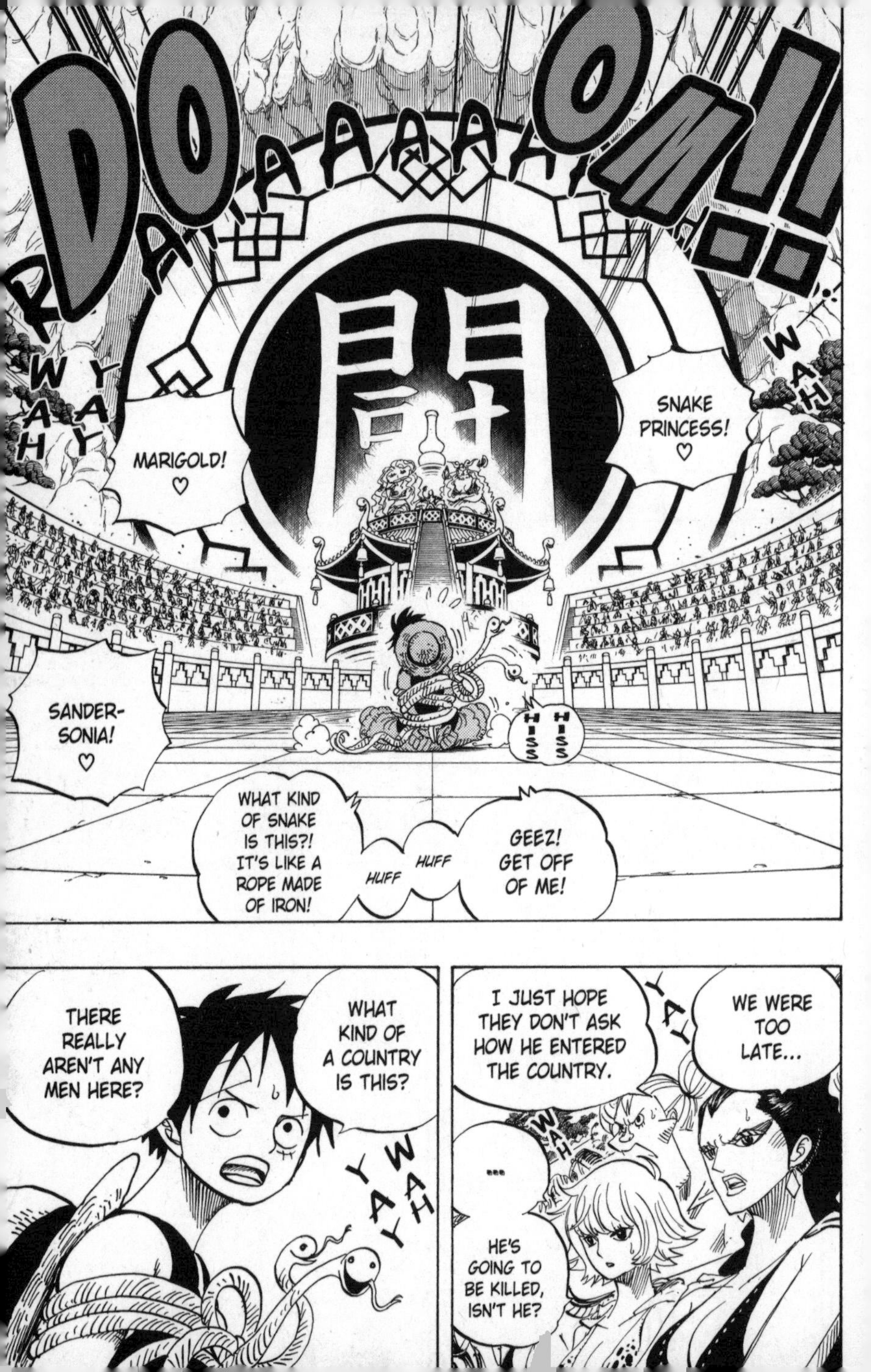
SNAKE PRINCESS! ♡
WAH
MARIGOLD! ♡
WAH YAY
SANDER-SONIA! ♡
HISS HISS
GEEZ! GET OFF OF ME!
HUFF HUFF
WHAT KIND OF SNAKE IS THIS?! IT'S LIKE A ROPE MADE OF IRON!
WE WERE TOO LATE...
YAY
I JUST HOPE THEY DON'T ASK HOW HE ENTERED THE COUNTRY.
WAH
...
HE'S GOING TO BE KILLED, ISN'T HE?
WHAT KIND OF A COUNTRY IS THIS?
THERE REALLY AREN'T ANY MEN HERE?
WAH YAY YAY

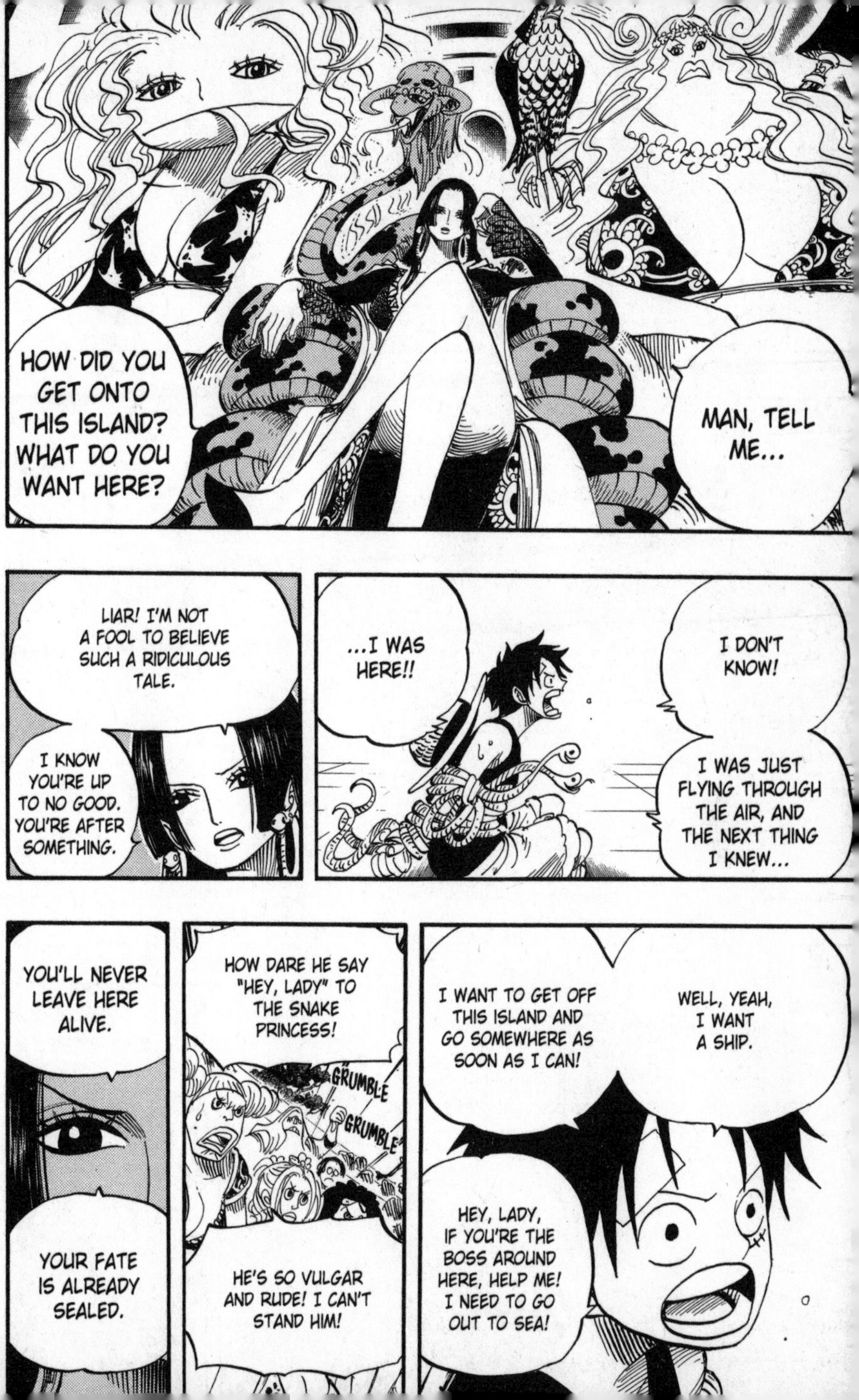
MAN, TELL ME...
HOW DID YOU GET ONTO THIS ISLAND? WHAT DO YOU WANT HERE?
I DON'T KNOW!
I WAS JUST FLYING THROUGH THE AIR, AND THE NEXT THING I KNEW...
...I WAS HERE!!
LIAR! I'M NOT A FOOL TO BELIEVE SUCH A RIDICULOUS TALE.
I KNOW YOU'RE UP TO NO GOOD. YOU'RE AFTER SOMETHING.
WELL, YEAH, I WANT A SHIP.
I WANT TO GET OFF THIS ISLAND AND GO SOMEWHERE AS SOON AS I CAN!
HEY, LADY, IF YOU'RE THE BOSS AROUND HERE, HELP ME! I NEED TO GO OUT TO SEA!
HOW DARE HE SAY "HEY, LADY" TO THE SNAKE PRINCESS!
GRUMBLE
GRUMBLE
HE'S SO VULGAR AND RUDE! I CAN'T STAND HIM!
YOU'LL NEVER LEAVE HERE ALIVE.
YOUR FATE IS ALREADY SEALED.

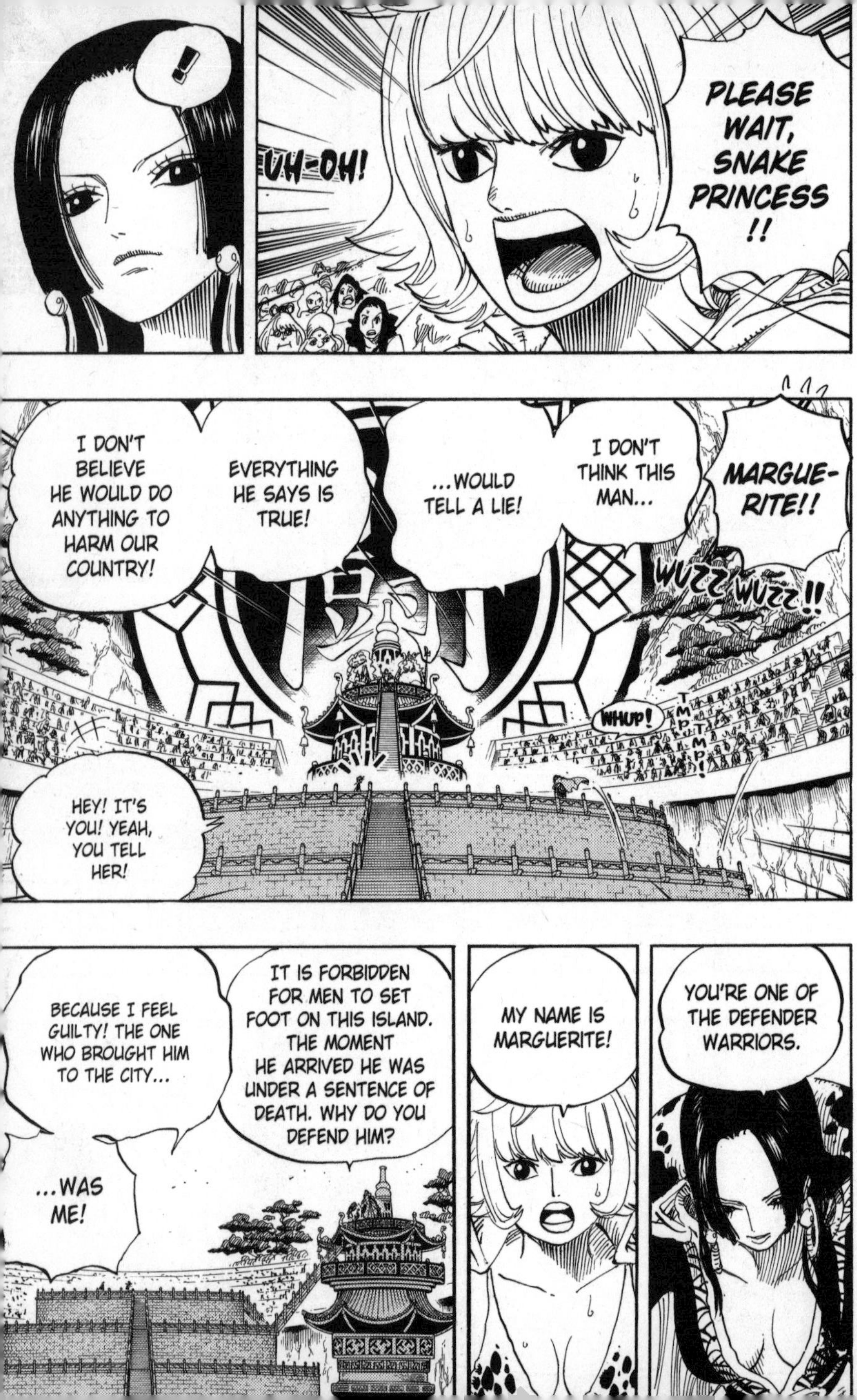
PLEASE WAIT, SNAKE PRINCESS!!
UH-OH!
!
MARGUE-RITE!!
WUZZ WUZZ!!
I DON'T THINK THIS MAN...
...WOULD TELL A LIE!
EVERYTHING HE SAYS IS TRUE!
I DON'T BELIEVE HE WOULD DO ANYTHING TO HARM OUR COUNTRY!
WHUP!
TMP TMP!
HEY! IT'S YOU! YEAH, YOU TELL HER!
YOU'RE ONE OF THE DEFENDER WARRIORS.
MY NAME IS MARGUERITE!
IT IS FORBIDDEN FOR MEN TO SET FOOT ON THIS ISLAND. THE MOMENT HE ARRIVED HE WAS UNDER A SENTENCE OF DEATH. WHY DO YOU DEFEND HIM?
BECAUSE I FEEL GUILTY! THE ONE WHO BROUGHT HIM TO THE CITY...
...WAS ME!

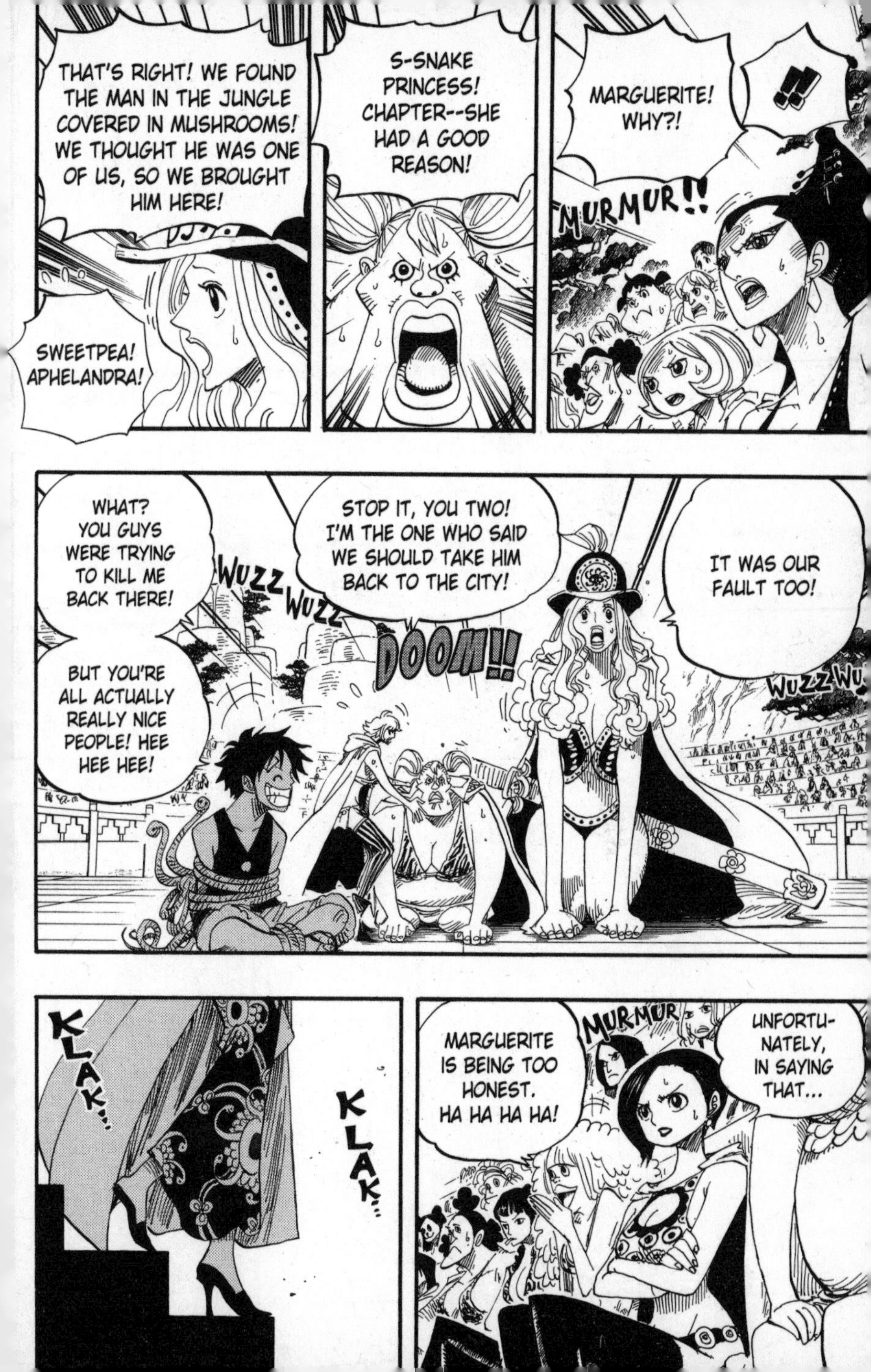
!!
MARGUERITE! WHY?!
MURMUR!!
S-SNAKE PRINCESS! CHAPTER--SHE HAD A GOOD REASON!
THAT'S RIGHT! WE FOUND THE MAN IN THE JUNGLE COVERED IN MUSHROOMS! WE THOUGHT HE WAS ONE OF US, SO WE BROUGHT HIM HERE!
SWEETPEA! APHELANDRA!
IT WAS OUR FAULT TOO!
WUZZ WU
STOP IT, YOU TWO! I'M THE ONE WHO SAID WE SHOULD TAKE HIM BACK TO THE CITY!
DOOM!!
WUZZ WUZZ
WHAT? YOU GUYS WERE TRYING TO KILL ME BACK THERE!
BUT YOU'RE ALL ACTUALLY REALLY NICE PEOPLE! HEE HEE HEE!
UNFORTU-NATELY, IN SAYING THAT...
MURMUR
MARGUERITE IS BEING TOO HONEST. HA HA HA HA!
KLAK...
KLAK...

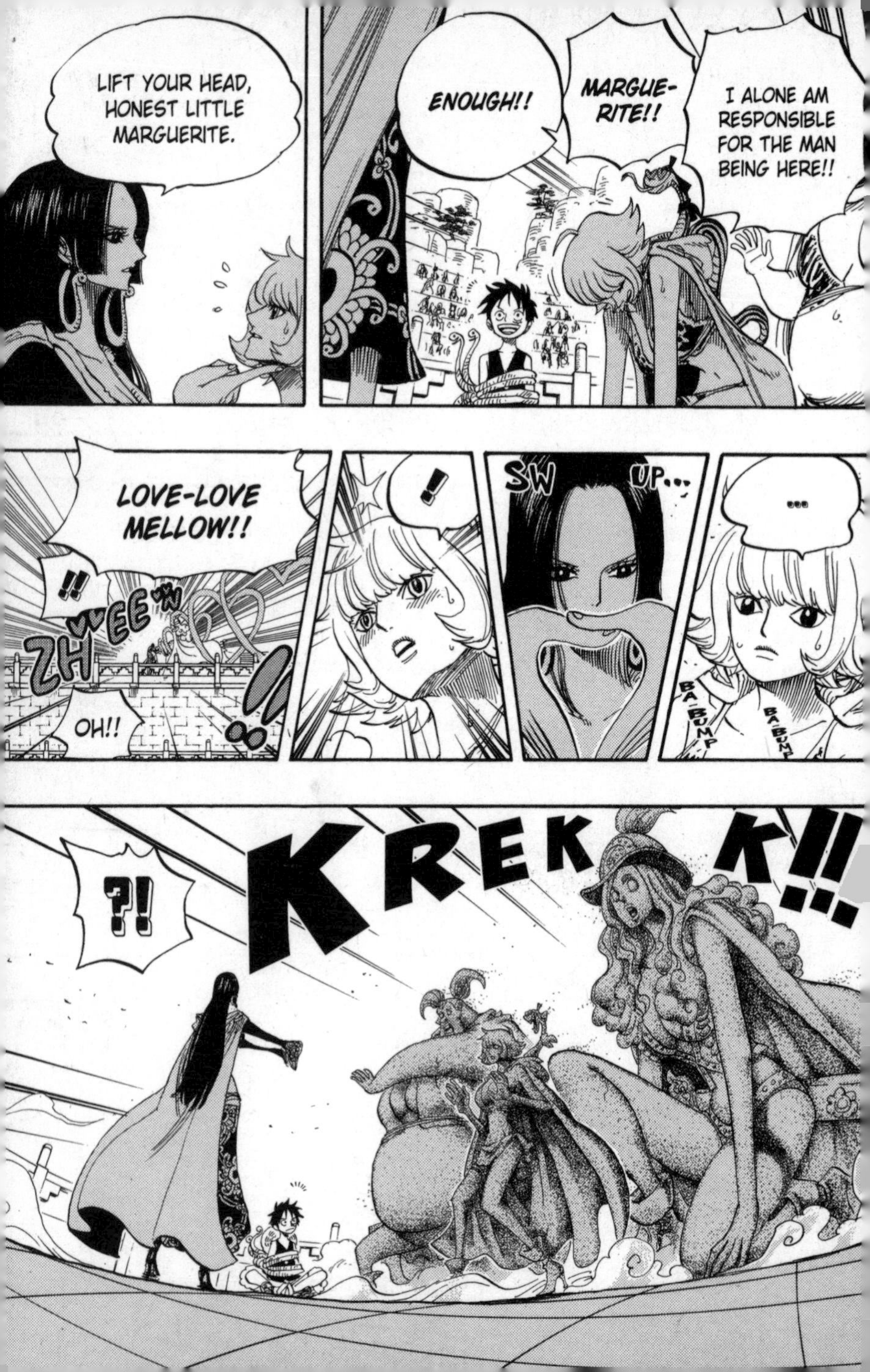
I ALONE AM RESPONSIBLE FOR THE MAN BEING HERE!!
MARGUE-RITE!!
ENOUGH!!
LIFT YOUR HEAD, HONEST LITTLE MARGUERITE.
...
BA-BUMP
BA-BUMP
SW
UP...
!
LOVE-LOVE MELLOW!!
!!
ZHWEEEN
!!
OH!!
KREKK!!
?!

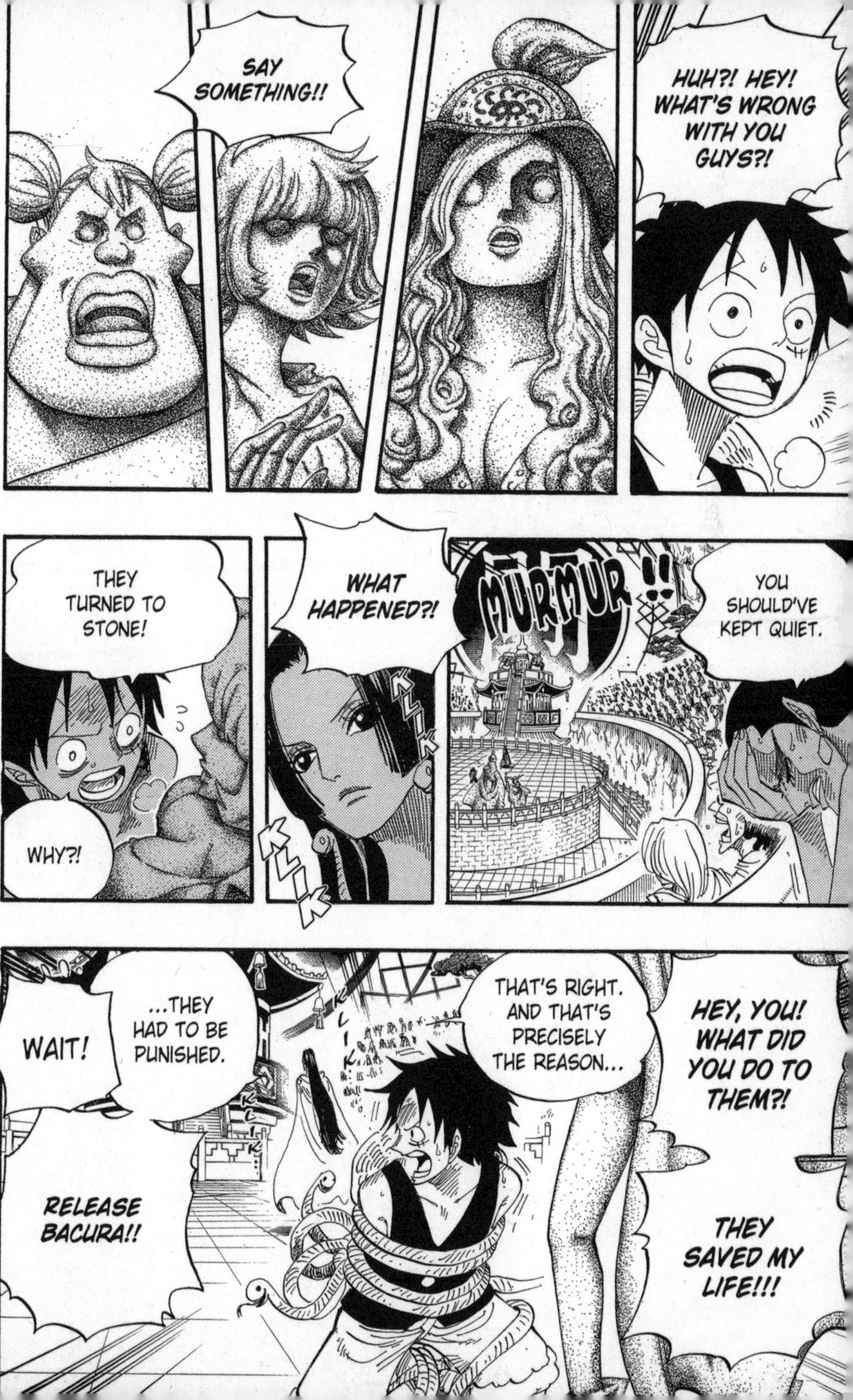
HUH?! HEY! WHAT'S WRONG WITH YOU GUYS?!
SAY SOMETHING!!
MURMUR!!
YOU SHOULD'VE KEPT QUIET.
WHAT HAPPENED?!
KLIK
KLIK
THEY TURNED TO STONE!
WHY?!
HEY, YOU! WHAT DID YOU DO TO THEM?!
THEY SAVED MY LIFE!!!
THAT'S RIGHT. AND THAT'S PRECISELY THE REASON...
KLIK
KLIK
...THEY HAD TO BE PUNISHED.
WAIT!
RELEASE BACURA!!

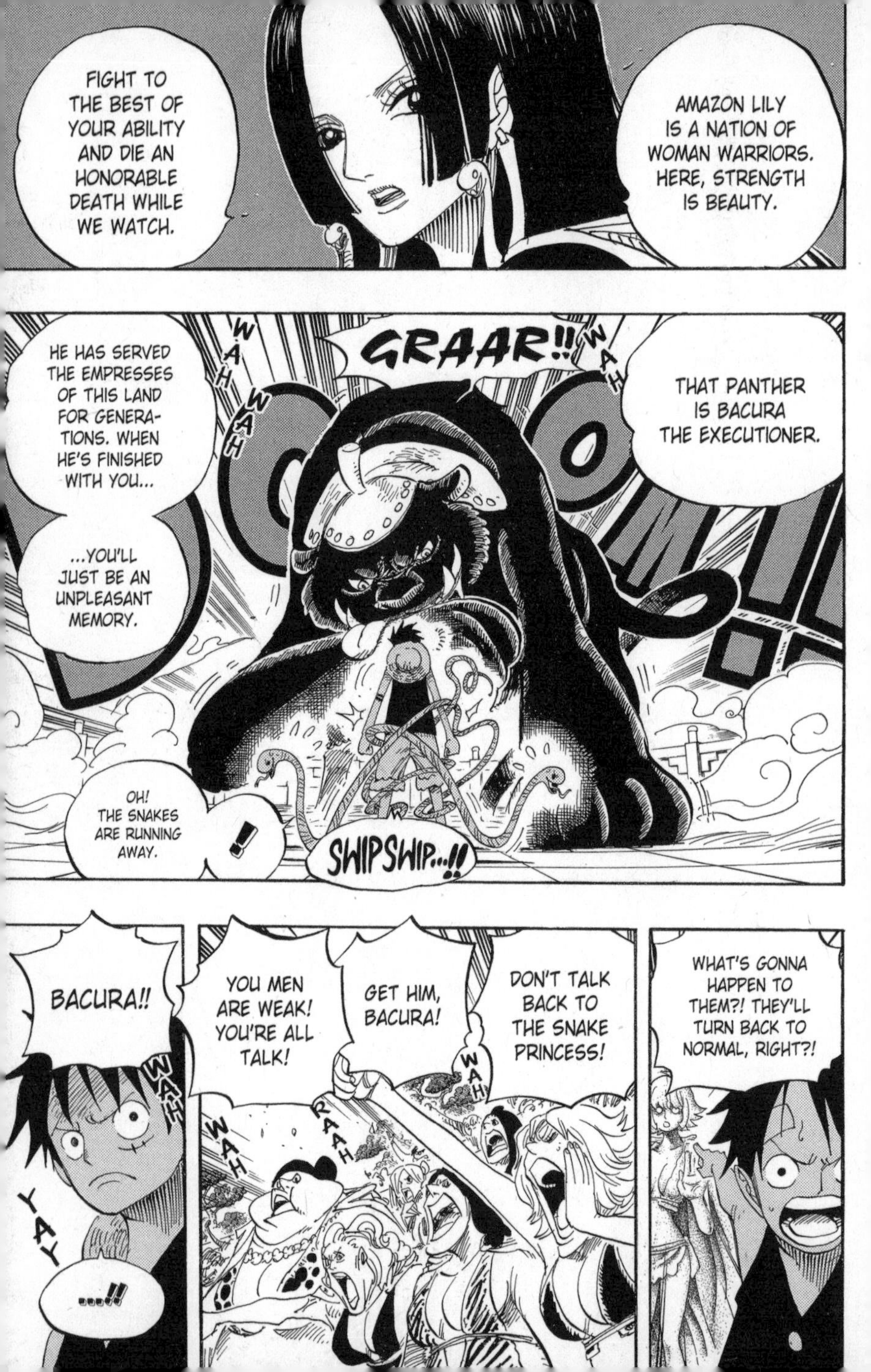
AMAZON LILY IS A NATION OF WOMAN WARRIORS. HERE, STRENGTH IS BEAUTY.
FIGHT TO THE BEST OF YOUR ABILITY AND DIE AN HONORABLE DEATH WHILE WE WATCH.
THAT PANTHER IS BACURA THE EXECUTIONER.
WAH
GRAAR!!
WAH WAH
HE HAS SERVED THE EMPRESSES OF THIS LAND FOR GENERATIONS. WHEN HE'S FINISHED WITH YOU...
...YOU'LL JUST BE AN UNPLEASANT MEMORY.
!
OH! THE SNAKES ARE RUNNING AWAY.
SHIPSHIP...!!
WHAT'S GONNA HAPPEN TO THEM?! THEY'LL TURN BACK TO NORMAL, RIGHT?!
DON'T TALK BACK TO THE SNAKE PRINCESS!
WAH
GET HIM, BACURA!
RAAH
YOU MEN ARE WEAK! YOU'RE ALL TALK!
WAH
BACURA!!
WAH
YAY
...!!

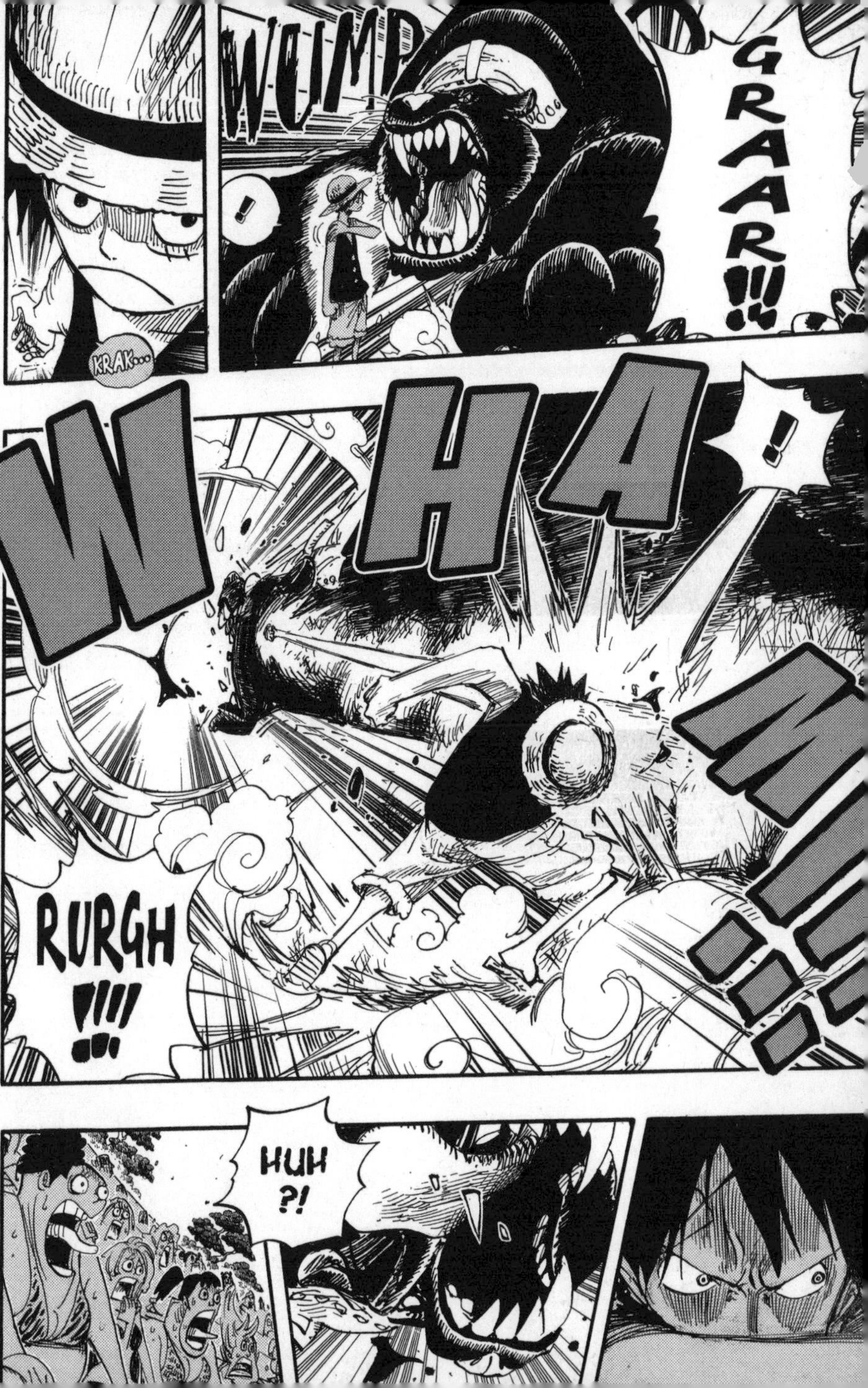
GRAAR!!!
WUMP
!
KRAK...
WHAM!!
RURGH!!!!...
HUH?!

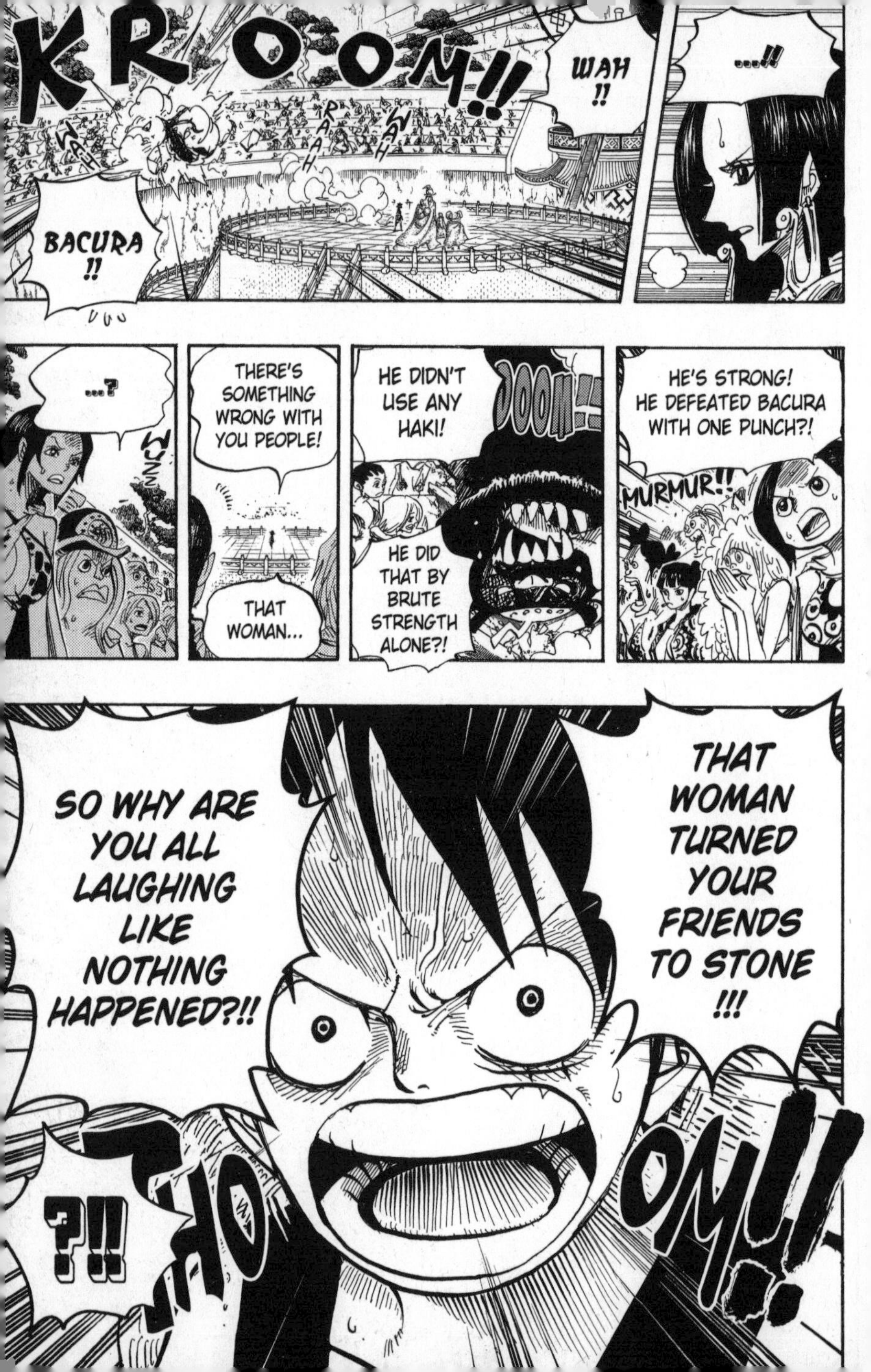
...!!
WAH !!
KROOOM!!
WAH
RAAH
WAH
BACURA !!
HE'S STRONG! HE DEFEATED BACURA WITH ONE PUNCH?!
MURMUR!!
HE DIDN'T USE ANY HAKI!
HE DID THAT BY BRUTE STRENGTH ALONE?!
THERE'S SOMETHING WRONG WITH YOU PEOPLE!
THAT WOMAN...
...?
THAT WOMAN TURNED YOUR FRIENDS TO STONE !!!
SO WHY ARE YOU ALL LAUGHING LIKE NOTHING HAPPENED?!!
WHOOM!!
?!!

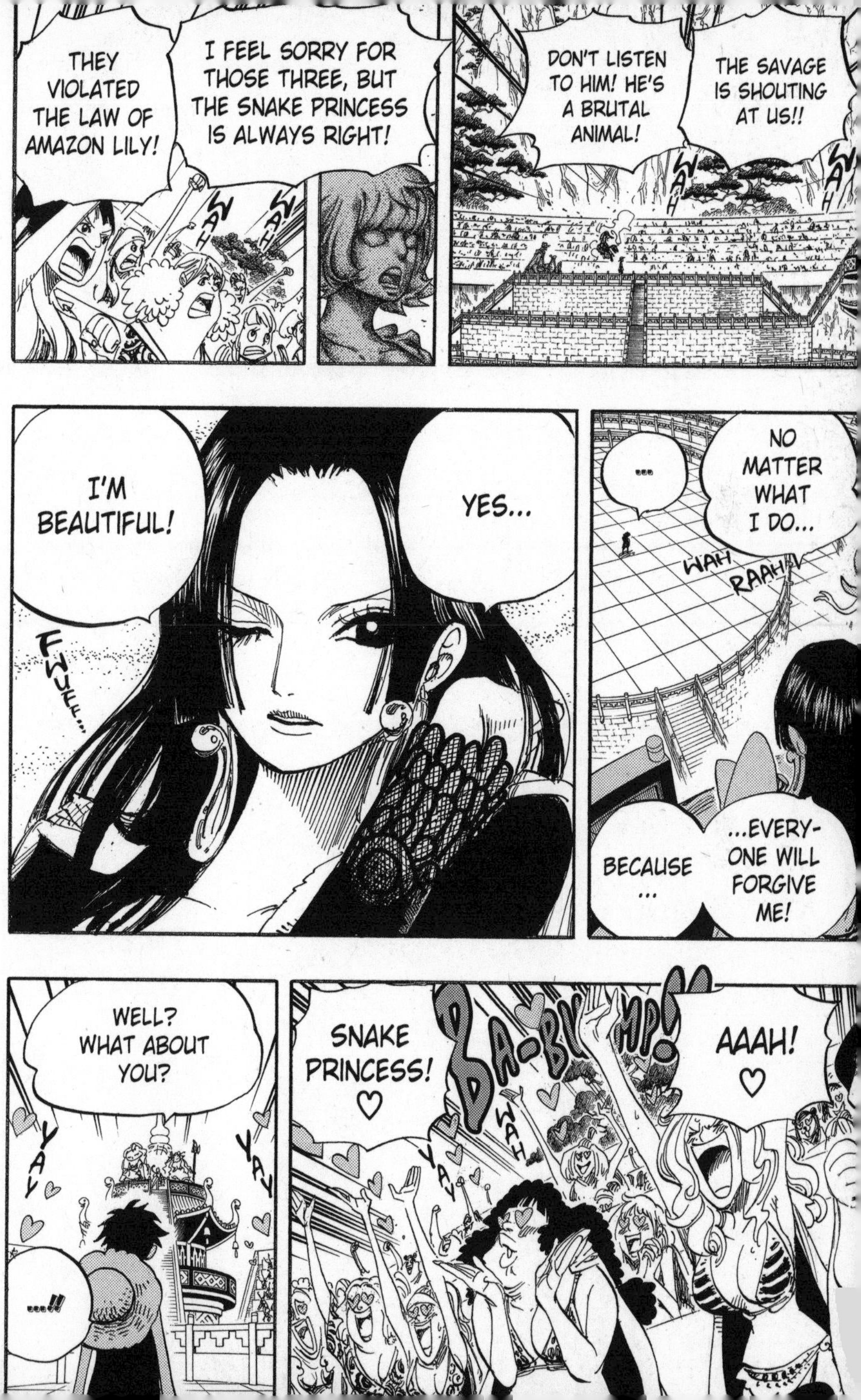
THE SAVAGE IS SHOUTING AT US!!
DON'T LISTEN TO HIM! HE'S A BRUTAL ANIMAL!
WAH
WAH
I FEEL SORRY FOR THOSE THREE, BUT THE SNAKE PRINCESS IS ALWAYS RIGHT!
THEY VIOLATED THE LAW OF AMAZON LILY!
WAH
WAH
NO MATTER WHAT I DO...
...
WAH
RAAH
...EVERY-ONE WILL FORGIVE ME!
BECAUSE ...
YES...
I'M BEAUTIFUL!
FWUFF...
AAAH! ♡
BA-BUMP!
SNAKE PRINCESS! ♡
WAH
YAY
WELL? WHAT ABOUT YOU?
YAY
YAY
...!!

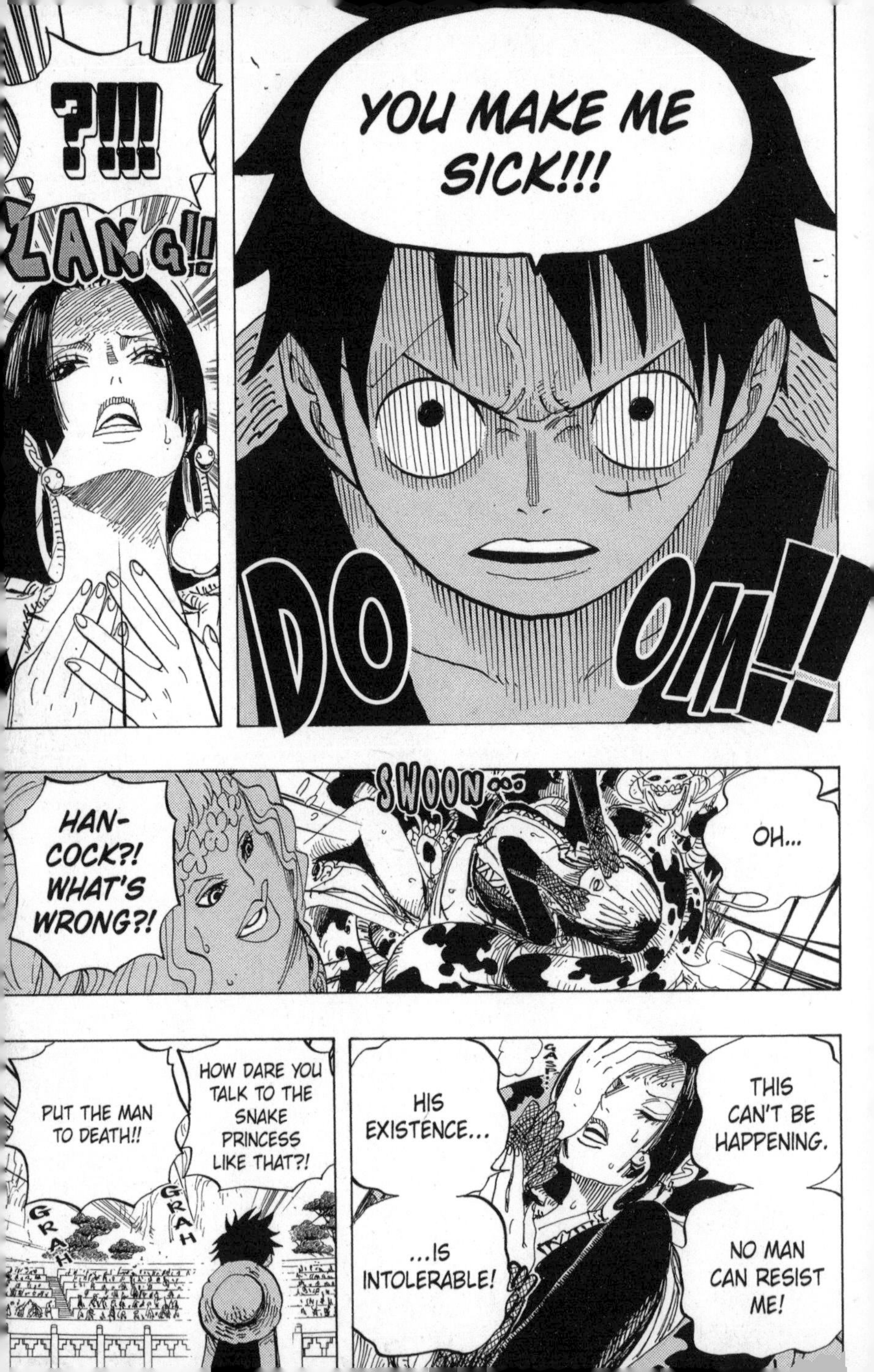
YOU MAKE ME SICK!!!
DOOM!!
?!!!
ZANG!!
OH...
SWOON...
HAN-COCK?! WHAT'S WRONG?!
THIS CAN'T BE HAPPENING.
NO MAN CAN RESIST ME!
GASP...
HIS EXISTENCE...
...IS INTOLERABLE!
HOW DARE YOU TALK TO THE SNAKE PRINCESS LIKE THAT?!
PUT THE MAN TO DEATH!!
GRAH
GRAH

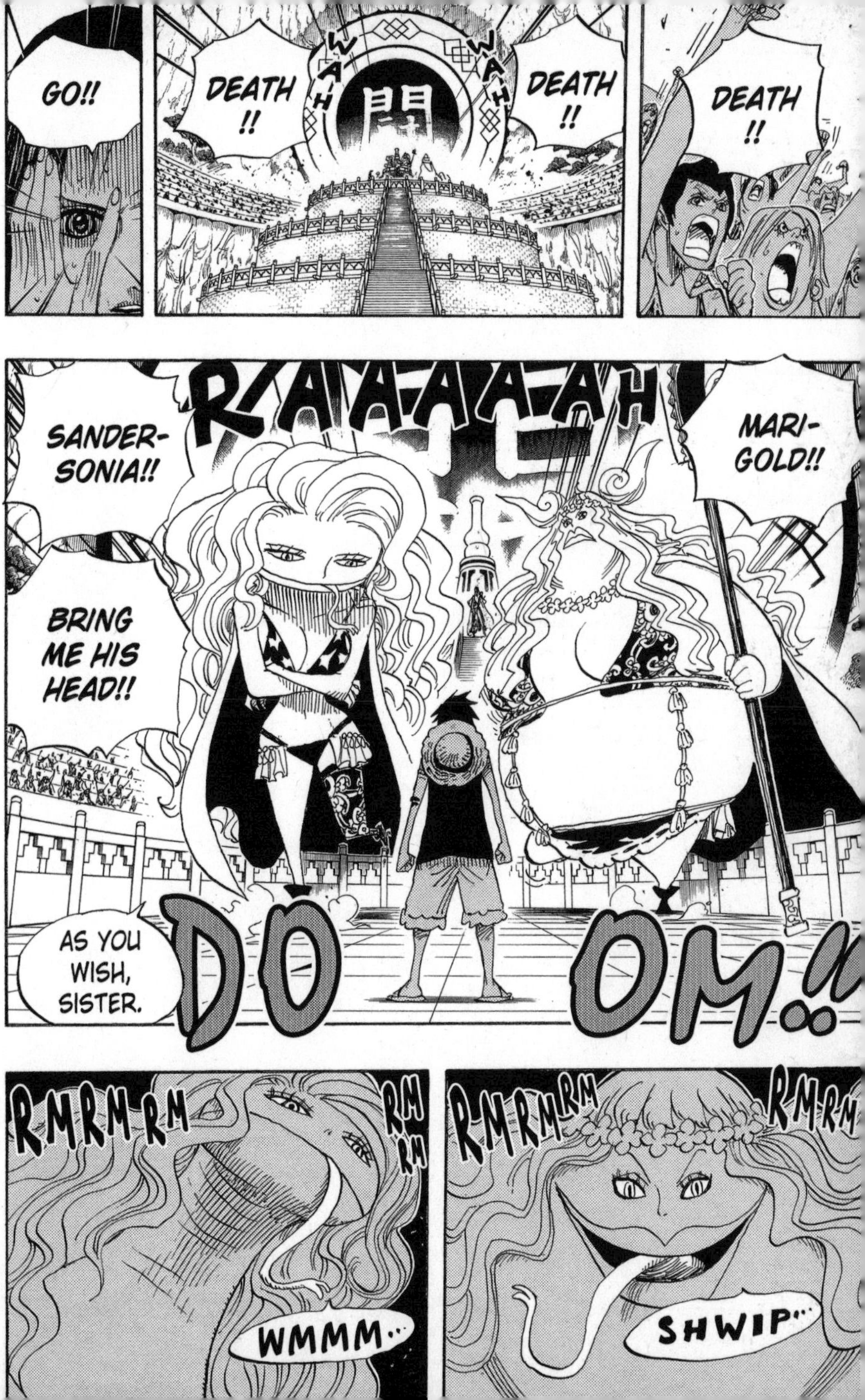
DEATH!!
WAH
DEATH!!
WAH
DEATH!!
GO!!
RAAAAH
MARI-GOLD!!
SANDER-SONIA!!
BRING ME HIS HEAD!!
AS YOU WISH, SISTER.
DOOM!!
RMRMRM
SHWIP...
RMRMRM
RMRM
WMMM...

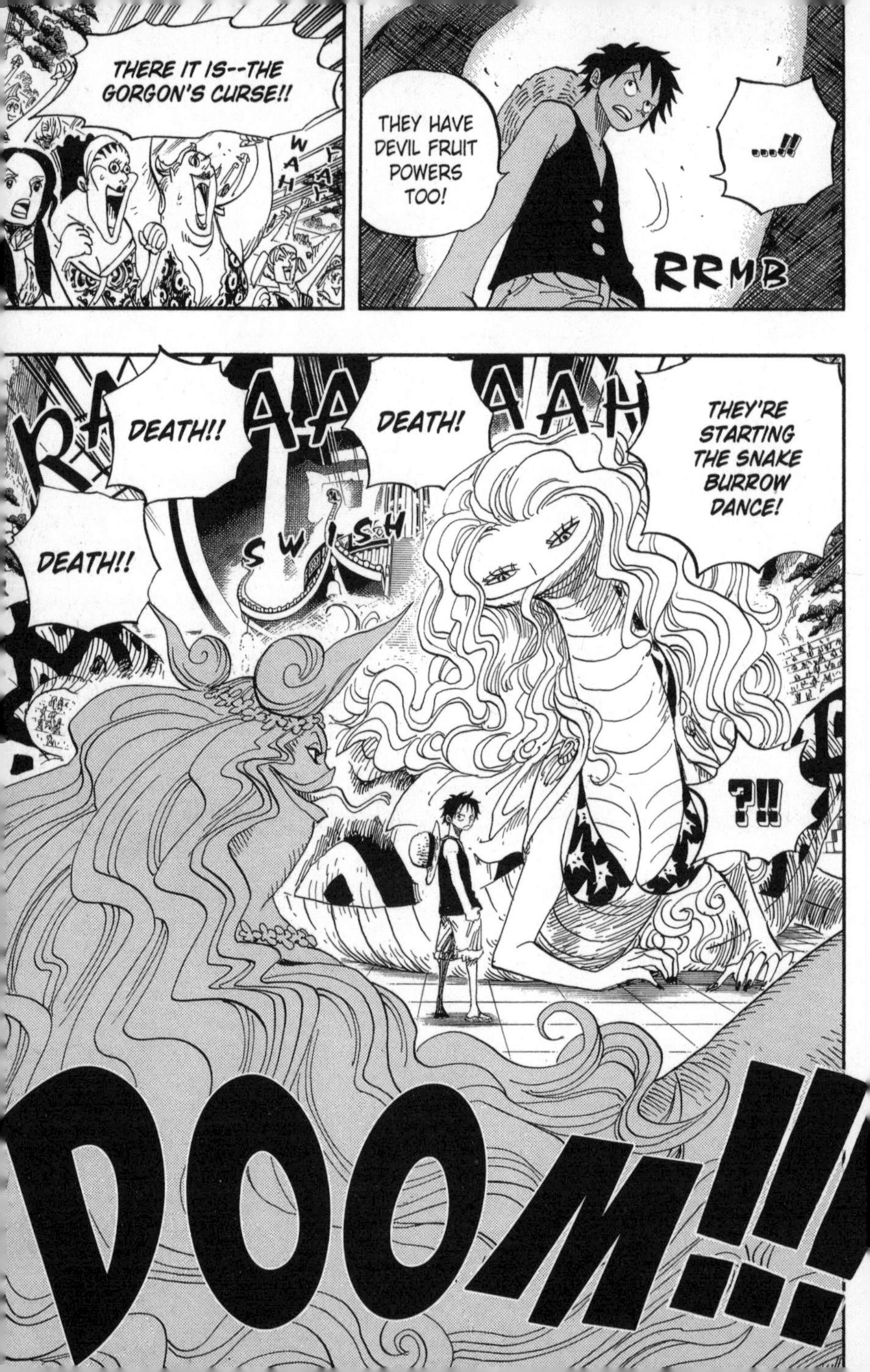
THEY HAVE DEVIL FRUIT POWERS TOO!
...!!
RRMB
THERE IT IS--THE GORGON'S CURSE!!
WAH
WAH
THEY'RE STARTING THE SNAKE BURROW DANCE!
AAH
DEATH!
AA
DEATH!!
DEATH!!
SWISH
?!!
DOOM!!!

SBS Question Corner

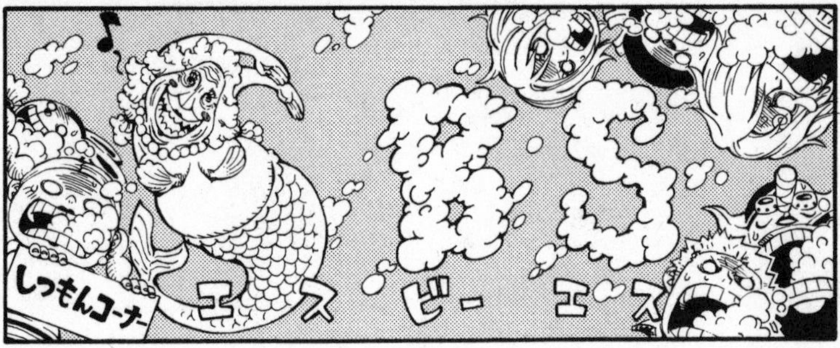
しつもんコーナー
エスビーエス

(Mall Osso, Tokyo)

Q: Hello, Oda Sensei! This may be sudden, but whose face is on the berry bills, the money that's used in the world of *One Piece*? I really want to know! You've never actually drawn them before. So please draw them here--with details, mind you!

--Cat Burglar Aki

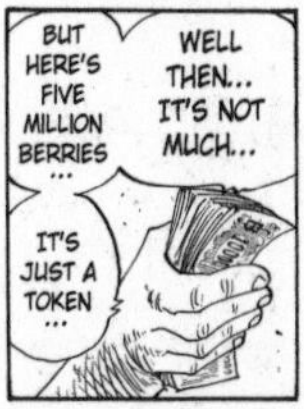
WELL THEN... IT'S NOT MUCH...
BUT HERE'S FIVE MILLION BERRIES...
IT'S JUST A TOKEN...

A: I see. I guess you're right.

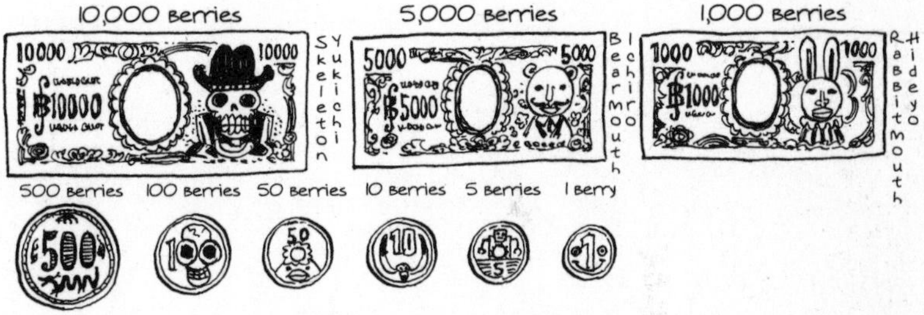
10,000 Berries
Skeleton Yukichi
5,000 Berries
Bearmouth Ichiro
1,000 Berries
Rabbitmouth Hideyo
500 Berries
100 Berries
50 Berries
10 Berries
5 Berries
1 Berry

There, that's all of them. What? I'm just winging it? No, I'm not! Wait! I guess I am! Anyway, I'm making this official right now.

Q: In chapter 487, "That Song," there was a skeleton with a polka dot shirt that Brook picked up. And the guy who asked Brook how to fight with a sword has a sword stuck in his head. He's supposed to have died while singing, so how did the sword get in his head? When did it happen? And who did it?

--Copin

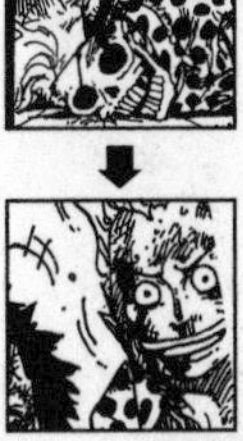
!!

A: My readers have such keen eyes for these things! I'm really surprised. I received a couple of letters about this, so let me introduce them to you! Meet the Mizuuta twins!

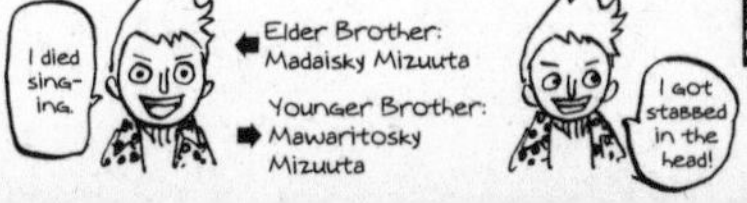
I died singing.
Elder Brother: Madaisky Mizuuta
Younger Brother: Mawaritosky Mizuuta
I got stabbed in the head!

Chapter 519: NATURAL BORN KING

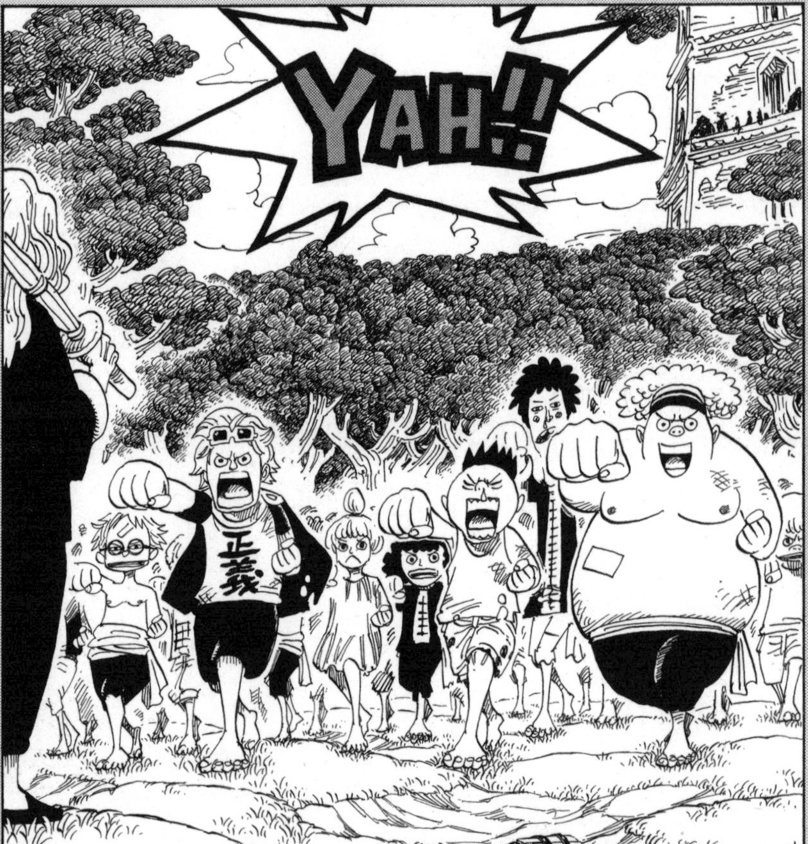
YAH!!

CP9'S INDEPENDENT REPORT, VOL. 26:
"NEXT GENERATION CP IN TRAINING"

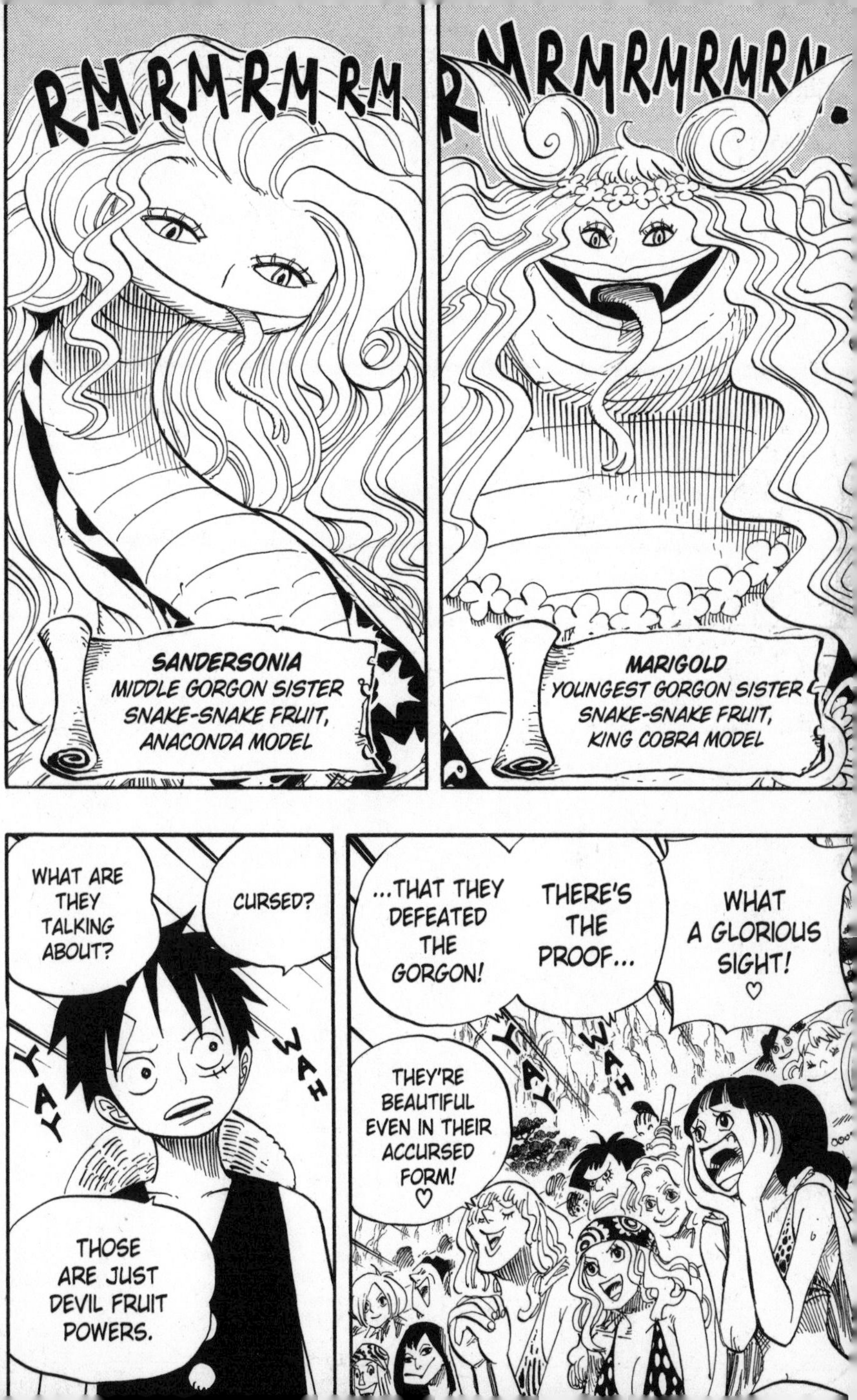
RMRMRMRMRMRN...
MARIGOLD
YOUNGEST GORGON SISTER
SNAKE-SNAKE FRUIT, KING COBRA MODEL
RMRMRMRMRM
SANDERSONIA
MIDDLE GORGON SISTER
SNAKE-SNAKE FRUIT, ANACONDA MODEL
WHAT A GLORIOUS SIGHT! ♡
THERE'S THE PROOF...
...THAT THEY DEFEATED THE GORGON!
WAH
YAY
THEY'RE BEAUTIFUL EVEN IN THEIR ACCURSED FORM! ♡
CURSED?
WHAT ARE THEY TALKING ABOUT?
WAH
YAY
THOSE ARE JUST DEVIL FRUIT POWERS.

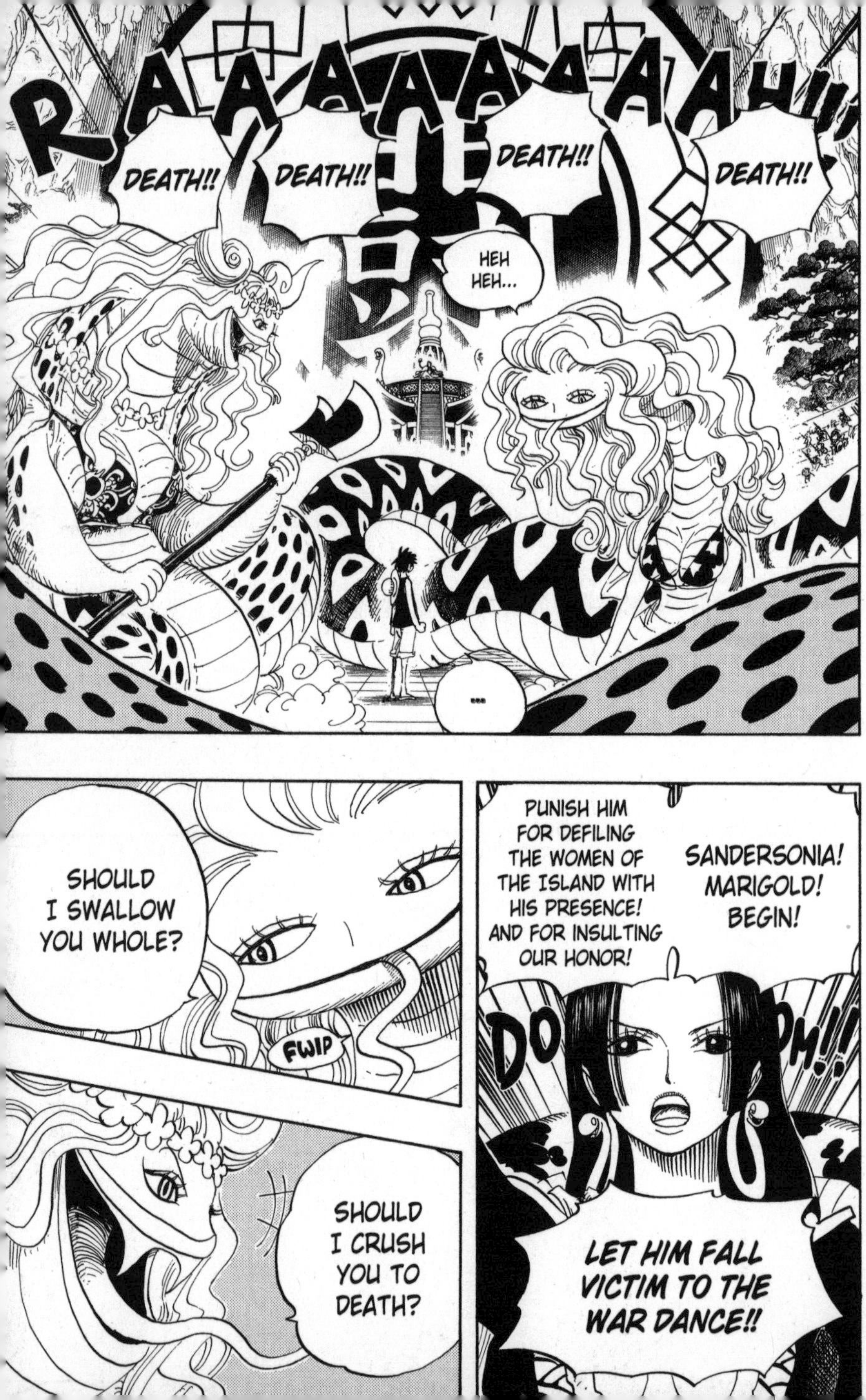
RAAAAAAAAH!!!
DEATH!!
DEATH!!
DEATH!!
DEATH!!
HEH HEH...
...
SANDERSONIA! MARIGOLD! BEGIN!
PUNISH HIM FOR DEFILING THE WOMEN OF THE ISLAND WITH HIS PRESENCE! AND FOR INSULTING OUR HONOR!
DO
OM!!!
LET HIM FALL VICTIM TO THE WAR DANCE!!
SHOULD I SWALLOW YOU WHOLE?
FWIP
SHOULD I CRUSH YOU TO DEATH?

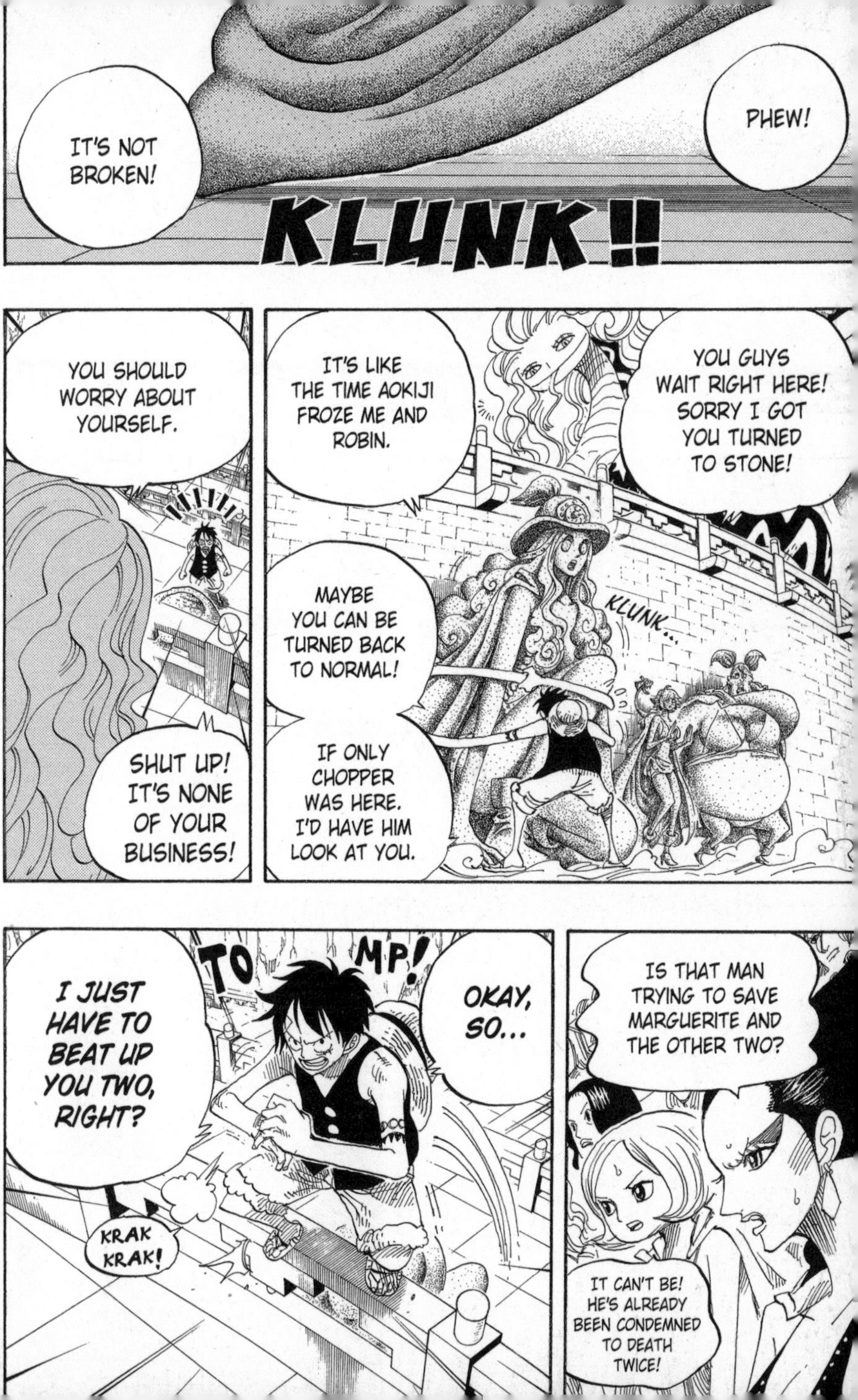
PHEW!
IT'S NOT BROKEN!
KLUNK!!
YOU GUYS WAIT RIGHT HERE! SORRY I GOT YOU TURNED TO STONE!
IT'S LIKE THE TIME AOKIJI FROZE ME AND ROBIN.
KLUNK...
MAYBE YOU CAN BE TURNED BACK TO NORMAL!
IF ONLY CHOPPER WAS HERE. I'D HAVE HIM LOOK AT YOU.
YOU SHOULD WORRY ABOUT YOURSELF.
SHUT UP! IT'S NONE OF YOUR BUSINESS!
IS THAT MAN TRYING TO SAVE MARGUERITE AND THE OTHER TWO?
IT CAN'T BE! HE'S ALREADY BEEN CONDEMNED TO DEATH TWICE!
TOMP!
OKAY, SO...
I JUST HAVE TO BEAT UP YOU TWO, RIGHT?
KRAK KRAK!

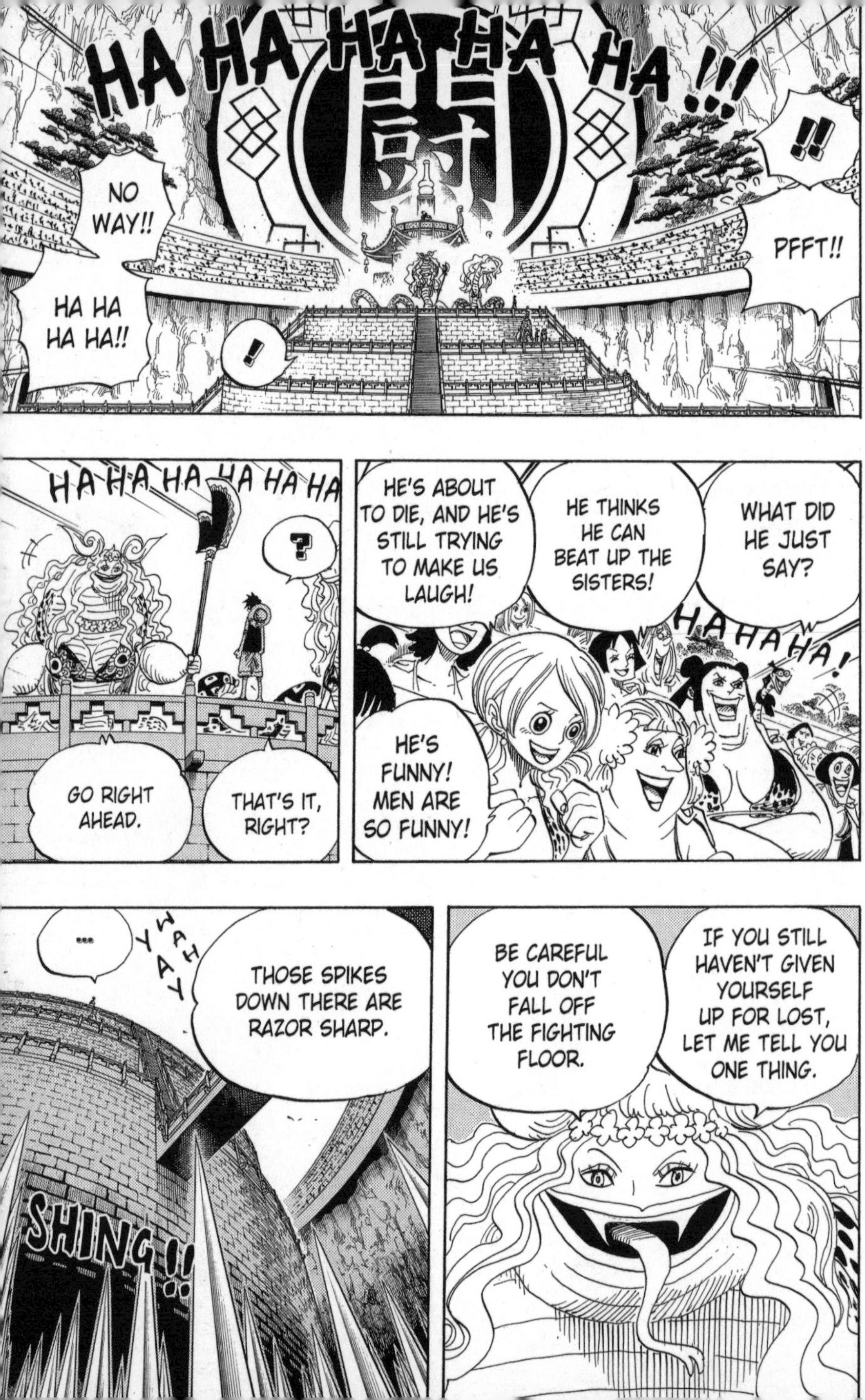
HA HA HA HA HA HA!!!
!!
PFFT!!
NO WAY!!
HA HA HA HA!!
!
WHAT DID HE JUST SAY?
HE THINKS HE CAN BEAT UP THE SISTERS!
HE'S ABOUT TO DIE, AND HE'S STILL TRYING TO MAKE US LAUGH!
HAHAHAHA!
HE'S FUNNY! MEN ARE SO FUNNY!
HA HA HA HA HA HA HA
?
THAT'S IT, RIGHT?
GO RIGHT AHEAD.
IF YOU STILL HAVEN'T GIVEN YOURSELF UP FOR LOST, LET ME TELL YOU ONE THING.
BE CAREFUL YOU DON'T FALL OFF THE FIGHTING FLOOR.
THOSE SPIKES DOWN THERE ARE RAZOR SHARP.
...
SHING!!

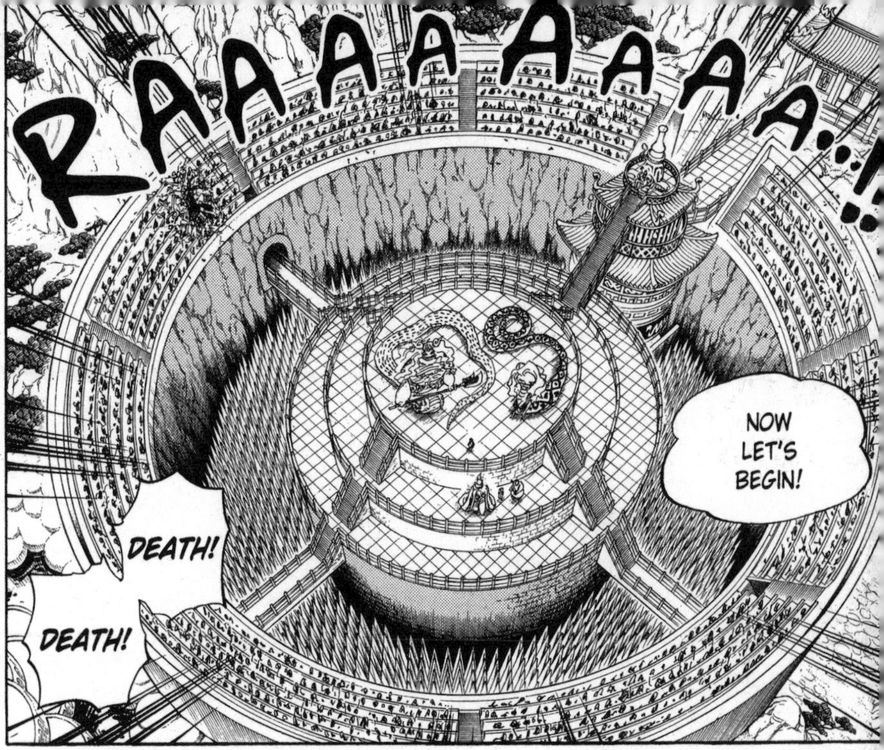
RAAAAAAAA..!!
NOW LET'S BEGIN!
DEATH!
DEATH!
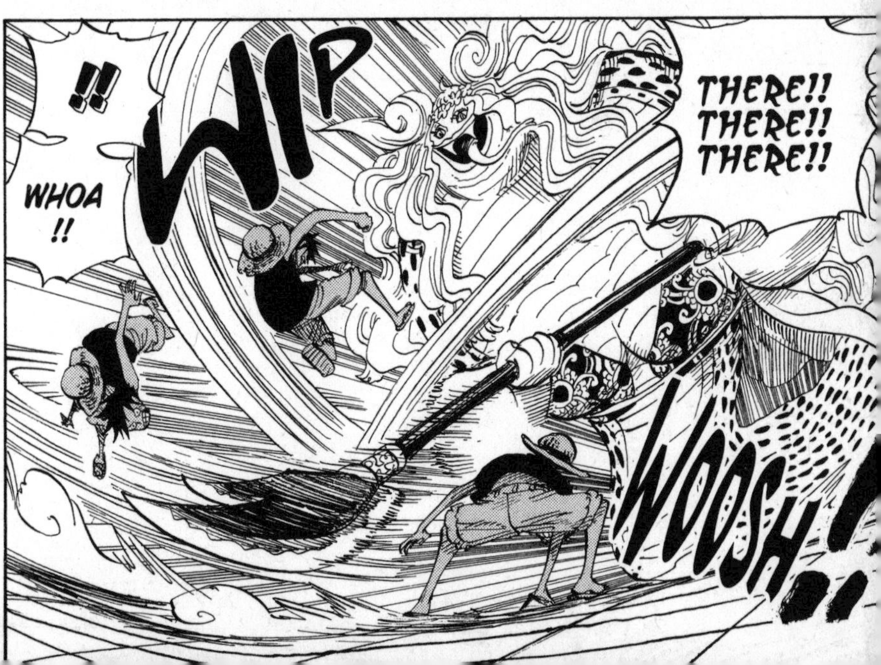
THERE!! THERE!! THERE!!
WOOSH!!
WHIP
!!
WHOA !!

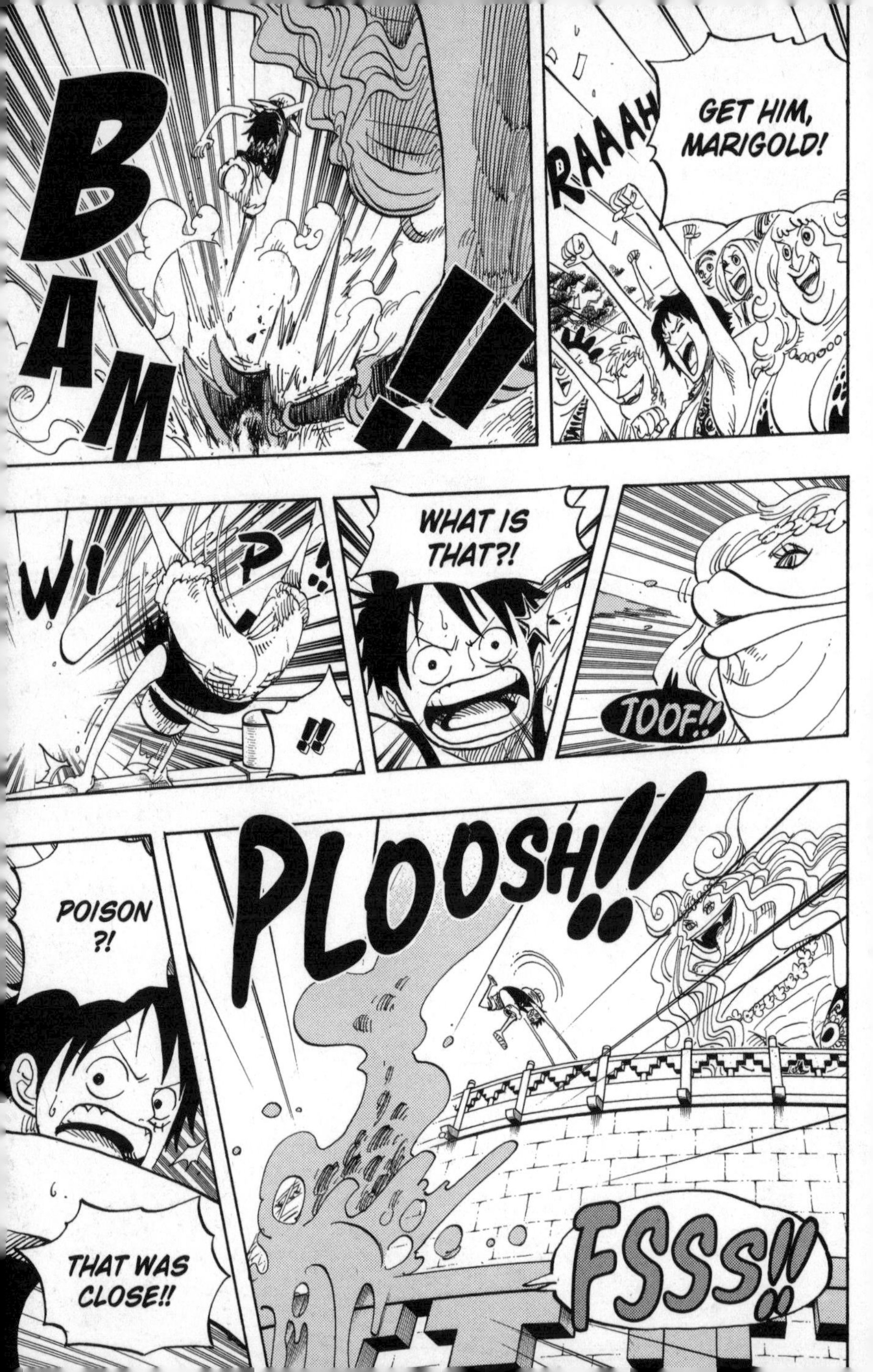
GET HIM, MARIGOLD!
RAAAH
BAM!!
TOOF!!
WHAT IS THAT?!
WIP!!
!!
PLOOSH!!
FSSS!!
POISON ?!
THAT WAS CLOSE!!

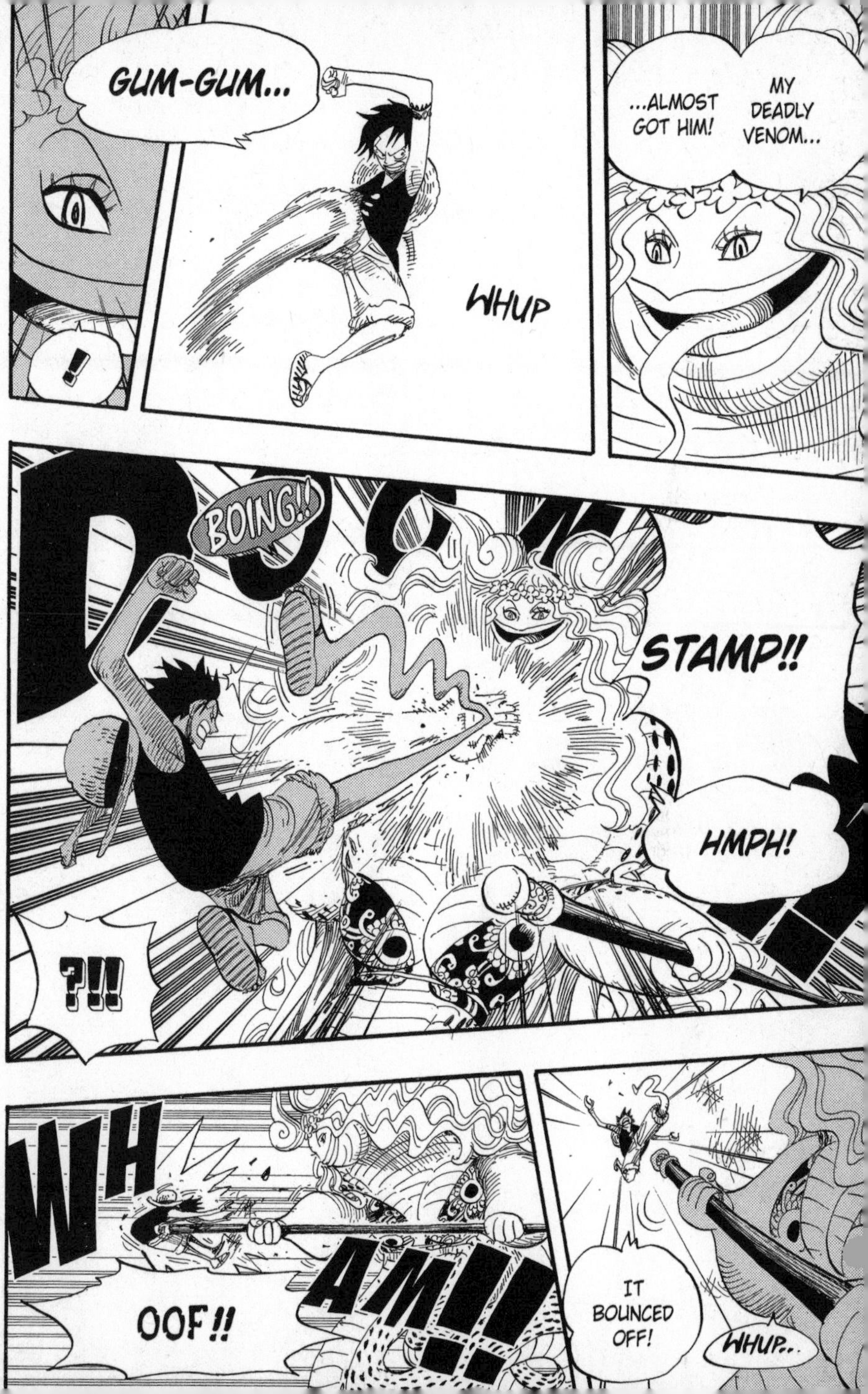
MY DEADLY VENOM...
...ALMOST GOT HIM!
GUM-GUM...
WHUP
!
BOING!!
STAMP!!
HMPH!
?!!
IT BOUNCED OFF!
WHUP..
WHAM!!
OOF!!

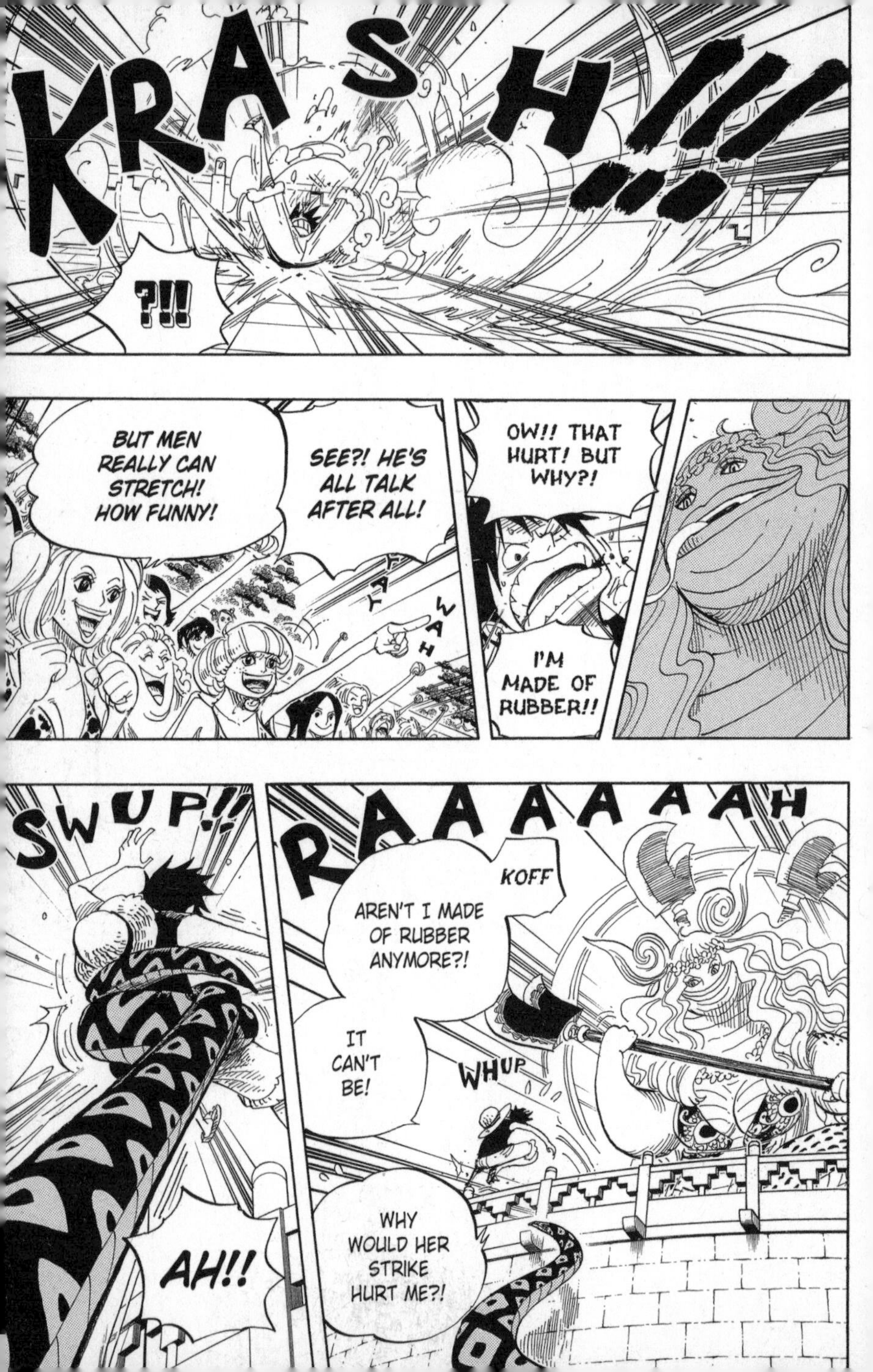
KRASH!!!
?!!
OW!! THAT HURT! BUT WHY?!
I'M MADE OF RUBBER!!
SEE?! HE'S ALL TALK AFTER ALL!
WAH
BUT MEN REALLY CAN STRETCH! HOW FUNNY!
RAAAAAAH
KOFF
AREN'T I MADE OF RUBBER ANYMORE?!
IT CAN'T BE!
WHUP
WHY WOULD HER STRIKE HURT ME?!
SWUP!!
AH!!

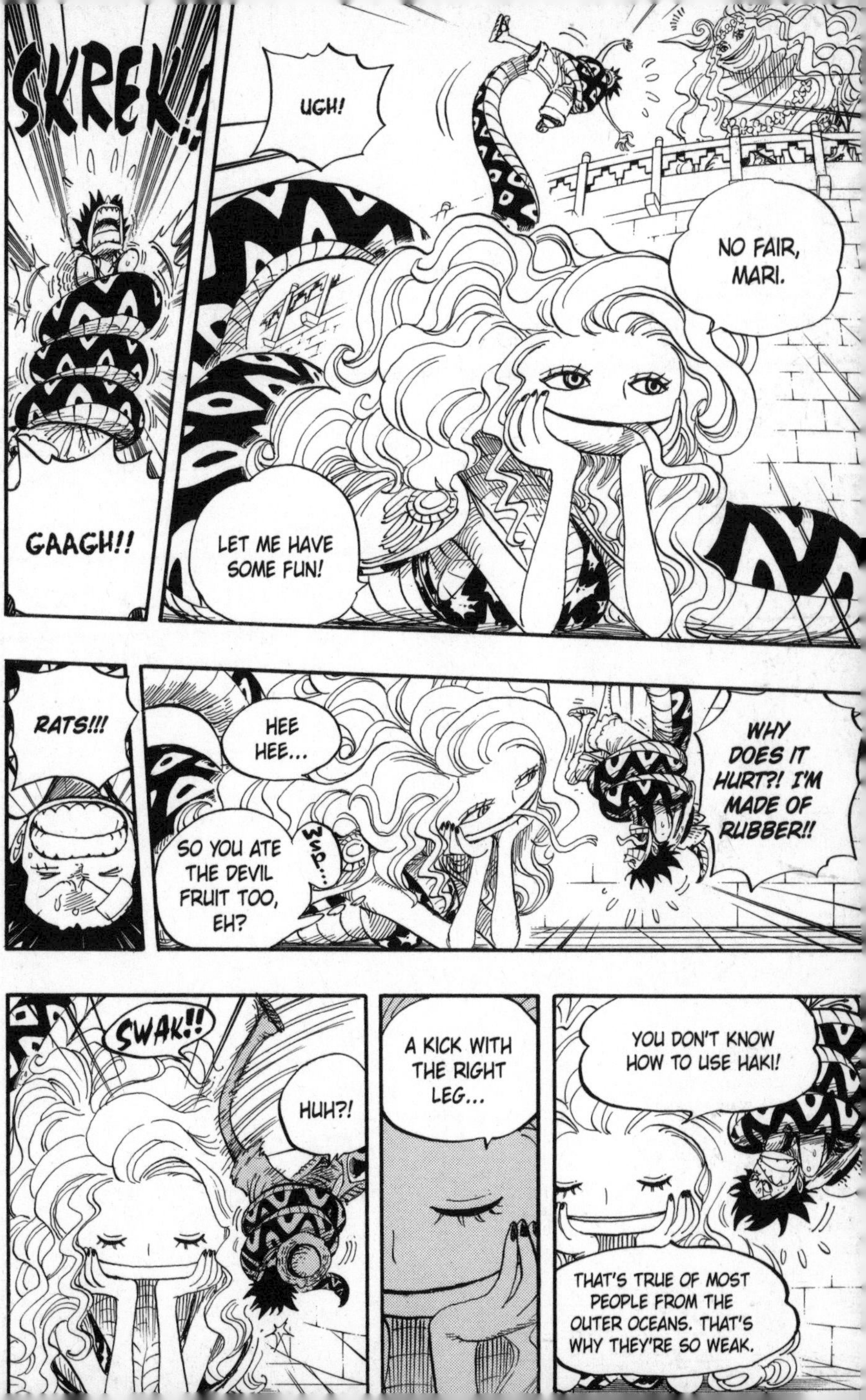
UGH!
NO FAIR, MARI.
LET ME HAVE SOME FUN!
SKREK!!
GAAGH!!
WHY DOES IT HURT?! I'M MADE OF RUBBER!!
HEE HEE...
WSP...
SO YOU ATE THE DEVIL FRUIT TOO, EH?
RATS!!!
YOU DON'T KNOW HOW TO USE HAKI!
THAT'S TRUE OF MOST PEOPLE FROM THE OUTER OCEANS. THAT'S WHY THEY'RE SO WEAK.
A KICK WITH THE RIGHT LEG...
SWAK!!
HUH?!

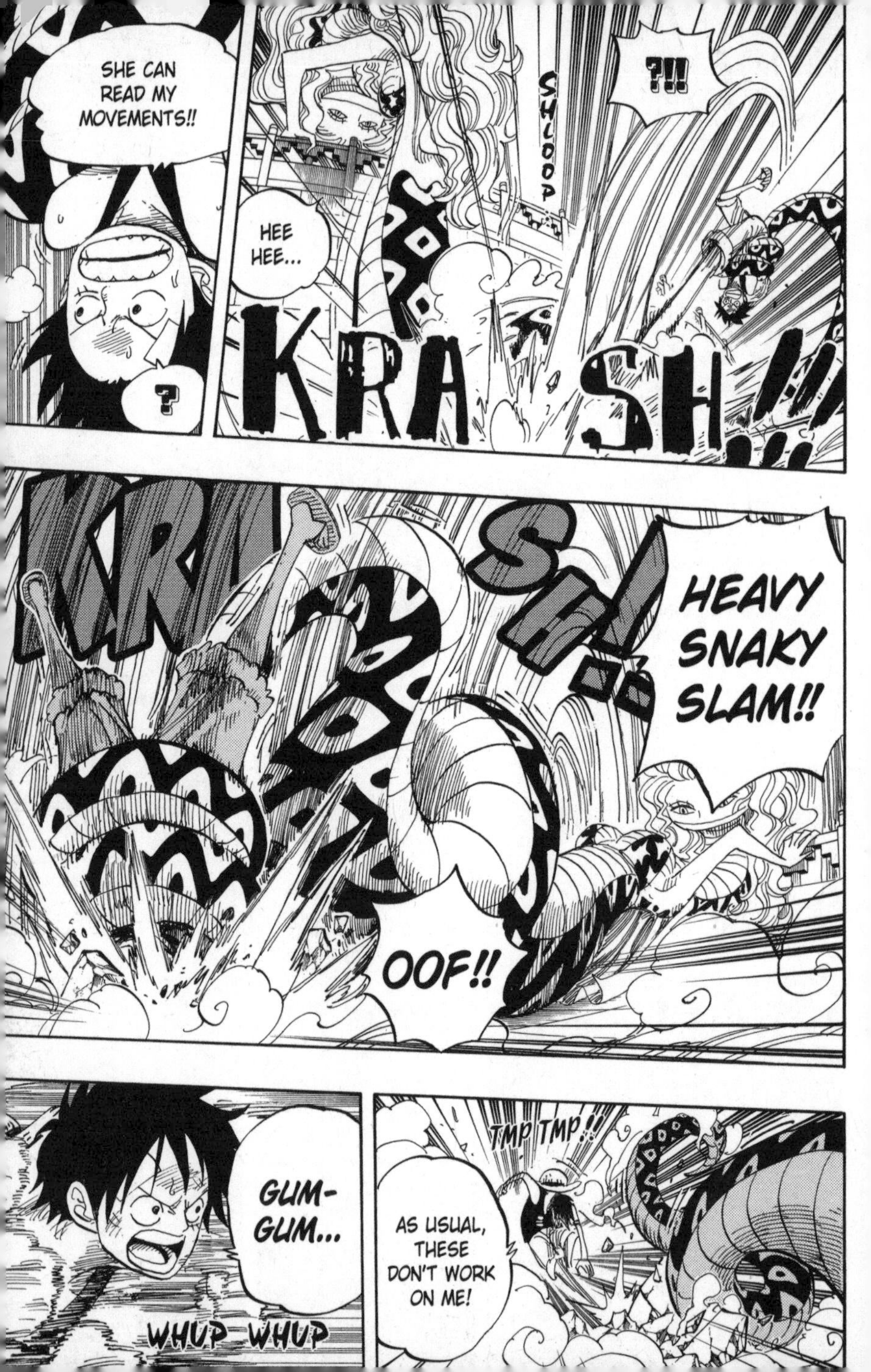
?!!
SHLOOP
HEE HEE...
KRASH!!
SHE CAN READ MY MOVEMENTS!!
?
HEAVY SNAKY SLAM!!
KRASH!!
OOF!!
TMP TMP!!
AS USUAL, THESE DON'T WORK ON ME!
GUM-GUM...
WHUP WHUP

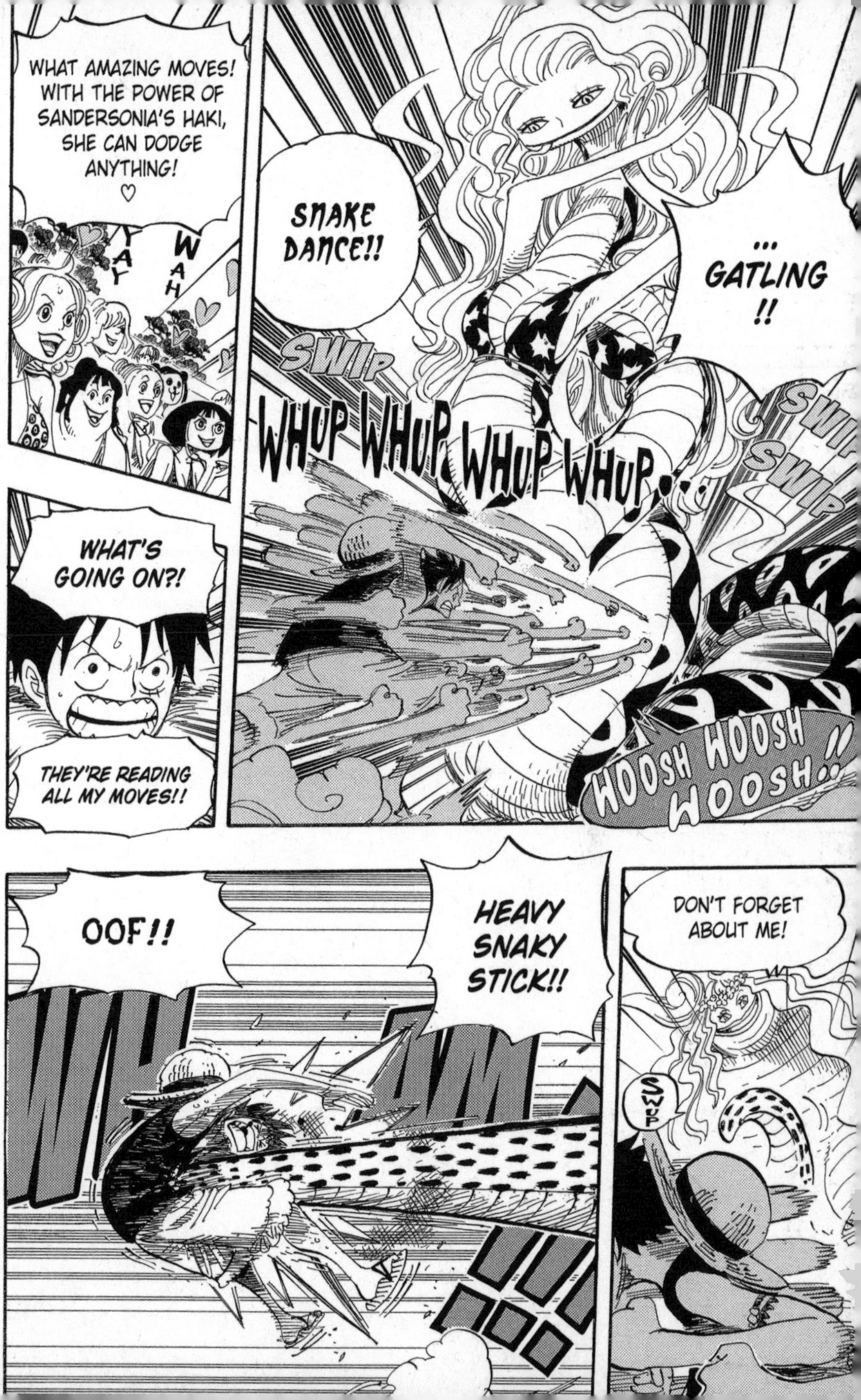

... GATLING !!
SWIP SWIP
SNAKE DANCE!!
SWIP
WHUP WHUP WHUP WHUP...
WOOSH WOOSH WOOSH..!!
WHAT AMAZING MOVES! WITH THE POWER OF SANDERSONIA'S HAKI, SHE CAN DODGE ANYTHING! ♡
YAY
WAH
WHAT'S GOING ON?!
THEY'RE READING ALL MY MOVES!!
DON'T FORGET ABOUT ME!
SWUP
HEAVY SNAKY STICK!!
OOF!!

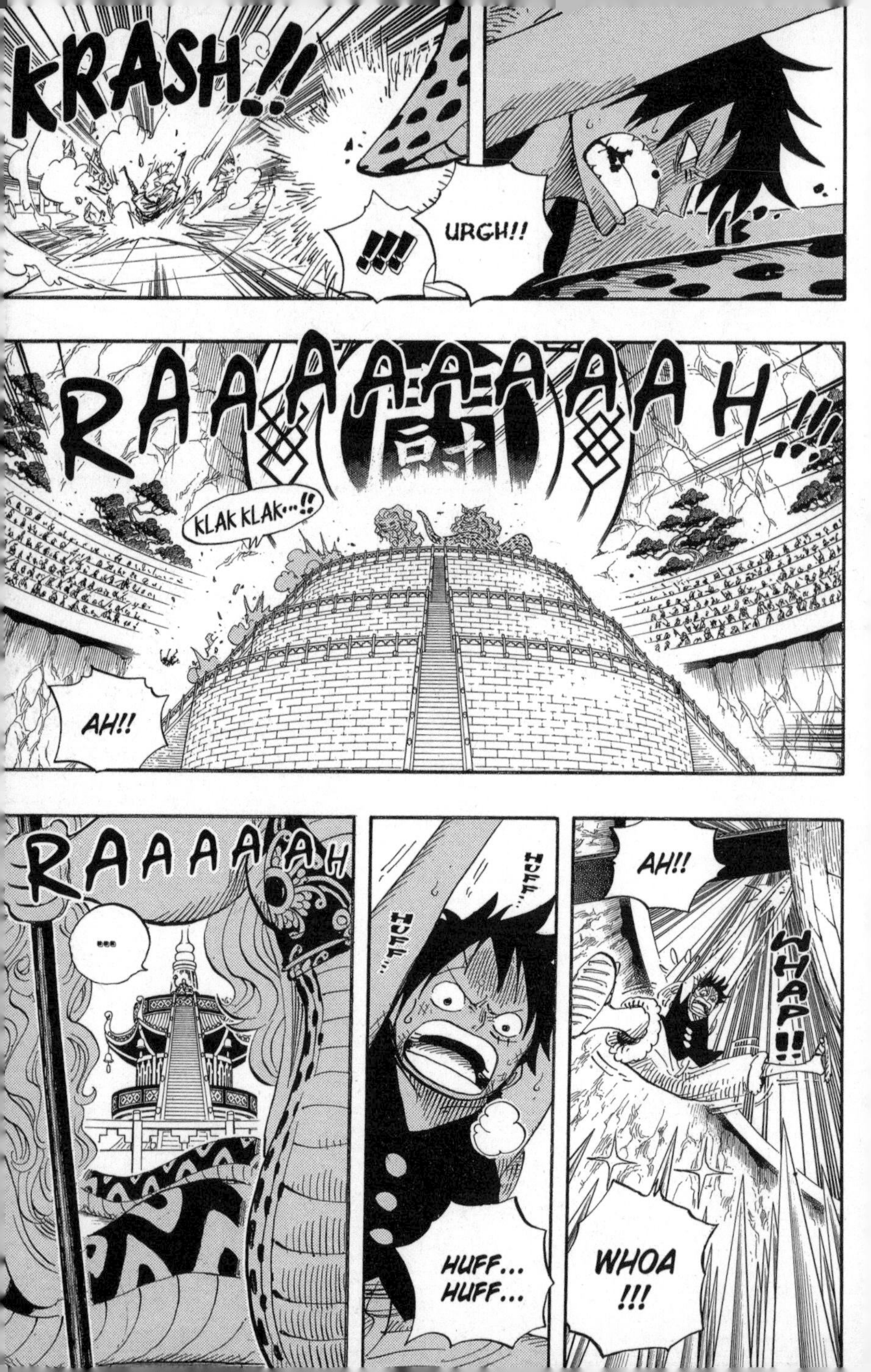
URGH!!
!!!
KRASH!!
RAAAAAAAAH!!!
KLAK KLAK...!!
AH!!
RAAAAAH
...
HUFF...
HUFF...
HUFF... HUFF...
AH!!
WHAP!!
WHOA !!!

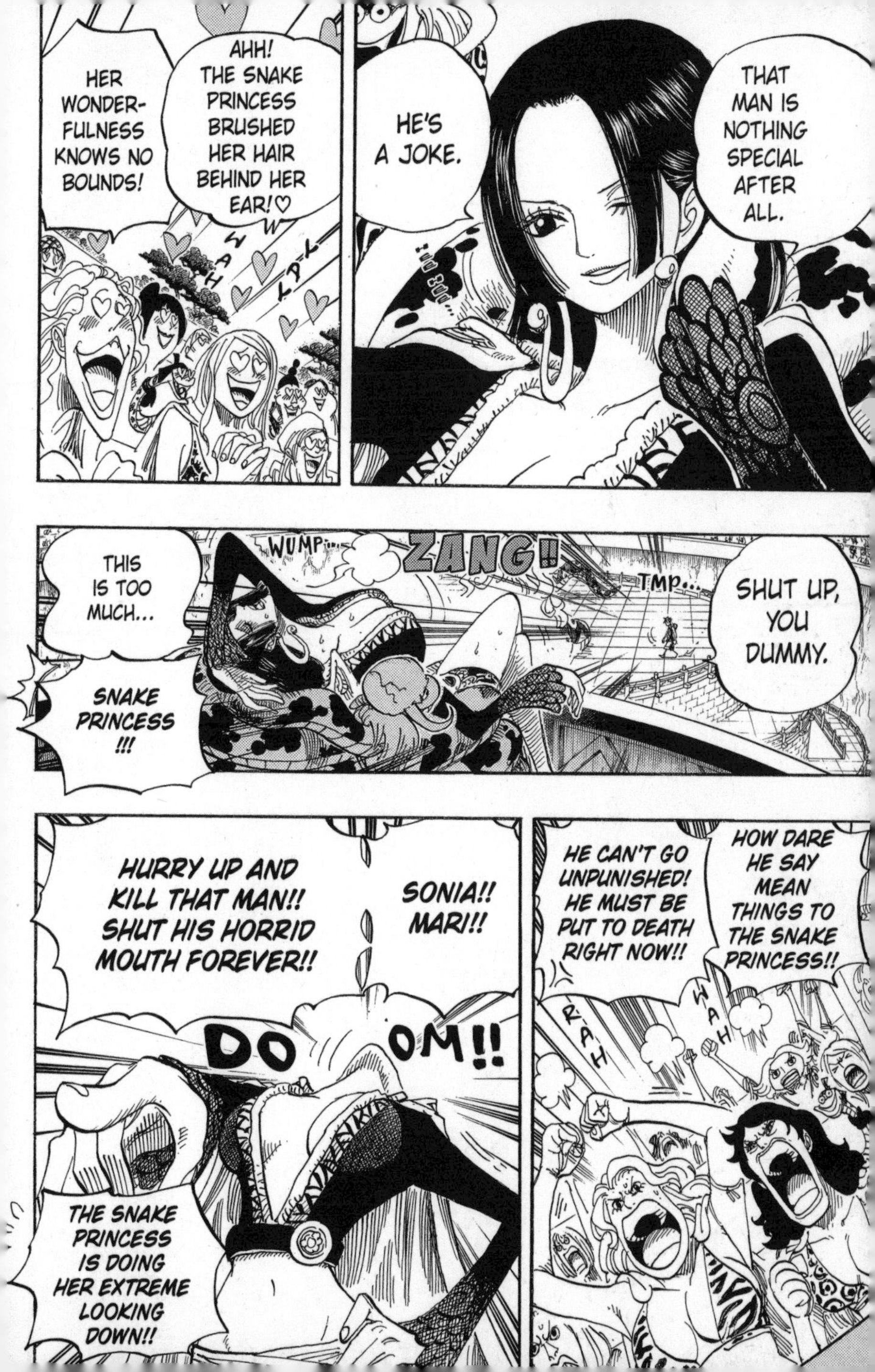
THAT MAN IS NOTHING SPECIAL AFTER ALL.
HE'S A JOKE.
AHH! THE SNAKE PRINCESS BRUSHED HER HAIR BEHIND HER EAR!♡
HER WONDER-FULNESS KNOWS NO BOUNDS!
SHUT UP, YOU DUMMY.
TMP...
ZANG!!
WUMP...
THIS IS TOO MUCH...
SNAKE PRINCESS !!!
HOW DARE HE SAY MEAN THINGS TO THE SNAKE PRINCESS!!
HE CAN'T GO UNPUNISHED! HE MUST BE PUT TO DEATH RIGHT NOW!!
WAH
RAH
SONIA!! MARI!!
HURRY UP AND KILL THAT MAN!! SHUT HIS HORRID MOUTH FOREVER!!
DOOM!!
THE SNAKE PRINCESS IS DOING HER EXTREME LOOKING DOWN!!

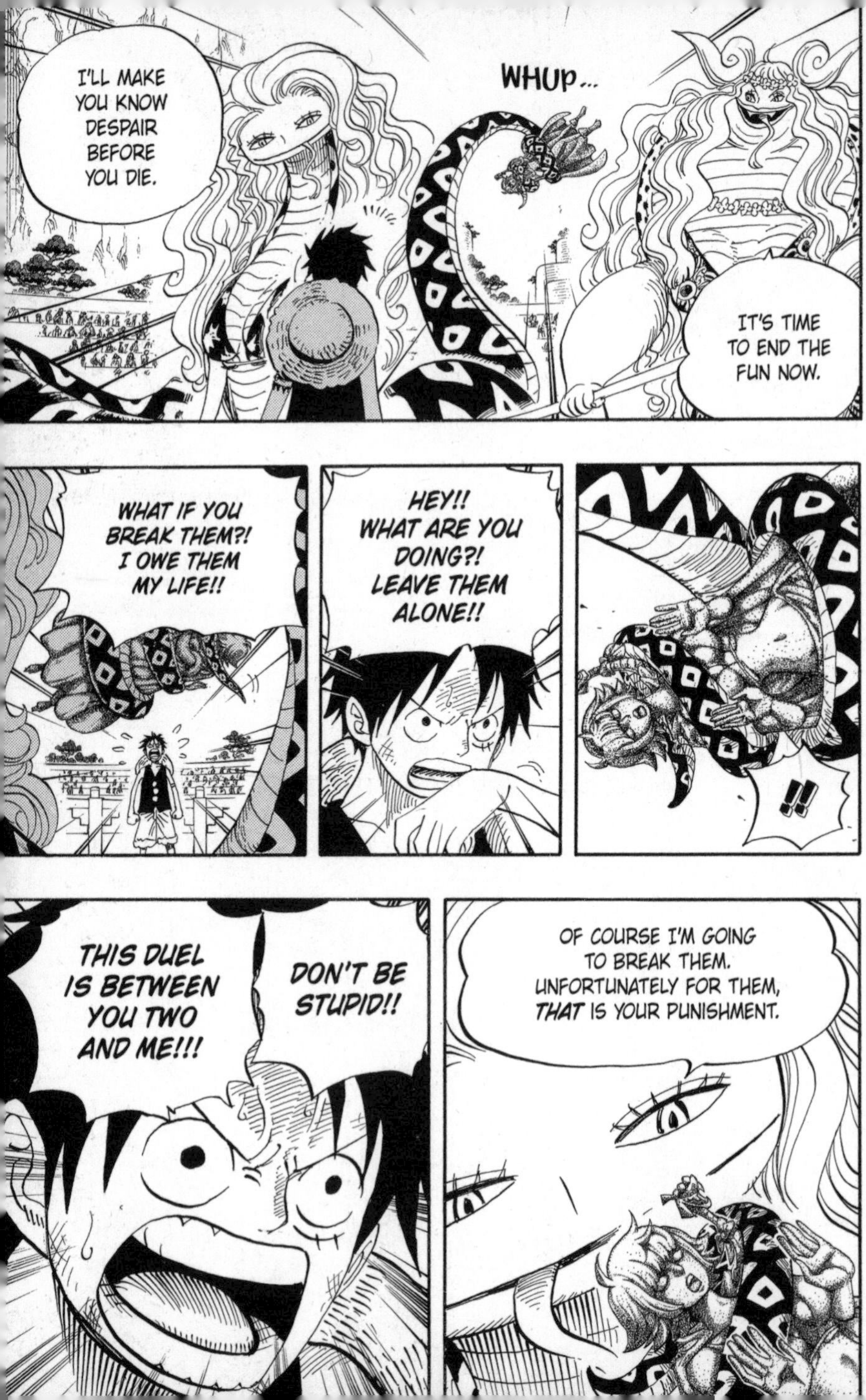
WHUP...
IT'S TIME TO END THE FUN NOW.
I'LL MAKE YOU KNOW DESPAIR BEFORE YOU DIE.
!!
HEY!! WHAT ARE YOU DOING?! LEAVE THEM ALONE!!
WHAT IF YOU BREAK THEM?! I OWE THEM MY LIFE!!
OF COURSE I'M GOING TO BREAK THEM. UNFORTUNATELY FOR THEM, THAT IS YOUR PUNISHMENT.
DON'T BE STUPID!!
THIS DUEL IS BETWEEN YOU TWO AND ME!!!

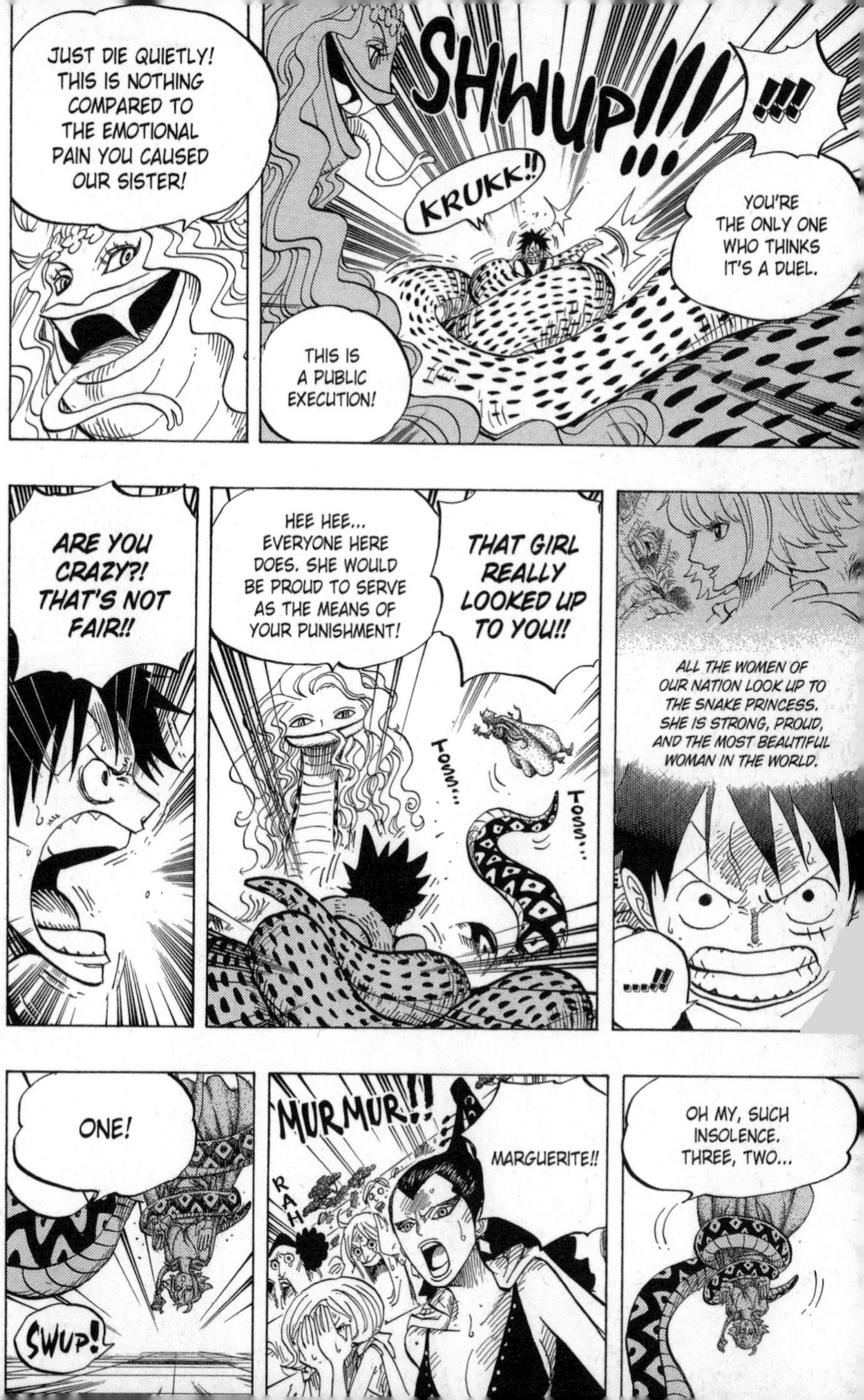
!!!
SHWUP!!!
YOU'RE THE ONLY ONE WHO THINKS IT'S A DUEL.
KRUKK!!
THIS IS A PUBLIC EXECUTION!
JUST DIE QUIETLY! THIS IS NOTHING COMPARED TO THE EMOTIONAL PAIN YOU CAUSED OUR SISTER!
ALL THE WOMEN OF OUR NATION LOOK UP TO THE SNAKE PRINCESS. SHE IS STRONG, PROUD, AND THE MOST BEAUTIFUL WOMAN IN THE WORLD.
....!!
THAT GIRL REALLY LOOKED UP TO YOU!!
HEE HEE... EVERYONE HERE DOES. SHE WOULD BE PROUD TO SERVE AS THE MEANS OF YOUR PUNISHMENT!
TOSS...
TOSS...
ARE YOU CRAZY?! THAT'S NOT FAIR!!
OH MY, SUCH INSOLENCE. THREE, TWO...
MARGUERITE!!
MURMUR!!
RAH
ONE!
SWUP!

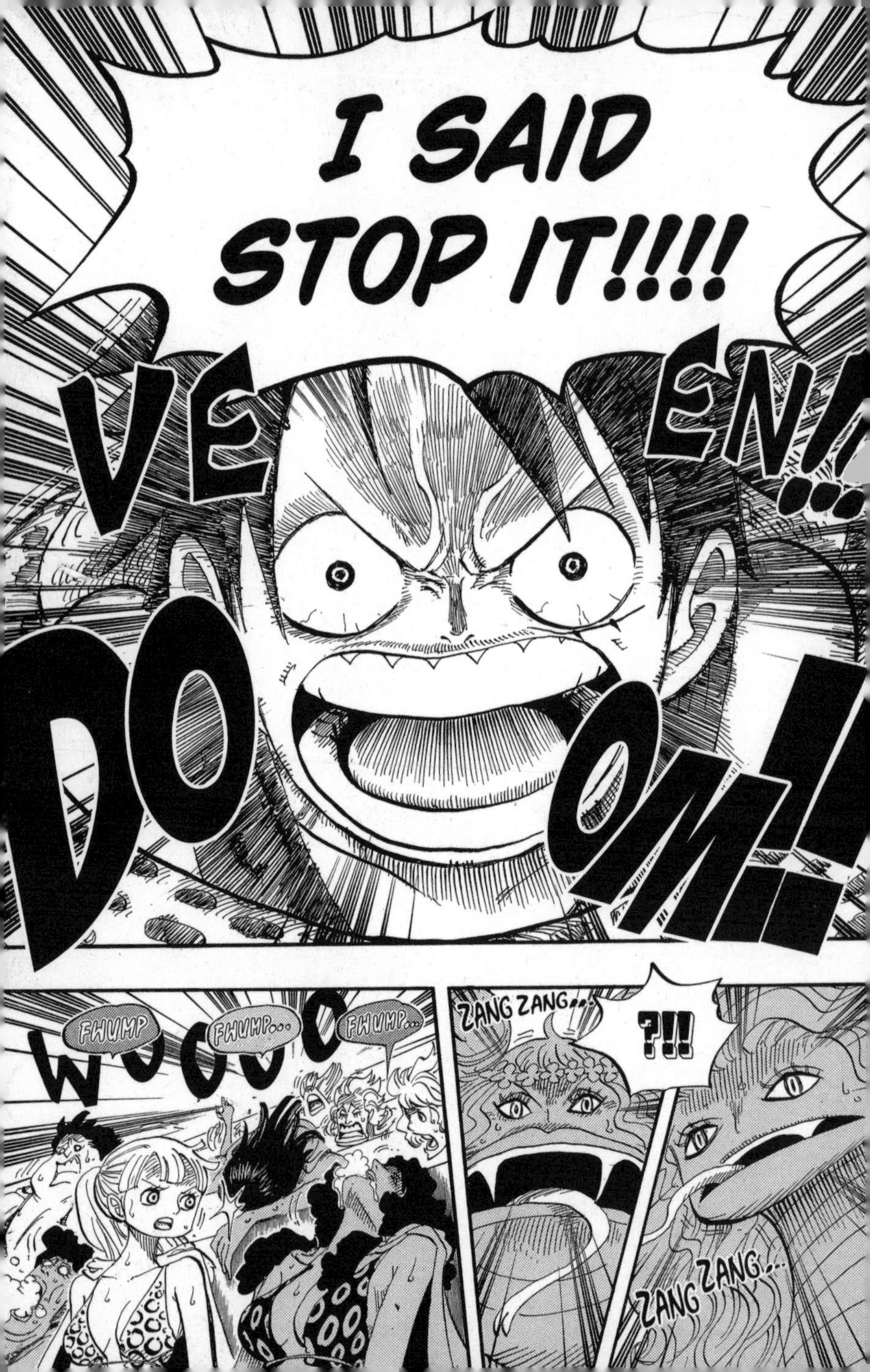
I SAID STOP IT!!!!
VEEEN!!
DOOOM!!
ZANG ZANG...
?!!
ZANG ZANG...
FWUMP
FWUMP...
FWUMP...
WOOOO

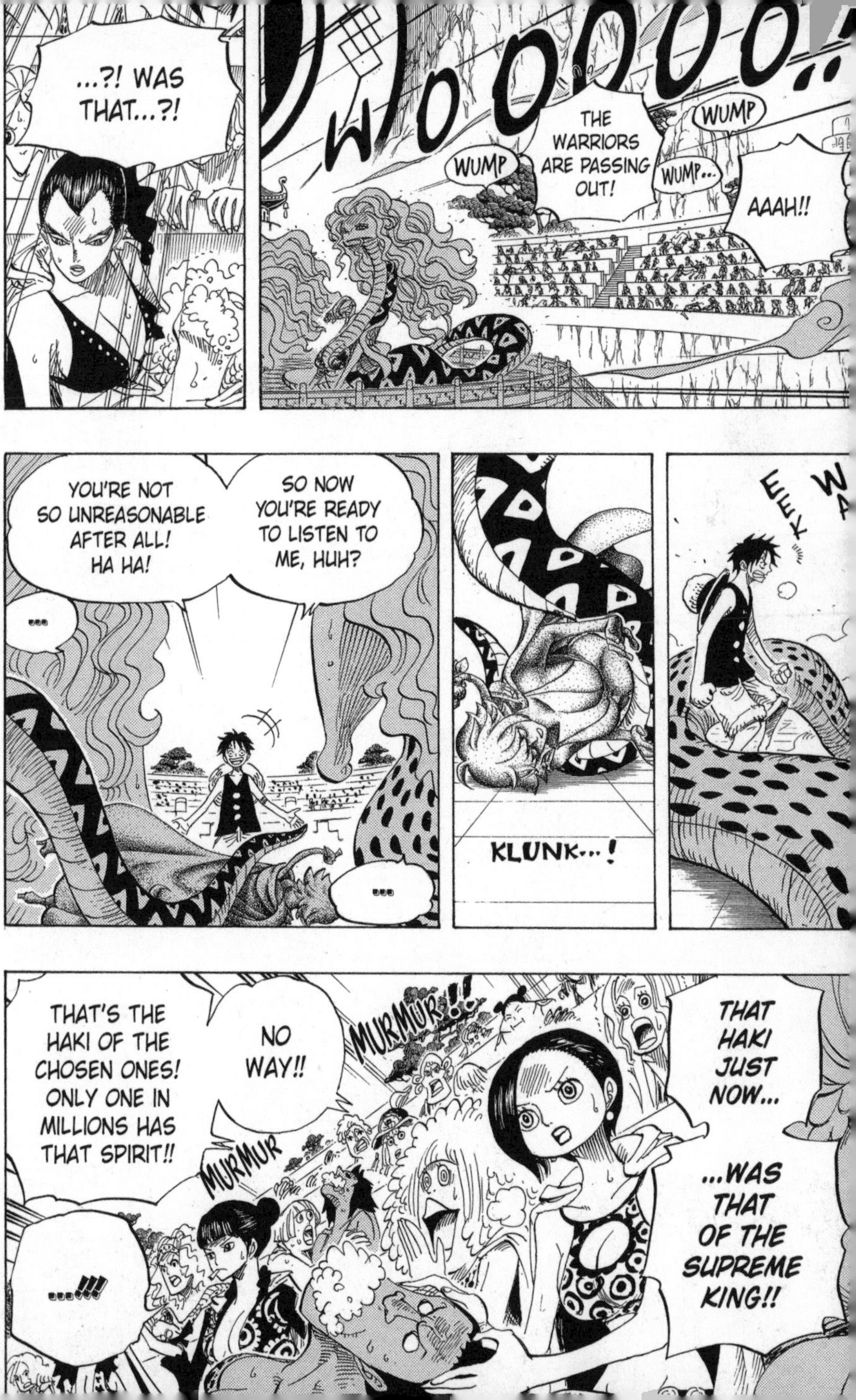
WOOOOOO!!
WUMP
THE WARRIORS ARE PASSING OUT!
WUMP...
WUMP
AAAH!!
...?! WAS THAT...?!
EEK
KLUNK...!
SO NOW YOU'RE READY TO LISTEN TO ME, HUH?
YOU'RE NOT SO UNREASONABLE AFTER ALL! HA HA!
...
...
THAT HAKI JUST NOW...
...WAS THAT OF THE SUPREME KING!!
MURMUR!!
NO WAY!!
THAT'S THE HAKI OF THE CHOSEN ONES! ONLY ONE IN MILLIONS HAS THAT SPIRIT!!
MURMUR
...!!!

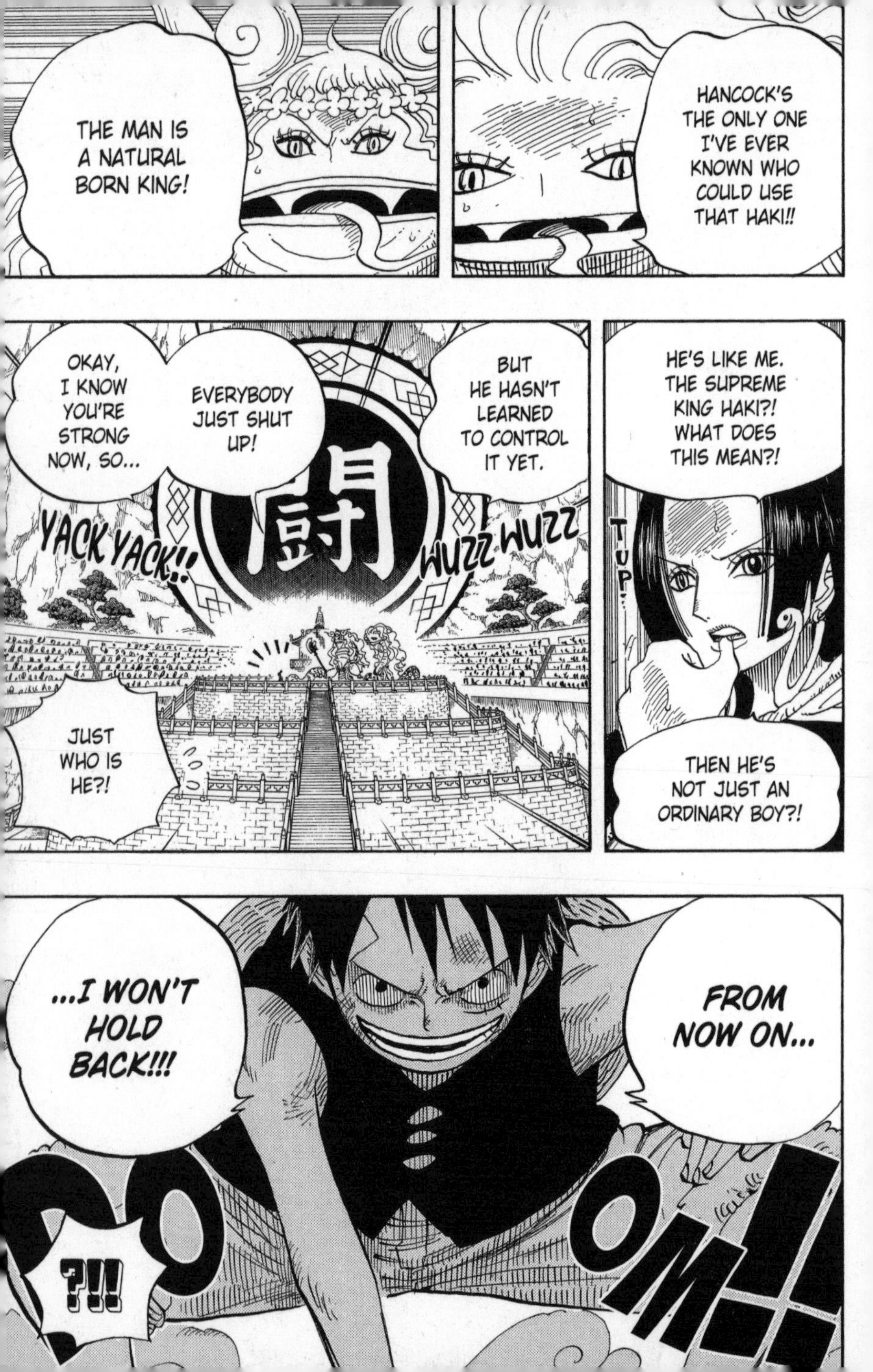
HANCOCK'S THE ONLY ONE I'VE EVER KNOWN WHO COULD USE THAT HAKI!!
THE MAN IS A NATURAL BORN KING!
HE'S LIKE ME. THE SUPREME KING HAKI?! WHAT DOES THIS MEAN?!
TUP
THEN HE'S NOT JUST AN ORDINARY BOY?!
BUT HE HASN'T LEARNED TO CONTROL IT YET.
WUZZ WUZZ
EVERYBODY JUST SHUT UP!
OKAY, I KNOW YOU'RE STRONG NOW, SO...
YACK YACK!!
JUST WHO IS HE?!
FROM NOW ON...
...I WON'T HOLD BACK!!!
GOOM!!
?!!

EYE OF THE GORGON

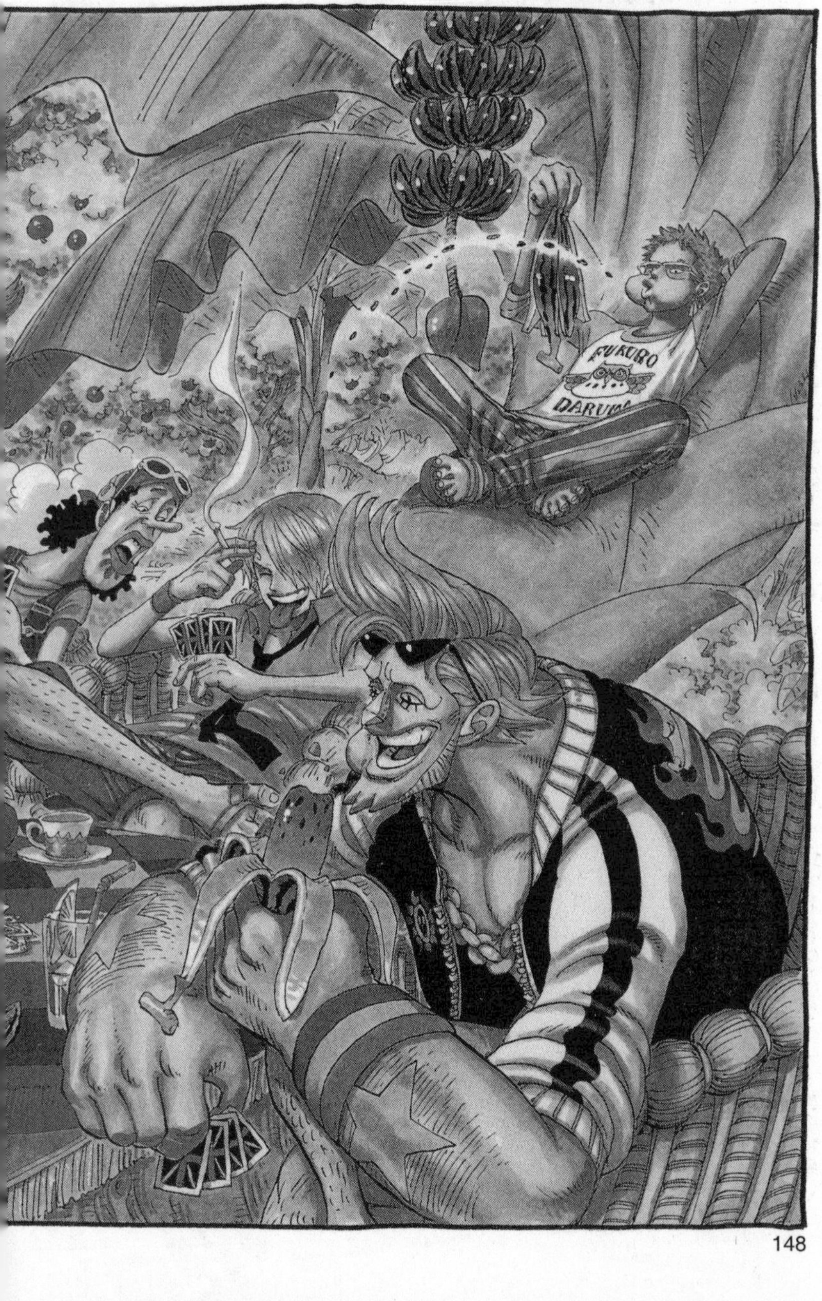
FUKURO
DARUMA

Chapter 520:

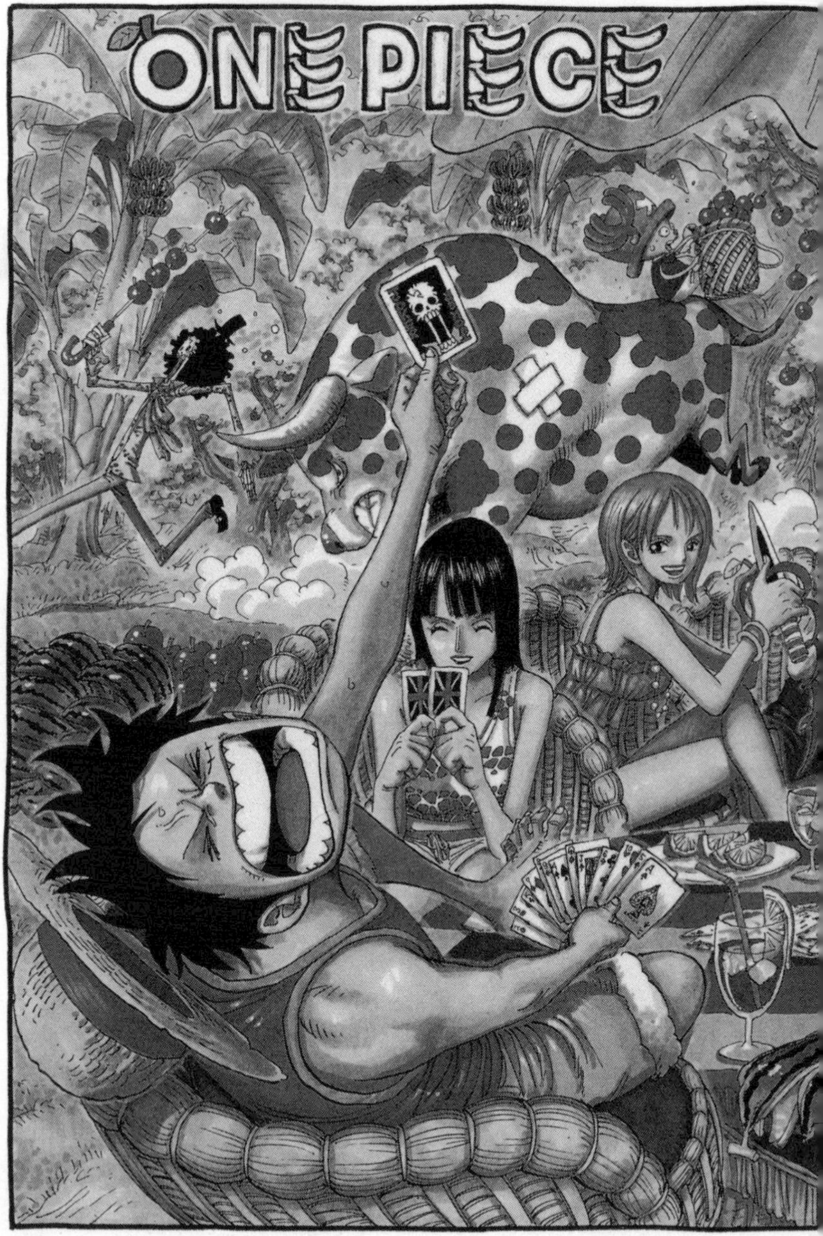
ONE PIECE

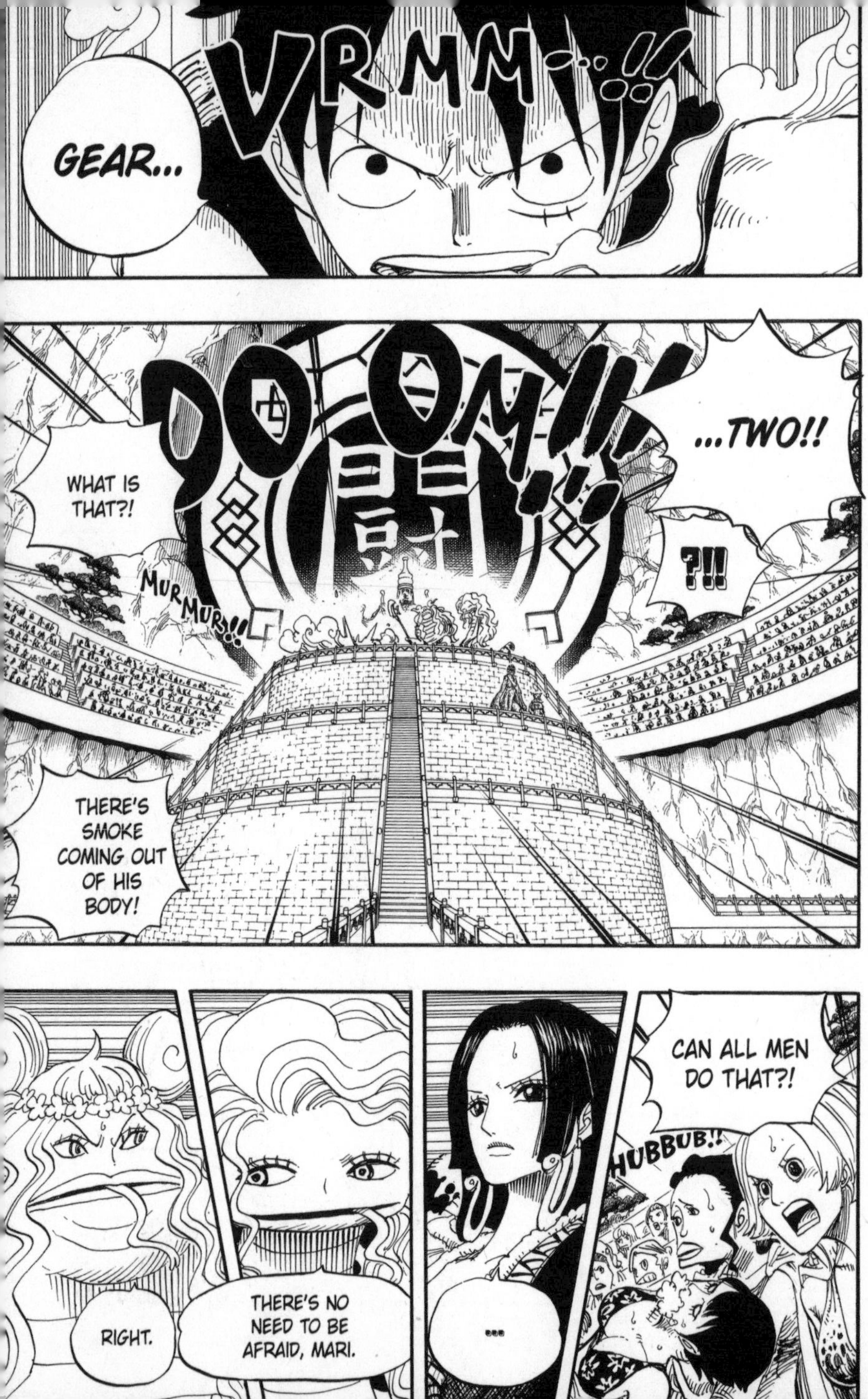
VRMM..!!
GEAR...
...TWO!!
DOOM!!
?!!
WHAT IS THAT?!
MURMUR!!
THERE'S SMOKE COMING OUT OF HIS BODY!
CAN ALL MEN DO THAT?!
HUBBUB!!
...
THERE'S NO NEED TO BE AFRAID, MARI.
RIGHT.

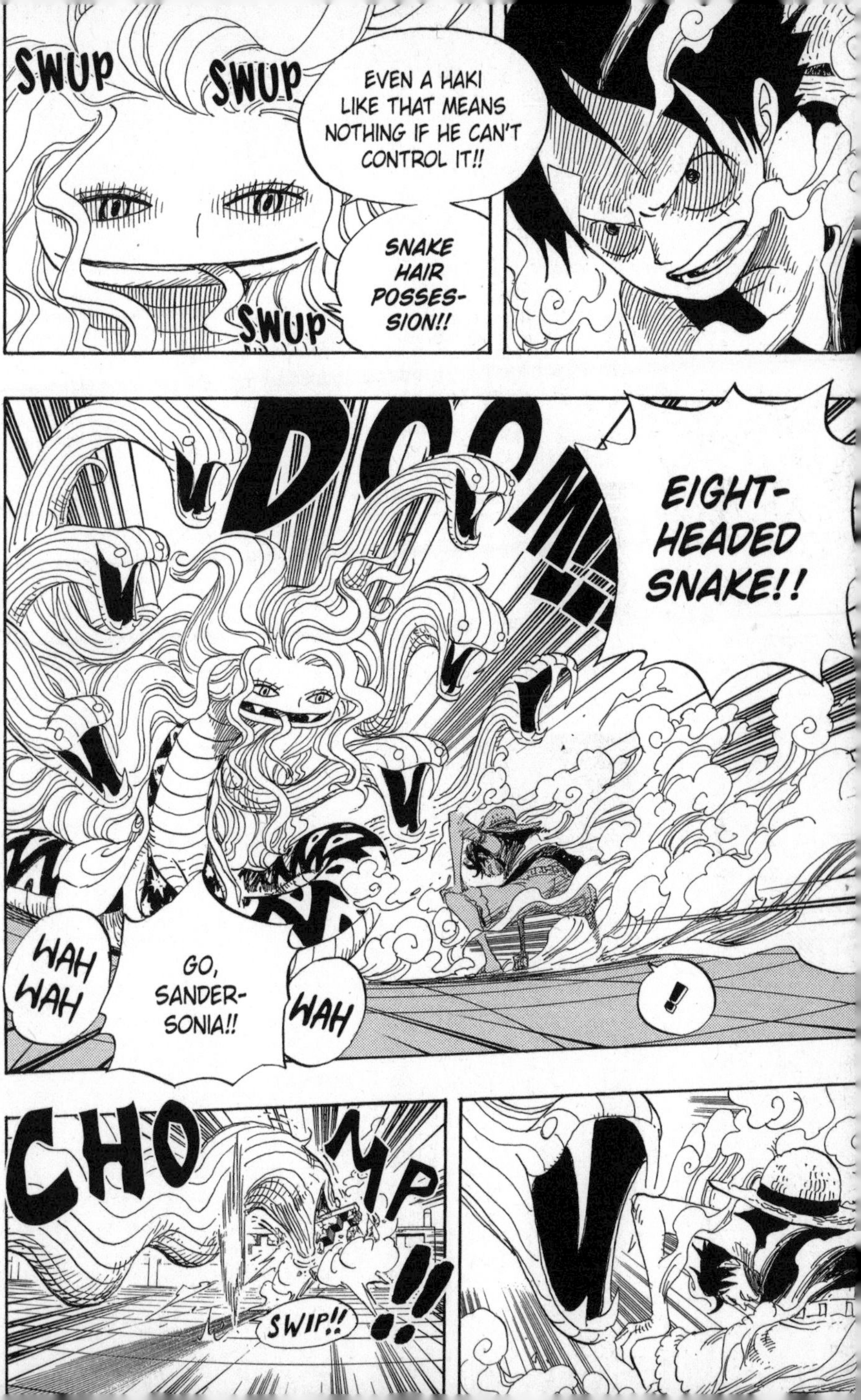
EVEN A HAKI LIKE THAT MEANS NOTHING IF HE CAN'T CONTROL IT!!
SWUP
SWUP
SNAKE HAIR POSSES-SION!!
SWUP
EIGHT-HEADED SNAKE!!
DOOM!!
!
WAH
GO, SANDER-SONIA!!
WAH WAH
CHOMP!!
SWIP!!

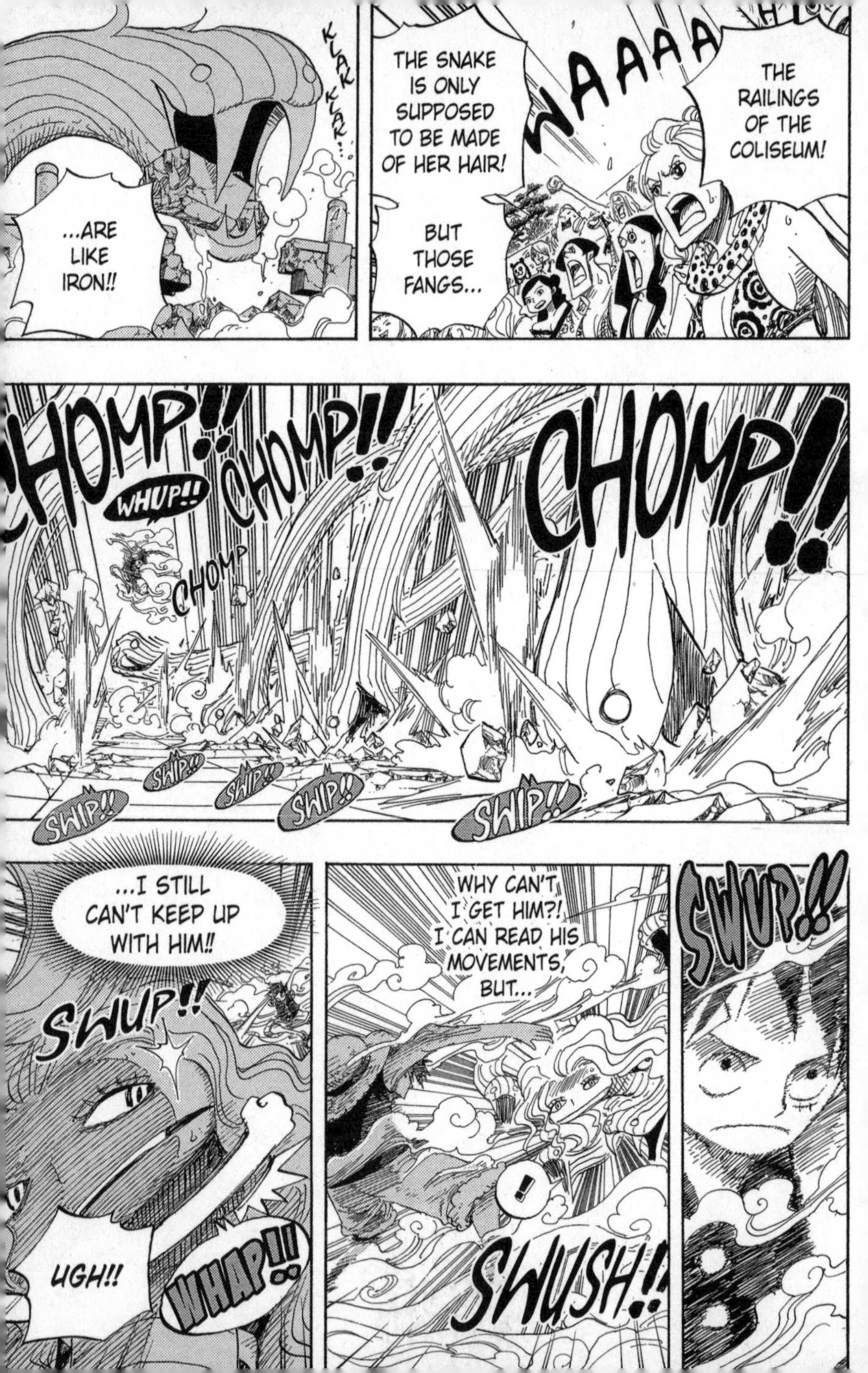
THE RAILINGS OF THE COLISEUM!
WAAAA
THE SNAKE IS ONLY SUPPOSED TO BE MADE OF HER HAIR!
BUT THOSE FANGS...
KLAK KLAK...
...ARE LIKE IRON!!
CHOMP!!
CHOMP!!
CHOMP!!
WHUP!!
CHOMP
SWIP!!
SWIP!!
SWIP!!
SWIP!!
SWIP!!
SWUP!!
WHY CAN'T I GET HIM?! I CAN READ HIS MOVEMENTS, BUT...
!
SWUSH!!
...I STILL CAN'T KEEP UP WITH HIM!!
SWUP!!
WHAP!!
UGH!!

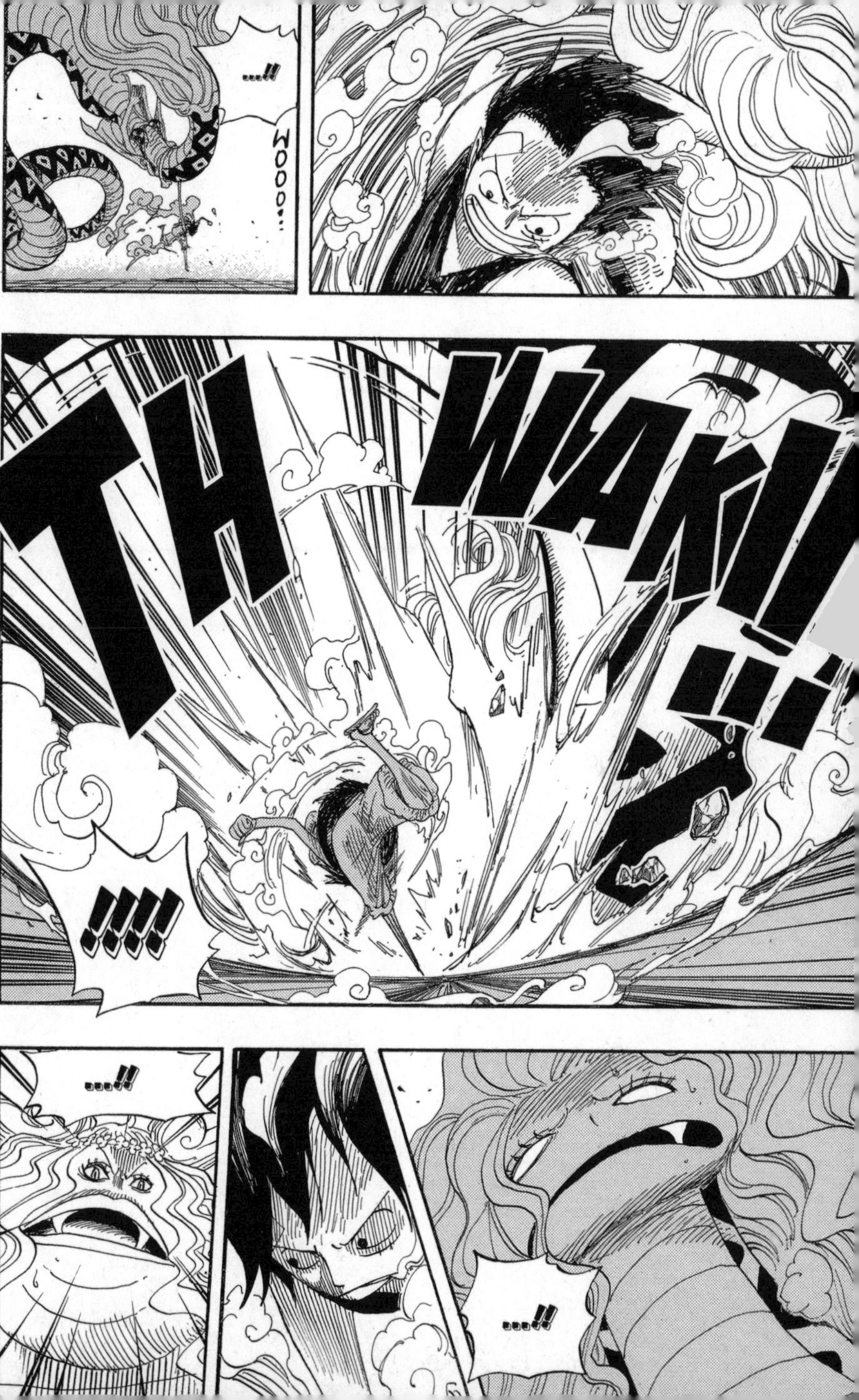
...!!
WOOO!!
THWAK!!!
!!!!
...!!
...!!

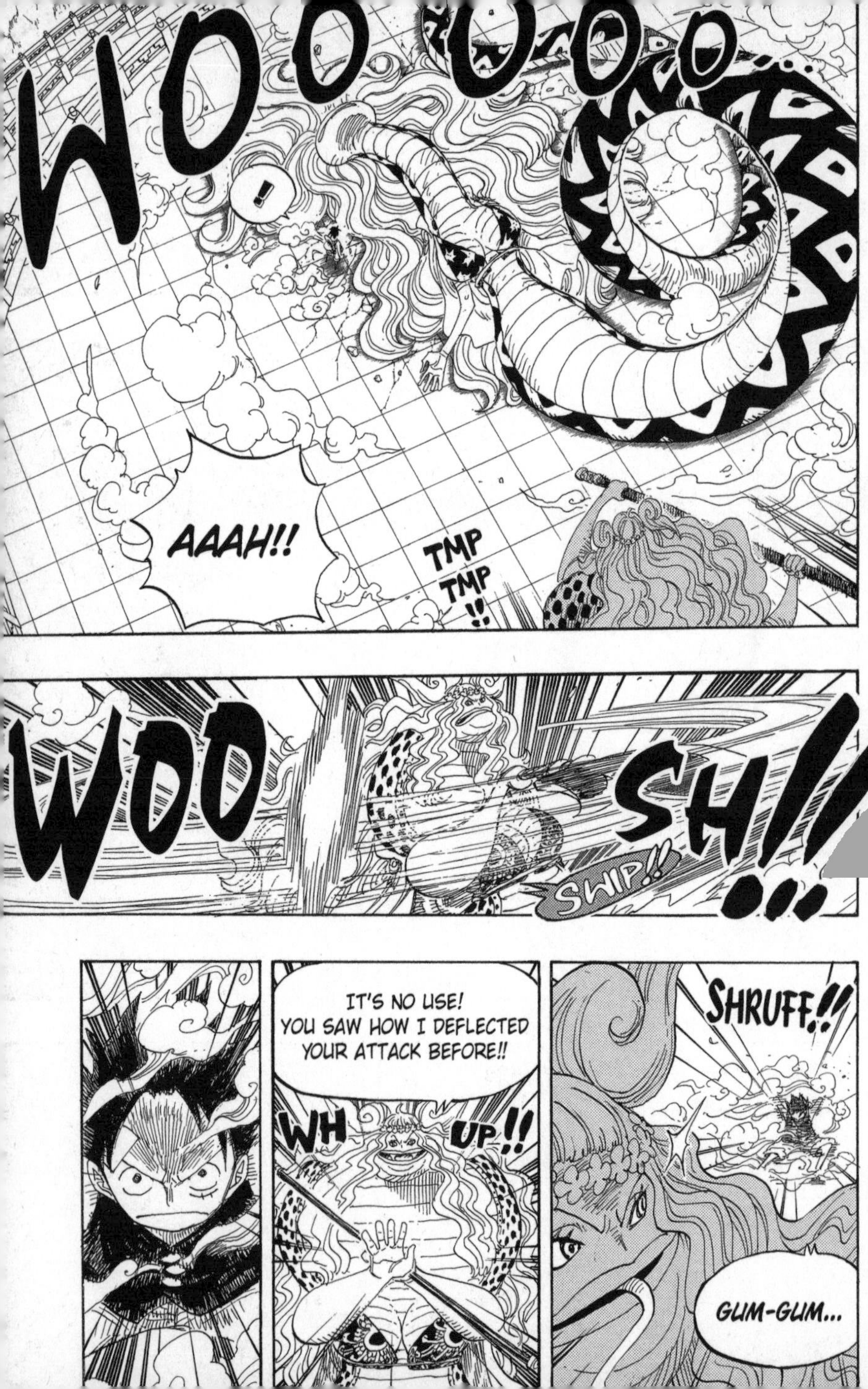
WOOOOOO...
AAAH!!
TMP TMP!!
WOOSH!!
SWIP!!
SHRUFF!!
GUM-GUM...
IT'S NO USE! YOU SAW HOW I DEFLECTED YOUR ATTACK BEFORE!!
WHUP!!

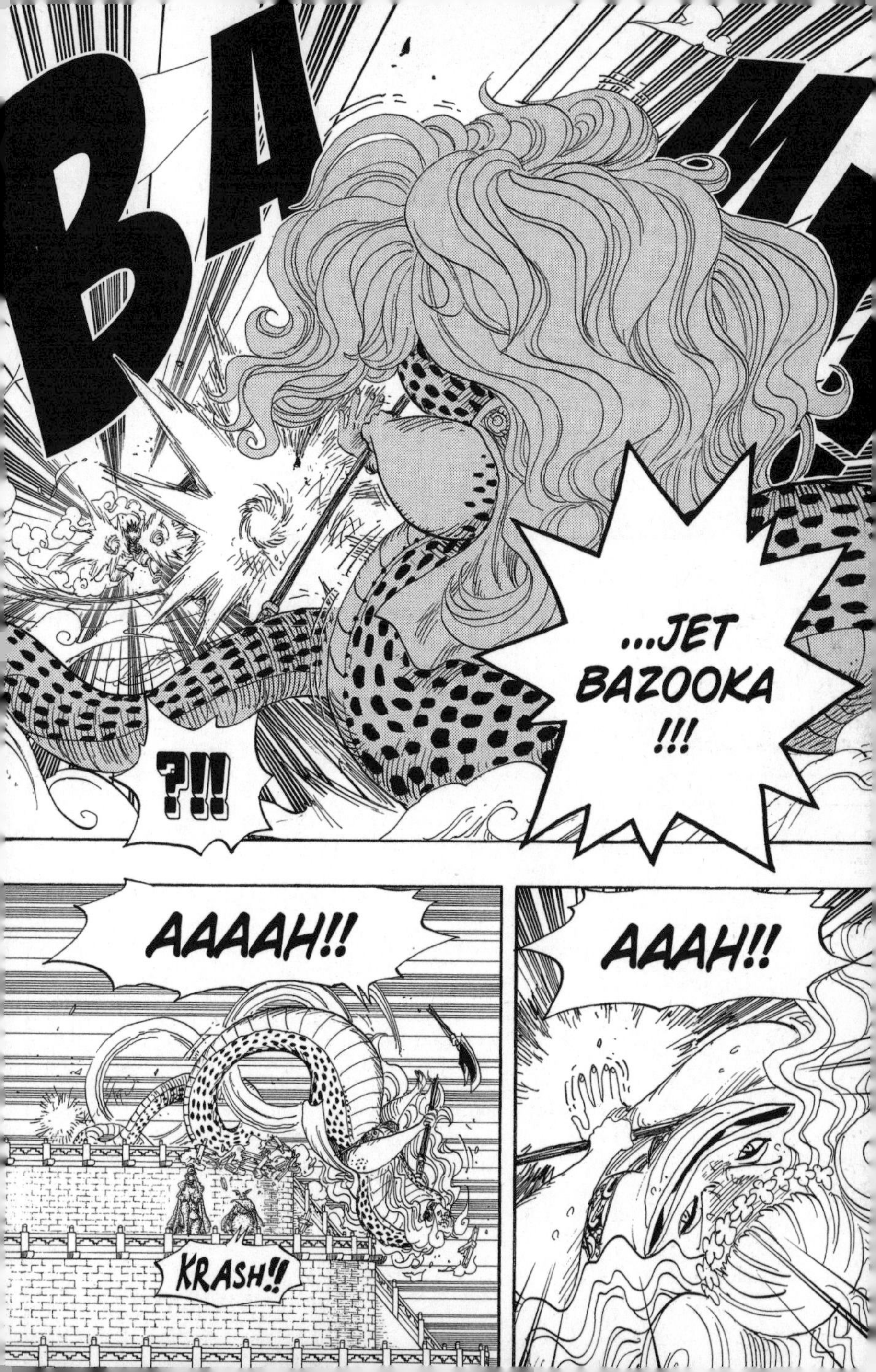
BAM
...JET BAZOOKA !!!
?!!
AAAH!!
AAAAH!!
KRASH!!

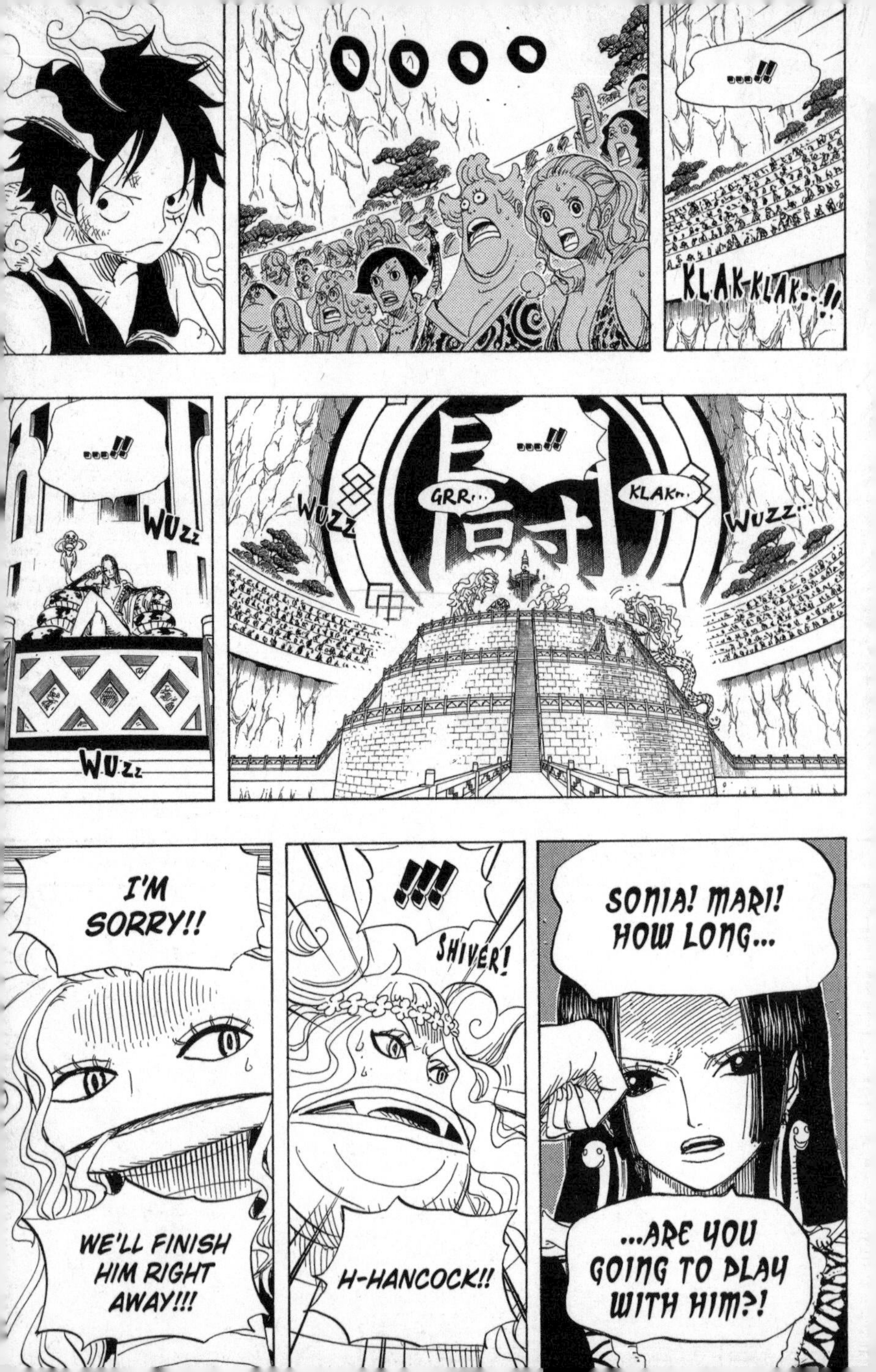
...!!
KLAK-KLAK...!!
...!!
GRR...
KLAK...
WUZZ
WUZZ...
...!!
WUZZ
WUZZ
SONIA! MARI! HOW LONG...
...ARE YOU GOING TO PLAY WITH HIM?!
!!!
SHIVER!
H-HANCOCK!!
I'M SORRY!!
WE'LL FINISH HIM RIGHT AWAY!!!

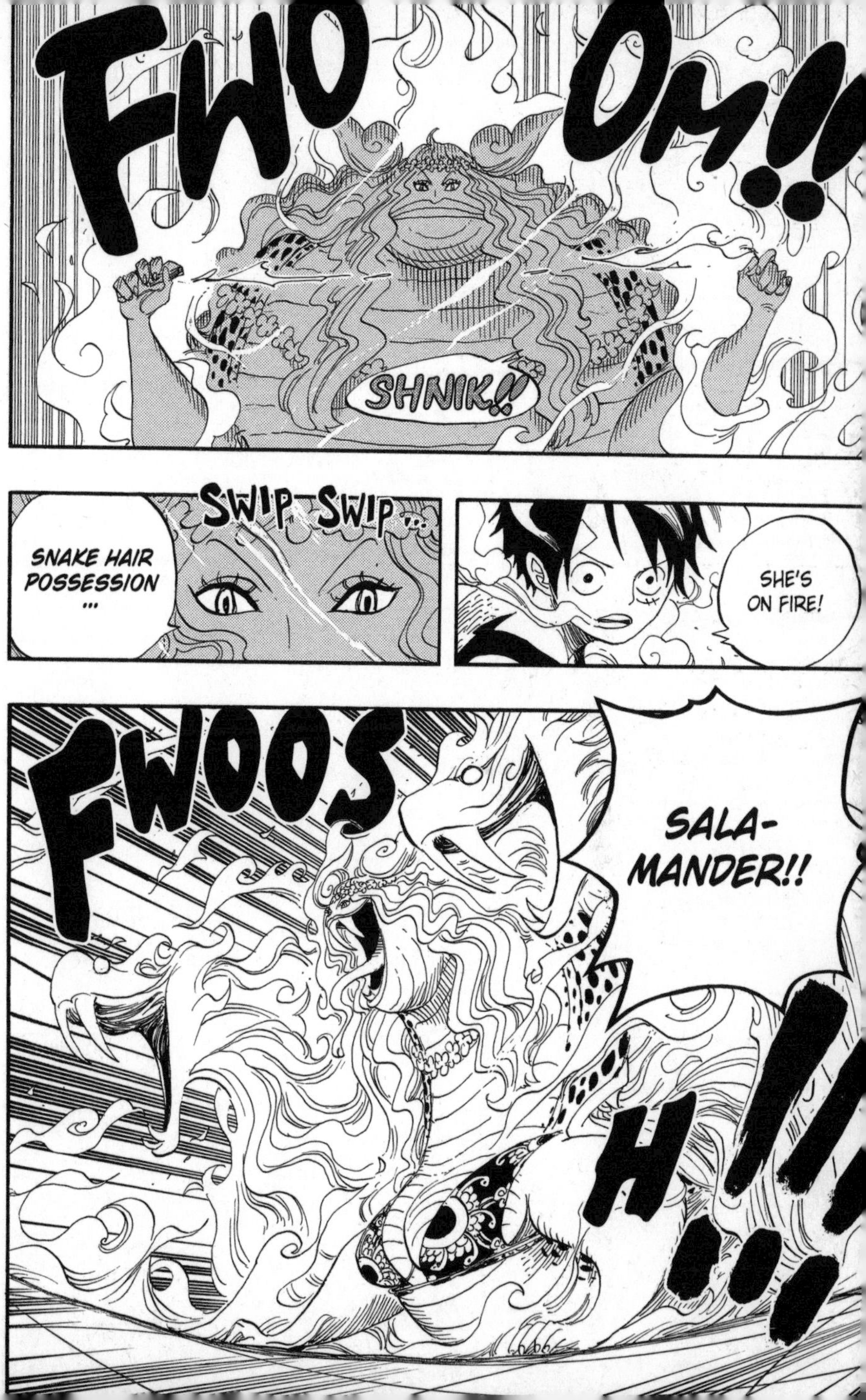
FWOOM!!!
SHNIK!!
SHE'S ON FIRE!
SWIP SWIP...
SNAKE HAIR POSSESSION ...
SALA-MANDER!!
FWOOSH!!!

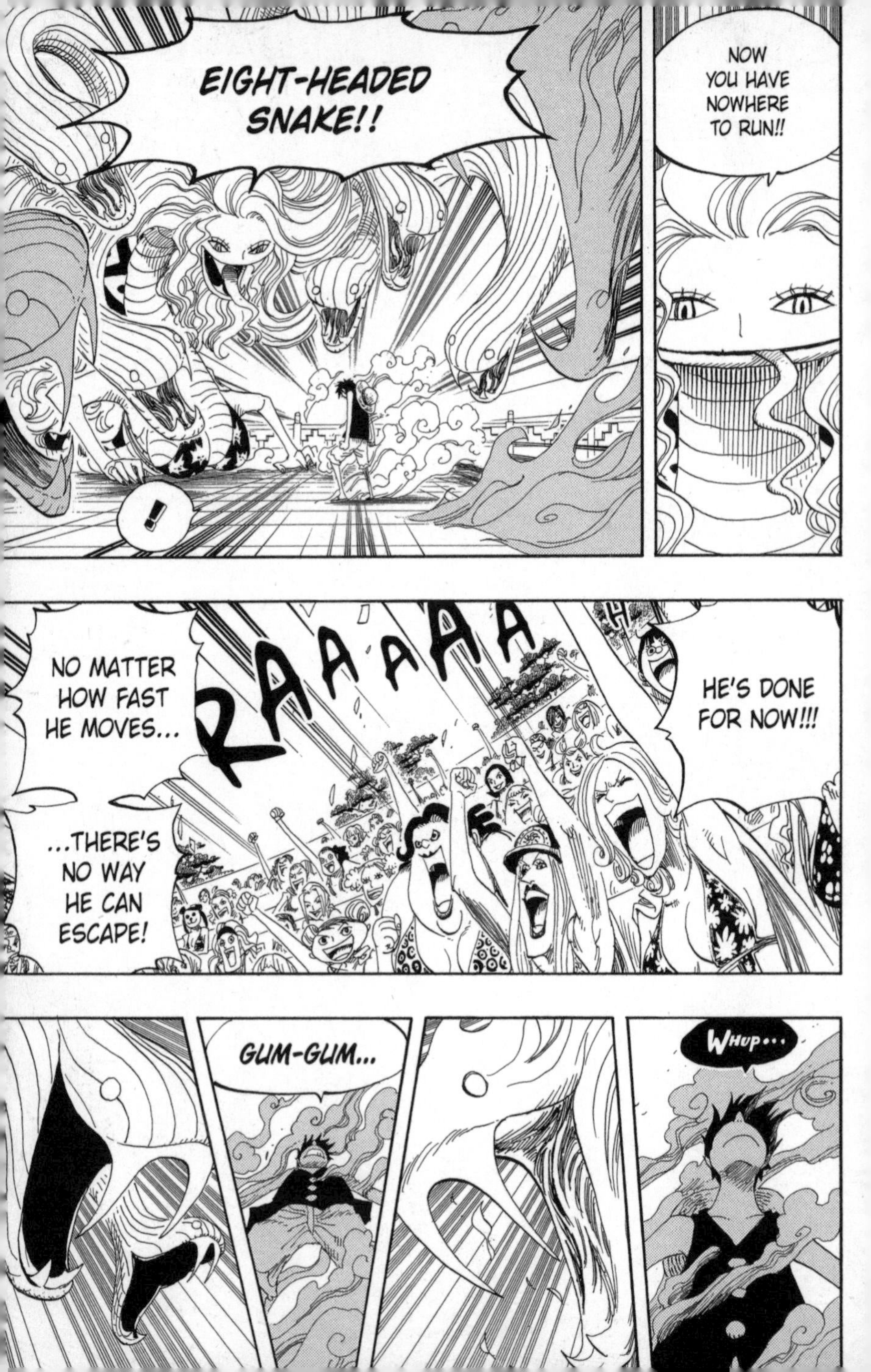
NOW YOU HAVE NOWHERE TO RUN!!
EIGHT-HEADED SNAKE!!
!
HE'S DONE FOR NOW!!!
RAAAAA
NO MATTER HOW FAST HE MOVES...
...THERE'S NO WAY HE CAN ESCAPE!
WHUP...
GUM-GUM...

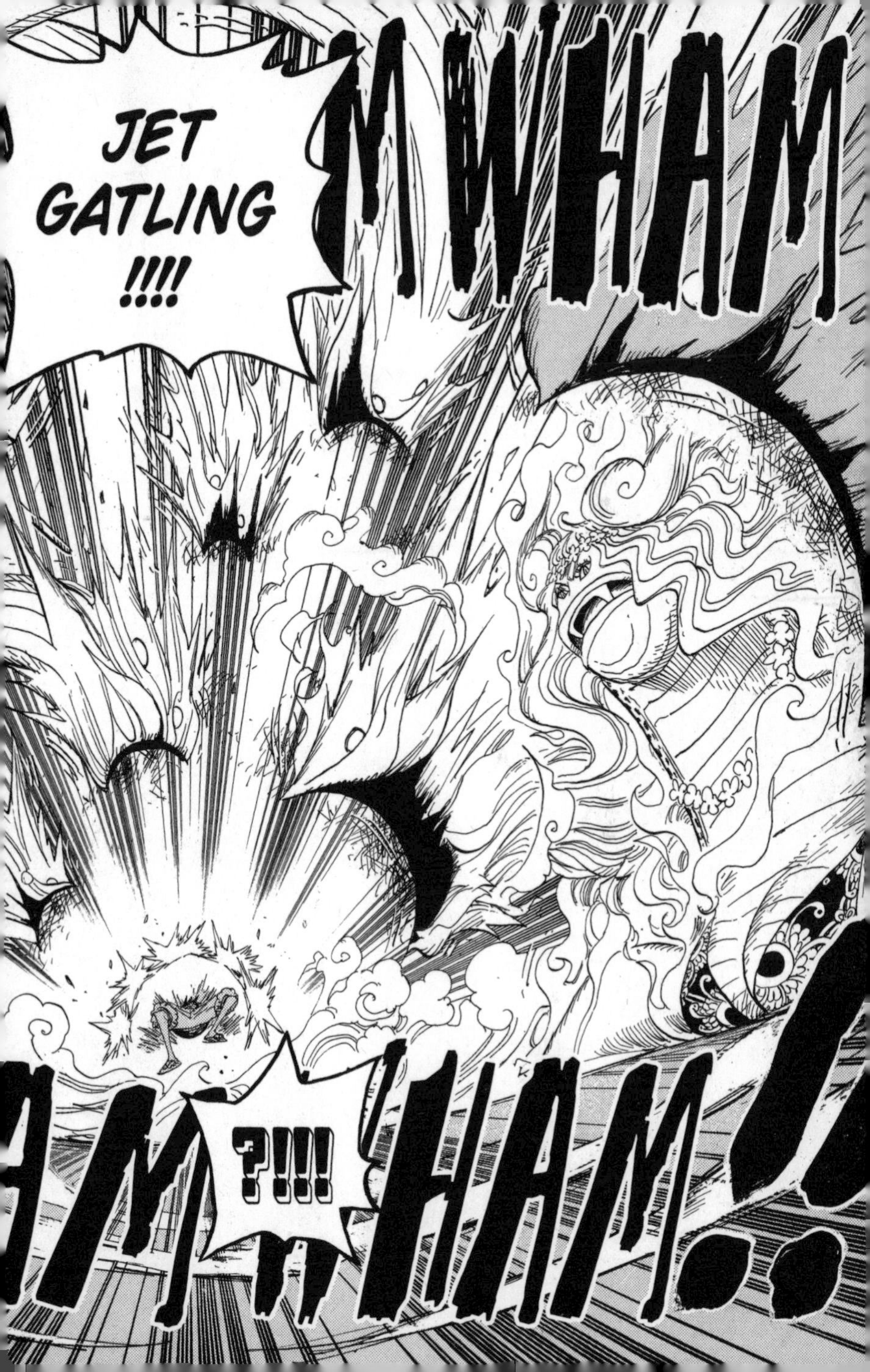
WHAM
JET GATLING !!!!
HAM!!
?!!!
AM!!

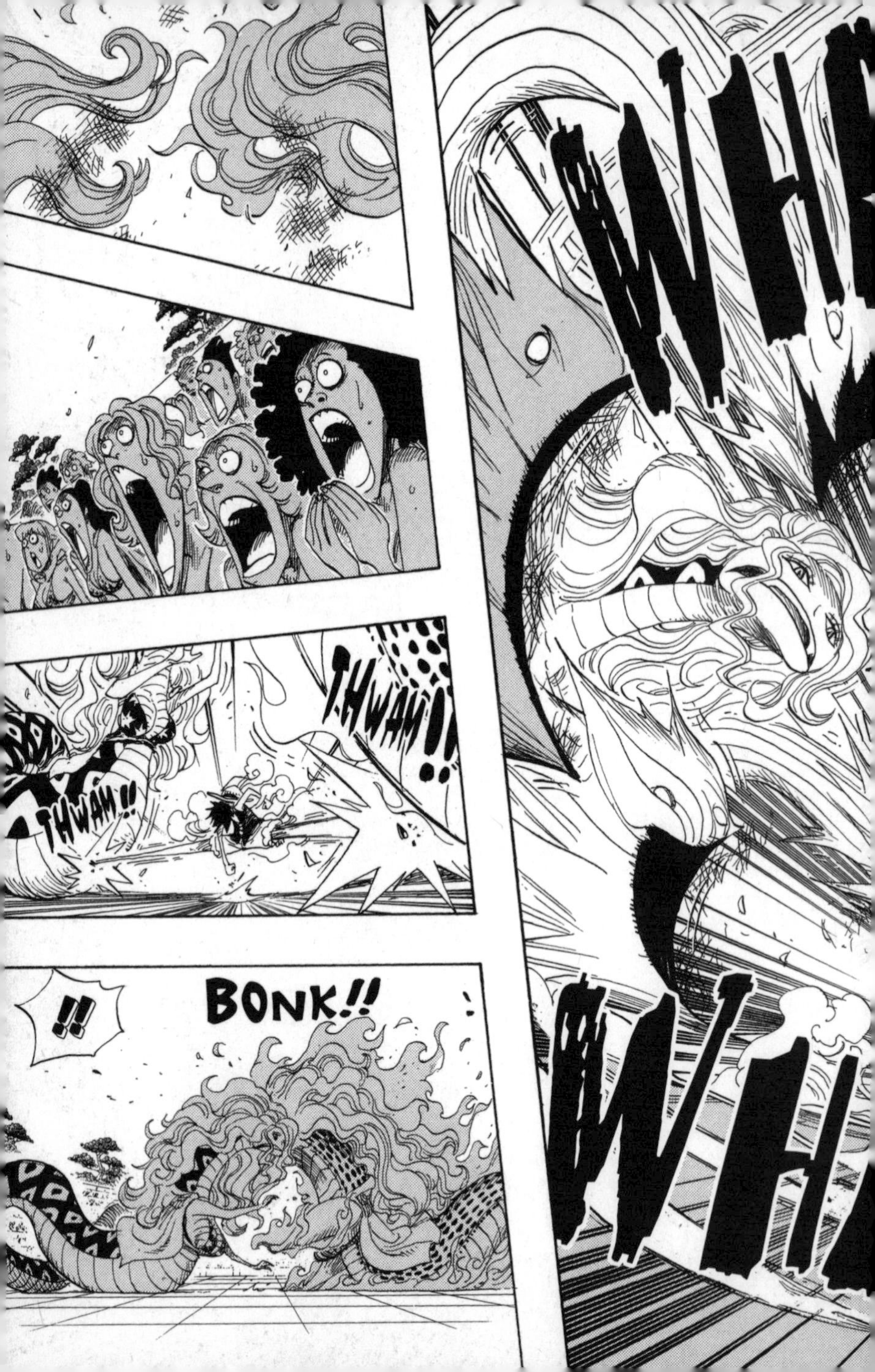
THWAM!!
THWAM!!
!!
BONK!!

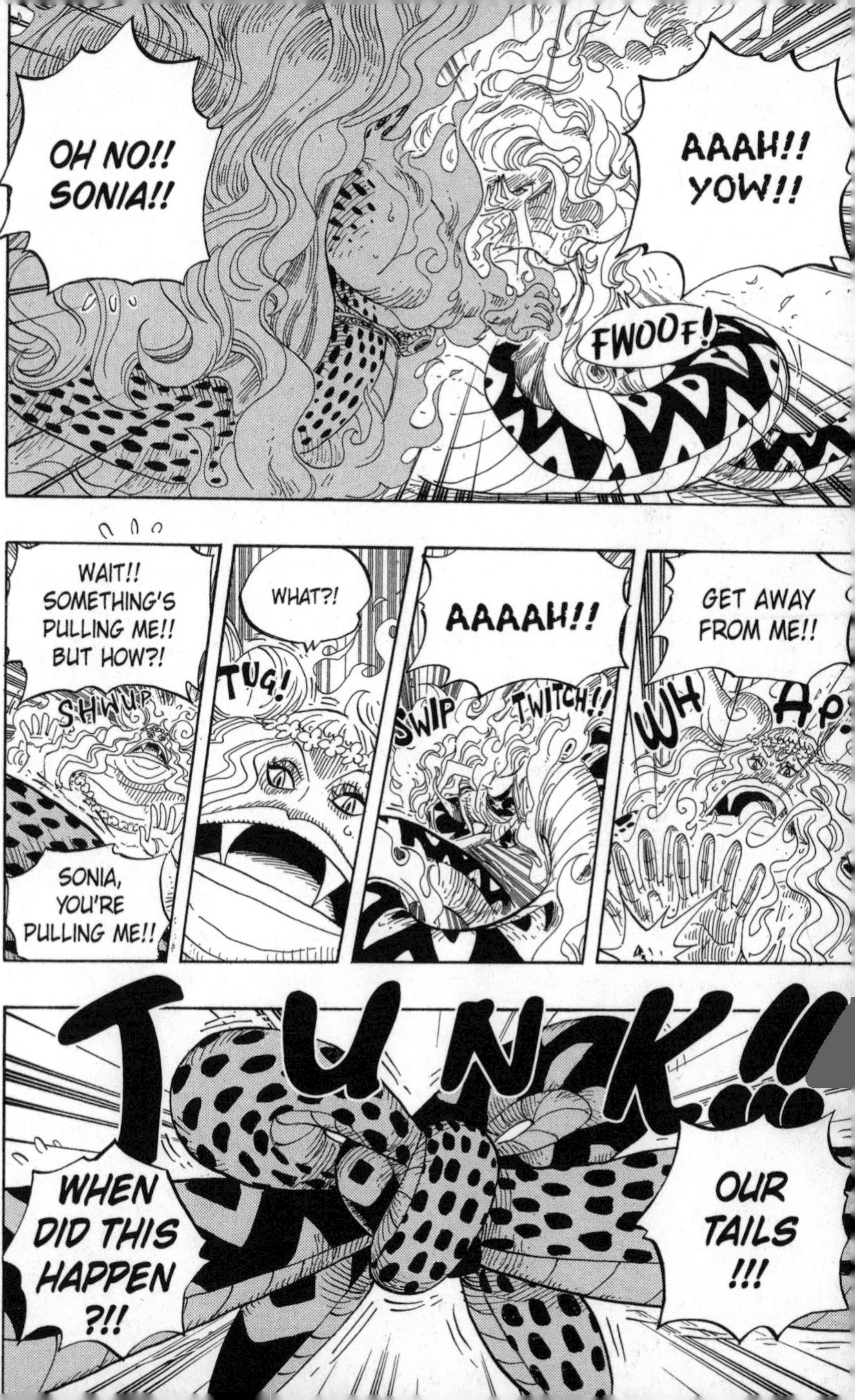
AAAH!! YOW!!
FWOOF!
OH NO!! SONIA!!
GET AWAY FROM ME!!
WHAP!
AAAAH!!
TWITCH!!
SWIP
WHAT?!
TUG!
WAIT!! SOMETHING'S PULLING ME!! BUT HOW?!
SHWUP
SONIA, YOU'RE PULLING ME!!
TUNK!!
OUR TAILS!!!
WHEN DID THIS HAPPEN?!!

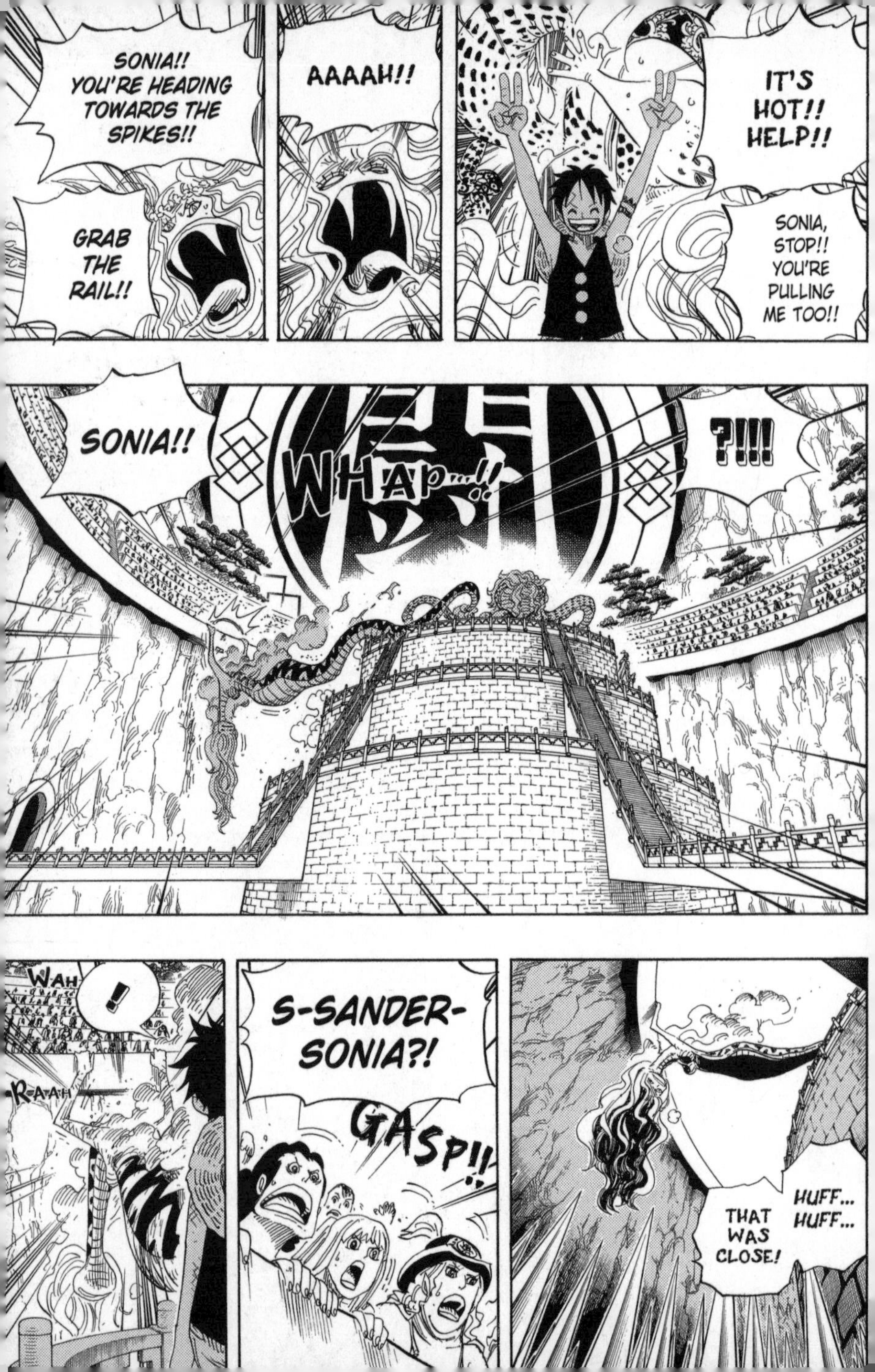
IT'S HOT!! HELP!!
SONIA, STOP!! YOU'RE PULLING ME TOO!!
AAAAH!!
SONIA!! YOU'RE HEADING TOWARDS THE SPIKES!!
GRAB THE RAIL!!
?!!!
SONIA!!
WHAP...!!
HUFF... HUFF...
THAT WAS CLOSE!
S-SANDER-SONIA?!
GASP!!
!
WAH
RAAH

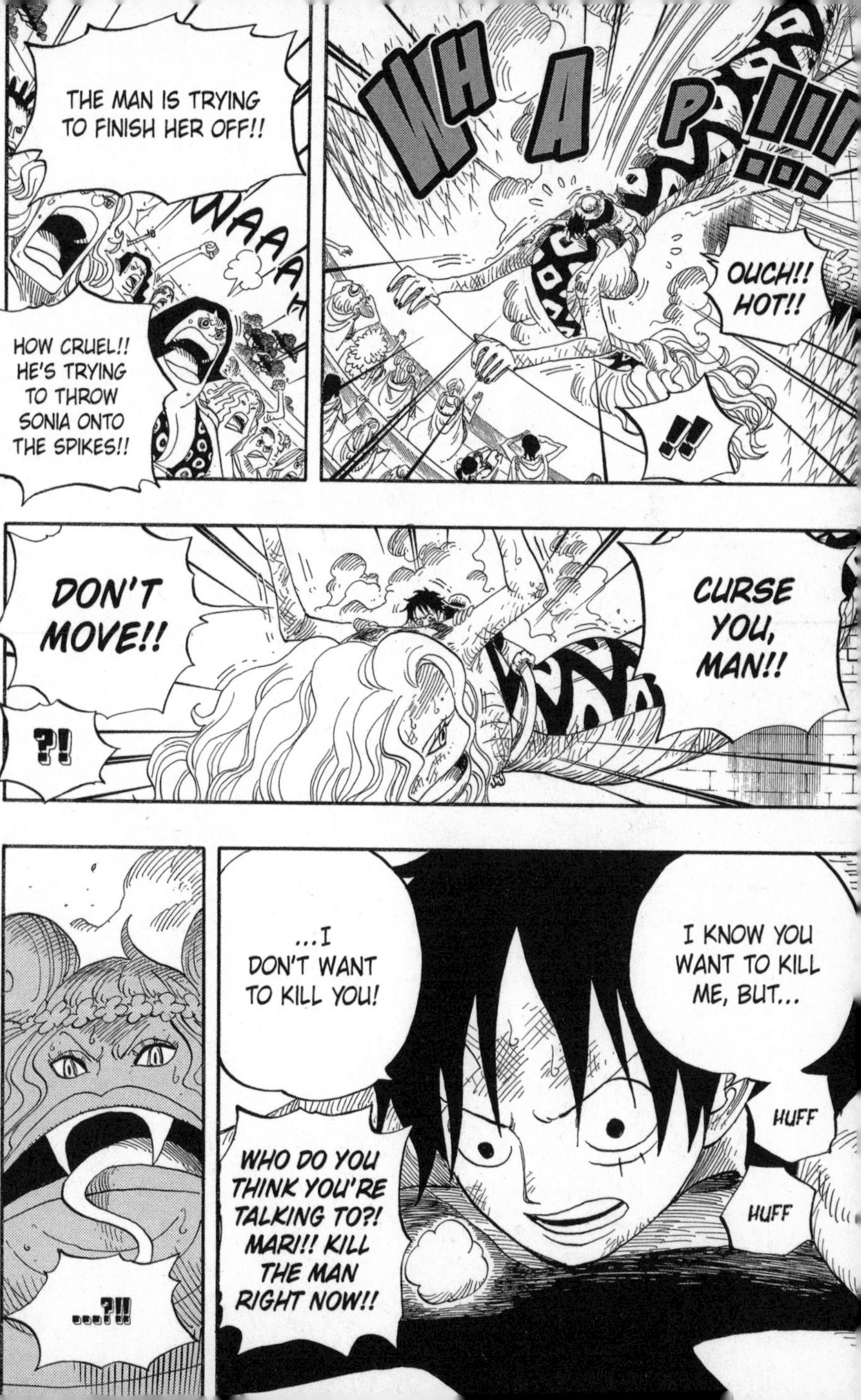
WHAP!!!
OUCH!! HOT!!
!!
THE MAN IS TRYING TO FINISH HER OFF!!
WAAAAH
HOW CRUEL!! HE'S TRYING TO THROW SONIA ONTO THE SPIKES!!
CURSE YOU, MAN!!
DON'T MOVE!!
?!
I KNOW YOU WANT TO KILL ME, BUT...
...I DON'T WANT TO KILL YOU!
HUFF
HUFF
WHO DO YOU THINK YOU'RE TALKING TO?! MARI!! KILL THE MAN RIGHT NOW!!
...?!!

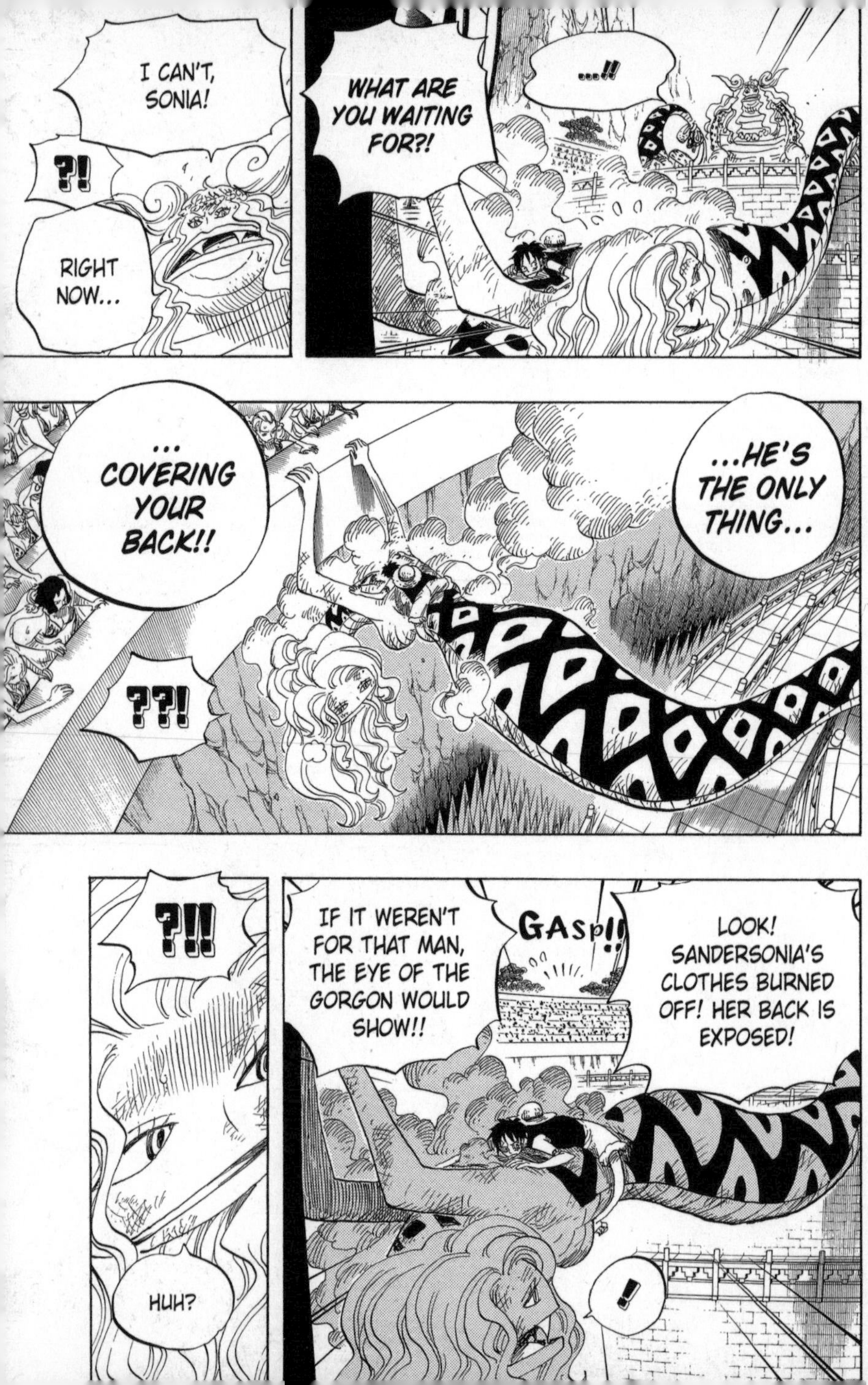
...!!
WHAT ARE YOU WAITING FOR?!
I CAN'T, SONIA!
?!
RIGHT NOW...
...HE'S THE ONLY THING...
...COVERING YOUR BACK!!
??!
LOOK! SANDERSONIA'S CLOTHES BURNED OFF! HER BACK IS EXPOSED!
GASp!!
IF IT WEREN'T FOR THAT MAN, THE EYE OF THE GORGON WOULD SHOW!!
!
?!!
HUH?

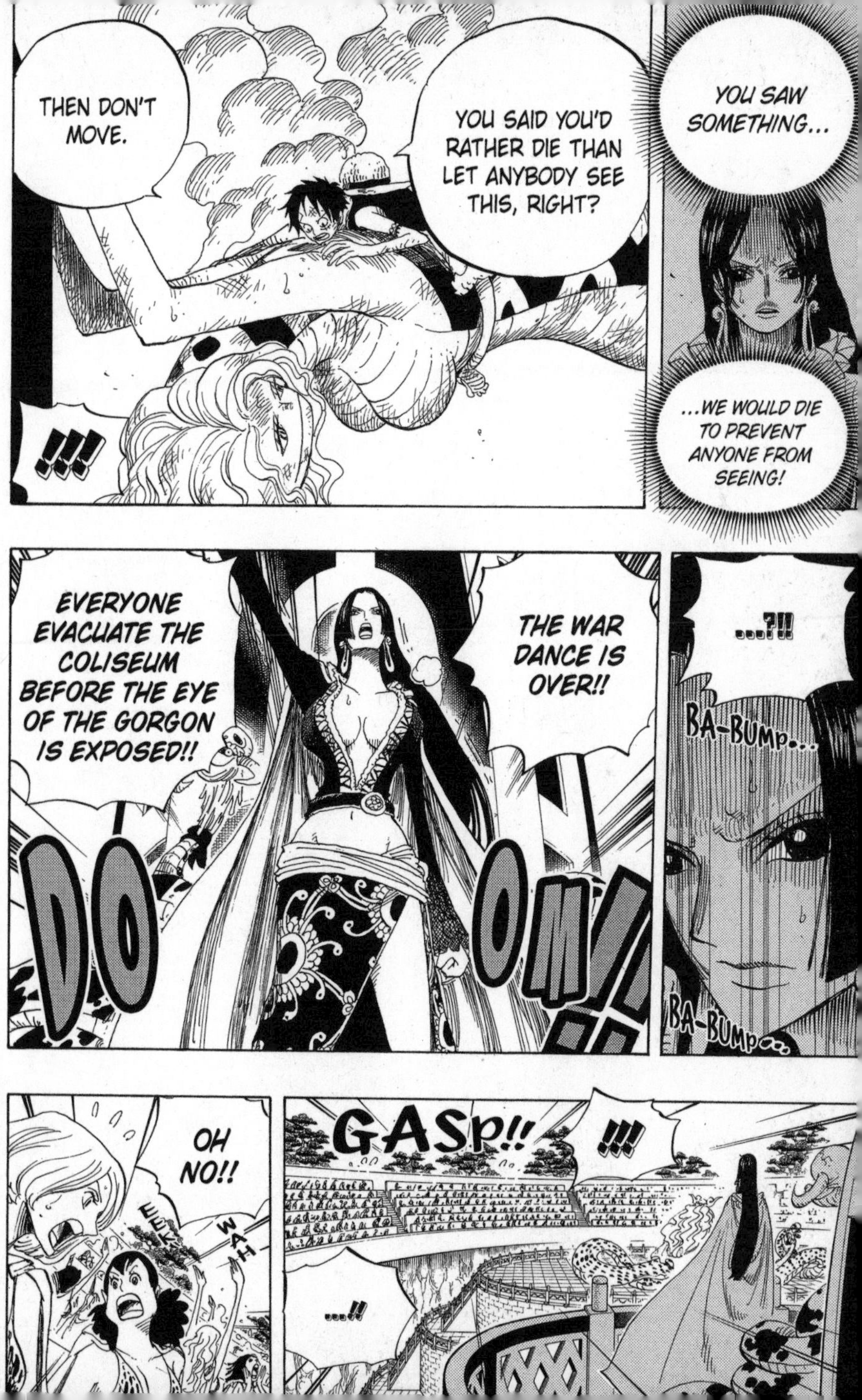
YOU SAW SOMETHING...
...WE WOULD DIE TO PREVENT ANYONE FROM SEEING!
YOU SAID YOU'D RATHER DIE THAN LET ANYBODY SEE THIS, RIGHT?
THEN DON'T MOVE.
!!!
...?!!
BA-BUMP...
BA-BUMP...
THE WAR DANCE IS OVER!!
EVERYONE EVACUATE THE COLISEUM BEFORE THE EYE OF THE GORGON IS EXPOSED!!
DOOM
!!!
GASP!!
...!!
OH NO!!
EEEK
WAH

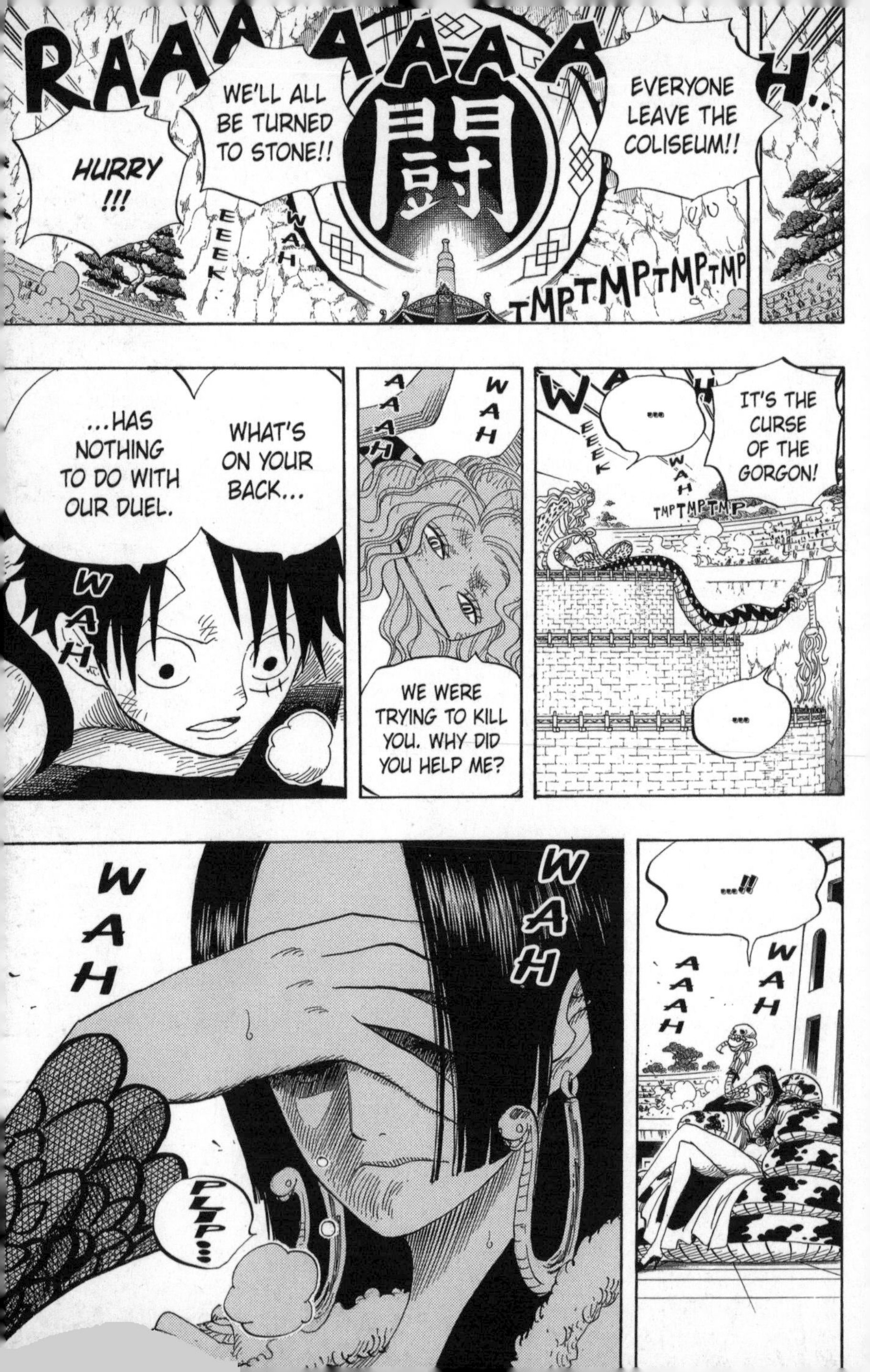
RAAAAAAAH..
闘
EVERYONE LEAVE THE COLISEUM!!
WE'LL ALL BE TURNED TO STONE!!
HURRY !!!
EEEEK
WAH
TMPTMPTMPTMP
WAAAH
...
IT'S THE CURSE OF THE GORGON!
EEEEK
WAH
TMPTMPTMP
...
WAH
AAAAH
WE WERE TRYING TO KILL YOU. WHY DID YOU HELP ME?
WHAT'S ON YOUR BACK...
...HAS NOTHING TO DO WITH OUR DUEL.
WAH
...!!
WAH
AAAAH
WAH
WAH
FLIP...

SBS Question Corner

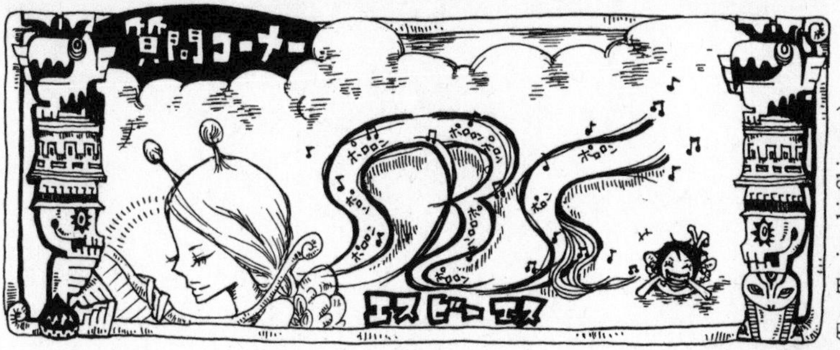
SBS

(Ena Taniguchi, Shimane)

Q: In chapter 519 of *One Piece*, you added tone to the title page, right? You painted one title page black too. After looking at the chapter number, I understood why. 519 is the final chapter of *Dragon Ball* by Akira Toriyama, an author you respect. In other words, that was your way of saying you'd caught up.

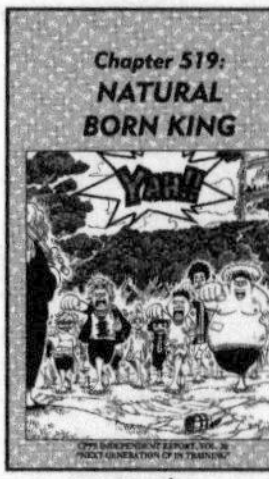
Chapter 519:
NATURAL BORN KING
YAH!!

A: Wow, you figured it out. You're exactly right. Well, it's more like a milestone for me than a message.
By the way, *Dragon Ball* only has 42 volumes out, so some people already think I'm way beyond that. But *Dragon Ball* started off as a humorous comic and only had 15 pages per chapter, while One Piece was a story comic with 19 pages per chapter. So even though we were both in serialization for 12 years, I did 53 volumes. I'm sorry I made you spend so much extra money. I want to wrap up One Piece soon, but I don't want to abandon the story until I've tied up the loose ends. So please be patient with me because I won't stop until I wrap everything up.

Q: Hello, Oda Sensei. CP9 is extremely popular at my school. There are Finger Pistol battles every single day, so our bodies are riddled with holes. By the way, I heard you're the legendary Seven Powers user who surpasses even the Six Powers. What's the last move? Please tell me.

--CP608

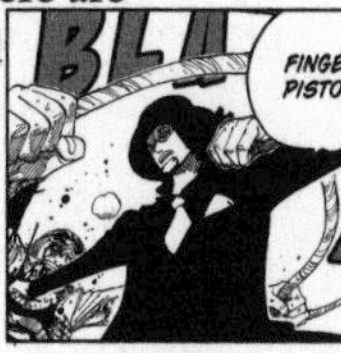
FINGER PISTOL.

A: You figured out my secret. Yes, that's right. I'm the legendary Seven Powers user. Six Powers means that you can use Finger Pistol, Moon Walk, Iron Body, Shave, Paper Art, and, uh... Tempest Kick! But there's one more special move that only I can use, and that's the Bother! When people are having a really serious fight, I get in between them and shout "Bother!" This gets really annoying really fast. So you got a problem with that?!

Q: Mr. Oda, if you were to take a trip, where would you go? ***Pop***!

--Junpei

A: !!... (See you in the next volume! Check out the special Question Corner section on page 188.)

Chapter 521:
HOOF OF THE CELESTIAL DRAGON

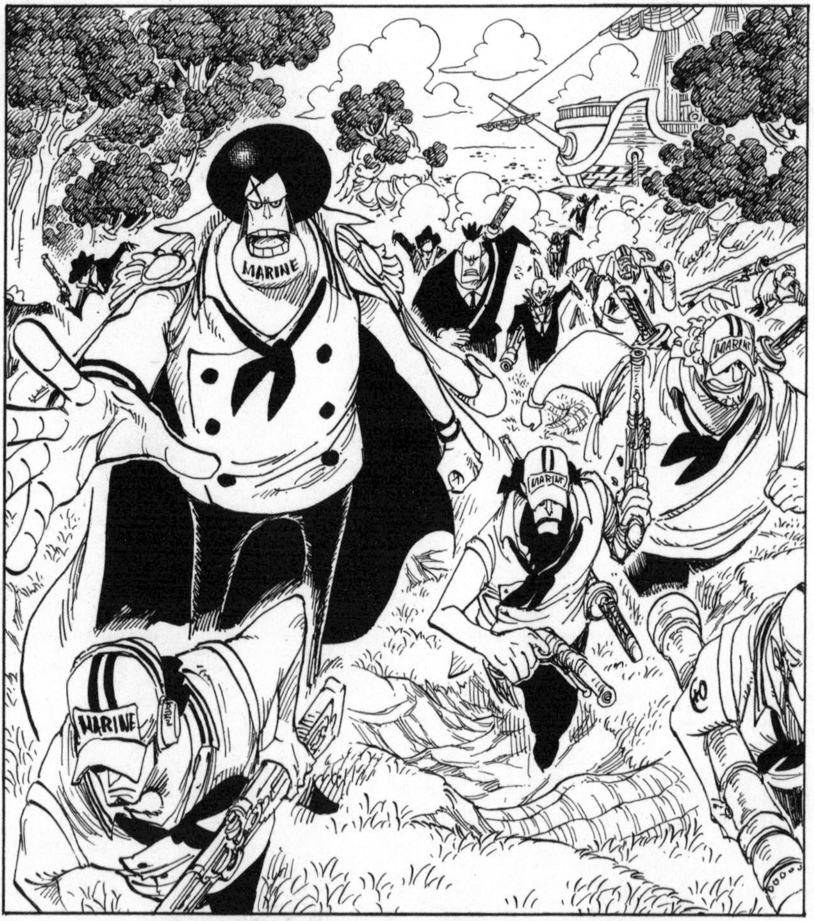
MARINE
MARINE
MARINE
MARINE

CP9'S INDEPENDENT REPORT, VOL. 27:
"PURSUERS ASHORE--CP9 CAPTURE MISSION"

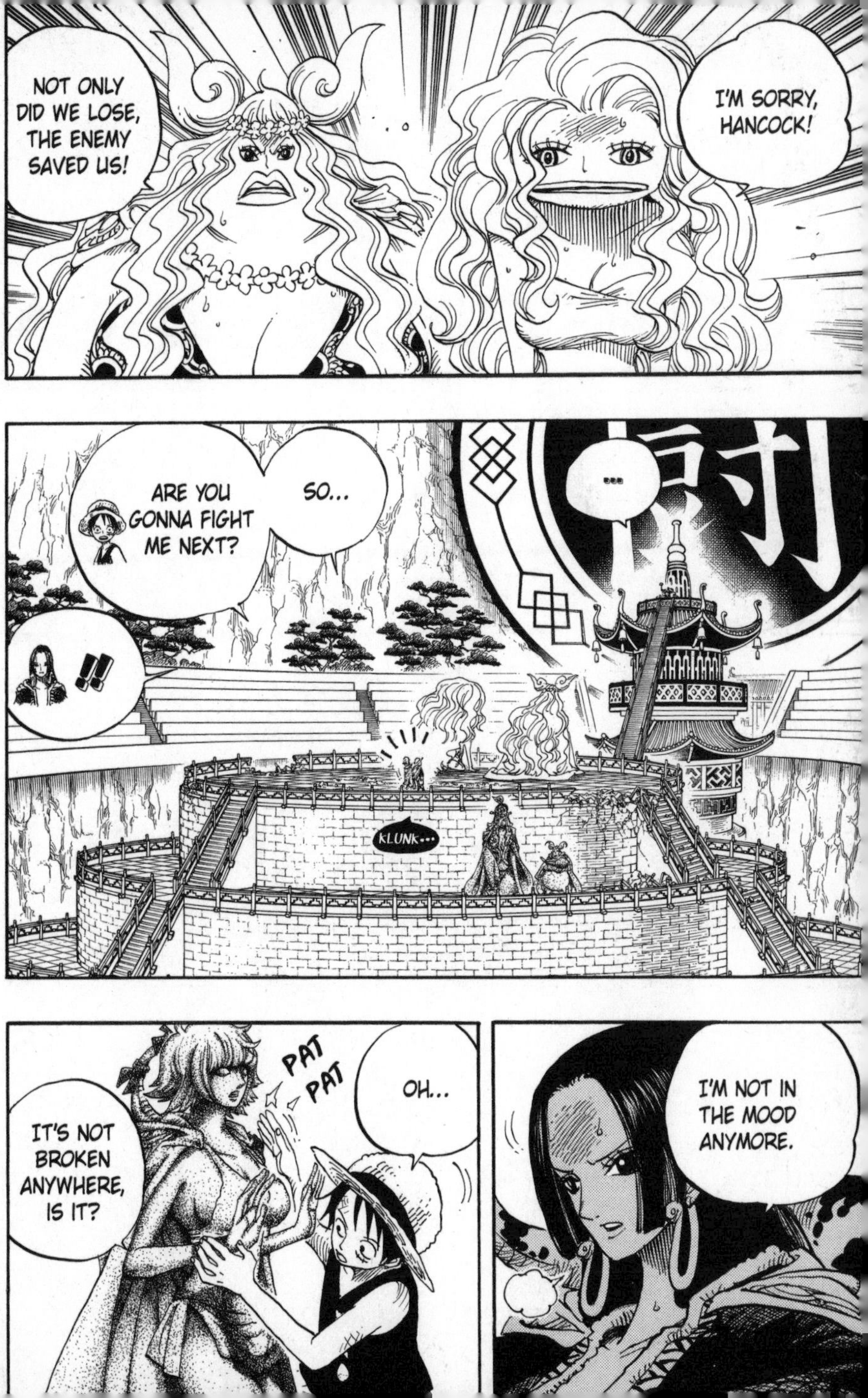
I'M SORRY, HANCOCK!
NOT ONLY DID WE LOSE, THE ENEMY SAVED US!
...
SO...
ARE YOU GONNA FIGHT ME NEXT?
!!
KLUNK...
I'M NOT IN THE MOOD ANYMORE.
OH...
PAT PAT
IT'S NOT BROKEN ANYWHERE, IS IT?

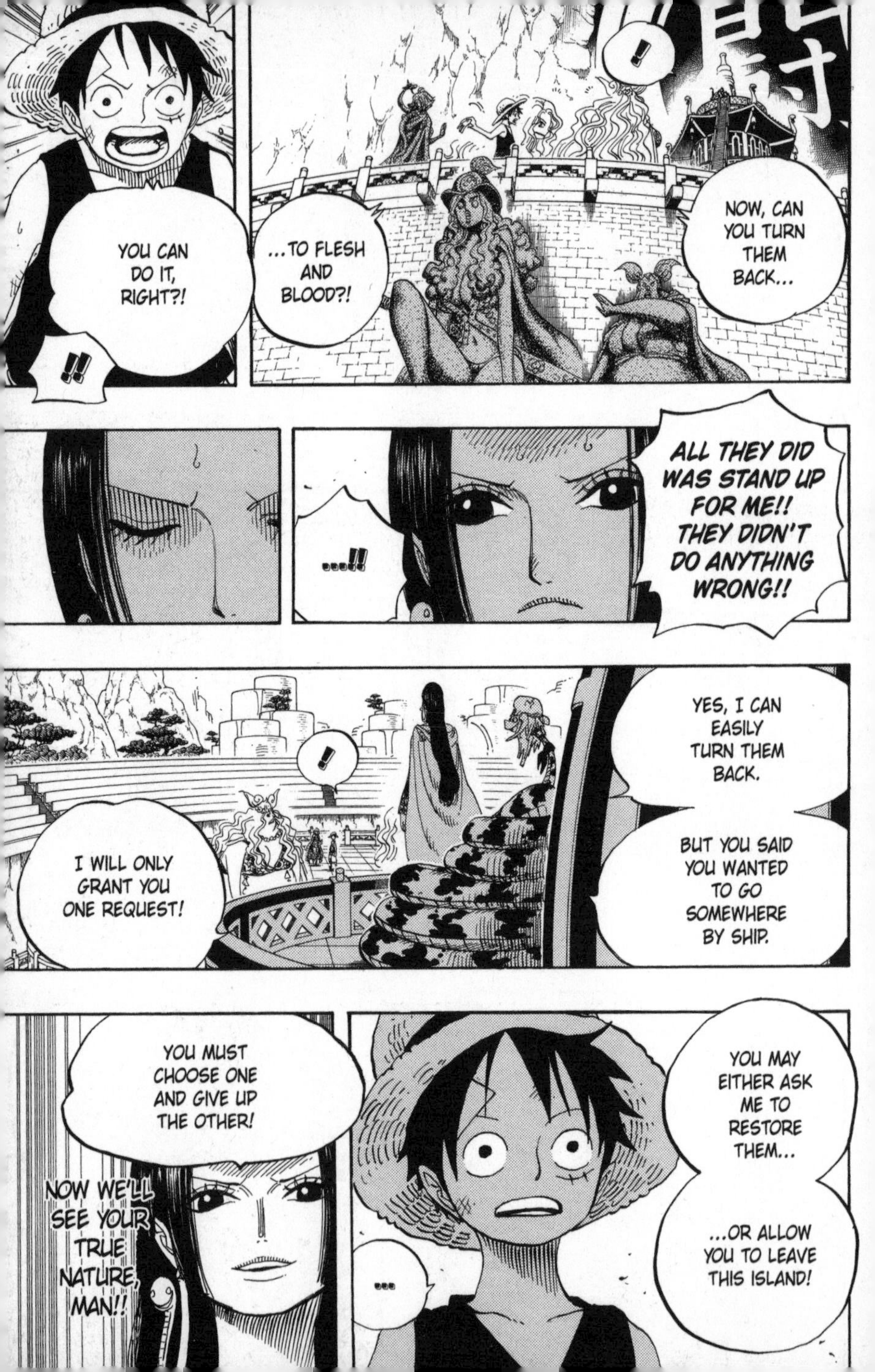
!
NOW, CAN YOU TURN THEM BACK...
...TO FLESH AND BLOOD?!
YOU CAN DO IT, RIGHT?!
!!
ALL THEY DID WAS STAND UP FOR ME!! THEY DIDN'T DO ANYTHING WRONG!!
...!!
YES, I CAN EASILY TURN THEM BACK.
BUT YOU SAID YOU WANTED TO GO SOMEWHERE BY SHIP.
!
I WILL ONLY GRANT YOU ONE REQUEST!
YOU MAY EITHER ASK ME TO RESTORE THEM...
...OR ALLOW YOU TO LEAVE THIS ISLAND!
...
YOU MUST CHOOSE ONE AND GIVE UP THE OTHER!
NOW WE'LL SEE YOUR TRUE NATURE, MAN!!

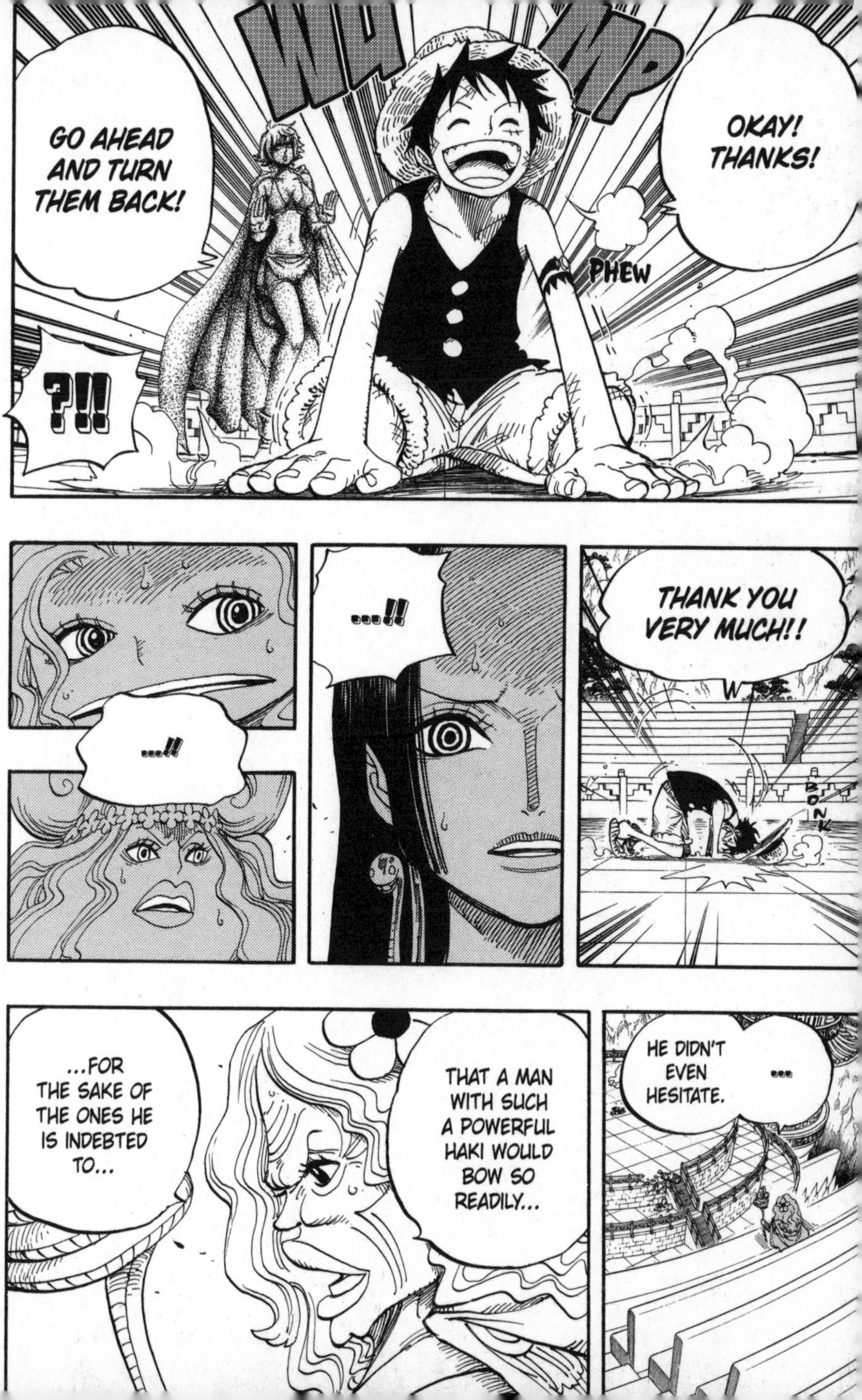
WHUMP
GO AHEAD AND TURN THEM BACK!
?!!
OKAY! THANKS!
PHEW
THANK YOU VERY MUCH!!
BONK
...!!
...!!
...
HE DIDN'T EVEN HESITATE.
THAT A MAN WITH SUCH A POWERFUL HAKI WOULD BOW SO READILY...
...FOR THE SAKE OF THE ONES HE IS INDEBTED TO...

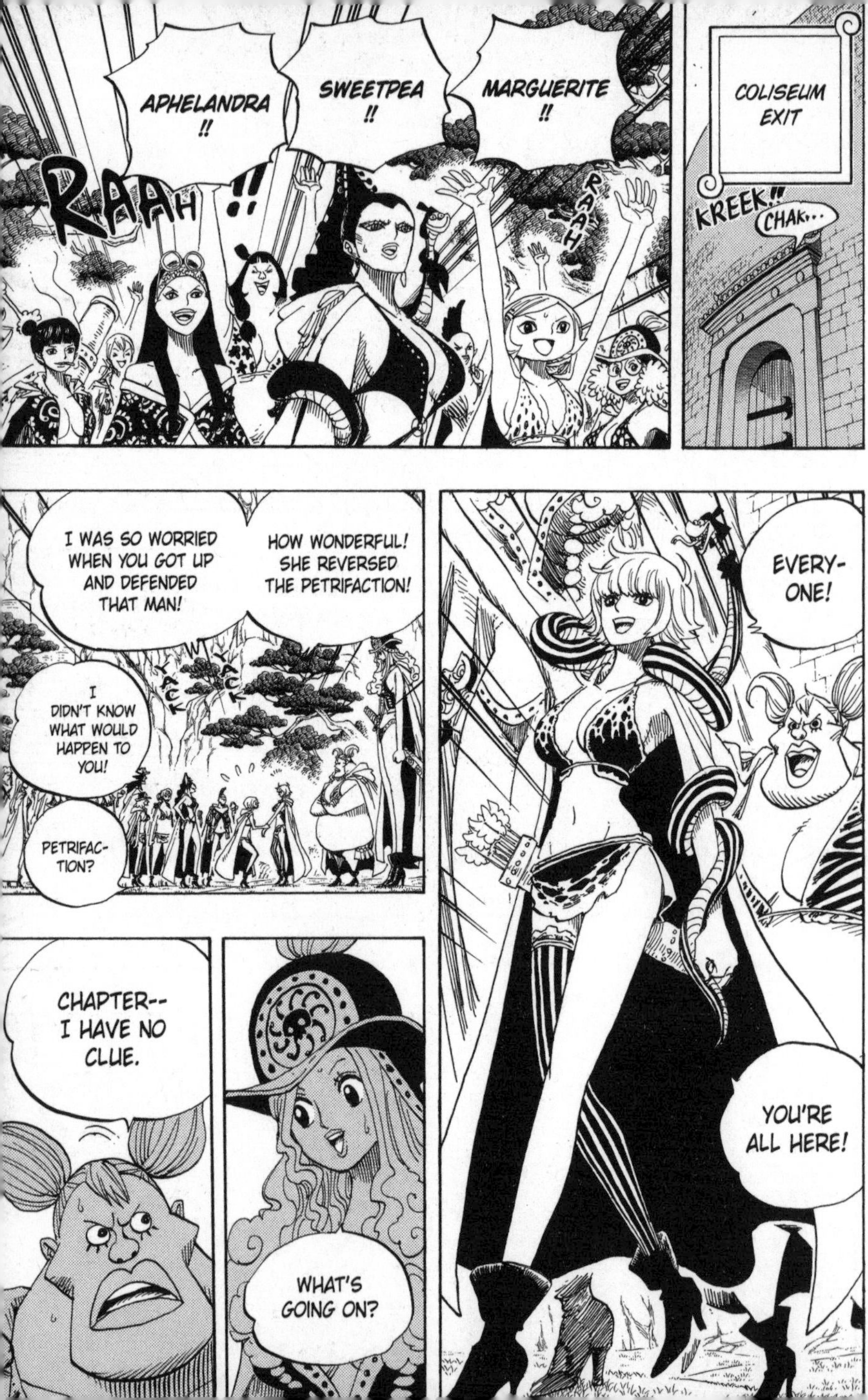
COLISEUM EXIT
KREEK!!
CHAK...
MARGUERITE !!
SWEETPEA !!
APHELANDRA !!
RAAAH !!
RAAAH
EVERY-ONE!
YOU'RE ALL HERE!
HOW WONDERFUL! SHE REVERSED THE PETRIFACTION!
I WAS SO WORRIED WHEN YOU GOT UP AND DEFENDED THAT MAN!
YACK YACK
I DIDN'T KNOW WHAT WOULD HAPPEN TO YOU!
PETRIFAC-TION?
WHAT'S GOING ON?
CHAPTER-- I HAVE NO CLUE.

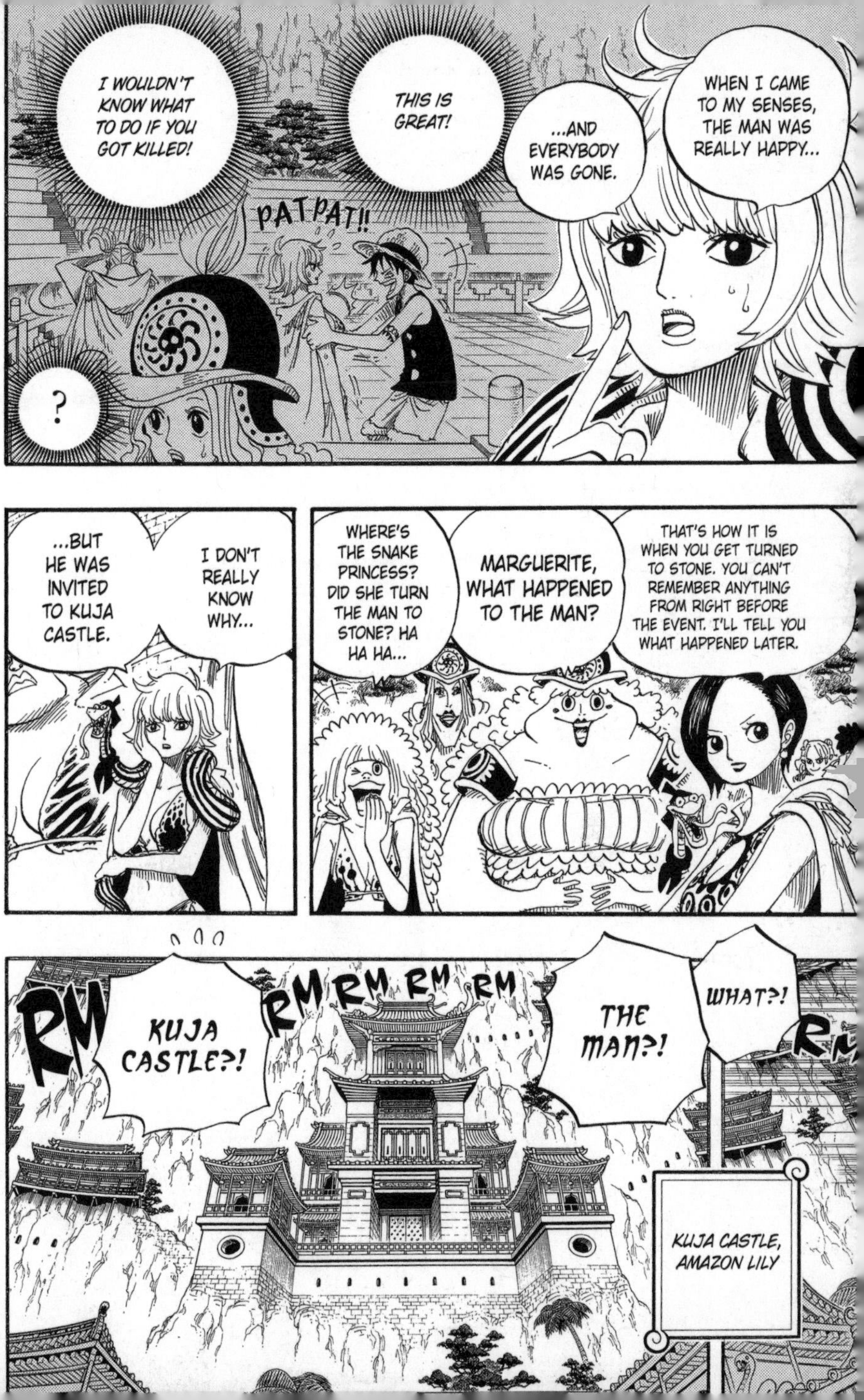
WHEN I CAME TO MY SENSES, THE MAN WAS REALLY HAPPY...
...AND EVERYBODY WAS GONE.
THIS IS GREAT!
PATPAT!!
I WOULDN'T KNOW WHAT TO DO IF YOU GOT KILLED!
?
THAT'S HOW IT IS WHEN YOU GET TURNED TO STONE. YOU CAN'T REMEMBER ANYTHING FROM RIGHT BEFORE THE EVENT. I'LL TELL YOU WHAT HAPPENED LATER.
MARGUERITE, WHAT HAPPENED TO THE MAN?
WHERE'S THE SNAKE PRINCESS? DID SHE TURN THE MAN TO STONE? HA HA HA...
I DON'T REALLY KNOW WHY...
...BUT HE WAS INVITED TO KUJA CASTLE.
WHAT?!
THE MAN?!
KUJA CASTLE?!
RM RM RM RM RM RM
KUJA CASTLE, AMAZON LILY

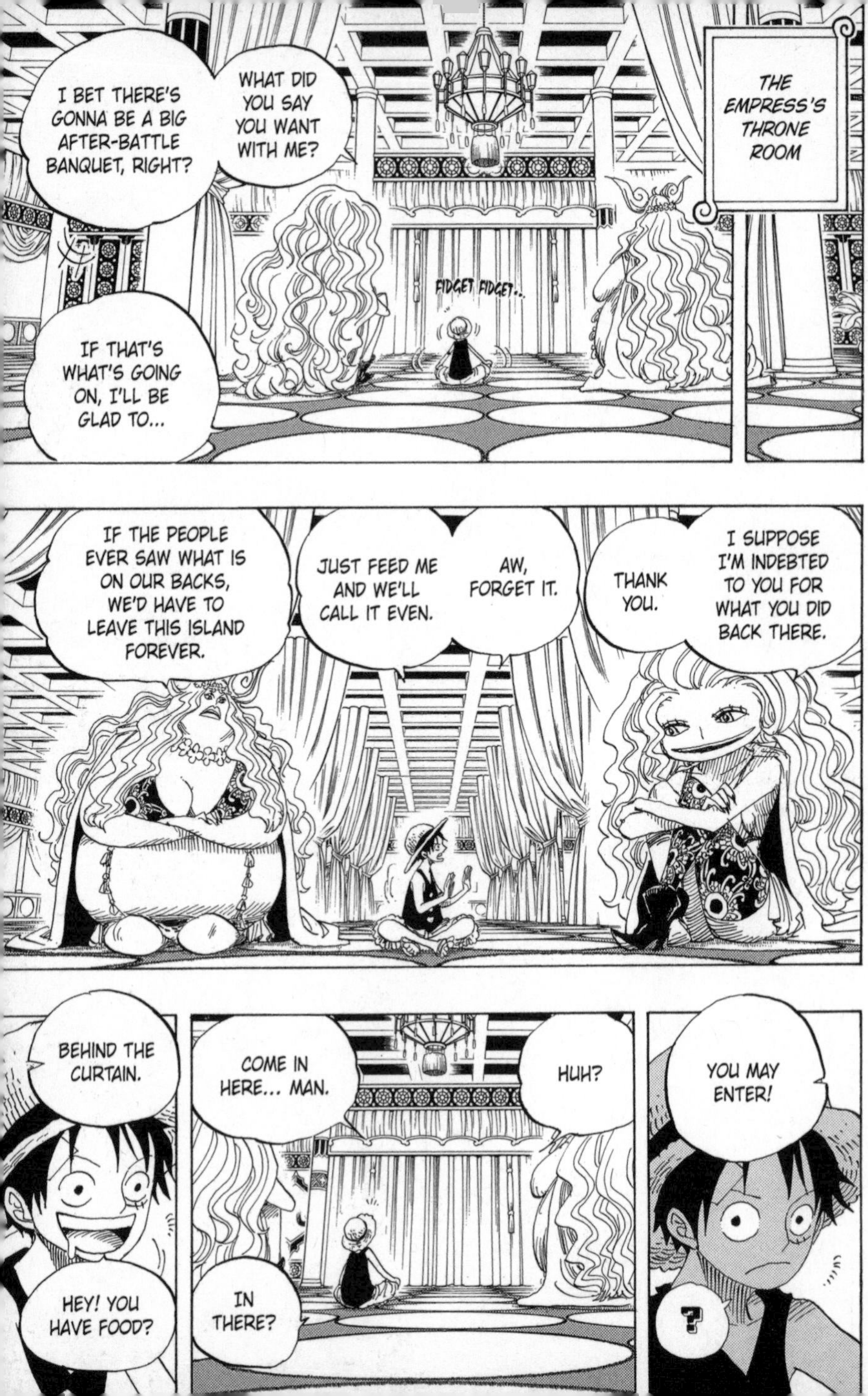
THE EMPRESS'S THRONE ROOM
WHAT DID YOU SAY YOU WANT WITH ME?
I BET THERE'S GONNA BE A BIG AFTER-BATTLE BANQUET, RIGHT?
FIDGET FIDGET...
IF THAT'S WHAT'S GOING ON, I'LL BE GLAD TO...
I SUPPOSE I'M INDEBTED TO YOU FOR WHAT YOU DID BACK THERE.
THANK YOU.
AW, FORGET IT.
JUST FEED ME AND WE'LL CALL IT EVEN.
IF THE PEOPLE EVER SAW WHAT IS ON OUR BACKS, WE'D HAVE TO LEAVE THIS ISLAND FOREVER.
YOU MAY ENTER!
?
HUH?
COME IN HERE... MAN.
IN THERE?
BEHIND THE CURTAIN.
HEY! YOU HAVE FOOD?

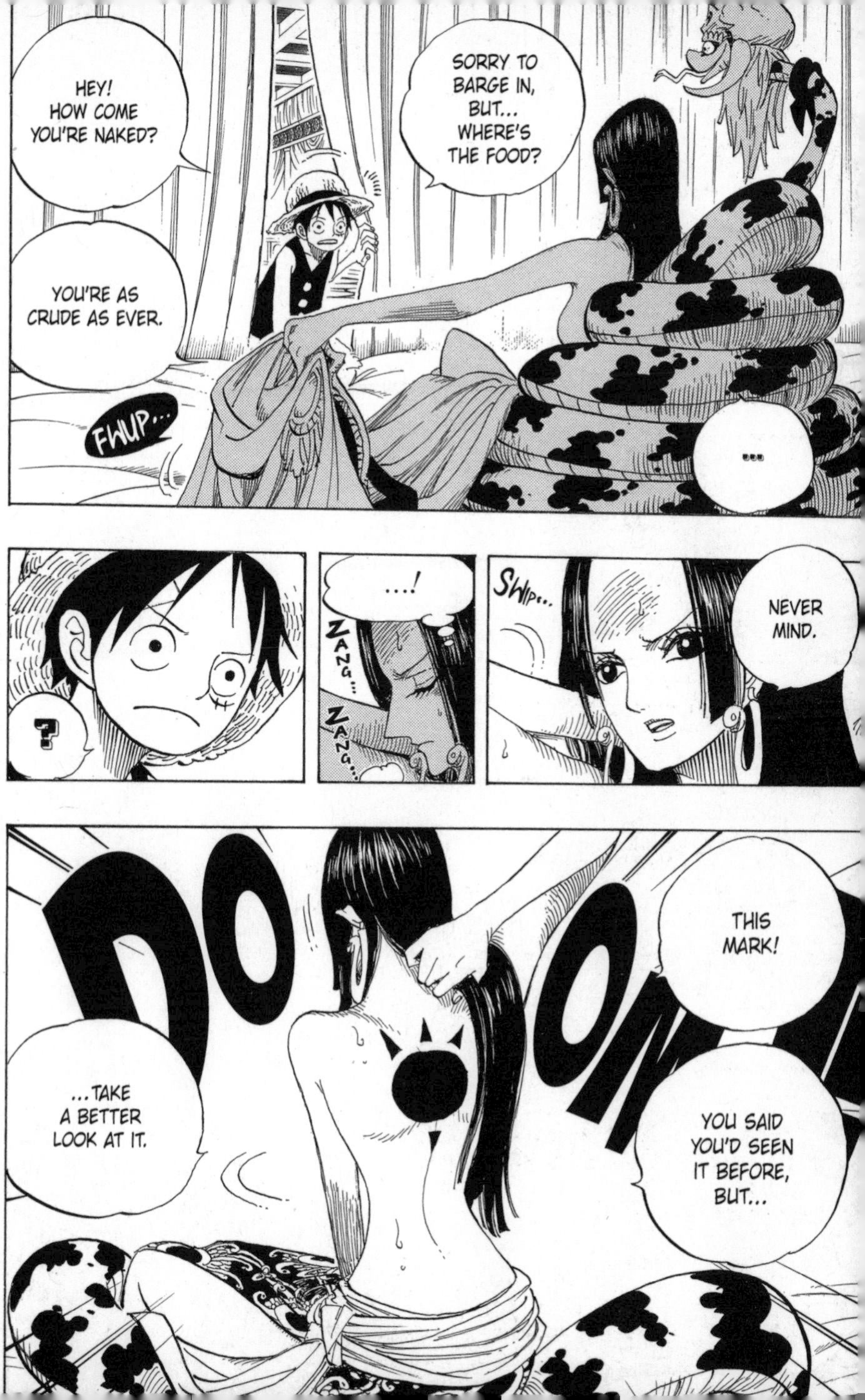

SORRY TO BARGE IN, BUT... WHERE'S THE FOOD?
HEY! HOW COME YOU'RE NAKED?
YOU'RE AS CRUDE AS EVER.
FWUP...
...
SWIP...
NEVER MIND.
...!
ZANG...
ZANG...
?
THIS MARK!
YOU SAID YOU'D SEEN IT BEFORE, BUT...
...TAKE A BETTER LOOK AT IT.

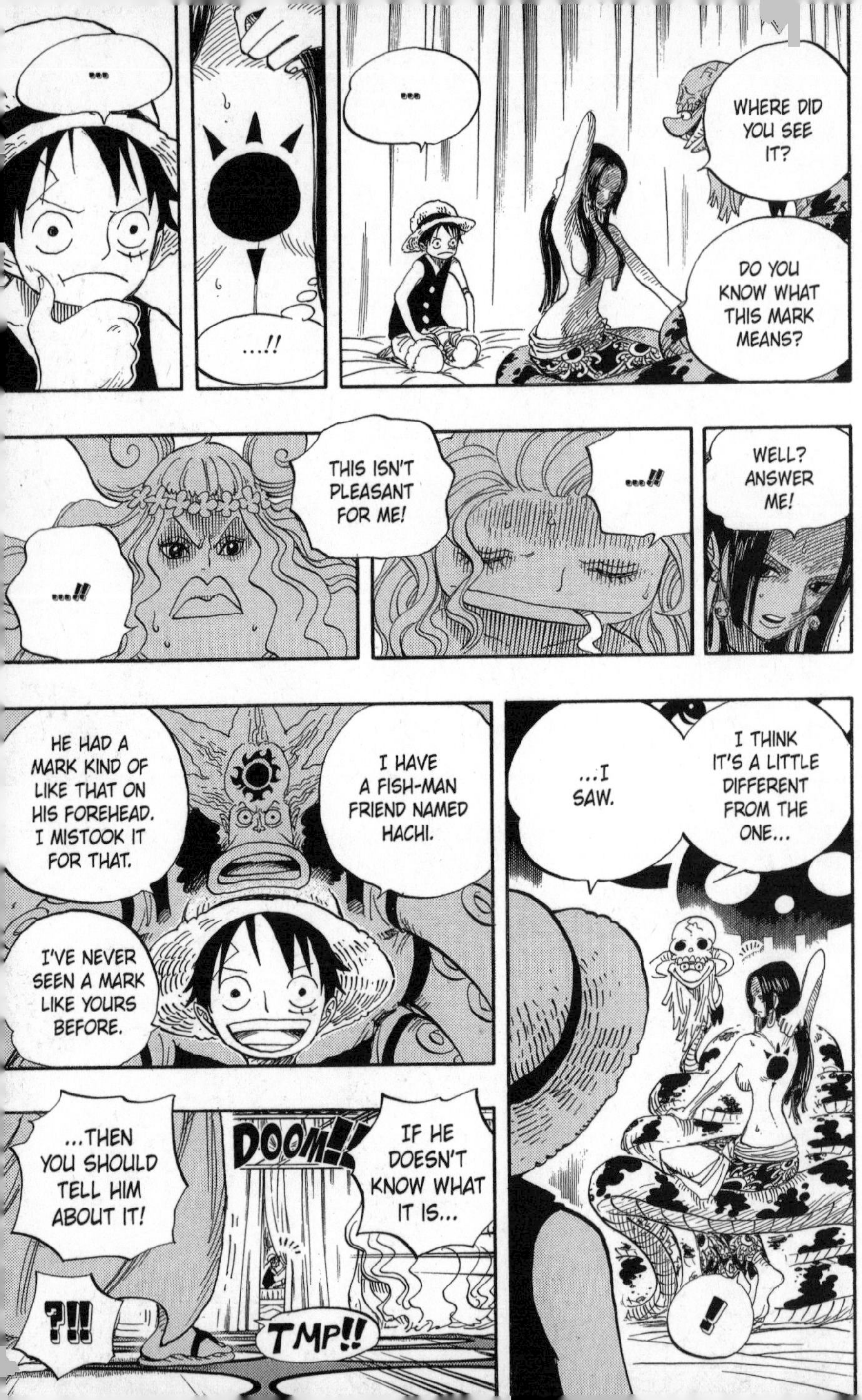
WHERE DID YOU SEE IT?
DO YOU KNOW WHAT THIS MARK MEANS?
...
....!!
...
WELL? ANSWER ME!
...!!
THIS ISN'T PLEASANT FOR ME!
...!!
I THINK IT'S A LITTLE DIFFERENT FROM THE ONE...
...I SAW.
!
I HAVE A FISH-MAN FRIEND NAMED HACHI.
HE HAD A MARK KIND OF LIKE THAT ON HIS FOREHEAD. I MISTOOK IT FOR THAT.
I'VE NEVER SEEN A MARK LIKE YOURS BEFORE.
IF HE DOESN'T KNOW WHAT IT IS...
DOOM!!
...THEN YOU SHOULD TELL HIM ABOUT IT!
TMP!!
?!!

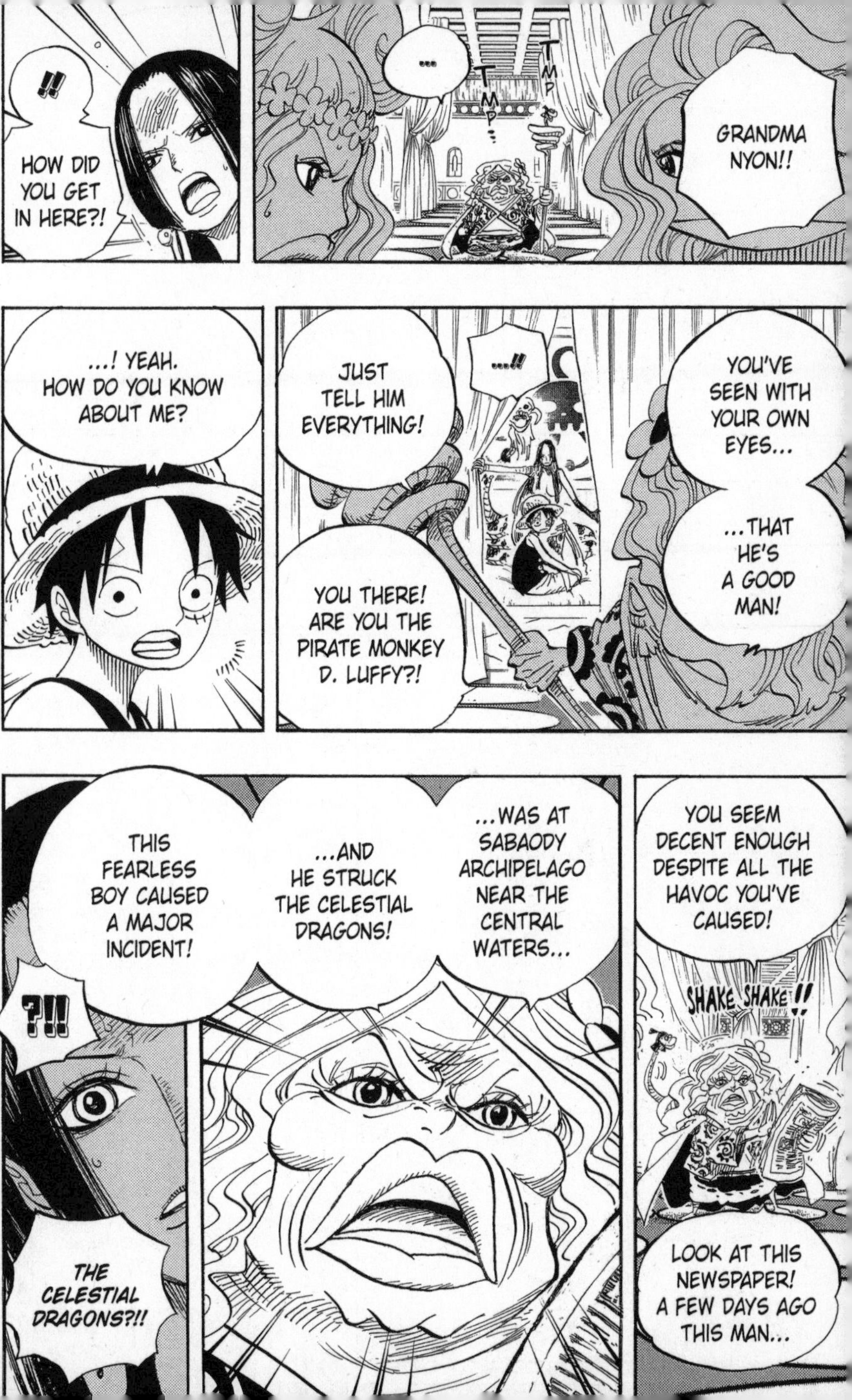
GRANDMA NYON!!
...
TMP
TMP
!!
HOW DID YOU GET IN HERE?!
YOU'VE SEEN WITH YOUR OWN EYES...
...THAT HE'S A GOOD MAN!
...!!
JUST TELL HIM EVERYTHING!
YOU THERE! ARE YOU THE PIRATE MONKEY D. LUFFY?!
...! YEAH. HOW DO YOU KNOW ABOUT ME?
YOU SEEM DECENT ENOUGH DESPITE ALL THE HAVOC YOU'VE CAUSED!
SHAKE SHAKE!!
LOOK AT THIS NEWSPAPER! A FEW DAYS AGO THIS MAN...
...WAS AT SABAODY ARCHIPELAGO NEAR THE CENTRAL WATERS...
...AND HE STRUCK THE CELESTIAL DRAGONS!
THIS FEARLESS BOY CAUSED A MAJOR INCIDENT!
?!!
THE CELESTIAL DRAGONS?!!

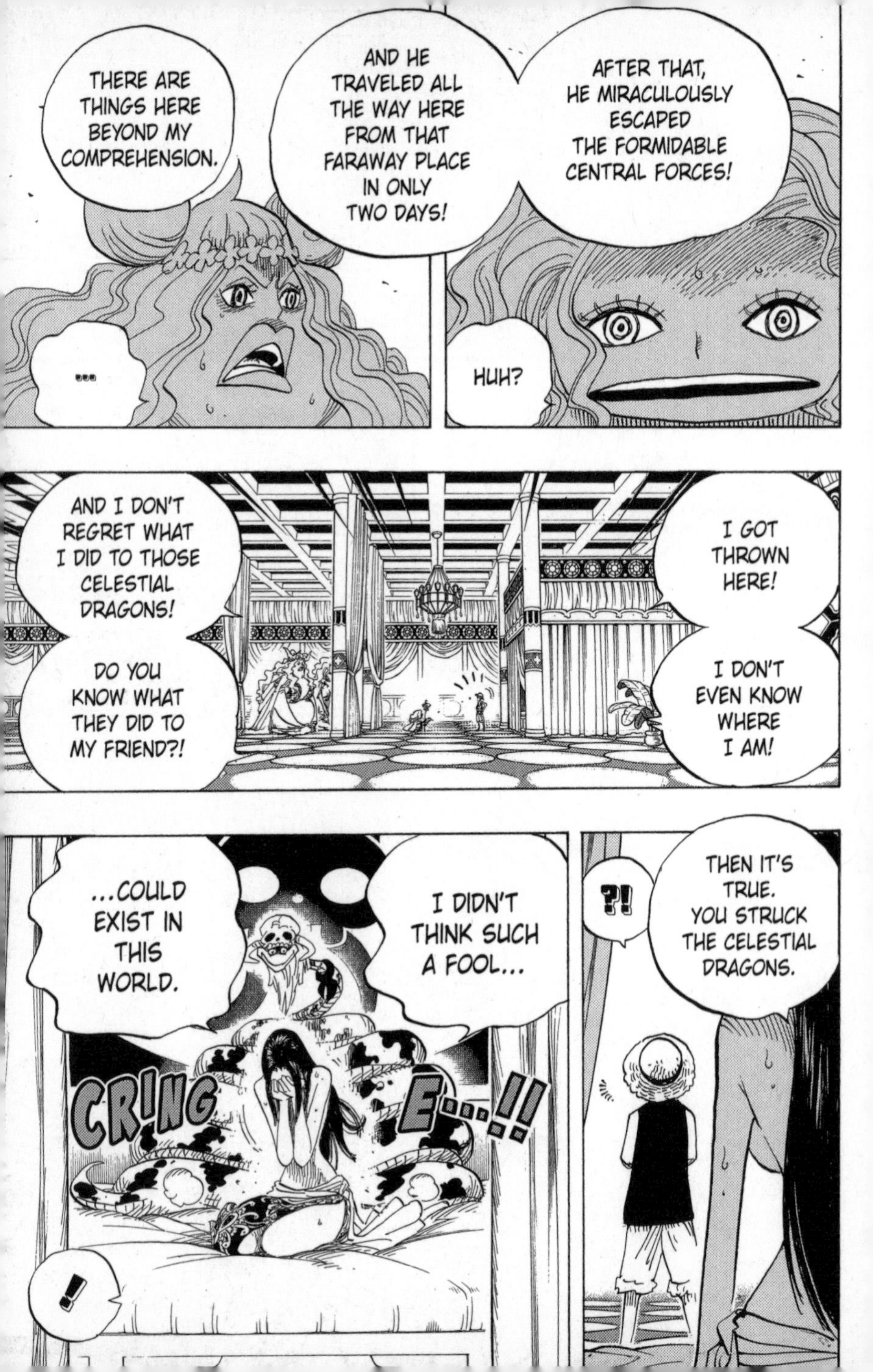
AFTER THAT, HE MIRACULOUSLY ESCAPED THE FORMIDABLE CENTRAL FORCES!
HUH?
AND HE TRAVELED ALL THE WAY HERE FROM THAT FARAWAY PLACE IN ONLY TWO DAYS!
THERE ARE THINGS HERE BEYOND MY COMPREHENSION.
...
I GOT THROWN HERE!
I DON'T EVEN KNOW WHERE I AM!
AND I DON'T REGRET WHAT I DID TO THOSE CELESTIAL DRAGONS!
DO YOU KNOW WHAT THEY DID TO MY FRIEND?!
THEN IT'S TRUE. YOU STRUCK THE CELESTIAL DRAGONS.
?!
I DIDN'T THINK SUCH A FOOL...
...COULD EXIST IN THIS WORLD.
CRINGE...!!
!

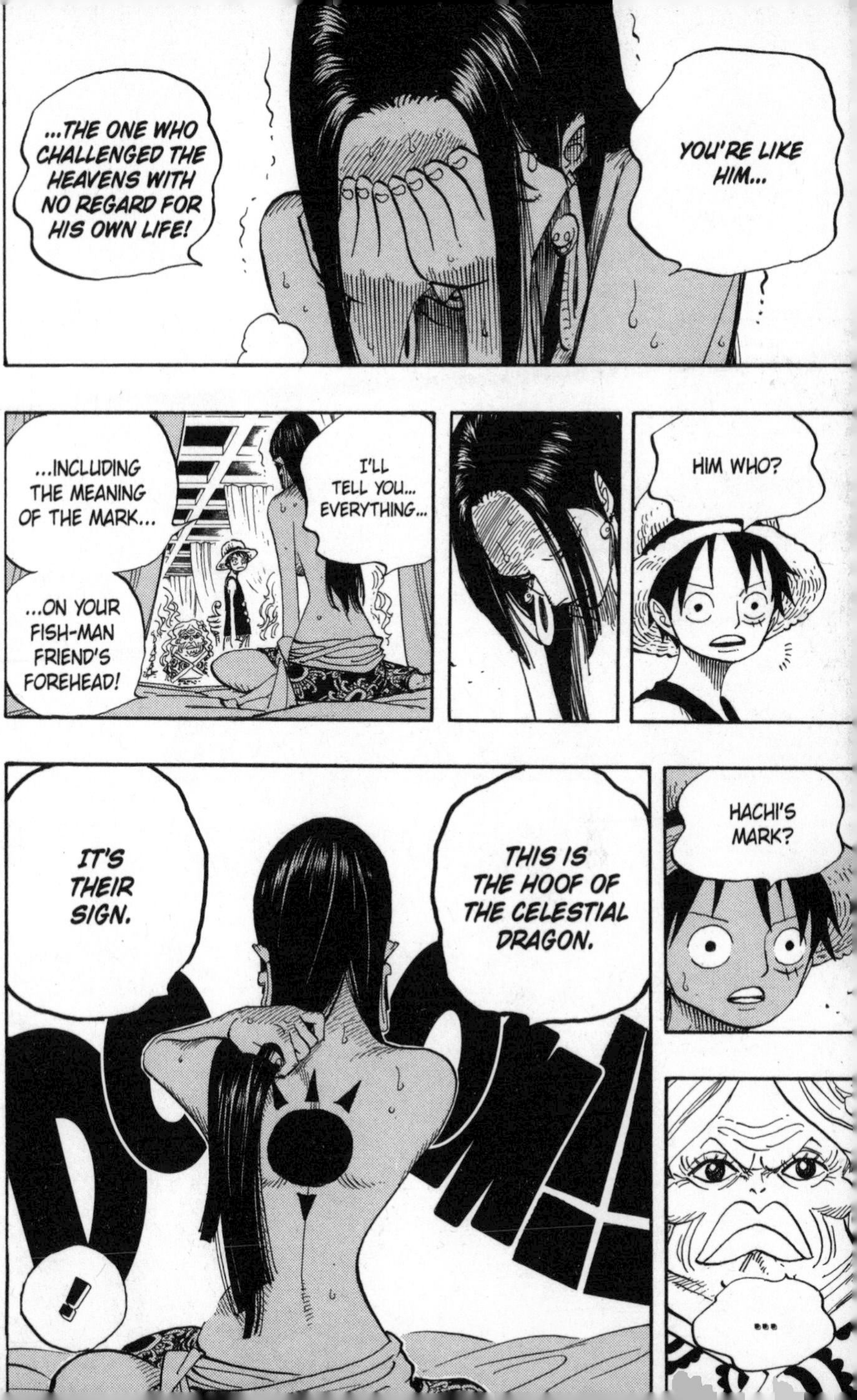
YOU'RE LIKE HIM...
...THE ONE WHO CHALLENGED THE HEAVENS WITH NO REGARD FOR HIS OWN LIFE!
HIM WHO?
I'LL TELL YOU... EVERYTHING...
...INCLUDING THE MEANING OF THE MARK...
...ON YOUR FISH-MAN FRIEND'S FOREHEAD!
HACHI'S MARK?
...
THIS IS THE HOOF OF THE CELESTIAL DRAGON.
IT'S THEIR SIGN.
!

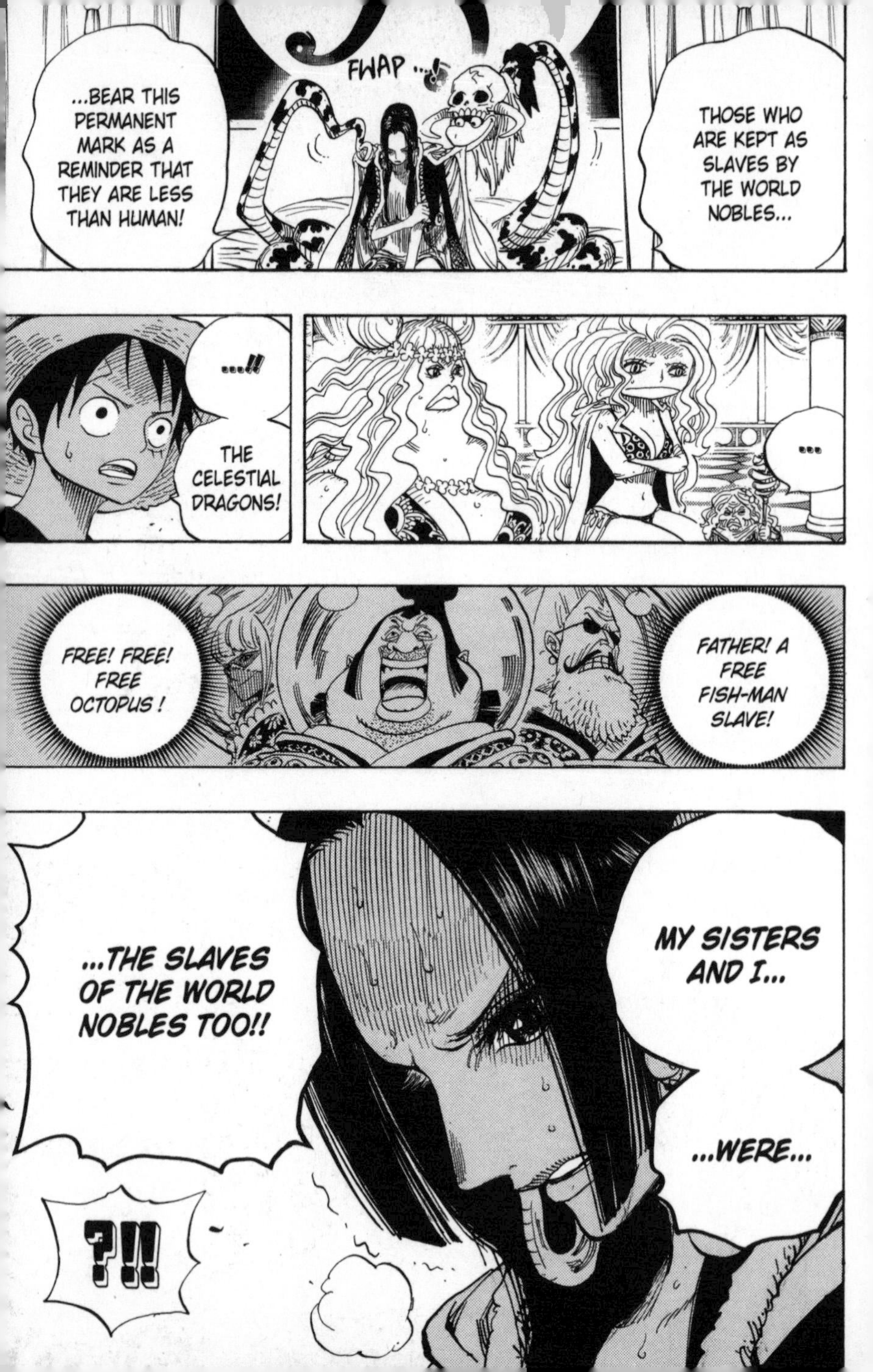
THOSE WHO ARE KEPT AS SLAVES BY THE WORLD NOBLES...
FWAP ...!
...BEAR THIS PERMANENT MARK AS A REMINDER THAT THEY ARE LESS THAN HUMAN!
...
...!!
THE CELESTIAL DRAGONS!
FATHER! A FREE FISH-MAN SLAVE!
FREE! FREE! FREE OCTOPUS!
MY SISTERS AND I...
...WERE...
...THE SLAVES OF THE WORLD NOBLES TOO!!
?!!

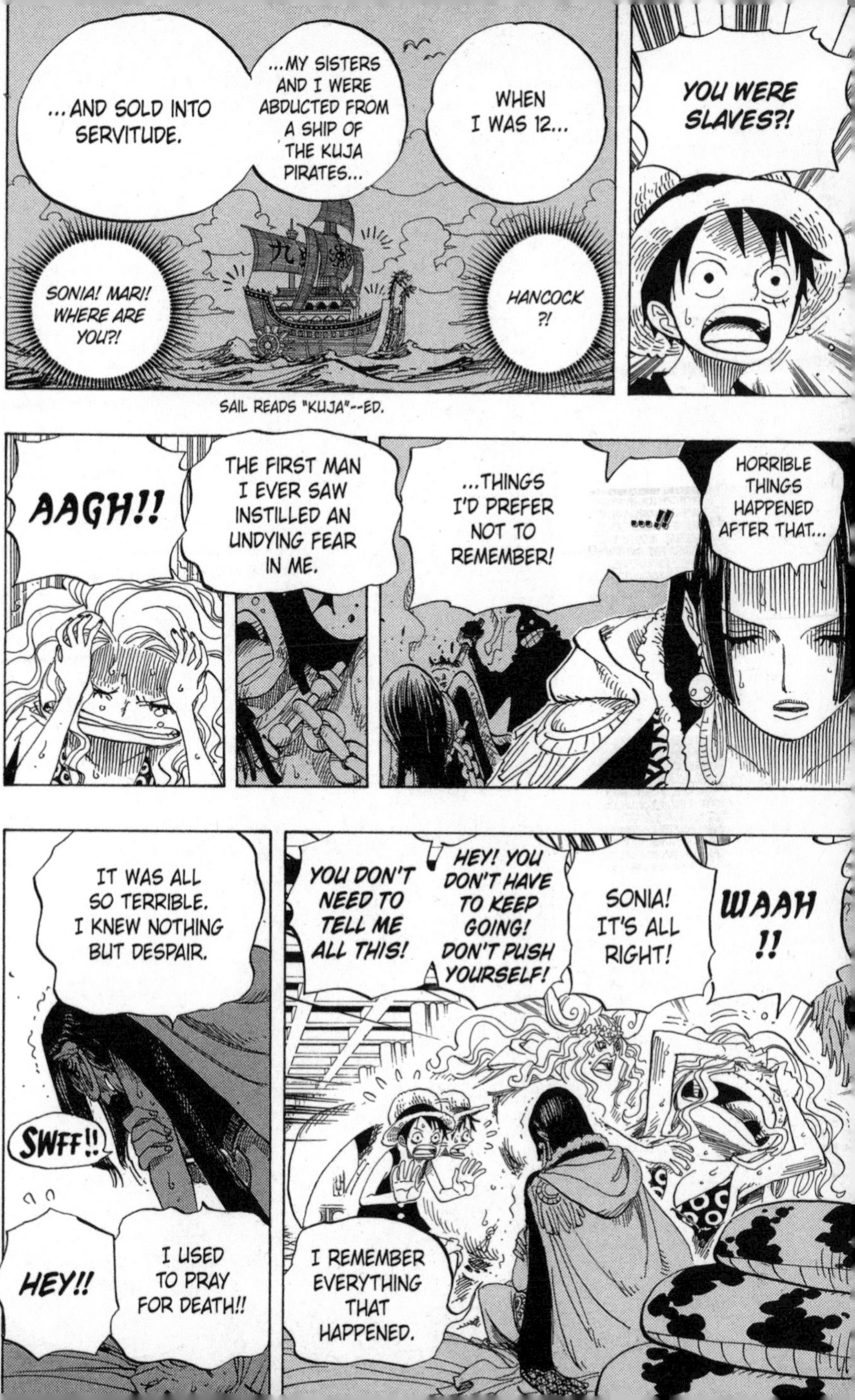
YOU WERE SLAVES?!
WHEN I WAS 12...
...MY SISTERS AND I WERE ABDUCTED FROM A SHIP OF THE KUJA PIRATES...
...AND SOLD INTO SERVITUDE.
HANCOCK ?!
SONIA! MARI! WHERE ARE YOU?!
SAIL READS "KUJA"--ED.
HORRIBLE THINGS HAPPENED AFTER THAT...
...!!
...THINGS I'D PREFER NOT TO REMEMBER!
THE FIRST MAN I EVER SAW INSTILLED AN UNDYING FEAR IN ME.
AAGH!!
WAAH !!
SONIA! IT'S ALL RIGHT!
HEY! YOU DON'T HAVE TO KEEP GOING! DON'T PUSH YOURSELF!
YOU DON'T NEED TO TELL ME ALL THIS!
I REMEMBER EVERYTHING THAT HAPPENED.
IT WAS ALL SO TERRIBLE. I KNEW NOTHING BUT DESPAIR.
SWFF!!
I USED TO PRAY FOR DEATH!!
HEY!!

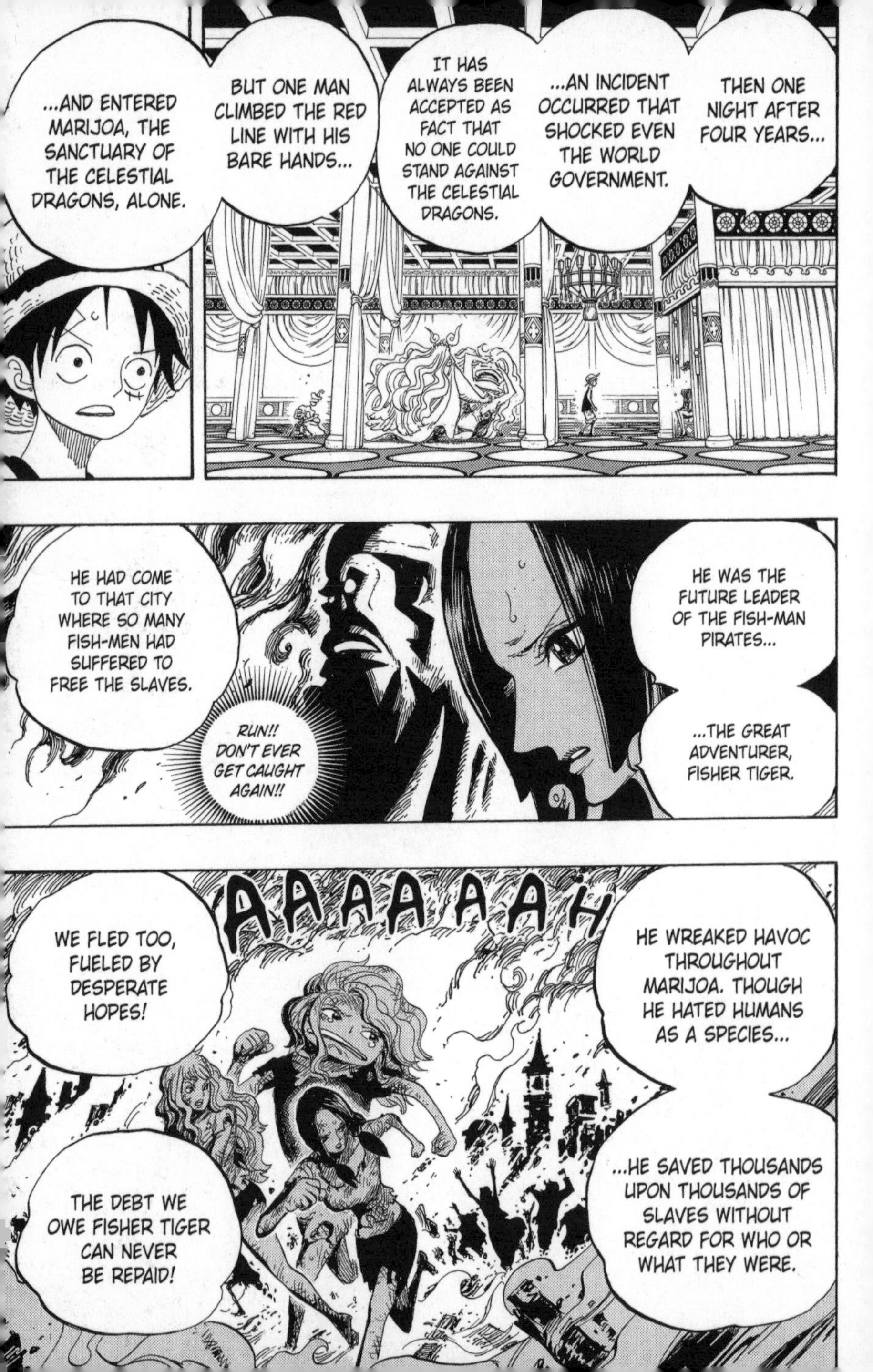
THEN ONE NIGHT AFTER FOUR YEARS...
...AN INCIDENT OCCURRED THAT SHOCKED EVEN THE WORLD GOVERNMENT.
IT HAS ALWAYS BEEN ACCEPTED AS FACT THAT NO ONE COULD STAND AGAINST THE CELESTIAL DRAGONS.
BUT ONE MAN CLIMBED THE RED LINE WITH HIS BARE HANDS...
...AND ENTERED MARIJOA, THE SANCTUARY OF THE CELESTIAL DRAGONS, ALONE.
HE WAS THE FUTURE LEADER OF THE FISH-MAN PIRATES...
...THE GREAT ADVENTURER, FISHER TIGER.
RUN!! DON'T EVER GET CAUGHT AGAIN!!
HE HAD COME TO THAT CITY WHERE SO MANY FISH-MEN HAD SUFFERED TO FREE THE SLAVES.
HE WREAKED HAVOC THROUGHOUT MARIJOA. THOUGH HE HATED HUMANS AS A SPECIES...
...HE SAVED THOUSANDS UPON THOUSANDS OF SLAVES WITHOUT REGARD FOR WHO OR WHAT THEY WERE.
AAAAAAAH
WE FLED TOO, FUELED BY DESPERATE HOPES!
THE DEBT WE OWE FISHER TIGER CAN NEVER BE REPAID!

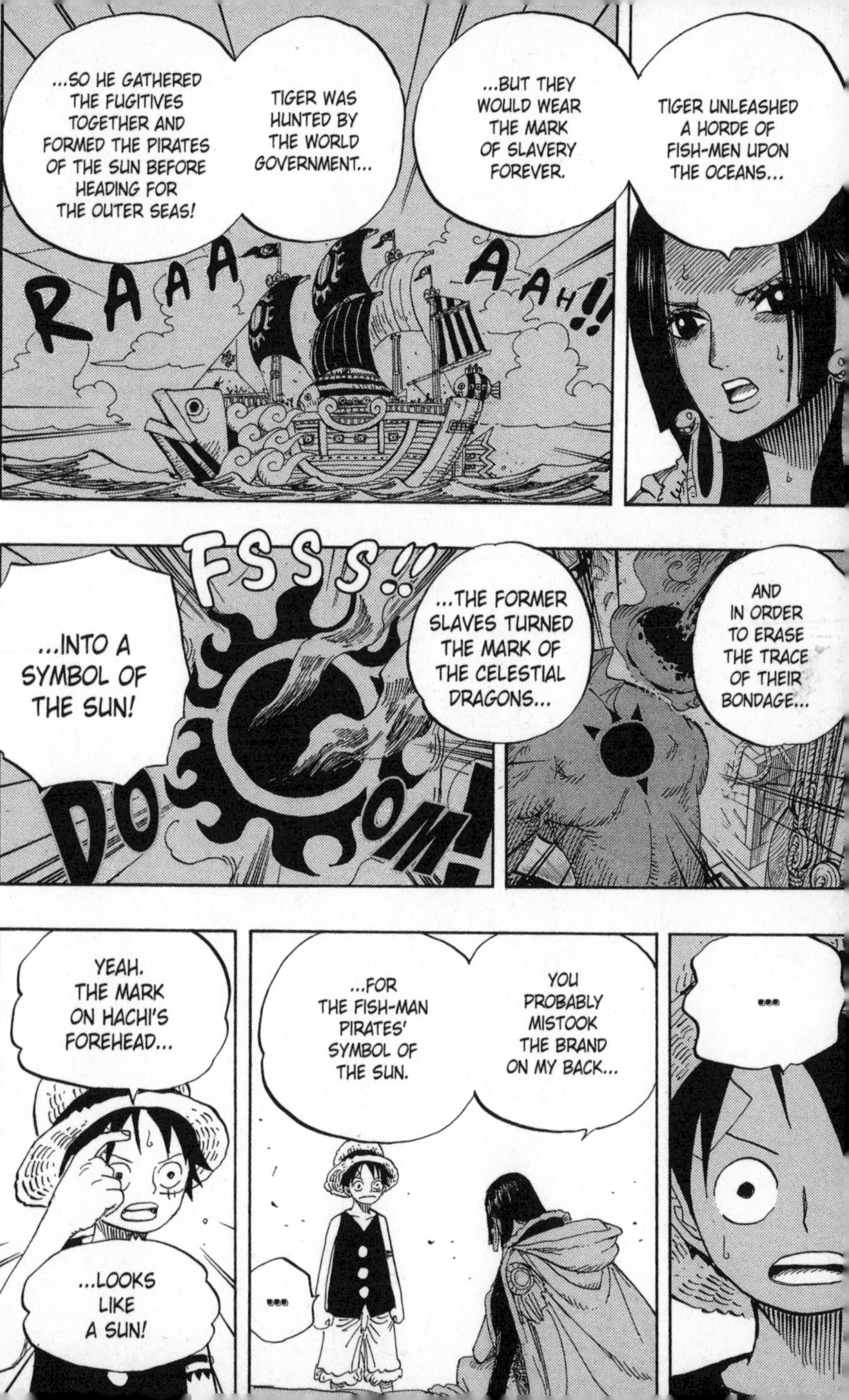
TIGER UNLEASHED A HORDE OF FISH-MEN UPON THE OCEANS...
...BUT THEY WOULD WEAR THE MARK OF SLAVERY FOREVER.
TIGER WAS HUNTED BY THE WORLD GOVERNMENT...
...SO HE GATHERED THE FUGITIVES TOGETHER AND FORMED THE PIRATES OF THE SUN BEFORE HEADING FOR THE OUTER SEAS!
RAAAAAH!!
AND IN ORDER TO ERASE THE TRACE OF THEIR BONDAGE...
...THE FORMER SLAVES TURNED THE MARK OF THE CELESTIAL DRAGONS...
FSSS!!
...INTO A SYMBOL OF THE SUN!
DOOOM!
...
YOU PROBABLY MISTOOK THE BRAND ON MY BACK...
...FOR THE FISH-MAN PIRATES' SYMBOL OF THE SUN.
...
YEAH. THE MARK ON HACHI'S FOREHEAD...
...LOOKS LIKE A SUN!

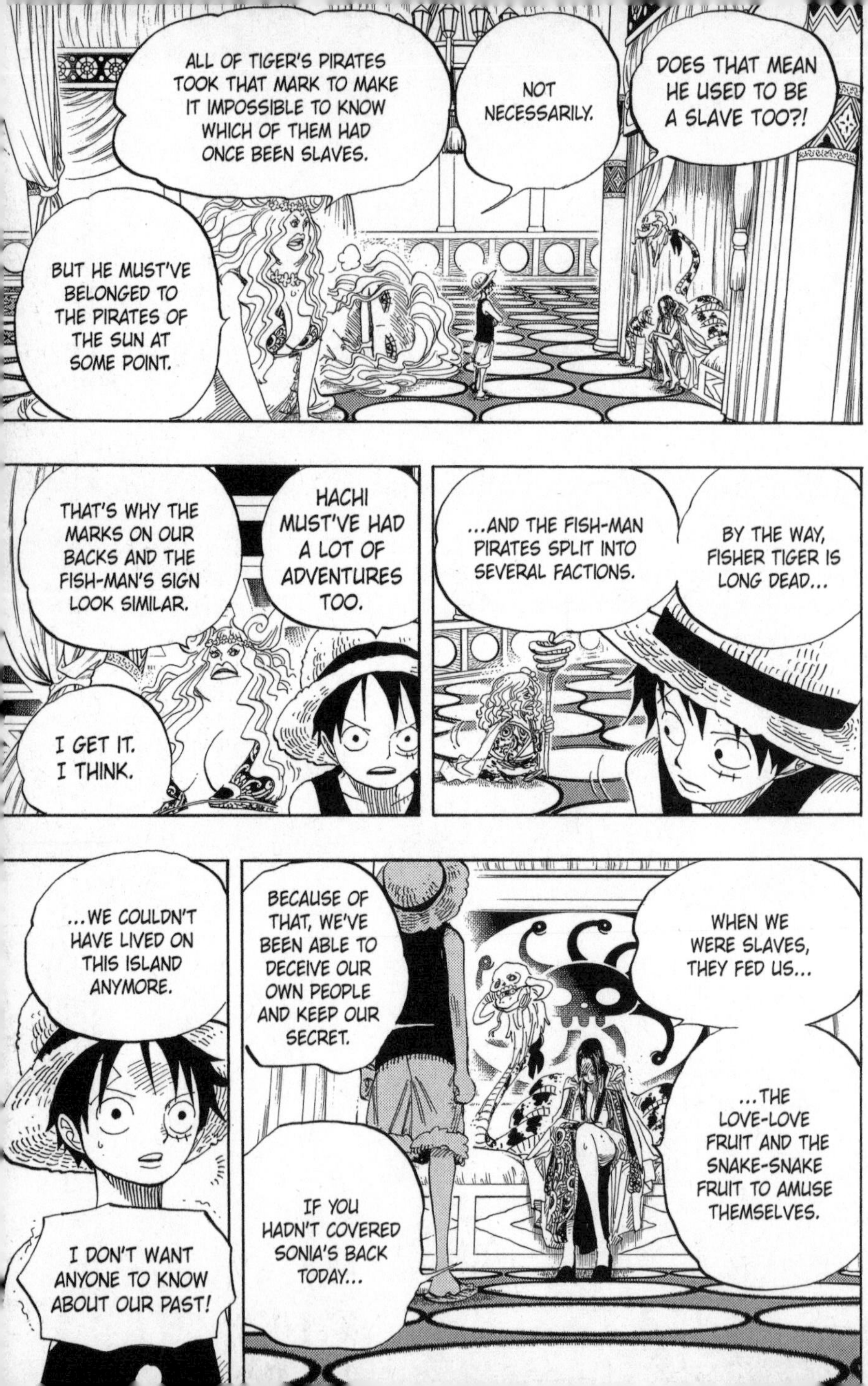
DOES THAT MEAN HE USED TO BE A SLAVE TOO?!
NOT NECESSARILY.
ALL OF TIGER'S PIRATES TOOK THAT MARK TO MAKE IT IMPOSSIBLE TO KNOW WHICH OF THEM HAD ONCE BEEN SLAVES.
BUT HE MUST'VE BELONGED TO THE PIRATES OF THE SUN AT SOME POINT.
BY THE WAY, FISHER TIGER IS LONG DEAD...
...AND THE FISH-MAN PIRATES SPLIT INTO SEVERAL FACTIONS.
HACHI MUST'VE HAD A LOT OF ADVENTURES TOO.
THAT'S WHY THE MARKS ON OUR BACKS AND THE FISH-MAN'S SIGN LOOK SIMILAR.
I GET IT. I THINK.
WHEN WE WERE SLAVES, THEY FED US...
...THE LOVE-LOVE FRUIT AND THE SNAKE-SNAKE FRUIT TO AMUSE THEMSELVES.
BECAUSE OF THAT, WE'VE BEEN ABLE TO DECEIVE OUR OWN PEOPLE AND KEEP OUR SECRET.
IF YOU HADN'T COVERED SONIA'S BACK TODAY...
...WE COULDN'T HAVE LIVED ON THIS ISLAND ANYMORE.
I DON'T WANT ANYONE TO KNOW ABOUT OUR PAST!

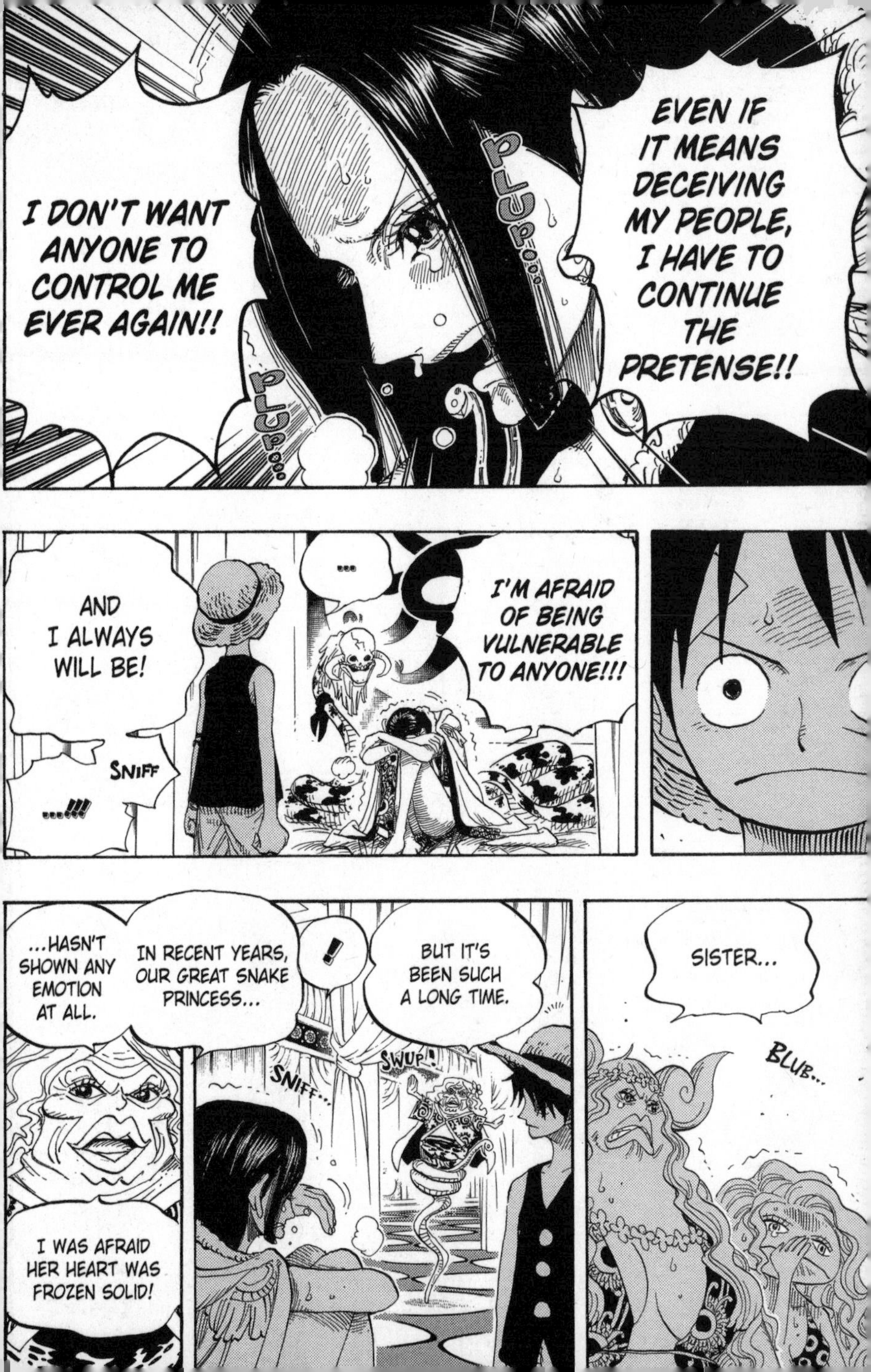
EVEN IF IT MEANS DECEIVING MY PEOPLE, I HAVE TO CONTINUE THE PRETENSE!!
PLUP...
I DON'T WANT ANYONE TO CONTROL ME EVER AGAIN!!
PLUP...
I'M AFRAID OF BEING VULNERABLE TO ANYONE!!!
...
AND I ALWAYS WILL BE!
SNIFF
...!!!
SISTER...
BLUB...
BUT IT'S BEEN SUCH A LONG TIME.
SWUP!
!
IN RECENT YEARS, OUR GREAT SNAKE PRINCESS...
SNIFF...
...HASN'T SHOWN ANY EMOTION AT ALL.
I WAS AFRAID HER HEART WAS FROZEN SOLID!

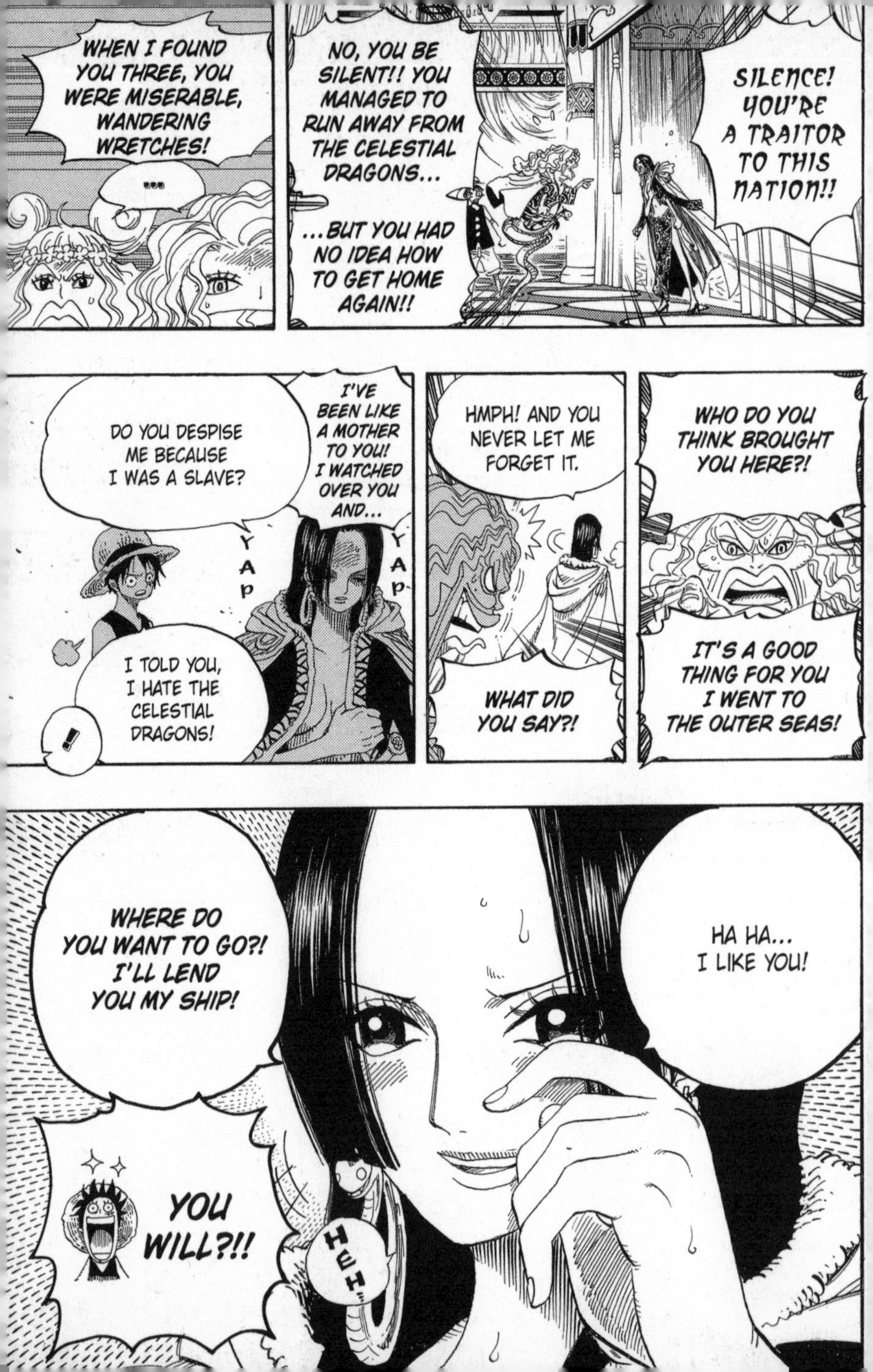
SILENCE! YOU'RE A TRAITOR TO THIS NATION!!
NO, YOU BE SILENT!! YOU MANAGED TO RUN AWAY FROM THE CELESTIAL DRAGONS...
...BUT YOU HAD NO IDEA HOW TO GET HOME AGAIN!!
WHEN I FOUND YOU THREE, YOU WERE MISERABLE, WANDERING WRETCHES!
...
WHO DO YOU THINK BROUGHT YOU HERE?!
IT'S A GOOD THING FOR YOU I WENT TO THE OUTER SEAS!
HMPH! AND YOU NEVER LET ME FORGET IT.
WHAT DID YOU SAY?!
I'VE BEEN LIKE A MOTHER TO YOU! I WATCHED OVER YOU AND...
YAP
YAP
DO YOU DESPISE ME BECAUSE I WAS A SLAVE?
I TOLD YOU, I HATE THE CELESTIAL DRAGONS!
!
HA HA... I LIKE YOU!
WHERE DO YOU WANT TO GO?! I'LL LEND YOU MY SHIP!
YOU WILL?!!
HEH

THE VOICE OF ZOLO, KAZUYA NAKAI!!

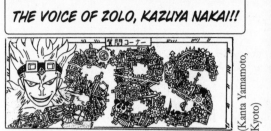

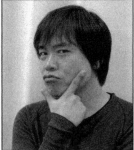

質問コーナー
SBS
(Kanta Yamamoto, Kyoto)

HDYD?! (How do you do?)
This is our second voice actor Question Corner. I'm happy to report that the first one was pretty popular. This time, we have the voice actor who voices our master swordsman, Roronoa Zolo. He's famous for farting while shouting out "Oni Giri!" We have Kazuya Nakai in the house!

Oda(O): Hello, here is Nakai. Please introduce yourself in a cool deep voice.

Nakai(N): Hello, this is Kazuya Nakai. My favorite dessert is Kashiwa-mochi.

O: Who asked you?

N: That's not very nice, Odachi.

O: Nice has nothing to do with it. We have limited space, so follow the script! Now then, do you know what SBS stands for?

N: (S)omething (B)latantly (S)enseless.

O: You don't know! Hey! Don't give me that "I was daydreaming" look!

N: Let me try again. (S)haved my head (B)ald but it (S)ucks.

O: Are you kidding me?! Never mind! Here. These are all letters with questions. (PLOP!) Have at them.

N: Sure.

More from Kazuya Nakai on page 208! ☞

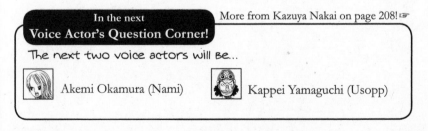

In the next
Voice Actor's Question Corner!

The next two voice actors will be...

Akemi Okamura (Nami)

Kappei Yamaguchi (Usopp)

Chapter 522:
FATAL ILLNESS

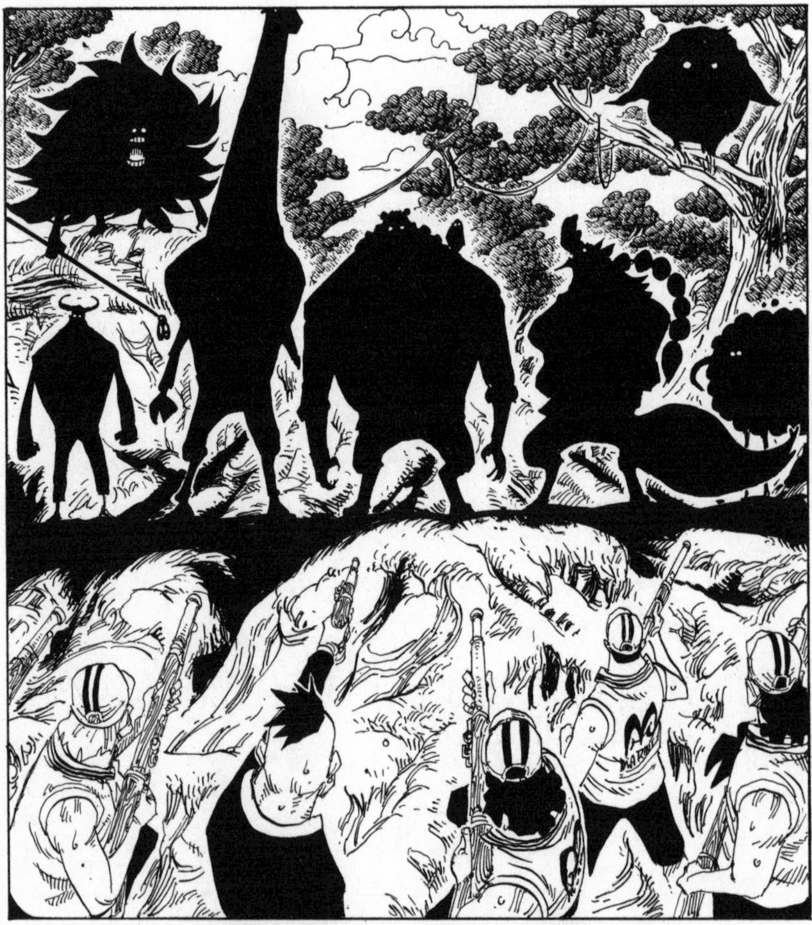

CP9'S INDEPENDENT REPORT, VOL. 28:
"DEFENDING OUR HOMETOWN"

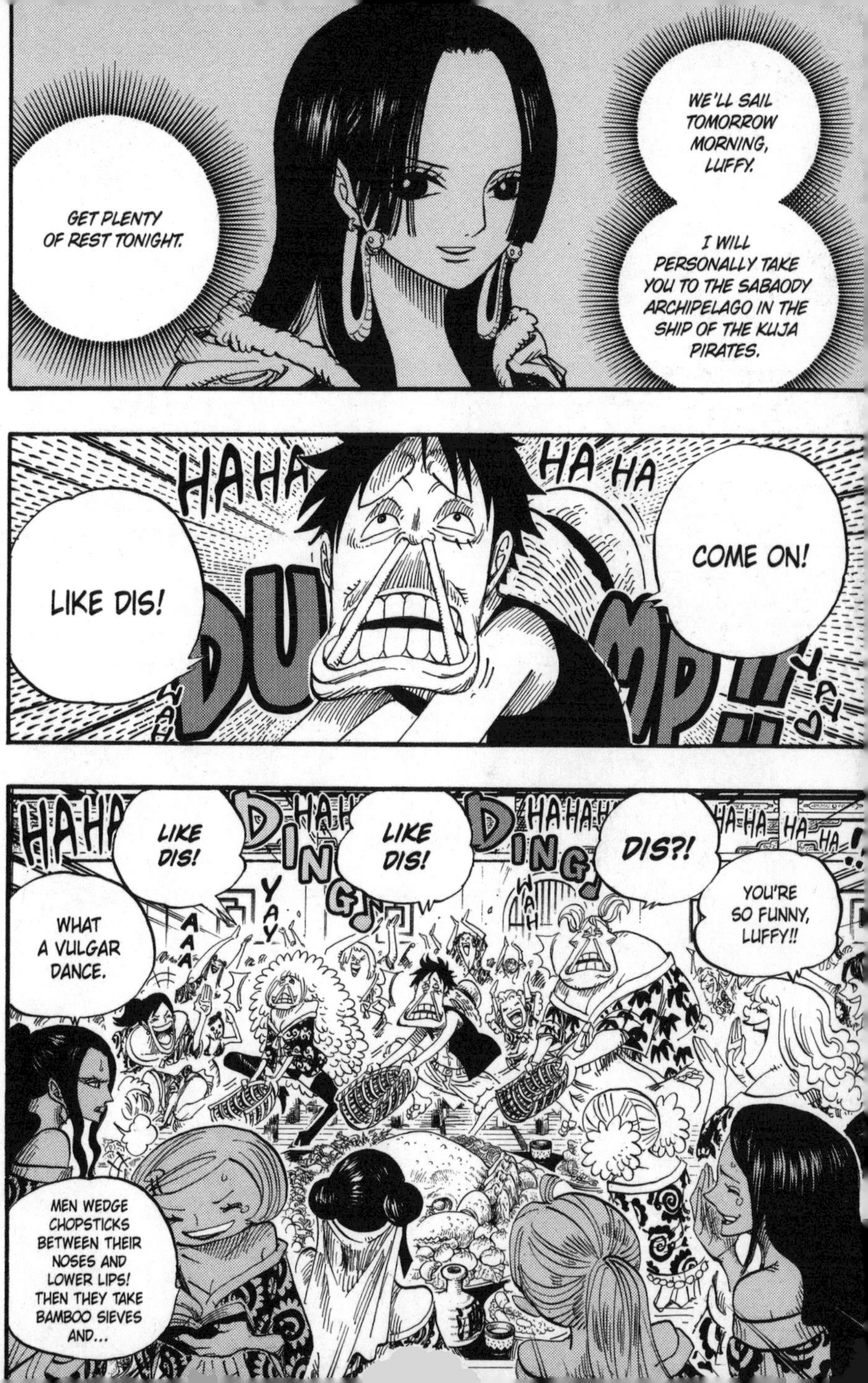

WE'LL SAIL TOMORROW MORNING, LUFFY.
I WILL PERSONALLY TAKE YOU TO THE SABAODY ARCHIPELAGO IN THE SHIP OF THE KUJA PIRATES.
GET PLENTY OF REST TONIGHT.
HA HA
COME ON!
DUMP!!
HAHA
LIKE DIS!
HA HA HA!
YOU'RE SO FUNNY, LUFFY!!
DIS?!
HAHAHA
DING!
WAH
LIKE DIS!
DING!
YAY
HAHA
LIKE DIS!
AAA
WHAT A VULGAR DANCE.
MEN WEDGE CHOPSTICKS BETWEEN THEIR NOSES AND LOWER LIPS! THEN THEY TAKE BAMBOO SIEVES AND...

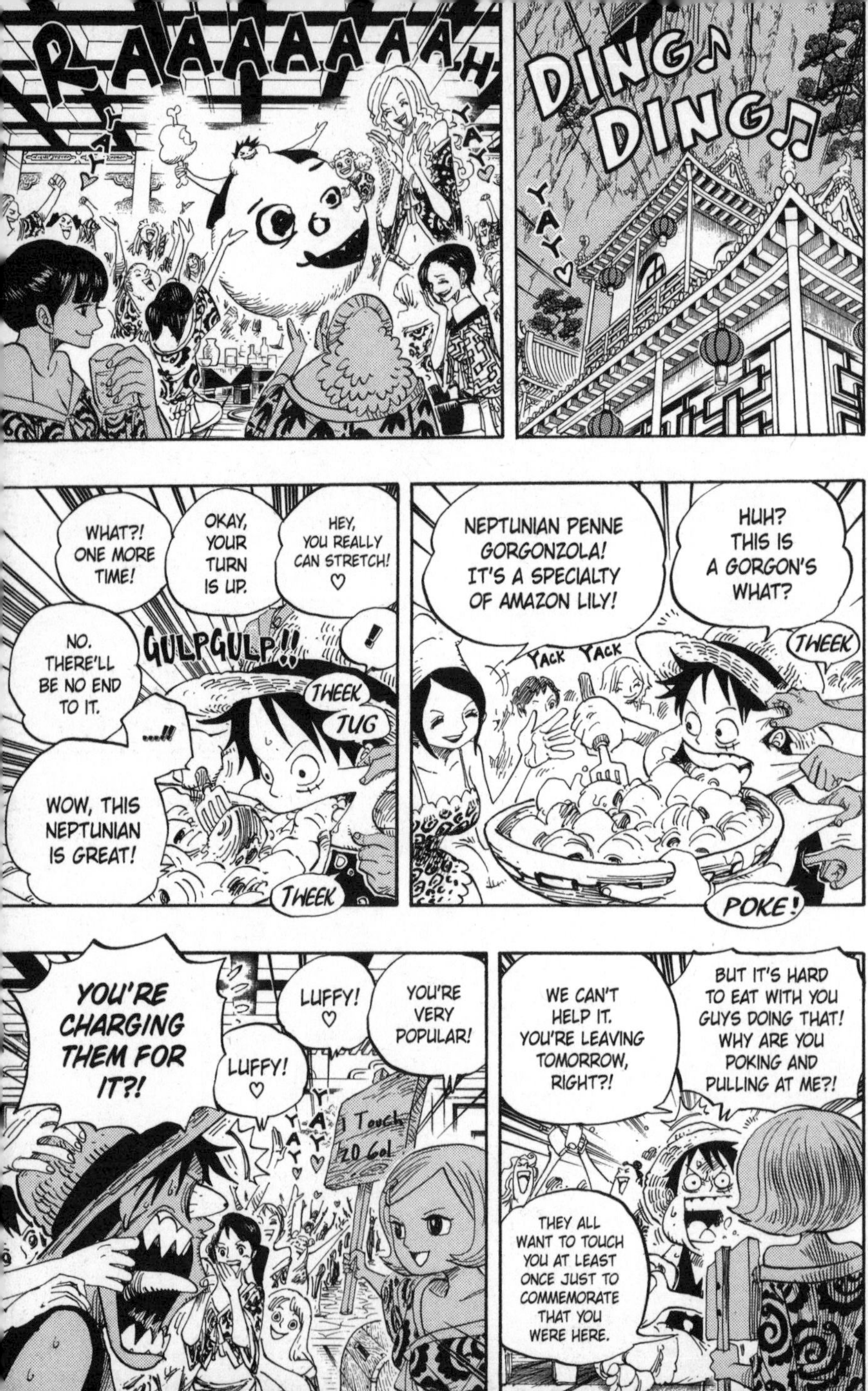
DING♪
DING♪
YAY♡
RAAAAAAAH
YAY
YAY♡
HUH? THIS IS A GORGON'S WHAT?
TWEEK
NEPTUNIAN PENNE GORGONZOLA! IT'S A SPECIALTY OF AMAZON LILY!
YACK YACK
POKE!
HEY, YOU REALLY CAN STRETCH! ♡
OKAY, YOUR TURN IS UP.
WHAT?! ONE MORE TIME!
!
GULPGULP!!
NO. THERE'LL BE NO END TO IT.
TWEEK
TUG
...!!
WOW, THIS NEPTUNIAN IS GREAT!
TWEEK
BUT IT'S HARD TO EAT WITH YOU GUYS DOING THAT! WHY ARE YOU POKING AND PULLING AT ME?!
WE CAN'T HELP IT. YOU'RE LEAVING TOMORROW, RIGHT?!
THEY ALL WANT TO TOUCH YOU AT LEAST ONCE JUST TO COMMEMORATE THAT YOU WERE HERE.
YOU'RE VERY POPULAR!
LUFFY! ♡
YOU'RE CHARGING THEM FOR IT?!
LUFFY! ♡
YAY
YAY♡
1 Touch 20 Gol

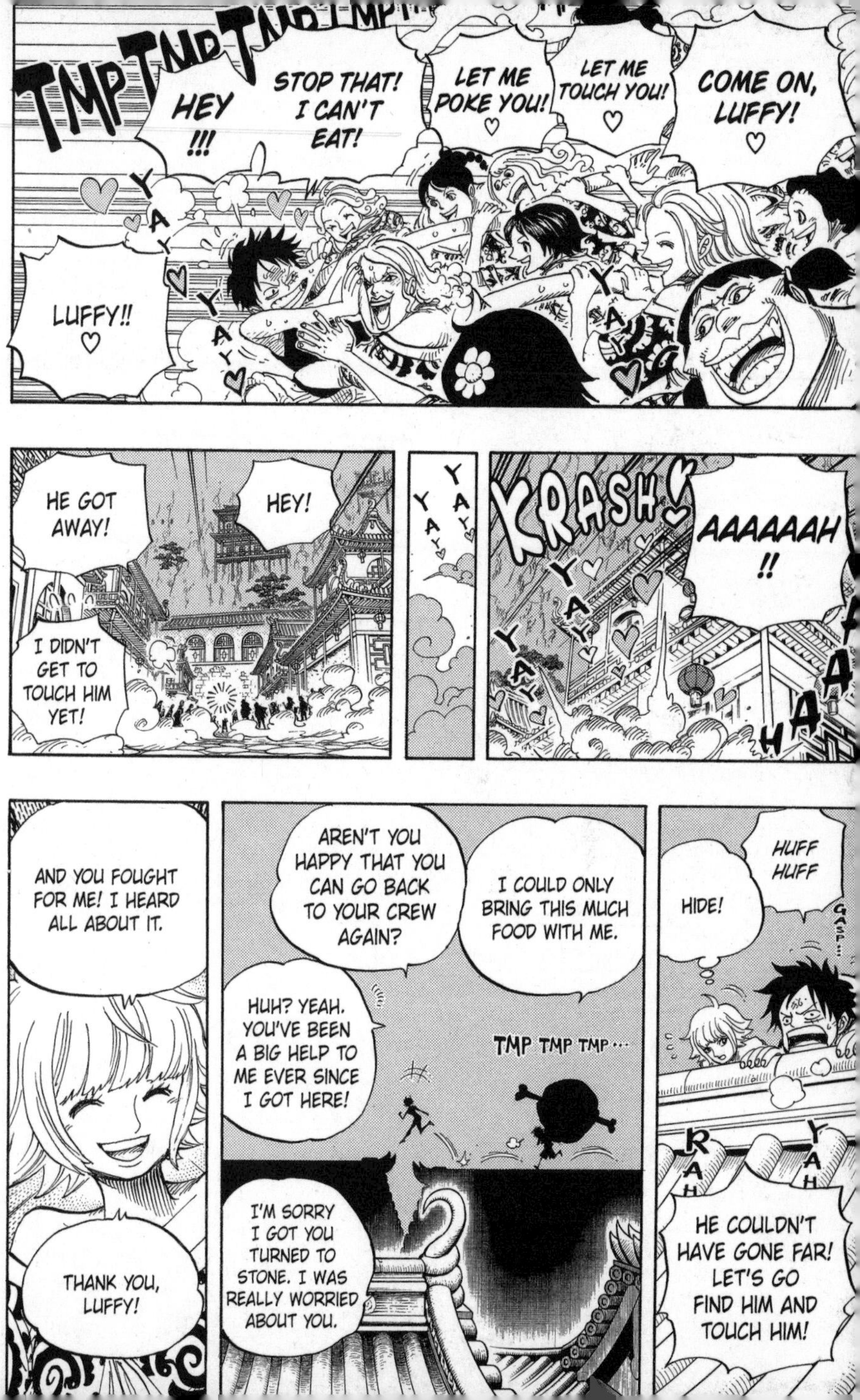
TMP TMP TMP TMP
COME ON, LUFFY! ♡
LET ME TOUCH YOU! ♡
LET ME POKE YOU! ♡
STOP THAT! I CAN'T EAT!
HEY!!!
YAY
YAY
LUFFY!! ♡
YAY
YAY
KRASH!
AAAAAAH!!
YAY
YAY
HAAA
YAY
YAY
HEY!
HE GOT AWAY!
I DIDN'T GET TO TOUCH HIM YET!
HUFF HUFF
HIDE!
GASP...
YAH
KRAH
HE COULDN'T HAVE GONE FAR! LET'S GO FIND HIM AND TOUCH HIM!
I COULD ONLY BRING THIS MUCH FOOD WITH ME.
AREN'T YOU HAPPY THAT YOU CAN GO BACK TO YOUR CREW AGAIN?
HUH? YEAH. YOU'VE BEEN A BIG HELP TO ME EVER SINCE I GOT HERE!
TMP TMP TMP...
I'M SORRY I GOT YOU TURNED TO STONE. I WAS REALLY WORRIED ABOUT YOU.
AND YOU FOUGHT FOR ME! I HEARD ALL ABOUT IT.
THANK YOU, LUFFY!

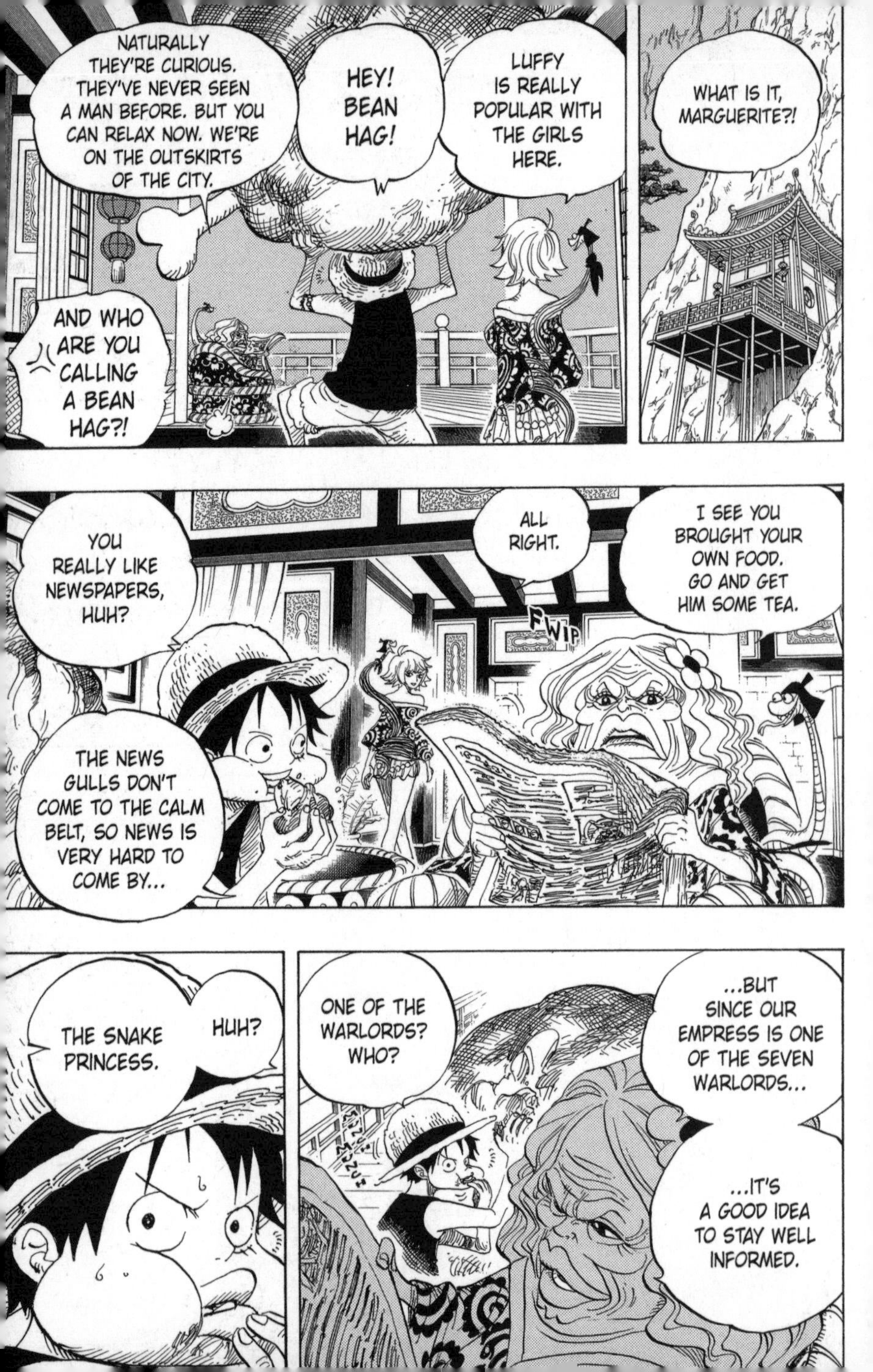
WHAT IS IT, MARGUERITE?!
LUFFY IS REALLY POPULAR WITH THE GIRLS HERE.
HEY! BEAN HAG!
NATURALLY THEY'RE CURIOUS. THEY'VE NEVER SEEN A MAN BEFORE. BUT YOU CAN RELAX NOW. WE'RE ON THE OUTSKIRTS OF THE CITY.
AND WHO ARE YOU CALLING A BEAN HAG?!
I SEE YOU BROUGHT YOUR OWN FOOD. GO AND GET HIM SOME TEA.
ALL RIGHT.
FWIP
YOU REALLY LIKE NEWSPAPERS, HUH?
THE NEWS GULLS DON'T COME TO THE CALM BELT, SO NEWS IS VERY HARD TO COME BY...
...BUT SINCE OUR EMPRESS IS ONE OF THE SEVEN WARLORDS...
...IT'S A GOOD IDEA TO STAY WELL INFORMED.
ONE OF THE WARLORDS? WHO?
HUH?
THE SNAKE PRINCESS.

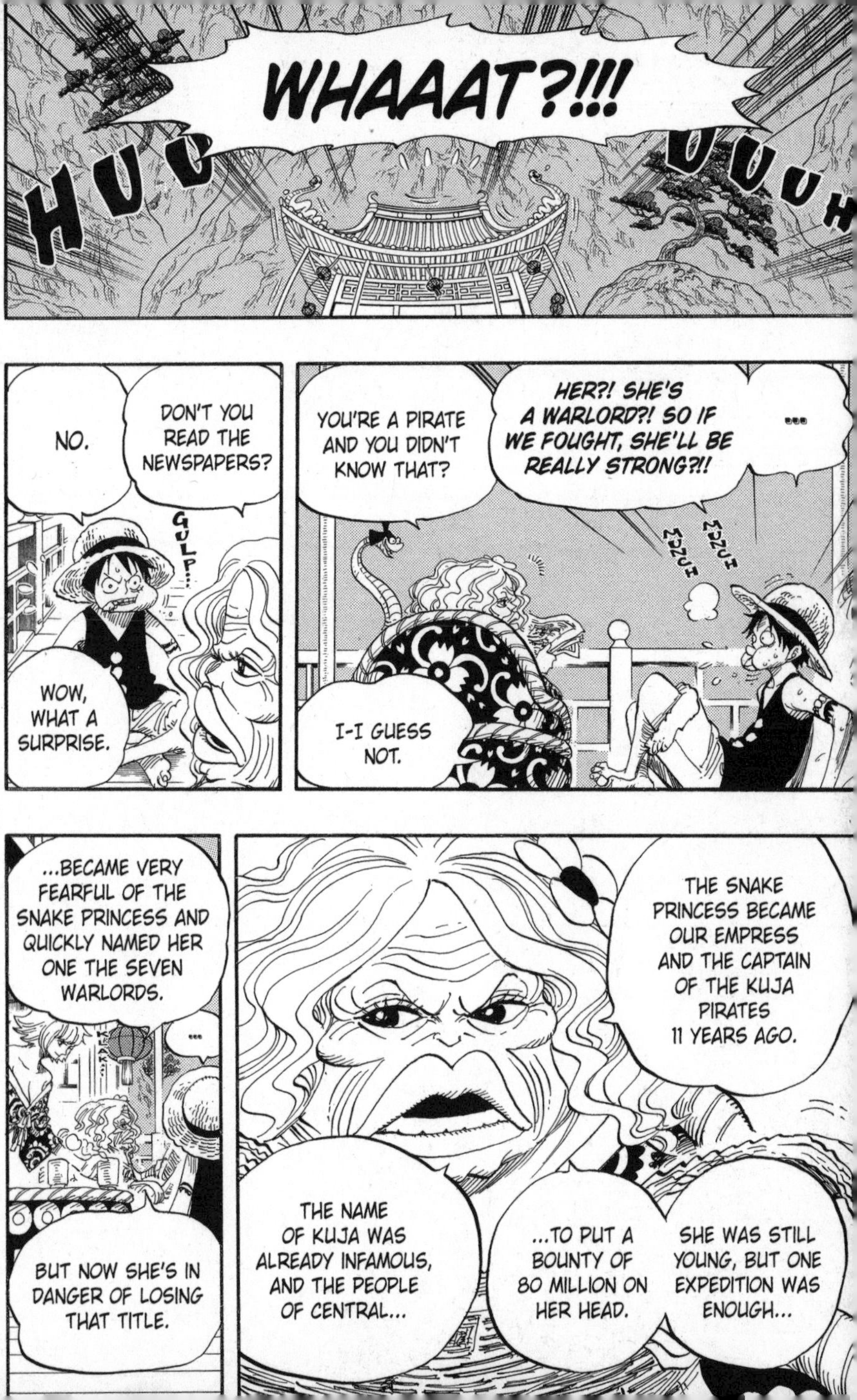
WHAAAT?!!!
UUUH
HUU
...
HER?! SHE'S A WARLORD?! SO IF WE FOUGHT, SHE'LL BE REALLY STRONG?!!
YOU'RE A PIRATE AND YOU DIDN'T KNOW THAT?
MUNCH
MUNCH
I-I GUESS NOT.
DON'T YOU READ THE NEWSPAPERS?
NO.
GULP...
WOW, WHAT A SURPRISE.
THE SNAKE PRINCESS BECAME OUR EMPRESS AND THE CAPTAIN OF THE KUJA PIRATES 11 YEARS AGO.
SHE WAS STILL YOUNG, BUT ONE EXPEDITION WAS ENOUGH...
...TO PUT A BOUNTY OF 80 MILLION ON HER HEAD.
THE NAME OF KUJA WAS ALREADY INFAMOUS, AND THE PEOPLE OF CENTRAL...
...BECAME VERY FEARFUL OF THE SNAKE PRINCESS AND QUICKLY NAMED HER ONE THE SEVEN WARLORDS.
...
KLAK...
BUT NOW SHE'S IN DANGER OF LOSING THAT TITLE.

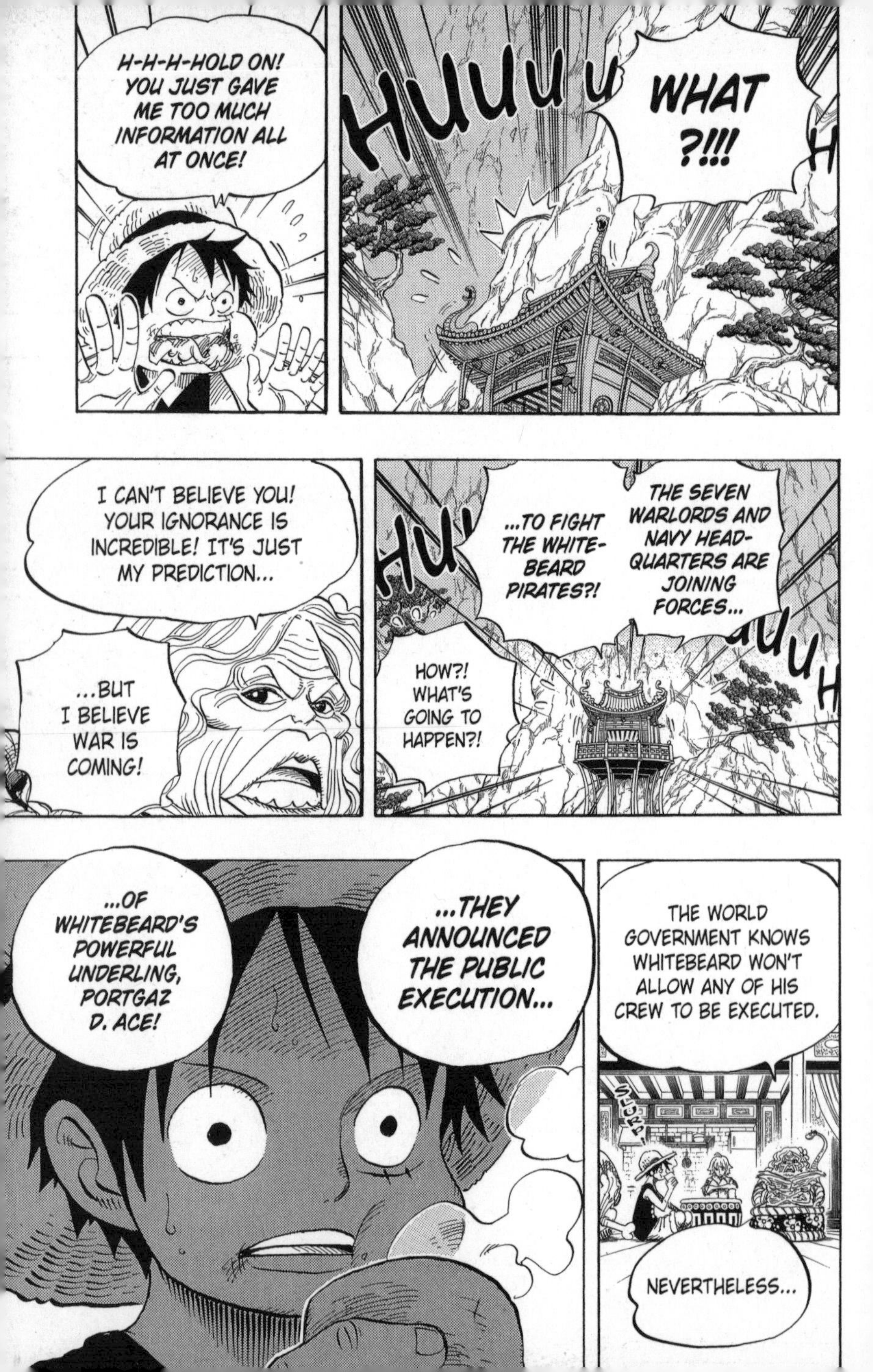

HUUUUU
WHAT ?!!!
H-H-H-HOLD ON! YOU JUST GAVE ME TOO MUCH INFORMATION ALL AT ONCE!
THE SEVEN WARLORDS AND NAVY HEAD-QUARTERS ARE JOINING FORCES...
...TO FIGHT THE WHITE-BEARD PIRATES?!
HOW?! WHAT'S GOING TO HAPPEN?!
I CAN'T BELIEVE YOU! YOUR IGNORANCE IS INCREDIBLE! IT'S JUST MY PREDICTION...
...BUT I BELIEVE WAR IS COMING!
THE WORLD GOVERNMENT KNOWS WHITEBEARD WON'T ALLOW ANY OF HIS CREW TO BE EXECUTED.
SLURP!
NEVERTHELESS...
...THEY ANNOUNCED THE PUBLIC EXECUTION...
...OF WHITEBEARD'S POWERFUL UNDERLING, PORTGAZ D. ACE!

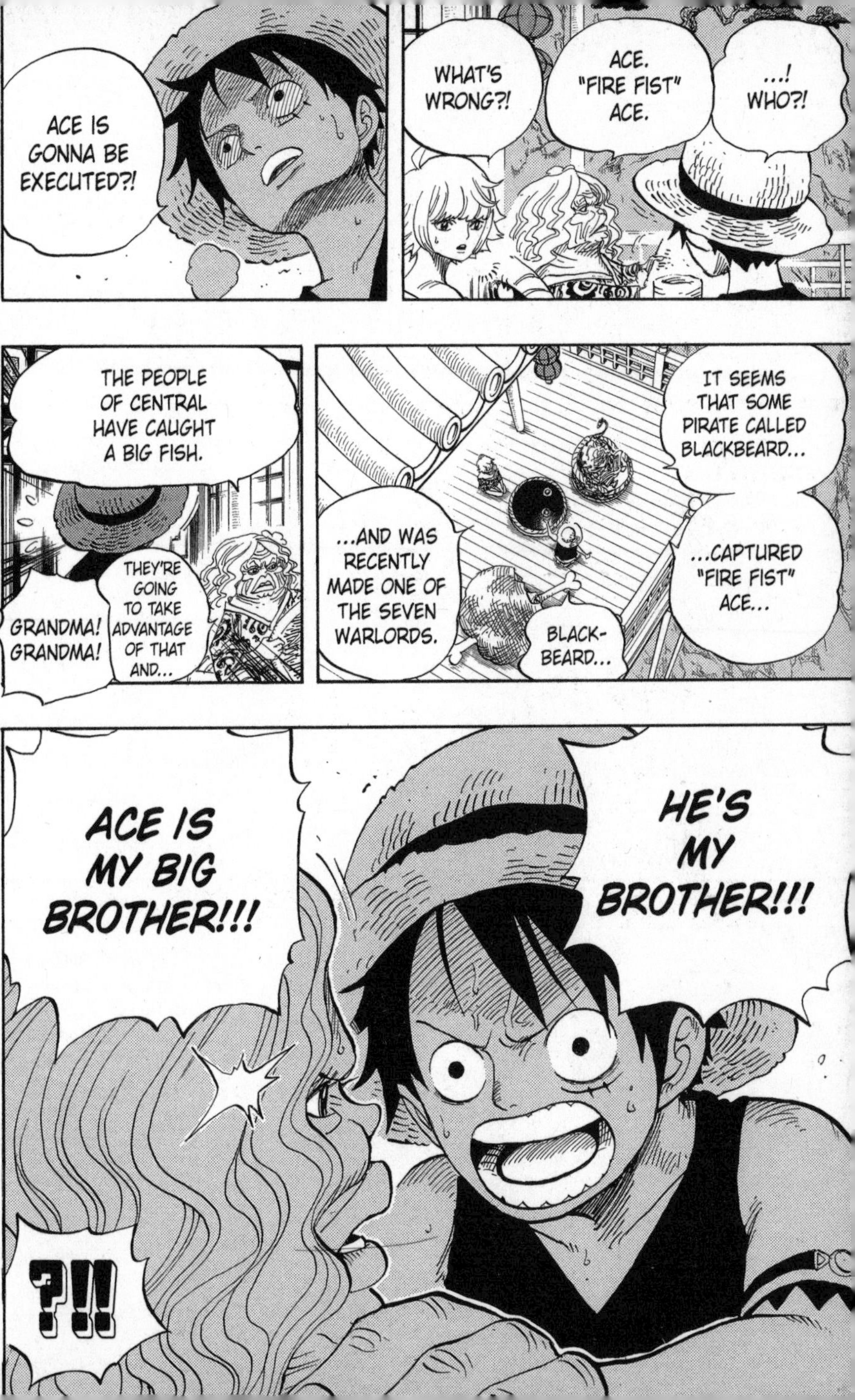
...! WHO?!
ACE. "FIRE FIST" ACE.
WHAT'S WRONG?!
ACE IS GONNA BE EXECUTED?!
IT SEEMS THAT SOME PIRATE CALLED BLACKBEARD...
...CAPTURED "FIRE FIST" ACE...
BLACK-BEARD...
...AND WAS RECENTLY MADE ONE OF THE SEVEN WARLORDS.
THE PEOPLE OF CENTRAL HAVE CAUGHT A BIG FISH.
THEY'RE GOING TO TAKE ADVANTAGE OF THAT AND...
GRANDMA! GRANDMA!
HE'S MY BROTHER!!!
ACE IS MY BIG BROTHER!!!
?!!

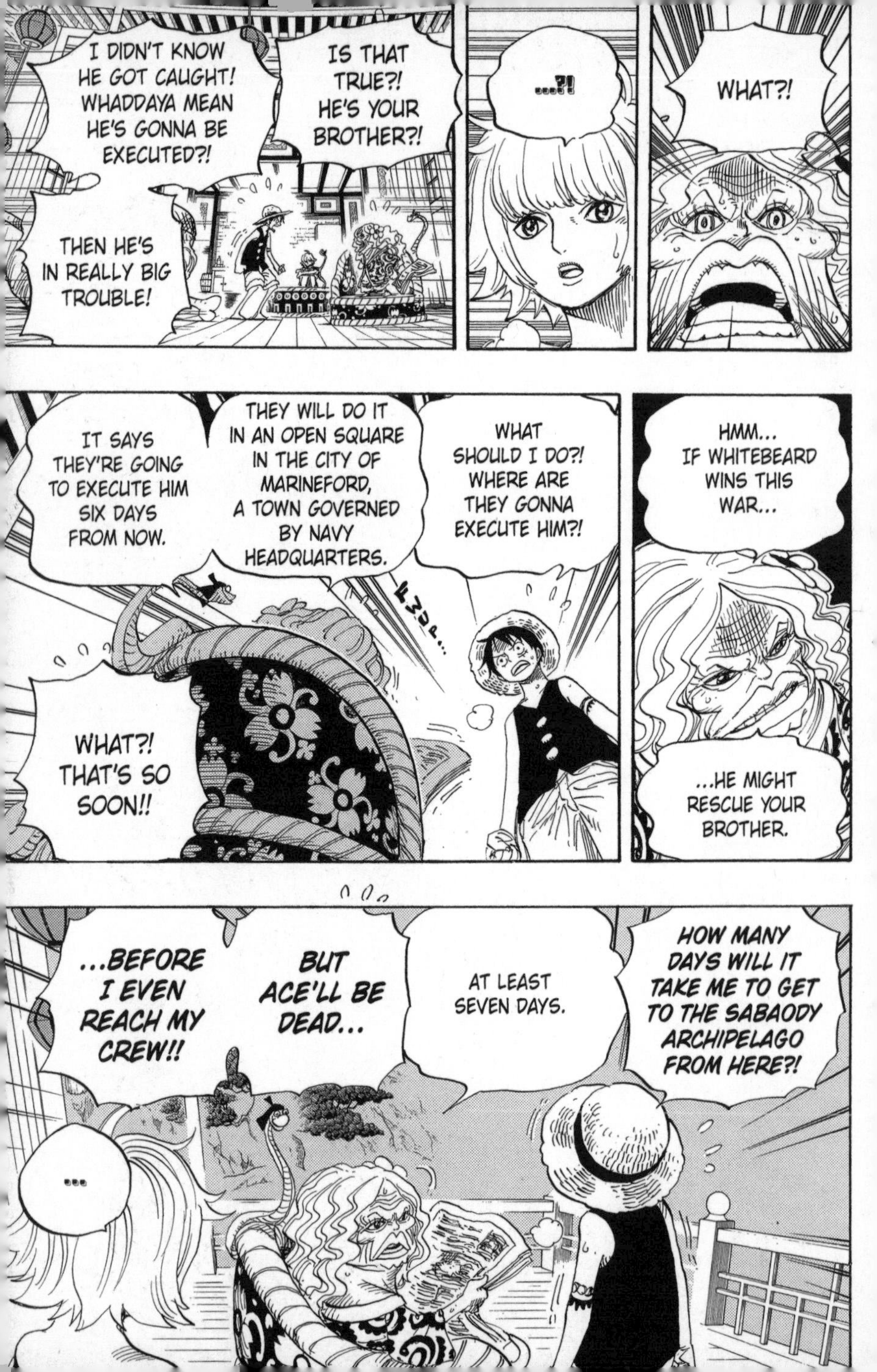
WHAT?!
...?!
IS THAT TRUE?! HE'S YOUR BROTHER?!
I DIDN'T KNOW HE GOT CAUGHT! WHADDAYA MEAN HE'S GONNA BE EXECUTED?!
THEN HE'S IN REALLY BIG TROUBLE!
HMM... IF WHITEBEARD WINS THIS WAR...
...HE MIGHT RESCUE YOUR BROTHER.
WHAT SHOULD I DO?! WHERE ARE THEY GONNA EXECUTE HIM?!
THEY WILL DO IT IN AN OPEN SQUARE IN THE CITY OF MARINEFORD, A TOWN GOVERNED BY NAVY HEADQUARTERS.
IT SAYS THEY'RE GOING TO EXECUTE HIM SIX DAYS FROM NOW.
WHAT?! THAT'S SO SOON!!
HOW MANY DAYS WILL IT TAKE ME TO GET TO THE SABAODY ARCHIPELAGO FROM HERE?!
AT LEAST SEVEN DAYS.
BUT ACE'LL BE DEAD...
...BEFORE I EVEN REACH MY CREW!!
...

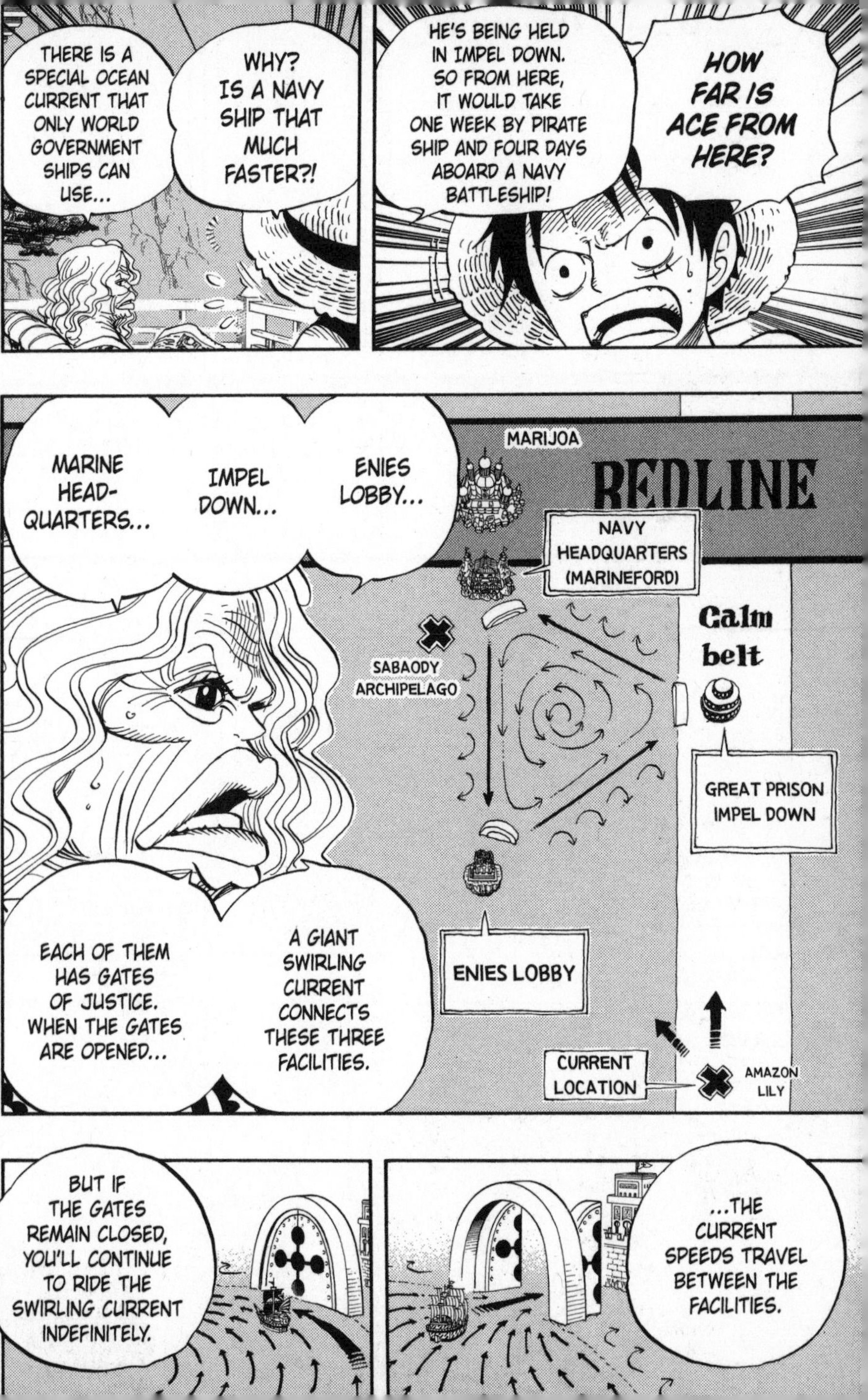
HOW FAR IS ACE FROM HERE?
HE'S BEING HELD IN IMPEL DOWN. SO FROM HERE, IT WOULD TAKE ONE WEEK BY PIRATE SHIP AND FOUR DAYS ABOARD A NAVY BATTLESHIP!
WHY? IS A NAVY SHIP THAT MUCH FASTER?!
THERE IS A SPECIAL OCEAN CURRENT THAT ONLY WORLD GOVERNMENT SHIPS CAN USE...
ENIES LOBBY...
IMPEL DOWN...
MARINE HEAD-QUARTERS...
MARIJOA
REDLINE
NAVY HEADQUARTERS (MARINEFORD)
Calm belt
SABAODY ARCHIPELAGO
GREAT PRISON IMPEL DOWN
ENIES LOBBY
CURRENT LOCATION
AMAZON LILY
A GIANT SWIRLING CURRENT CONNECTS THESE THREE FACILITIES.
EACH OF THEM HAS GATES OF JUSTICE. WHEN THE GATES ARE OPENED...
...THE CURRENT SPEEDS TRAVEL BETWEEN THE FACILITIES.
BUT IF THE GATES REMAIN CLOSED, YOU'LL CONTINUE TO RIDE THE SWIRLING CURRENT INDEFINITELY.

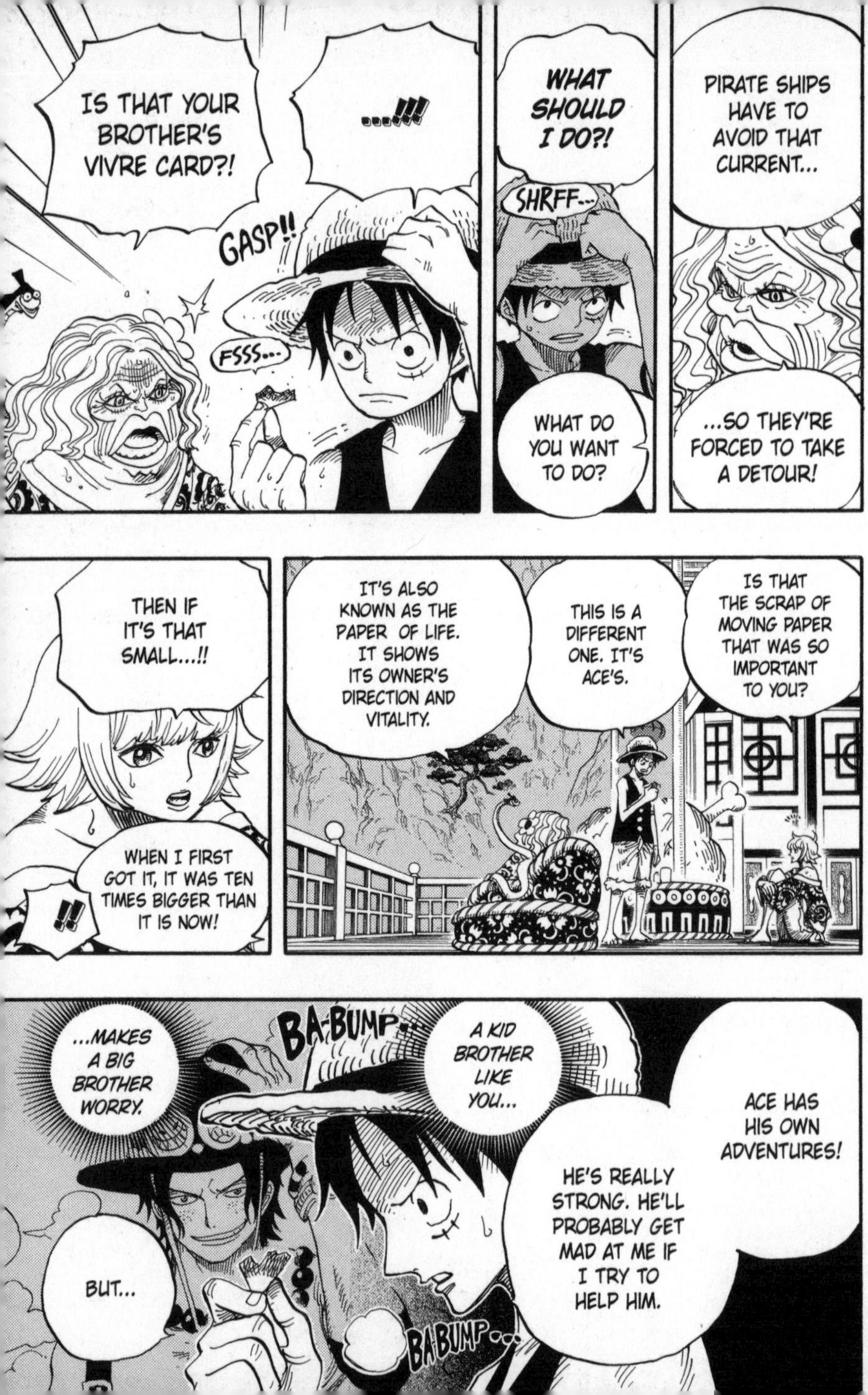
PIRATE SHIPS HAVE TO AVOID THAT CURRENT...
...SO THEY'RE FORCED TO TAKE A DETOUR!
WHAT SHOULD I DO?!
SHRFF...
WHAT DO YOU WANT TO DO?
...!!!
IS THAT YOUR BROTHER'S VIVRE CARD?!
GASP!!
FSSS...
IS THAT THE SCRAP OF MOVING PAPER THAT WAS SO IMPORTANT TO YOU?
THIS IS A DIFFERENT ONE. IT'S ACE'S.
IT'S ALSO KNOWN AS THE PAPER OF LIFE. IT SHOWS ITS OWNER'S DIRECTION AND VITALITY.
THEN IF IT'S THAT SMALL...!!
WHEN I FIRST GOT IT, IT WAS TEN TIMES BIGGER THAN IT IS NOW!
!!
ACE HAS HIS OWN ADVENTURES!
HE'S REALLY STRONG. HE'LL PROBABLY GET MAD AT ME IF I TRY TO HELP HIM.
A KID BROTHER LIKE YOU...
BA-BUMP...
...MAKES A BIG BROTHER WORRY.
BUT...
BA-BUMP...

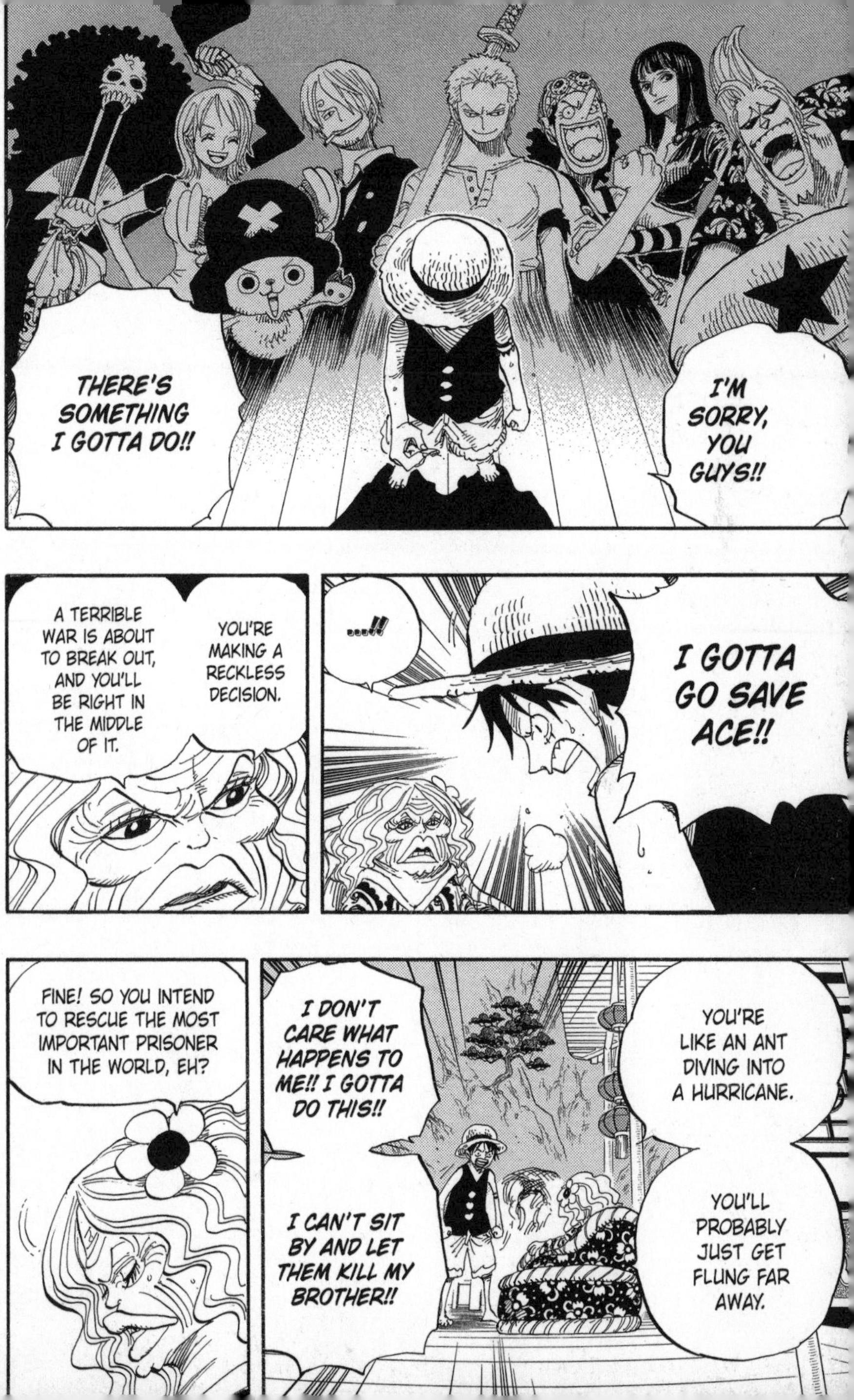
I'M SORRY, YOU GUYS!!
THERE'S SOMETHING I GOTTA DO!!
I GOTTA GO SAVE ACE!!
...!!
YOU'RE MAKING A RECKLESS DECISION.
A TERRIBLE WAR IS ABOUT TO BREAK OUT, AND YOU'LL BE RIGHT IN THE MIDDLE OF IT.
YOU'RE LIKE AN ANT DIVING INTO A HURRICANE.
YOU'LL PROBABLY JUST GET FLUNG FAR AWAY.
I DON'T CARE WHAT HAPPENS TO ME!! I GOTTA DO THIS!!
I CAN'T SIT BY AND LET THEM KILL MY BROTHER!!
FINE! SO YOU INTEND TO RESCUE THE MOST IMPORTANT PRISONER IN THE WORLD, EH?

NARUTO

Story and Art by
Masashi Kishimoto

Naruto is determined to become the greatest ninja ever!

Twelve years ago the Village Hidden in the Leaves was attacked by a fearsome threat. A nine-tailed fox spirit claimed the life of the village leader, the Hokage, and many others. Today, the village is at peace and a troublemaking kid named Naruto is struggling to graduate from Ninja Academy. His goal may be to become the next Hokage, but his true destiny will be much more complicated. The adventure begins now!

WORLD'S BEST SELLING MANGA!

www.shonenjump.com

www.viz.com

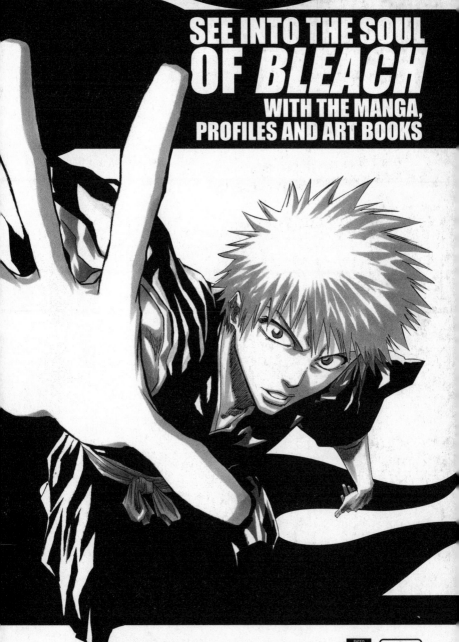

SEE INTO THE SOUL
OF *BLEACH*
WITH THE MANGA, PROFILES AND ART BOOKS

COMING NEXT VOLUME:

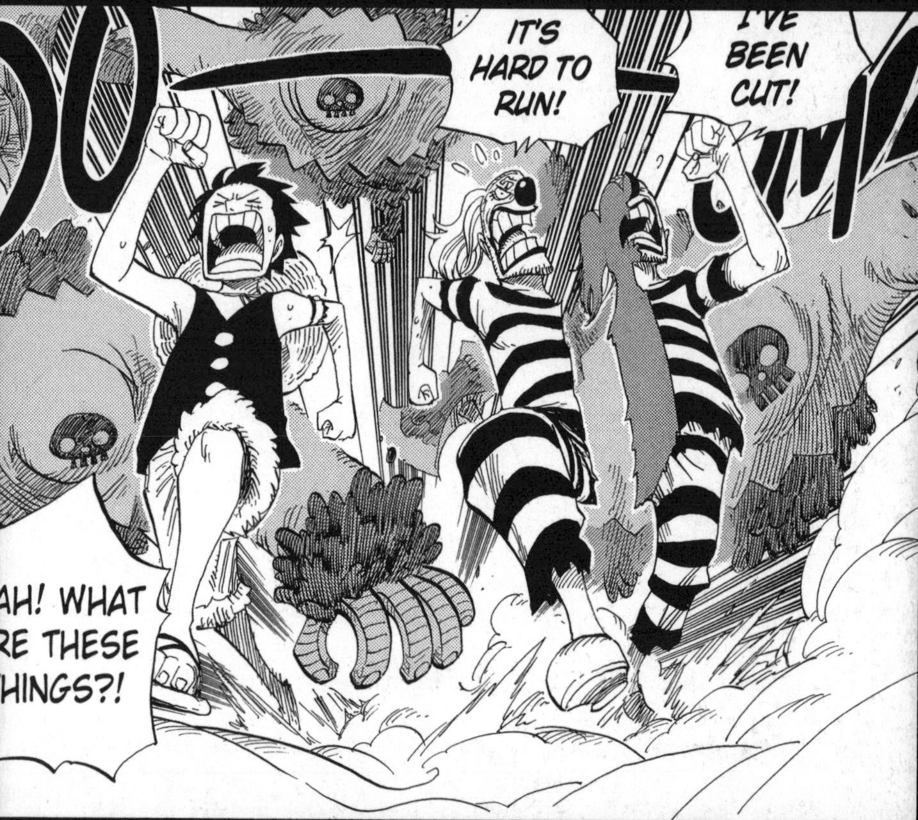
I'VE BEEN CUT!
IT'S HARD TO RUN!
AH! WHAT RE THESE HINGS?!

Luffy's racing against time to rescue his brother, "Fire Fist" Ace, from execution by the Navy forces at Impel Down. He may have found a way to sneak into the maximum-security prison, but it seems that finding Ace won't be quite that easy…until Luffy runs into some old enemies who just may be able to help!

ON SALE NOW!

R: Mr. Nakai, I have a question! Zolo is a weight-training freak, right? So do you lift weights to get into character? Oh! I know! I'll do the same thing I did with Mayumi Tanaka! Take this! Negative Hollow!

--Naocchi

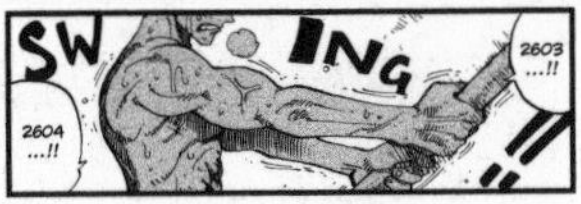
2603 ...!!
SWING
2604 ...!!

N: Ugh... Sorry, I may be Zolo, but I have 23% body fat.

R: Nakai! Take this! Oni Giri!! *Broot!!*
*Don't hold in your farts, just let them out! *Broot!!*

--Tony

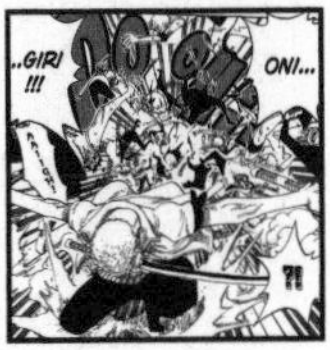
ONI...
..GIRI !!!
?!

N: That was a devious special attack I used only once way back in the day! Use it with the greatest care: it can easily backfire.

R: I have a question for Kazuya Nakai. Do you and the voice actor for Sanji really get into fights? In the comic (and anime), you always seem to be at each other's throats.

--The South

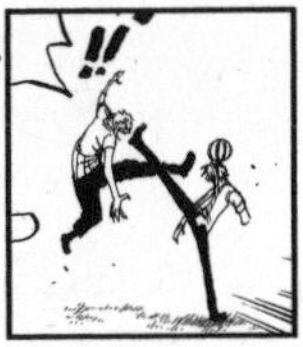
!!

N: Who's Sanji?

R: Please put a sword in your mouth and say, "Oni Giri!!"

--Kendo Club Spearhead

N: Mmrf! "Sword!" Oops! I mixed it up.

Oda: Thank you very much! Times about up, Mr. Nakai. Hey! Why are you munching on rice balls?! Let's make the next postcard the last. Hey! Stop eating! And stop shouting "sword!" You're spraying rice everywhere!

R: Please think of a Zolo move that's also a pun. Thanks!

--By a thread

N: Leech! Loiter! Last!

Oda: That's useless! That ends this Voice Actor Question Corner! See you next time!

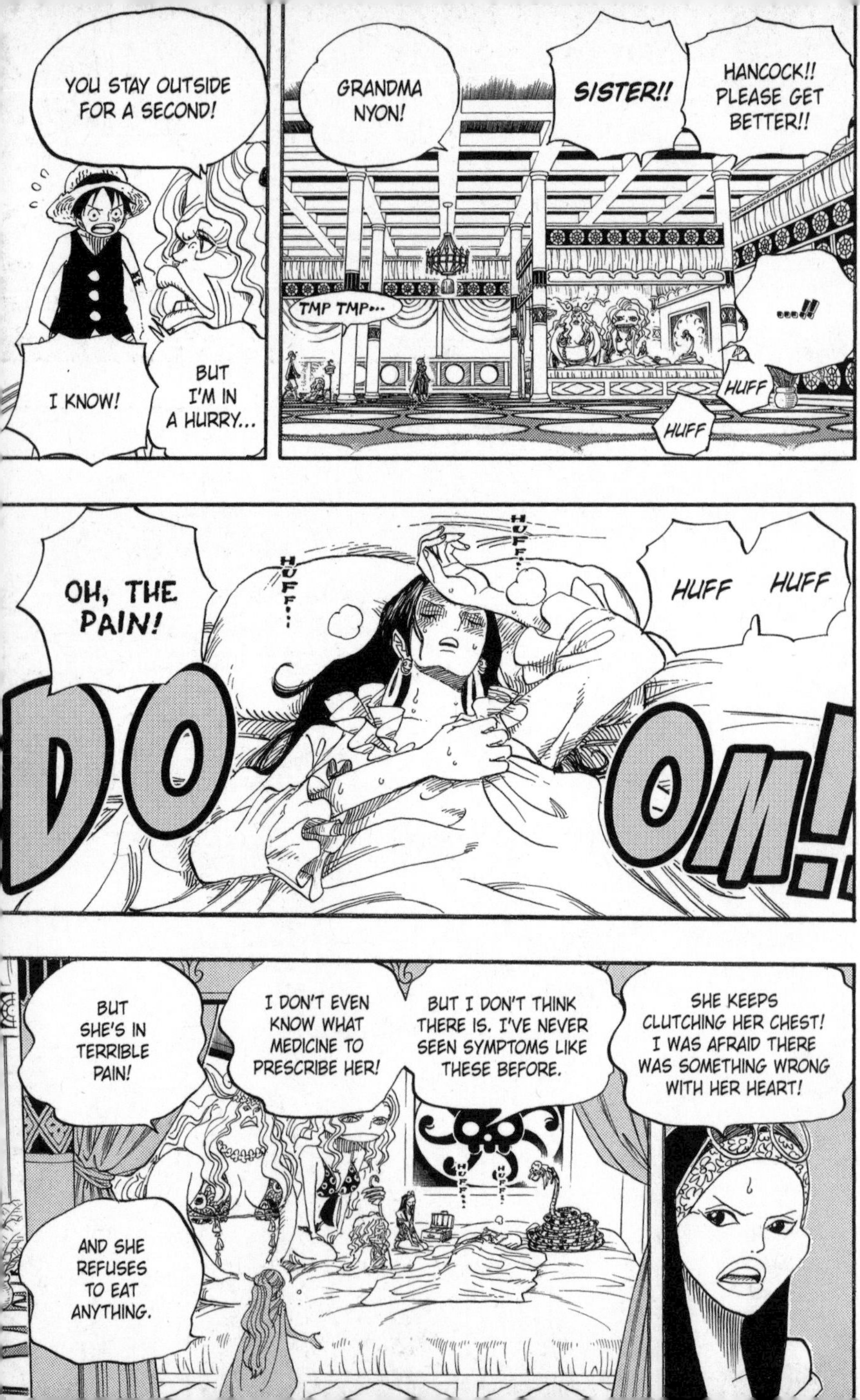
HANCOCK!! PLEASE GET BETTER!!
SISTER!!
GRANDMA NYON!
...!!
TMP TMP...
HUFF
HUFF
YOU STAY OUTSIDE FOR A SECOND!
BUT I'M IN A HURRY...
I KNOW!
HUFF HUFF
HUFF...
HUFF...
OH, THE PAIN!
DOOM!!
SHE KEEPS CLUTCHING HER CHEST! I WAS AFRAID THERE WAS SOMETHING WRONG WITH HER HEART!
BUT I DON'T THINK THERE IS. I'VE NEVER SEEN SYMPTOMS LIKE THESE BEFORE.
I DON'T EVEN KNOW WHAT MEDICINE TO PRESCRIBE HER!
BUT SHE'S IN TERRIBLE PAIN!
HUFF...
HUFF...
AND SHE REFUSES TO EAT ANYTHING.

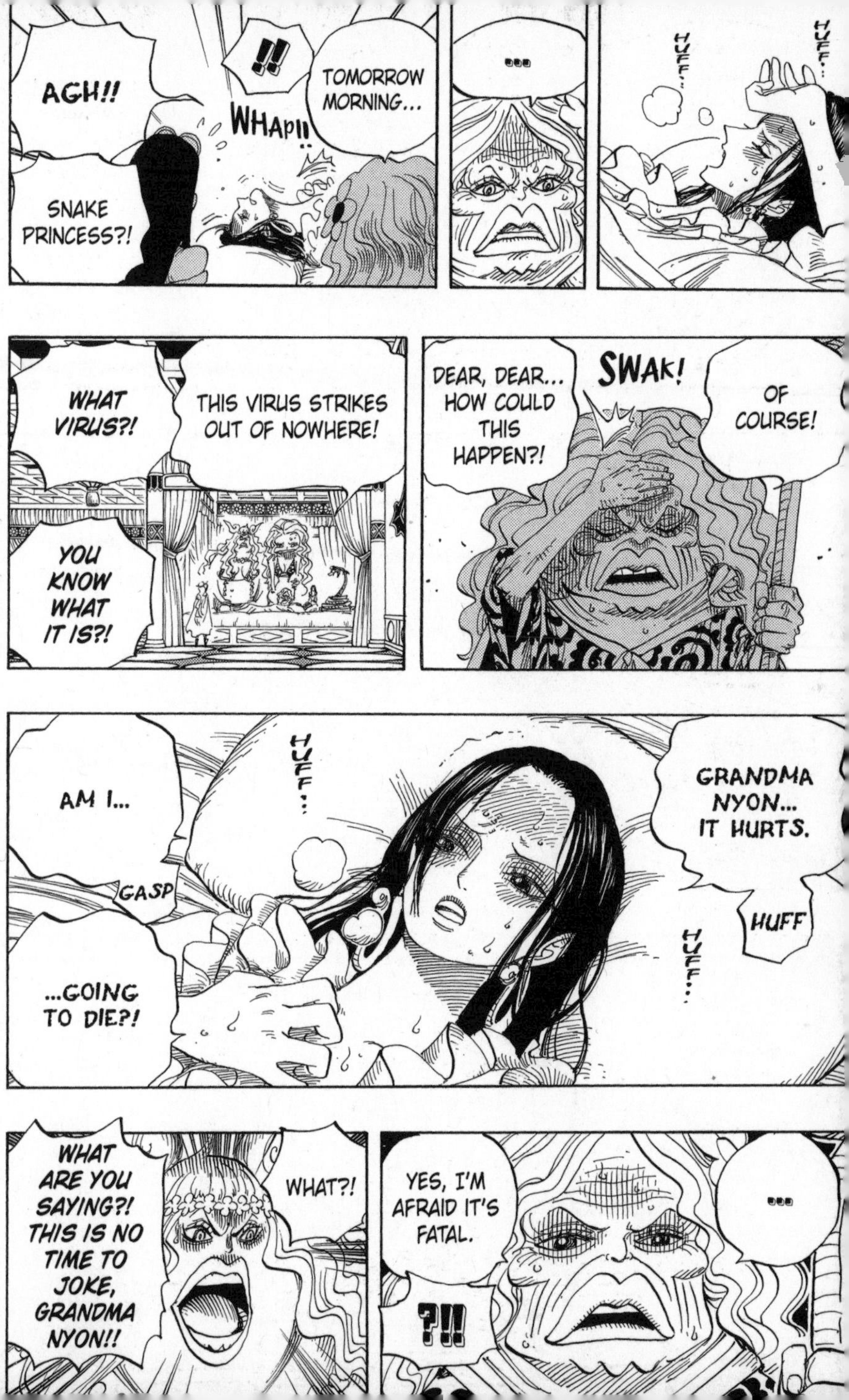
HUFF...
HUFF...
...
TOMORROW MORNING...
!!
WHAP!!
AGH!!
SNAKE PRINCESS?!
OF COURSE!
SWAK!
DEAR, DEAR... HOW COULD THIS HAPPEN?!
THIS VIRUS STRIKES OUT OF NOWHERE!
WHAT VIRUS?!
YOU KNOW WHAT IT IS?!
GRANDMA NYON... IT HURTS.
HUFF
HUFF...
HUFF...
AM I...
GASP
...GOING TO DIE?!
...
YES, I'M AFRAID IT'S FATAL.
?!!
WHAT?!
WHAT ARE YOU SAYING?! THIS IS NO TIME TO JOKE, GRANDMA NYON!!

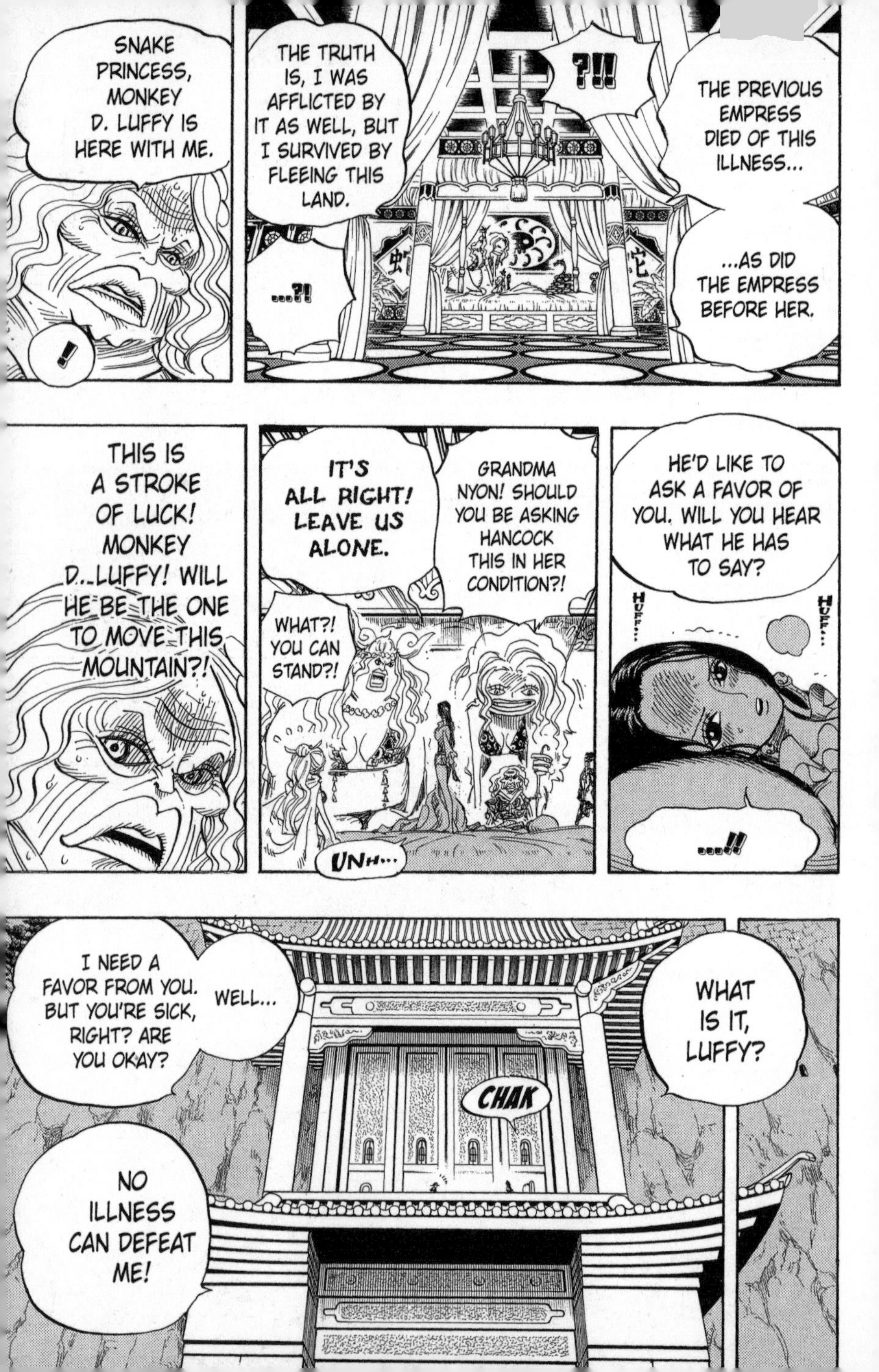
THE PREVIOUS EMPRESS DIED OF THIS ILLNESS...
...AS DID THE EMPRESS BEFORE HER.
?!!
THE TRUTH IS, I WAS AFFLICTED BY IT AS WELL, BUT I SURVIVED BY FLEEING THIS LAND.
...?!
SNAKE PRINCESS, MONKEY D. LUFFY IS HERE WITH ME.
!
HE'D LIKE TO ASK A FAVOR OF YOU. WILL YOU HEAR WHAT HE HAS TO SAY?
HUFF...
HUFF...
...!!
GRANDMA NYON! SHOULD YOU BE ASKING HANCOCK THIS IN HER CONDITION?!
IT'S ALL RIGHT! LEAVE US ALONE.
WHAT?! YOU CAN STAND?!
UNH...
THIS IS A STROKE OF LUCK! MONKEY D..LUFFY! WILL HE BE THE ONE TO MOVE THIS MOUNTAIN?!
WHAT IS IT, LUFFY?
CHAK
WELL...
I NEED A FAVOR FROM YOU. BUT YOU'RE SICK, RIGHT? ARE YOU OKAY?
NO ILLNESS CAN DEFEAT ME!

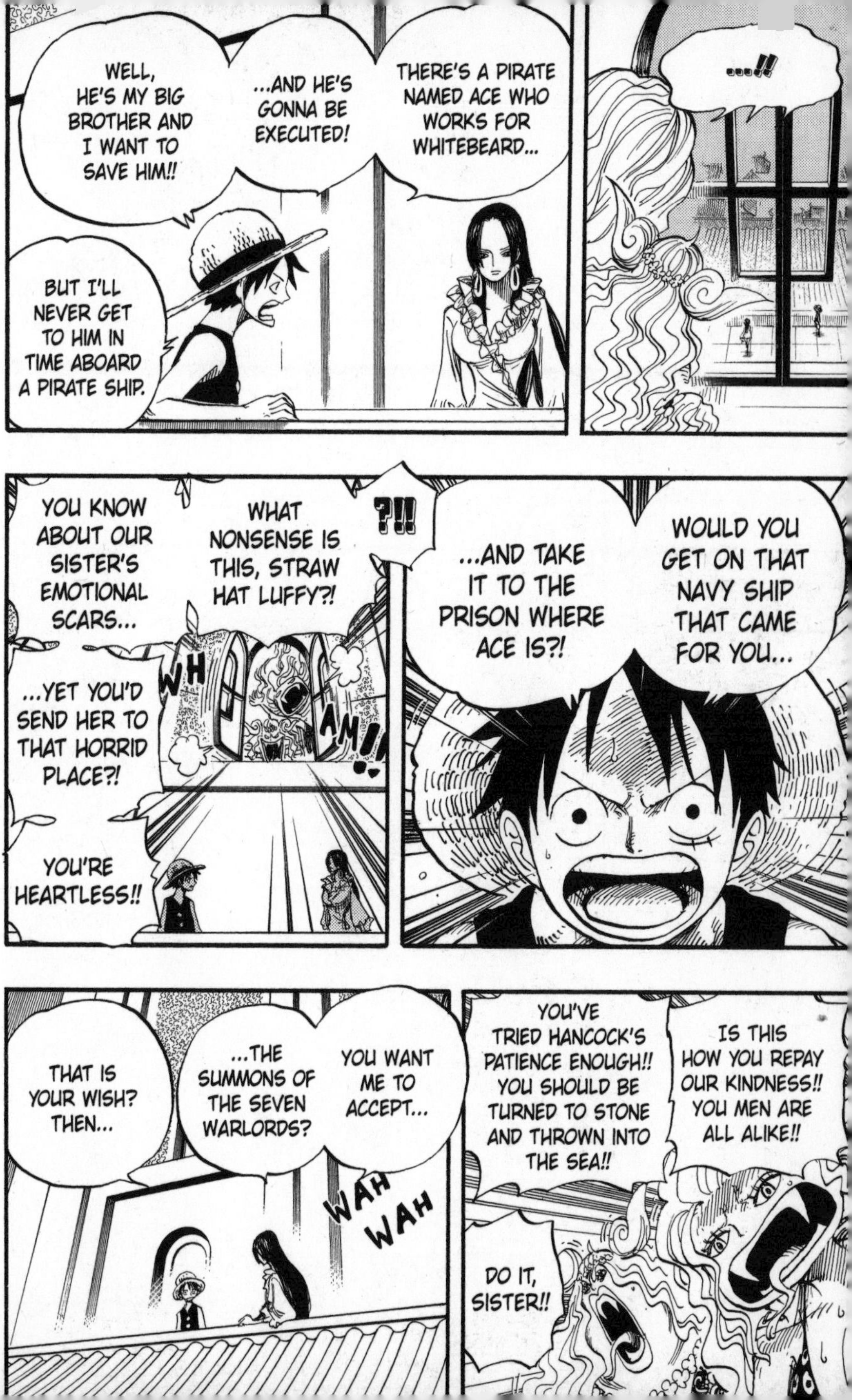
...!!
THERE'S A PIRATE NAMED ACE WHO WORKS FOR WHITEBEARD...
...AND HE'S GONNA BE EXECUTED!
WELL, HE'S MY BIG BROTHER AND I WANT TO SAVE HIM!!
BUT I'LL NEVER GET TO HIM IN TIME ABOARD A PIRATE SHIP.
WOULD YOU GET ON THAT NAVY SHIP THAT CAME FOR YOU...
...AND TAKE IT TO THE PRISON WHERE ACE IS?!
?!!
WH AM!!
WHAT NONSENSE IS THIS, STRAW HAT LUFFY?!
YOU KNOW ABOUT OUR SISTER'S EMOTIONAL SCARS...
...YET YOU'D SEND HER TO THAT HORRID PLACE?!
YOU'RE HEARTLESS!!
IS THIS HOW YOU REPAY OUR KINDNESS!! YOU MEN ARE ALL ALIKE!!
YOU'VE TRIED HANCOCK'S PATIENCE ENOUGH!! YOU SHOULD BE TURNED TO STONE AND THROWN INTO THE SEA!!
DO IT, SISTER!!
YOU WANT ME TO ACCEPT...
...THE SUMMONS OF THE SEVEN WARLORDS?
THAT IS YOUR WISH? THEN...
WAH WAH

SBS Question Corner

OUR GREAT SWORDSMAN, KAZUYA NAKAI!!

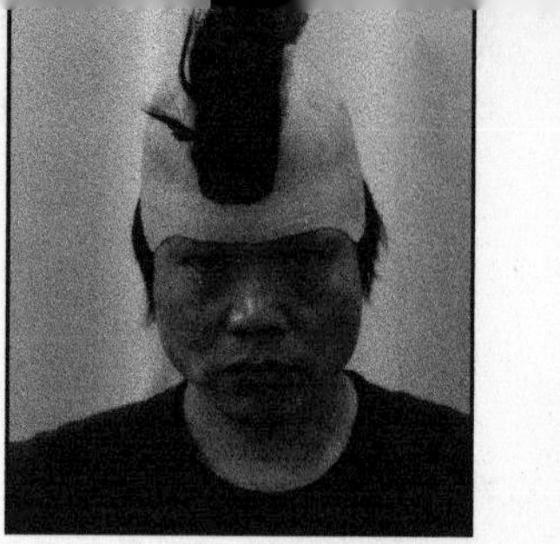

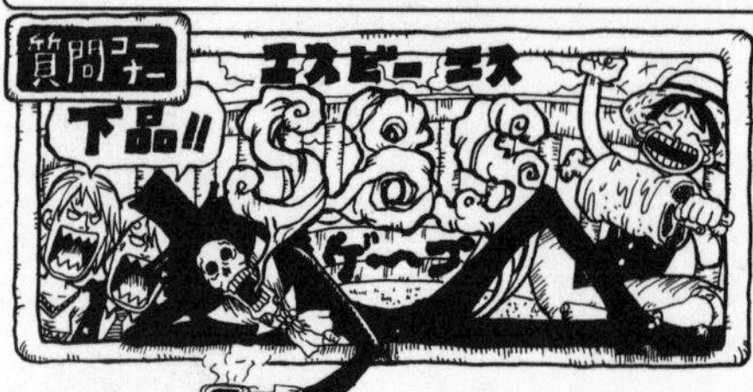
質問コーナー
エスビーエス
下品!!

(Moto-Chan, Tokyo)

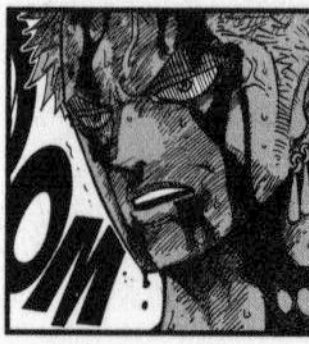

Reader(R): I always enjoy reading *One Piece*! I have a question for Mr. Nakai. Of all the characters in *One Piece*, Zolo seems to get injured the most. So do you suffer any kind of damage when he does? Please tell me!

--Spirit of Zero

Nakai(N): You remember how our captain said we aim for realism? Everybody beats on me in those scenes!

R: Nakai, please be my brother!

--Marimokorigori

N: Don't call me Brother! I have the heart of a girl! (Spoken on impulse)

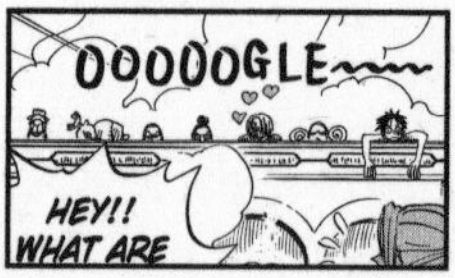
OOOOOOGLE~~
HEY!!
WHAT ARE

R: Hello, Mr. Nakai. In the Alabasta arc, all the guys except Zolo were peeping at the bathing women. Would you have peeped if you'd been there?

--Harason Beam

N: No. I'm a grown man. It's more fun to listen to the peepers talk about it and fantasize. Because I'm a grown-up.

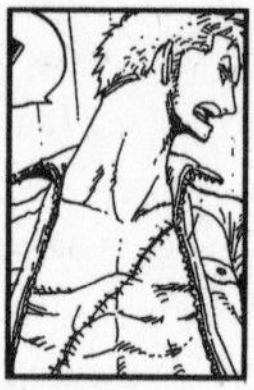

R: Mr. Nakai, I bet your abs are as cut as Zolo's! Tell me exactly how great they are!

--Yo

N: I don't know about my abs, but my butt has a deep cut down the center.

R: Mr. Nakai, have you ever cut your hair? I have. My hair used to be down to my waist, but I cut it to shoulder length.

--Snake

N: If you don't have anything to say, don't call me.

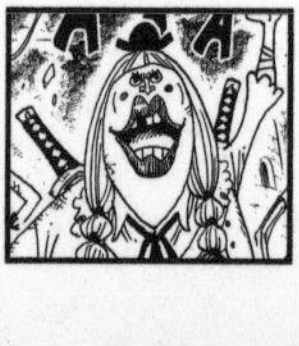

R: Nakai, I love you! Marry me! (voice of Lola the Proposer) Please answer me in a manly way, like Zolo. (Hee)

--Vague Suii

N: Streaming Wolf-Swords!!

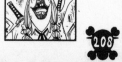

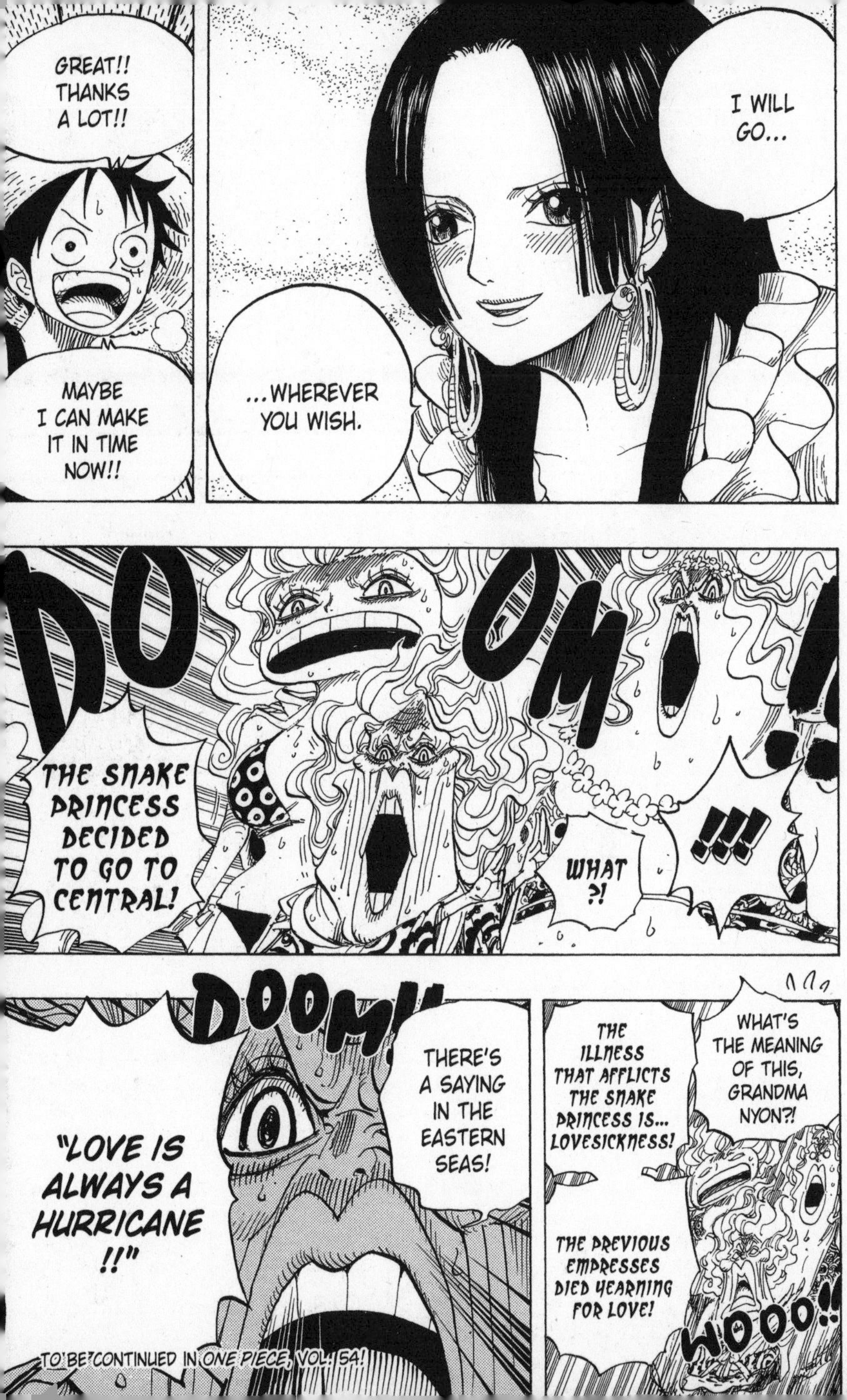
I WILL GO...
...WHEREVER YOU WISH.
GREAT!! THANKS A LOT!!
MAYBE I CAN MAKE IT IN TIME NOW!!
DOOM!!
WHAT?!
!!!
THE SNAKE PRINCESS DECIDED TO GO TO CENTRAL!
WHAT'S THE MEANING OF THIS, GRANDMA NYON?!
THE ILLNESS THAT AFFLICTS THE SNAKE PRINCESS IS... LOVESICKNESS!
THE PREVIOUS EMPRESSES DIED YEARNING FOR LOVE!
WOOO!!
DOOM!!
THERE'S A SAYING IN THE EASTERN SEAS!
"LOVE IS ALWAYS A HURRICANE!!"
TO BE CONTINUED IN ONE PIECE, VOL. 54!

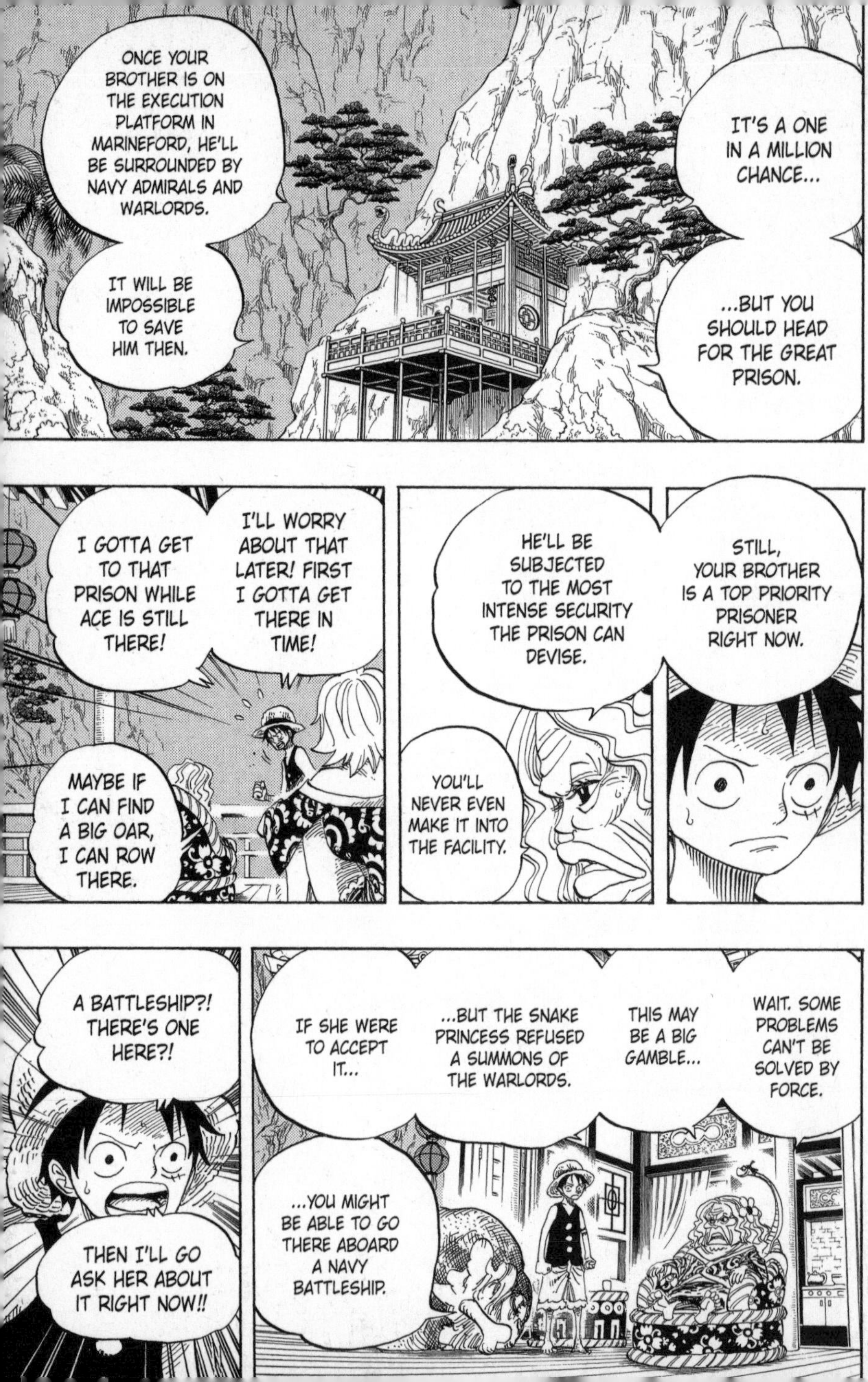
IT'S A ONE IN A MILLION CHANCE...
...BUT YOU SHOULD HEAD FOR THE GREAT PRISON.
ONCE YOUR BROTHER IS ON THE EXECUTION PLATFORM IN MARINEFORD, HE'LL BE SURROUNDED BY NAVY ADMIRALS AND WARLORDS.
IT WILL BE IMPOSSIBLE TO SAVE HIM THEN.
STILL, YOUR BROTHER IS A TOP PRIORITY PRISONER RIGHT NOW.
HE'LL BE SUBJECTED TO THE MOST INTENSE SECURITY THE PRISON CAN DEVISE.
YOU'LL NEVER EVEN MAKE IT INTO THE FACILITY.
I'LL WORRY ABOUT THAT LATER! FIRST I GOTTA GET THERE IN TIME!
I GOTTA GET TO THAT PRISON WHILE ACE IS STILL THERE!
MAYBE IF I CAN FIND A BIG OAR, I CAN ROW THERE.
WAIT. SOME PROBLEMS CAN'T BE SOLVED BY FORCE.
THIS MAY BE A BIG GAMBLE...
...BUT THE SNAKE PRINCESS REFUSED A SUMMONS OF THE WARLORDS.
IF SHE WERE TO ACCEPT IT...
...YOU MIGHT BE ABLE TO GO THERE ABOARD A NAVY BATTLESHIP.
A BATTLESHIP?! THERE'S ONE HERE?!
THEN I'LL GO ASK HER ABOUT IT RIGHT NOW!!

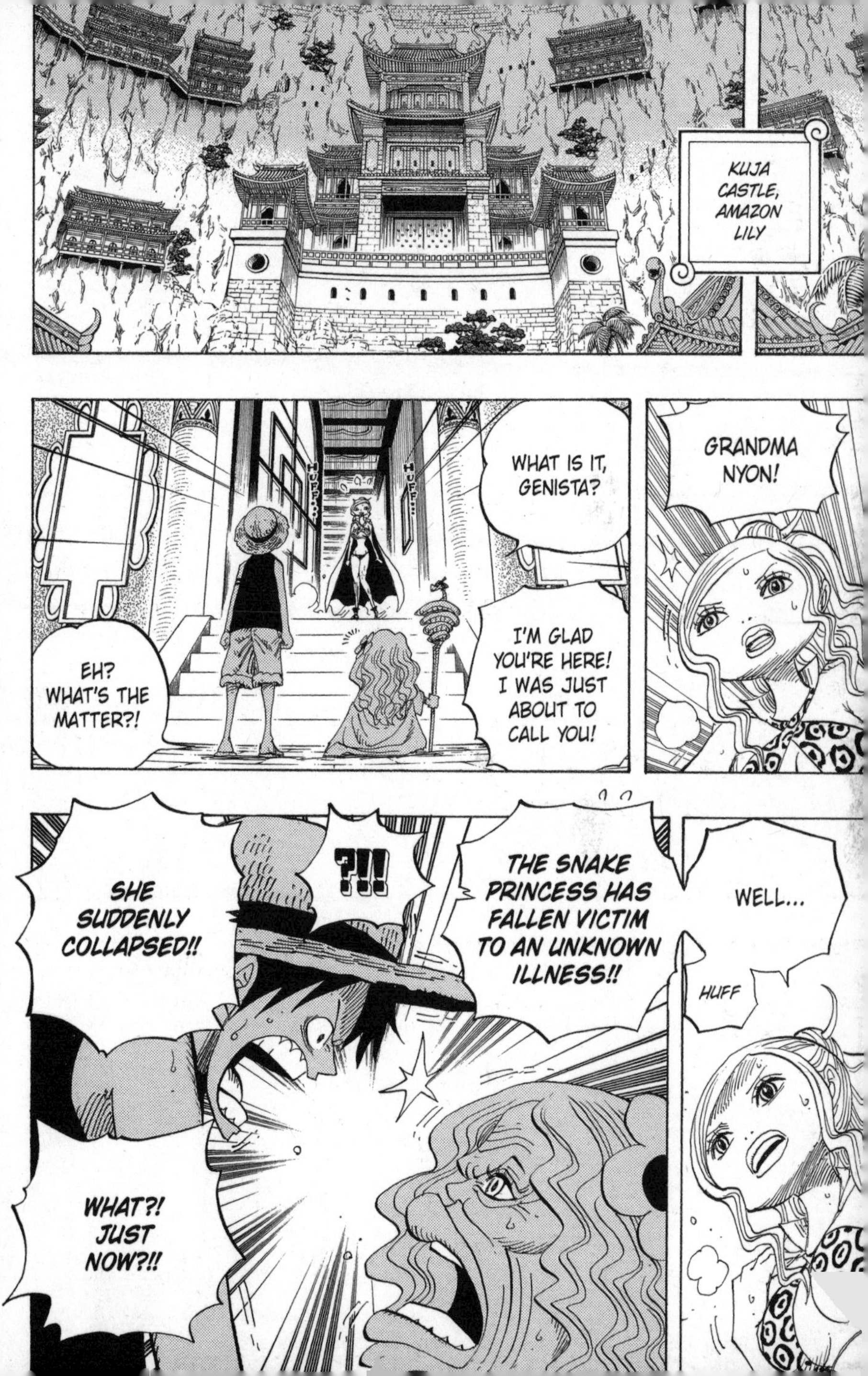
KUJA CASTLE, AMAZON LILY
GRANDMA NYON!
HUFF...
HUFF...
WHAT IS IT, GENISTA?
I'M GLAD YOU'RE HERE! I WAS JUST ABOUT TO CALL YOU!
EH? WHAT'S THE MATTER?!
WELL...
HUFF
THE SNAKE PRINCESS HAS FALLEN VICTIM TO AN UNKNOWN ILLNESS!!
?!!
SHE SUDDENLY COLLAPSED!!
WHAT?! JUST NOW?!!

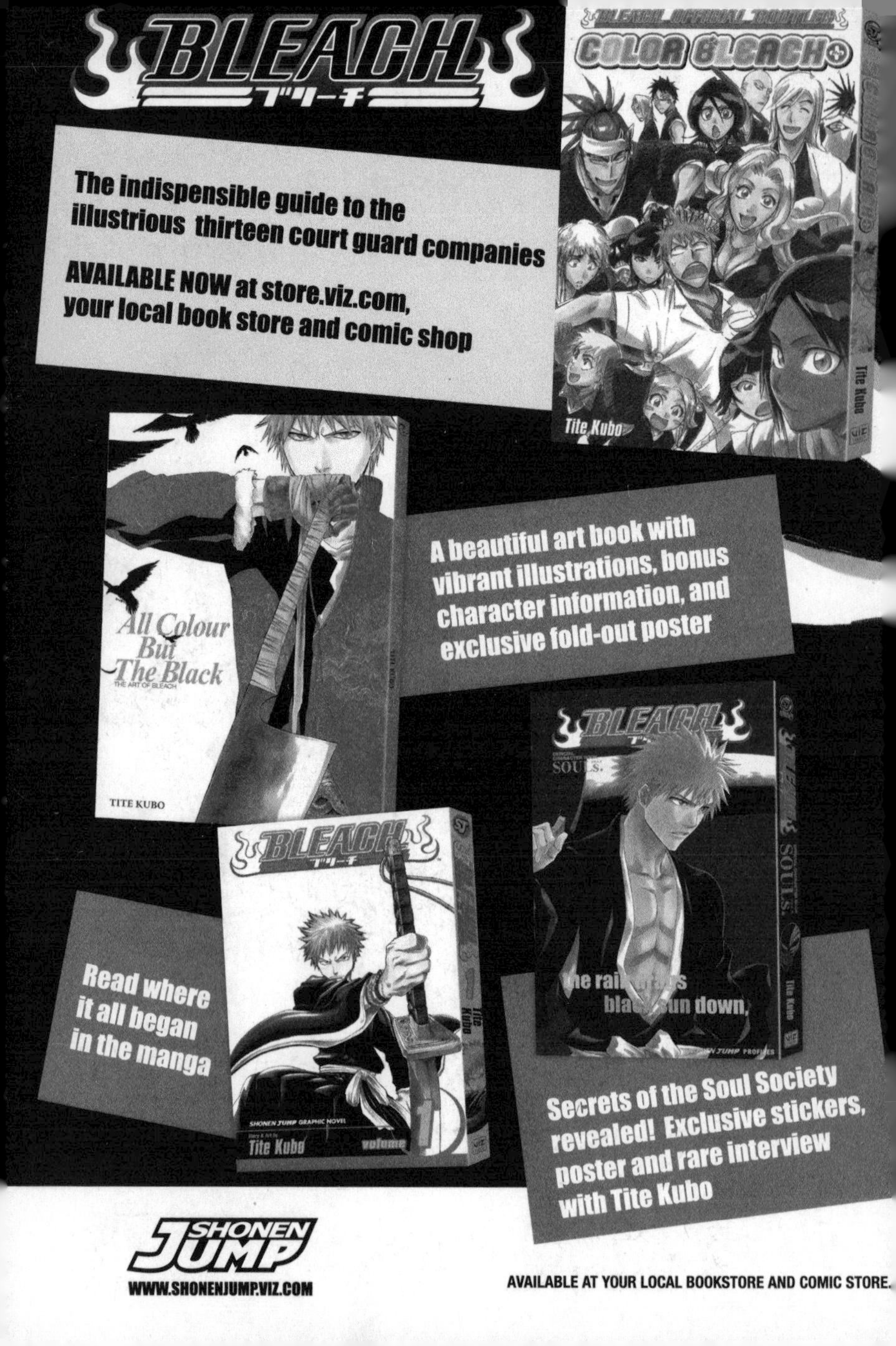
BLEACH
ブリーチ
The indispensible guide to the illustrious thirteen court guard companies
AVAILABLE NOW at store.viz.com, your local book store and comic shop
COLOR BLEACH+
Tite Kubo
All Colour But The Black
THE ART OF BLEACH
TITE KUBO
A beautiful art book with vibrant illustrations, bonus character information, and exclusive fold-out poster
BLEACH
SOULS.
BLEACH
ブリーチ
SHONEN JUMP GRAPHIC NOVEL
Tite Kubo
volume
Read where it all began in the manga
Secrets of the Soul Society revealed! Exclusive stickers, poster and rare interview with Tite Kubo
SHONEN JUMP
WWW.SHONENJUMP.VIZ.COM
AVAILABLE AT YOUR LOCAL BOOKSTORE AND COMIC STORE.

YuYu HAKUSHO

Story and Art by *Yoshihiro Togashi*

Yusuke Urameshi was a tough teen delinquent until one selfless act changed his life...by ending it. When he died saving a little kid from a speeding car, the afterlife didn't know what to do with him, so it gave him a second chance at life. Now, Yusuke is a ghost with a mission, performing good deeds at the behest of Botan, the spirit guide of the dead, and Koenma, her pacifier-sucking boss from the other side.

The Shonen Jump classic by Yoshihiro Togashi, the creator of *Hunter x Hunter*

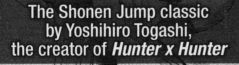

www.viz.com

www.shonenjump.com